W9-AOE-799

HAROLD PINTER

A Bibliographical History

HAROLD PINTER

A Bibliographical History

WILLIAM BAKER & JOHN C. ROSS

THE BRITISH LIBRARY
and
OAK KNOLL PRESS
2005

DEDICATION

For Donald Hawes, gentleman and scholar, whose generous help has done so much to make this work viable.

First published 2005 by
The British Library
96 Euston Road
London NW1 2DB

and

Oak Knoll Press
310 Delaware Street
New Castle
DE 19720

Cataloguing-in-Publication Data is available from both The British Library and the Library of Congress

ISBN 0-7123-4885-9 (BL)
ISBN 1-58456-156-4 (OKP)

Typeset by Cambridge Photosetting Services, Cambridge
Printed and bound in Great Britain by St Edmundsbury Press, Bury St Edmunds

Contents

Introduction

This bibliographical history aims to provide as comprehensive and as complete an account of the published writings, and other texts, wholly or partly authored by Harold Pinter, as can be managed in relation to certain conditions, among them the absence of closure, and the imperative of having to stop somewhere. At the time of our compiling it, he is still very much a living author, creating new texts, and capable of modifying the forms in which previously composed works may appear. Hence the closure usually present for a substantial author-bibliography is lacking; and effectively, the *terminus ad quem* for this present volume is October 2004.

At this point in time, if one takes into account his published juvenilia, from 1947 onward, Pinter's authorial career already extends fifty-seven years. He is widely regarded as the outstanding English dramatist of the later twentieth century; and one can affirm that his major stature owes much to the sheer cumulative magnitude of his *œuvre*, over this period, as well as to its often very high quality.

Harold Pinter is pre-eminently a playwright, a creator of texts in dramatic form for live theatre, radio, television or cinema, and yet he has also composed a significant body of poetry, a number of short stories, a novel, and a large number of non-fictional prose writings, in the forms of essays or articles, published speeches, letters to periodicals, and items in sundry lesser modes. He has given many interviews, recorded in print or in other media; and this type of mixed authorship has here been interpreted generously to include interview-based articles by journalists which quote passages of direct speech. The "Miscellaneous" section comprehends various kinds of minor contributions, such as forewords or short notes, and those of collaborative, joint or implicitly joint authorship, such as examples of the many petitions or letters to newspapers for which he has been one of a number of signatories. In seeking to be inclusive, this section ventures into areas of shared or implied authorship of varying shades of grey.

Comprehensiveness in the early years of the twenty-first century requires the coverage of authored or partially authored texts in other media as well as print, including for Pinter sound and audiovisual recorded forms, and also items on websites, especially in cases for which at the time of compilation no print-medium publication is known.[1] However, we have sought to exclude instances

---

[1]Cf. D. F. McKenzie, *The Panizzi Lectures 1985: Bibliography and the Sociology of Texts* (London: The British Library, 1986): "Bibliography is the discipline that studies texts as recorded forms, and the processes of their transmission, including their production and reception...It seems to me it would now be more useful to describe bibliography as the study of the sociology of texts...I define `texts' to include verbal, visual, oral, and numeric data, in the form of maps, prints and music, of archives of recorded sound, of films, videos, and any computer-stored information" (pp. 4–5).

where Pinter was simply a performer, narrator or director, rather than to some degree the author. (The more important of these instances are noticed in the *Chronology*.)

Generally, we have excluded translations into languages other than English from the body of the bibliography, although, where known of, they are noticed in *Appendix One* (designated the letter "W"). That is, we have not sought to offer a full coverage of them, but have provided it where the data has been readily available. However, items with the texts in English, print-published in non-Anglophone countries, are included in the relevant sections.

While a virtually complete coverage can otherwise be provided for publication of his dramatic works, and writings in other literary genres, it cannot be assured for other categories. Harold Pinter has given interviews very widely, in the United Kingdom, the United States of America, and other countries, and has delivered numerous speeches. From the mid-1970s onward he has involved himself in movements opposing violations of human rights, in anti-war and anti-nuclear weapons events, and with left-wing radical magazines, such as *Red Pepper*. While many of his writings relating to these causes and interests have been noticed here, we cannot claim to have identified them all, and in some cases information is incomplete. As observed above, one has to stop somewhere.

In compiling listings of items, especially in non-literary categories, we have been much assisted by several existing enumerative bibliographies which cover Pinter's writings (as well as secondary sources), notably Rüdiger Imhof's *Pinter: A Bibliography* (London: TQ Publications,1975), Steven H. Gale's *Harold Pinter: An Annotated Bibliography* (Boston, MA: G. K. Hall & Co.,1978), and, from 1989 onward, Susan Hollis Merritt's bibliographies in the annual volumes of *The Pinter Review*. Malcolm Page's *File on Pinter* (London: Methuen Drama, 1993) has also been useful. We have also benefitted from the work of Ms Letitia Dace, who has kindly permitted us to draw upon her notes. To these scholars we are very much indebted, and gratefully acknowledge their fine work.

A bibliographical history goes beyond the scope of a descriptive author bibliography, in seeking to offer a kind of documentary biography of the author, in terms of his or her published writings, to signal connections between these writings, and (as appropriate) to document the history of each of them. In approaching this task, for Harold Pinter's works, the application of the concepts of authorship, text and publication can often prove problematic.

With his works in dramatic modes, for live theatre, radio or television, his authorship of the texts is usually clear-cut, with only a few, clearly acknowledged cases of explicit collaboration. They were initially designed as scripts for productions, and in most of their subsequent print manifestations have been modified for reading, although acting editions retain the function of scripts. He has sought to retain firm control over their dialogue, and has himself cut or re-written it, as it has appeared in revised printed editions, with little if any direct input from directors or actors. However, presentations in the various media naturally involve significant dimensions of collaboration and social production; and these cuts and re-writings have sometimes manifestly resulted from experience within the production process, as can be seen from promptbooks, especially when Pinter himself was involved as the director, or was working closely with a director, with a particular cast of actors, and evaluating audience responses. Thus some degree of indirect influence from other agents cannot be wholly ruled out.

Moreover, given that a dramatic text comprises not only lines of dialogue, but also stage directions, and other "apparatus," then in the American acting editions especially, where these features sometimes diverge from those of the standard editions, the variants may well have originated from some director's notations on a script being used as a copy-text, perhaps with Pinter's approval. Still, the most extensive re-writing and re-formatting have come about when Pinter himself has adapted a work initially designed for one medium for one of the others, responding to its differing exigencies.

With Pinter's screenplays, the authorship situation is more complex than for his works in other dramatic modes. Although he has adapted four of his own plays for film (*The Caretaker, The Birthday Party, The Homecoming* and *Betrayal*), the adapted scripts have not appeared in print, and nearly all of his screenplays so far published have been adaptations from novels by other authors (the one exception, *The Dreaming Child,* derived from a short story; another screen adaptation, unpublished, that of Simon Gray's *Butley,* was of a play he had directed for the stage). Moreover the final form of the shooting script inevitably involves input from other agents. In two relatively extreme cases, he has not published the screenplay of Margaret Atwood's *The Handmaid's Tale,* because so little of his original script was retained unchanged; and he declined to appear as one of the authors of the eventual script of the film of Kazuo Ishiguro's *The Remains of the Day,* although "there are still seven or eight scenes in the finished film that [he] wrote" (Billington 304, 324). Nonetheless, he could claim in 1995 that of the "twenty-two film scripts" he had written, up to that time, "seventeen have been made exactly as written; that's not too bad a statistic, given the nature of the movie industry" (Billington 324). Since then he has written two more.

In relation to some of the other genres, grey areas of mixed, shared or implied authorship have already been noticed. And what is one to make of the contents of theatre programmes for stage productions for which Pinter was the director? While not necessarily their author, he may be assumed to have authorised them. However, we have come across only one instance in which a programme note was signed (for the 1980 first production of his own play *The Hothouse*); otherwise, this genre has been disregarded.

The status of Pinter's works and of their publication can also be problematic, raising challenges for devising appropriate methodologies for documenting them. Any such work may be a play, a poem, a radio talk, a television interview, or whatever, and its text manifested in one or more recorded verbal forms (in some categories, involving sound or audiovisual elements as well). The work and its essential text can appear in two or more distinct versions, either because he has adapted a work written for one medium to suit another, or because he has substantially revised the text, while it still remains within the same medium and genre (or sub-genre).

With Pinter's texts in dramatic form inherently scripts for performance, it could, on one hand, be claimed that in the fullest sense the text may be the performance itself. However, for live theatre, any such performance is an ephemeral happening, and strongly distinct in its nature from any form of recording that could be made of it. On the other hand, a sound recording of a radio presentation preserves what the listeners heard, and the video-recording of a television production, or a copy of a film, similarly has a semi-permanence as the recorded and replayable form of the fully realised work to which the script was aiming. Hence these recorded forms must be given some coverage; nonetheless, they can not be said to be "authored," and accordingly they are given attention within *Appendix One*, rather than within the main sections.

Taking only the narrow definition of publication as print-publishing for public sale, a published entity may be constituted by its containing the text of just one particular work, or by its containing the texts of a particular combination of works, whether two, or three, or many. Any such published entity may have concrete forms in a number of manifestations, either as different editions or reprintings of the same textual version(s), or including editions to some extent revised, incorporating different versions of one or more of the one or more texts contained. Where the entity contains the text of a single work, other manifestations of this entity can include an appearance in print of the text within a serial, or within an anthology, along with works by other authors.

For example, the published entity *Landscape and Silence (A28)*, as first published by Methuen in 1969, includes the texts of three works, the third being the sketch "Night." It was reprinted in Britain in 1970, and subsequently, and by Grove Press in the United States, with the first of a series of printings in 1970. Each of these reprints or printings is a further manifestation. However, in this case, the American acting edition entitled *Landscape and Silence (A33)*, published by Samuel French, New York, in 1971, is a distinctly different entity, because it does not include "Night." Moreover, *Landscape* has also appeared as a separately published text *(A27)*, in book form, and other manifestations of this entity include publication within an issue of the magazine *Evergreen Review*, and within an educational anthology.

For another example, *The Dwarfs* as a dramatic work first appeared as a radio play written and broadcast in 1960, and published in 1961, and as a stage play first published in 1966, and then in a revised form in 1968. This can be considered a single work, with one radio version and two stage versions; but the published entities are the particular combinations of texts, such as *A Slight Ache and Other Plays* (Methuen, 1961) *(A12)*, *Three Plays* (Grove, 1962) *(A13)*, or *The Dwarfs and Eight Revue Sketches* (Dramatists Play Service, 1965) *(A21)*, in which it has appeared.

This bibliography is primarily concerned with documenting such published entities, in their various manifestations. It identifies substantially different versions of the text of each work, but does not notice the presence of minor textual variations. *Sections A* to *I* are concerned essentially with print-published entities. *Section J* deals with "sound" entities, mainly involving works published in a wider sense by being broadcast on radio, and in most cases preserved in recorded forms, either on long-playing records, tapes, or CD discs, or at least as typescript transcripts of the verbal texts. *Section K* deals with audiovisual entities, for the most part television items, published by being transmitted, and potentially or actually preserved on film, videotape, or videodisc. In addition, some items up to this time have been "published" only on a website (often www.haroldpinter.org); nonetheless, they are too few to justify the creation of a separate section, hence are included within the relevant generic sections.

While *Sections A* to *K* cover these categories of entities, more can still be done to bring together the "histories" of the more substantial works to fulfil some of the other functions of a bibliographical history. This task is undertaken in *Appendix One*, which addresses these works, in terms of their estimated order of composition, and provides for each of them brief documentation of the various recorded forms in which its textual versions may have appeared. For the sake of bringing such documentation coherently together, details of radio, television or film productions, presentations or recordings of works which have also been print-published are documented here rather than within *Sections J* or *K*, which are confined to those items which have manifestations only in the sound or audiovisual domains, with their appropriately recorded forms.

Moreover, while it is not the business of a bibliography to document the composition of the texts of works, in the case of Pinter, a contemporary author who has deposited most of his manuscripts and pre-publication typescripts in the Pinter Archive in the British Library, relatively brief notice can be given to these in *Appendix One*. They include not only holograph and typescript drafts, but also duplicated typescripts (in a few cases, limited-issue printed scripts) which have been created for use for the earliest stage productions, prior to the first editions being issued for public sale. There are also some duplicated typescripts used for radio, television or film productions. These documents can be said to be "published" in the very broad sense of being duplicated in multiple copies and distributed. Nonetheless, it is useful to retain a distinction between this sense and the normal sense of print-publication, of being issued for public sale; hence they are dealt with in *Appendix One*, rather than in the main body of the bibliography.

In relation especially to the print-publication for public sale of dramatic works, dealt with in *Section A*, it can be seen that Pinter's career has bridged a major transition in technology. The earliest printings of his first dramatic works would have been typeset using a linotype or Monotype machine, or the equivalent, and printed offset with photolithographical plates, with subsequent revisions carried out through cutting and pasting of the plates, and patching-in of new material. Certain later titles were photoset, using a process whereby keying-in each letter led to its reproduction on a photographic negative. Later still, the works have been computer typeset, and exist in the first instance on a computer file, from which print-publication can be carried out. The practical consequences of textual revision have derived from the technical processes involved; for example, in revised editions of *The Birthday Party*, the process of cutting and pasting of litho plates has sometimes observably resulted in uneven vertical spacing, and the short-term retention of brief stage-directions that have no longer related to their contexts (see *A1c*, notes).

At each stage, the standard American editions published by Grove Press in New York have largely followed the British editions line-for-line, hence it may be that in the earlier period a duplicate set of the plates was sometimes made available to Grove; however, no information has been obtained as to what kinds of commercial cooperation may have occurred between the British and American publishers. In any event, revisions in the British editions have been followed soon after in the successive printings of the Grove editions.

Very brief accounts of such revisions are provided in *Appendix Two, A*. However, fully detailed documentation and discussion of textual revisions of dramatic texts would be beyond the scope of this bibliography. For a few plays, these revisions have aleady been the subject of article-length studies, e.g., Gerald M. Berkowitz, "Pinter's Revisions of *The Caretaker*," *Journal of Modern Literature*, 5: 1 (February 1976): 109–116.

The basic ordering principle within all sections and appendices is chronological. Within *Sections A to I*, this entails the order of publication of the first manifestations in print of published entities, with the first entry for each entity then followed by those for its subsequent manifestations. With *Sections J and K*, it normally entails chronology of first presentation, by radio broadcast or television transmission, although sometimes the only relevant or known date is of recording.

This ordering sometimes differs quite substantially from the order of composition or from that of first live theatre performance, or of first radio or television presentation. For example, Pinter's first written and performed play was *The Room*, premièred at the University of Bristol on 15 May 1957, but it was not published until 1960 *(A4; W5)*; his first published play was *The Birthday Party*, premièred in Cambridge on 28 April 1958 and first published in 1959 *(A1; W6)*. Both of these other kinds of ordering are addressed in *Appendix One*, where the basic order is by general period of composition, and first performances or presentations are noted within the biographical timeline in the *Chronology*.

Within the main body of the bibliography, the essential division between sections is generic. All the same, it must be acknowledged that, as an adventurous writer working in a number of genres, Pinter has published some writings that cross over these generic boundaries. For example, "Dialogue for Three" *(A15)* was published as a prose piece in dialogue form, and also broadcast on radio, and printed, as a dramatic sketch. "Tess" *(D13)* has been staged as a sketch and print-published as a short story. "Episode," published as a poem, is a series of monologues in verse, reflecting a dramatic situation of sexual jealousy (see *18, Note one*). Published collections also belie their titles, with, for example, *Poems* (1968) including the short story "Kullus," and the Methuen *Plays* volumes including prose pieces (see *13, 11*). Indeed, any organising principle for this bibliography encounters a few exceptions; and such items have to be assigned to one section or another on the basis of common sense, with noting of their generic double nature. Items which came to our recent attention in the later stages of work on the bibliographical history are assigned an "A" as part of their designations (for instance *H2A* is Pinter's contribution to the National Book League [NBL] pamphlet *Celebrities' Choice*).

Section A brackets plays for the stage, radio and television, firstly because some of the published volumes contain dramatic works designed for more than one of these media, and secondly because some of the plays, initially composed for one of them, were then adapted for presentation in one of the others, with the later versions sometimes replacing the first versions in the published volumes. The distinction between plays and sketches derives solely from relative length, and in practice there is no clear division between sketches and very short plays. Hence, sketches have generally been treated in the same way as plays.

As indicated, entities in *Section A* are dealt with in chronological order in terms of the estimated earliest publication in print of each play (when it occurs in a single-play volume, or within a periodical, or, for one sketch, within a book), or of each volume containing a combination of two or more plays. Then follow all subsequent publication of this play (in a single-play volume, or periodical), or of this combination of plays. Where several entities received first publication in the same year, in the United Kingdom or in the United States of America, the precise datings of their earliest publication are not always known, and accordingly the relative ordering of them is based upon estimated rather than definitely known datings, and cannot always be definitive.

Where the play has appeared in more than one manifestation, the order of categories adopted is: standard (i.e., readers', or, trade) editions, educational (or, students') editions with notes, acting editions, and anthologies. Within each category, British publication precedes American publication, except for one or two cases of anthologies where the American publication clearly appeared first (e.g., *A2n, A2o*). In most cases, the American publication of an entity corresponds to the British ones. Occasionally, however, a particular combination of plays was published only in the United States, constituting a distinct entity (see, e.g., *A10, A11*). For some titles, in addition to the standard (trade) editions, there are collectors' editions, numbered and signed by the author; these are ordered within the series of standard editions. The one sub-category which has not been systematically pursued (one of relatively minor significance) is that of Grove Press Book Club or Book of the Month Club editions, although a few examples have been recorded. For another category, informally published items, two exceptionally interesting instances are included (*A3, A9*); others, however, are included in *Appendix One*.

Section B covers Harold Pinter's published screenplays. While they have an obvious affinity with play-texts written for television, in practice there is a clear division, in that virtually all the works designated on their title pages as screenplays are adaptations from other authors' novels, or, in the case of *The Dreaming Child,* from a short story (moreover, many of them are structured in terms of shots). Inevitably, there is an exception, the television version of *Party Time,* designated on its title page as a screenplay, but dealt with in *Section A* (as *A49b*) instead of *Section B,* to associate it with the stage version of this work (*A49a*), and with the other television plays.

A number of the screenplays Pinter has written have remained unpublished. They include his adaptations for cinema of four of his own plays initially written for the stage, or for television, as mentioned above (for details, see *Appendix One*); and several other screenplays that Pinter has written have not been published, either because they were not used at all, as in the case of *Lolita,* or were made use of in such a partial or mangled way that Pinter declined to acknowledge his share in authorship of the final shooting script; these are noticed only in *Appendix One*. His recent film adaptation of Shakespeare's play *The Tragedy of King Lear* has not yet been filmed or published.

However, *The Compartment (B1)* does merit inclusion in *Section B,* because of its great interest as Pinter's only original screenplay, and one of his earliest efforts in the genre, despite the fact that it has only been informally published, in duplicated typescript. And given that a number of the volumes recorded in this section are, already, groups of screenplays, the three-volume Faber and Faber *Collected Screenplays* is also dealt with within it, rather than in the *Collections* section. Of the screenplays included in this collected edition, only *The Dreaming Child* had not been previously published.

Section C deals with Pinter's poems, published individually, within serials, as opposed to some which were first published within collections of his poems, which are covered in subsection 2 of the *Collections* section. Regrettably, it has not always been practical to pursue the full details of pagination, or even of precise dating, for all items; or example, for the poem "Restaurant" (*C26*), the list of first publication, given in *Collected Poems and Prose* (Faber and Faber, 1991), p. [119], cites only "*Daily Telegraph,* 1989," and a search of earlier issues of this newspaper, for that year, did not discover it. It may be that earlier publication of some poems remain unidentified. The Pinter Archive in the British Library contains drafts of some poems for which no publication has been identified; it may be that one or two of them did get published somewhere.

Section D deals with Pinter's prose fiction, including one novel, *The Dwarfs,* but otherwise short stories. His earlier stories and poems are of particular interest because they explore certain themes, such as dominance-struggles for territory or sexual possession, later given fuller exploration in the plays.

Section E covers published articles, essays and speeches, bracketing these because a text originally composed for delivery as a speech could then become part or all of the text of an article or essay. From the 1980s onward, many of these items have had to do with radical political causes and protests. Some have come into being as acceptance speeches for honorary degrees. As with the poems, it has not always been practical to ascertain details such as pagination, notably in cases in which the item has been seen on a newspaper's website, where it is not provided. Some very short, or jointly authored, prose pieces are to be found in *Section H* ("Miscellaneous") rather than here.

Section F deals with Pinter's letters to editors published in newspapers or magazines. This excludes letters for which he is only one of the signatories, and which are covered in *Section H*.

Section G covers print-published interviews and interview-based articles, in newspapers or magazines. The second category comprises articles by journalists which do not have a question-response structure, and yet incorporate substantial passages of direct speech, deriving from an interview with Pinter, rather than merely being reproduced from some previously published source.

Section H ("Miscellaneous") covers a wide range of kinds of items. As already indicated, they include brief contributions to various publications, letters to newspapers or petitions with multiple signatures, volumes edited by Pinter, and so forth.

Section I ("Collections and Selections") is divided into two sequences, one of collected plays (but with the volumes including also some short prose pieces), and the other of volumes of poetry and prose.

Sections J and *K* deal with sound and audiovisual entities, respectively, such as are not broadcastings of works also published in print (which are dealt with in *Appendix One*).

Appendix One, as indicated, deals with the individual works, ordered in chronology of estimated order of composition, in accord with the "Chronology" list published in the Methuen *Plays* volumes. *Appendix Two* addresses briefly the issues of substantial revisions of some play-texts and promptbooks.

The formatting and conventions of description employed differ for the different sections, as appropriate to their generic areas and modes of publication. For *Section A*, where the majority of the items described are books, the formatting generally follows that of Donald Gallup's *Ezra Pound: A Bibliography* (Charlottesville, VA: University of Virginia Press, 1983), Number 7 in the St Paul's Bibliographies series, and of other publications in this series, including B. C. Bloomfield's *Philip Larkin: A Bibliography 1933–1994,* Revised and enlarged edition (London: The British Library; New Castle, DE: Oak Knoll Press, 2002) (first edition 1979). However, more fully-detailed descriptions are provided of bindings and dust jackets, and fuller accounts of contents, to clarify the disparities between different manifestations. Where the notes to an entry deal with very disparate topics, they are sometimes presented in separately numbered notes, rather than being juxtaposed within a single paragraph.

Given that the majority of publications are British, this situation is the "default," and the country of publication is identified only when it is not the United Kingdom. Similarly, where theatres are referred to, they are London theatres unless otherwise indicated.

In transcription of lettering, the use of italic is identified, but not of bold type, because of the difficulty of doing so consistently, given that the standard modes of some typefaces appear bolder than those of others do. Use of bold lettering on bindings is sometimes quite common, and some features, such as "ff" used as a device for Faber and Faber, are normally in bold. Uses of decorative typefaces are noted, with no attempt to identify the face. Typesize difference is represented only when two sizes of type occur in the same line. The colour of lettering, rules, devices or decoration on title pages, bindings and dust jackets is black unless otherwise indicated; in some instances where other colours are present it is specified that some words, etc., are in black. Indications within square brackets of colour of lettering, or of an unusual typeface, apply only to the line of lettering immediately following, unless otherwise specified (where the lettering is down the spine, they apply to all lettering up to an indication of a change in colour or style). Similarly, reproduced photographs are black-and-white unless otherwise specified.

For binding-modes, the stock terms "hardback" and "paperback" are employed, although for the latter the cover material is usually light card, off-white or unpigmented on the inside (Dramatists Play Service volumes are bound with coloured card). Some hardbacks are "quarter-bound," that is, bound with coloured cloth (or sometimes leather) around the spine of the book, and extending several centimetres across the front and back boards, with the rest of the boards bound in some other cloth, or coloured paper. Where the same edition has appeared in both hardback and paperback bindings, where seen, both are described. Dust jackets for hardback copies are described when these have been seen; however, for copies in libraries, they have often been disposed of, and it has not always been practical to pursue copies retaining them. Usually, the dust jacket is similar to the paperback binding, with some material on the front and back flaps of the jacket that is to be found on the back cover of the paperback.

Pagination conventions broadly follow those of the St Paul's Bibliographies series. The fact that some of the first pages in the preliminaries are unpaginated is disregarded in the account of pagination, where they clearly have implied pagination within the main sequence, in relation to the first numbered page, or do so within an established preliminaries sequence in small Roman numerals (unlike Gallup, we take no account of whether the first numbered page is a recto or a verso). On the other hand, preliminaries leaves that precede either kind of sequence, and that bear printed matter, are identified simply as "leaves," and those with none as "blank leaves." At the end of the book, if the last page bearing printed matter of any kind is paginated, then the pagination extends only to its page number; thus, if this last page, p.65, say, is a recto, and the verso is blank, the pagination account would be 65 pp. If there were to be some printed matter on this verso, it would be 65, [1] pp. If there were to be one or more further leaves bearing some printed matter, they would be noted as "1 leaf," or, as it may be, "2 leaves," etc., with blank leaves also counted. Where there are single blank leaves at both the beginnings and the ends of books, these are generally noticed simply as endpapers, except in cases where they clearly belong to the gatherings bearing text. The abbreviation "pp." is used for "pages," rather than "p.," to avoid confusion with that for "pence."

Within the "Contents" note, unpaginated pages are designated by their implied page-numbers being within square brackets; and preliminaries pages that precede any identified sequence are designated with small Roman numerals within square brackets, where these numerals are not already being used, otherwise with "a," "b," etc. Inserted leaves are designated by the addition of "a," "b," etc. to the number of the preceding page.

With typescript items, typed matter and pagination are usually present on the rectos of leaves only. Hence, for example, "36 pp." indicates thirty-six leaves, paginated on the rectos 1–36, with the versos blank.

Measurements of leaf-dimensions are in centimetres, height by width. Rules that extend across a full width are not measured; otherwise their length is normally indicated in centimetres (sometimes simply as "short rule"). In many instances it has been impractical to include detailed signature statements, however, in some cases, where especially interesting, these are noted (see for instance A20a, A34a).

Data as to exact publication dates, subsequent printings, and numbers of copies printed are provided when known, usually derived from publishers' records (for some of them, we gratefully acknowledge indebtedness to Ms Letitia Dace's research notes). However, it has often not been possible to find out these details. Such information is usually provided only for the first impression or printing of the first edition, but when they are readily available for others, they are included. A rough indication of the month and day of publication is usually provided by the British Library accession date-stamp, or, for American editions, by the Library of Congress registration date. However, for first impressions of British publications, sometimes the British Library accession slightly precedes the official publication date, provided to us by the publisher, and for later reprints, or for American editions, may follow long after it.

Whenever possible, copies described have been of the first impressions of the first British editions, and of revised editions, and the first printings of American editions, and the first to incorporate revisions, but in a few cases, mainly with American editions, the nearest printing has been described. Generally, little attention has been accorded to subsequent straight reprints, even though these can sometimes involve a change of publisher (for example, recently various Grove Press publications have appeared for sale in Britain through Avalon Travel Publications; and an edition of the collected plays has been issued by Penguin Books Canada). Locations of copies are given only in the case of special copies, that is, authorially signed and numbered copies, or other significant association copies.

We have where practical examined two or more copies in each instance. Many of those seen have been in the British Library (which has not preserved dust-wrappers of hardback copies), or in the personal collection of Dr William Baker. Where copies of American editions have been interloaned from American libraries, some have had dust jackets and others have not, which has in a few cases caused uncertainty about the status of a Grove Press volume with a special setting, since the only explicit identification of a Book Club edition is to be found on the dust jacket.

In referring briefly to publishers, "Methuen" is being used as a blanket term for Methuen & Co., and its successor firms Eyre Methuen, Methuen London, etc., "Faber" for Faber and Faber, and "Grove" for Grove Press and Grove Weidenfeld (with the Evergreen and Black Cat series).

With *Sections B* and *I* the same degree of detail is provided as for *Section A*, except that in the first subsection of *Section I* a simplified form of the contents is provided. With *Sections C* to *H*, a simplified form of titles is provided, except for those items which are books. Where the title is that of a poem, short story, article or interview within a periodical or newspaper, where it has been seen, it is given in the form in which it occurs. Otherwise it is given in a standardised style, with capitals and lower case; so, this style does not necessarily represent that in which the title appeared. Similarly, other details are provided in a standardised, simplified form. A few items, which are books, such as the novel *The Dwarfs* in *Section D*, are given more detailed descriptions.

With *Appendix One*, an ad hoc format has been adopted to provide summary information about the composition, live performance or presentation via radio, television or film, and publication, of the various works. Given that for the films later reproductions are of the nature of copies with a different technology, no attention is given to video cassettes or DVD videodiscs.

The primary items of concern for an author bibliography are, properly, published items, but in the case of Pinter, a modern author still active in the early years of the twenty-first century, some notice needs to be accorded to the availability of other resources.

Outstandingly, there is the Pinter Archive (PA), lodged as Loan 110 in the British Library. This major collection of manuscript and typescript materials, for most of his works, was handed over by Harold Pinter on long-term loan to the British Library on 13 September 1993. These materials were initially divided up into 61 boxes, with later lodgings of documents relating to later writings up to the end of 2001 bringing the collection up to 74 boxes.

Some composition documents for the earliest plays had been left in the house in Hanover Terrace, Regent's Park, which Pinter had shared with his first wife, Vivien Merchant, and although he later returned to look for them, he could not find them. No materials survive for *The Room*, *The Dumb Waiter*, *The Birthday Party* (as a play), *A Slight Ache*, *A Night Out*, or for most of the early sketches. Three typescripts of *The Caretaker* as a stage play were sold to the Lilly Library, University of Indiana, Bloomington (which also has a few documents relating to radio sketches); however, the *Caretaker* box in the Pinter Archive does include one such typescript, with the remaining items relating to the adaptation for the film.

The contents of the collection have been listed in the British Library finding list, compiled by Dr Sally Brown; and they have been the subject of two substantial articles in *The Pinter Review*: by Susan Hollis Merritt, "The Harold Pinter Archive in the British Library," *TPR 1994*: 14–53; and by Steven H. Gale and Christopher C. Hudgins, "The Harold Pinter Archives II: A Description of the Filmscript Materials in the Archive in the British Library," *TPR 1995*: 101–142. In providing a summary account of documents relating to Pinter's screenplays, we are glad to acknowledge further information provided by Steven Gale and Christopher Hudgins. In our listing of items within each box, we are sometimes simply reduced to a "best-guess" rendition of their proper chronological order. The contents of the boxes may change from time to time as new material is deposited.

A significant cache of uncorrected proof copies of published volumes, and of duplicated typescripts issued for hire for early theatre-productions of stage-plays, can be found in the Pinter Collection in the Harry Ransom Humanities Research Centre at the University of Texas, Austin.

The British National Sound Archive (*NSA*), lodged in the British Library, includes an extensive collection of recordings of Harold Pinter's works in performance, or of performances or occasions in which he was involved, many of them from the BBC, as preserved recordings of radio broadcasts. Most are acoustic recordings but there are also a few video cassettes, including a video reproduction of the film of *The Caretaker*, and a video of the television production of *Mountain Language*.

The National Theatre Museum in London contains in its theatre-related material relevant to Pinter three folders of press-cuttings, one prompt book (for a Prospect Theatre production of *The Birthday Party*, using leaves from French's first edition, interleaved with unlined leaves on which there are many stage-directions in pencil), and a large number of theatre programmes of plays by Pinter, or authored by others and directed by him. Relatively few of these programmes, that have been seen, contain programme notes about the plays, and very few of these notes are evidently or possibly by Pinter.

The Shakespeare Centre in Stratford-upon-Avon holds some prompt-scripts used for Royal Shakespeare Company productions of Pinter's plays. Likewise, the Archives Centre of the Royal National Theatre in London holds prompt-copies of National Theatre productions of them. The BBC's Written Archives Centre at Caversham Park, Reading, has documents about many of Pinter's dealings with the BBC, for performances as an actor or narrator, talks, and recordings and broadcasts of his plays, as well as scripts preserved in its script library. Some resources relating to live theatre productions in New York are held in the New York Public Library, especially in the Billy T. Rose Theatre Collection.

The British Film Institute, with the associated British Film Library and Information Services, in London, holds in the National Film and Television

Archive some viewing copies of films, as well as some videos of television items, and, in the Library and Information Services, copies of film-scripts and press-books for the films for which Pinter wrote the screenplays which were produced by British companies, and a file of press-cuttings. Comparably the American Film Institute may hold some copies of films, and related materials, for films produced by American producers; certainly very substantial resources in this area are held by the Library of Congress in Washington. Some further material for the four films on which Pinter worked with Joseph Losey are in the British Film Institute, in the Joseph Losey Special Collection.

What one can propose, from pursuing this study, is that Harold Pinter may well have derived from his writing of poetry in the 1950s, before he came to the writing of plays, a degree of confidence and competence in the constituting of texts from a concatenation of disjunctive utterances and verbally-evoked images, held together by complex rhythms. From his early experiences as an actor he derived a sense of what can be made to work in the theatre, together with much reading, notably of Samuel Beckett.

Thereafter, while his manifold activities as a director of, or actor in, numerous stage-plays, television and radio dramas, or films, scripted by other writers, can be noticed here, when at all, only in the *Chronology*, nonetheless, a recognition of the extent to which he has been, and to some extent continues to be, a man of the theatre, in a broad sense, is vital for an adequate appreciation of the progress of his own dramatic writings. His increasing eminence has meant that he has been able to select which projects he would direct or act in, and yet there is plenty of testimony to his gift for engaging with the spirit of works by other authors, and for respecting and seeking to preserve their integrity. Hence, while he has developed his own distinctive authorial "voice," he has remained open to the challenges and stimuli deriving from such engagement. Shifting ideas and techniques have advanced dialectically through such engagement and openness.

Since 1973, when he was responding to the shock of the United States-induced military coup that overthrew the democratic government of Chile, and installed a murderous military dictatorship, Pinter's progressive engagements with political and humanitarian causes, though not with any political party, have led to a large body of non-literary writings; and these concerns have spread over to most of his later plays as well. He has, evidently, however, retained a grasp of the distance between art and propaganda.

Some of the political articles have been made available in the volume *Various Voices* (London: Penguin, 1998); yet we can dare to hope that the more comprehensive guide to these writings provided in our bibliographical history, with its annotations of entries, will serve to encourage people to seek wider understandings of the dialectic between Pinter's literary and non-literary writings.

This study remains however in several senses work in progress. For some items, mainly in *Sections E, G, J* and *K*, certain details remain undiscovered; yet we have provided whatever information has been available, to advance the search for them. From another perspective, Harold Pinter is still writing, and long may he continue to do so.

Acknowledgements

First, we thank Harold Pinter for his consent to our embarking on this project. It is an honour and a privilege to investigate the fine work documented here, and to add to the body of knowledge about it. Our publishers, David Way, Kathleen Houghton and Charlotte Lochhead at the British Library have been patient and understanding.

The circumstances of our working upon it have been fairly eccentric, with one of us based, for much of the time, in a provincial university city in New Zealand, and the other in a provincial university city in the United States, with relatively brief and very busy periods spent elsewhere in major research libraries or archive centres. We have accordingly owed much to the generosity of a number of individuals who have either answered our inquiries or have smoothed the way to our making good use of our time.

We have benefitted greatly from the kindness of Steven Gale and Christopher Hudgins in allowing us to draw upon their bibliographical resources, especially in relation to the archival material for Pinter's screenplays in the British Library, as well as upon their published works. We have also have benefitted from being able to draw upon the annual bibliographies compiled for *The Pinter Review* by Susan Hollis Merritt since 1987. We have been conscious of building upon the efforts of other predecessors as well, most notably Letitia (Tish) Dace who graciously allowed us to make use of her research notes, including data from publishers' records and extensive collection of plays and other works by and about Harold Pinter. This collection is now owned by William Baker. The "*Chronology*" draws upon several previous "Chronologies," especially those compiled by: Lois Gordon in *Harold Pinter: A Casebook*, edited by Lois Gordon (New York & London: Garland Publishing, Inc., 1990); D. Keith Peacock in *Harold Pinter and the New British Theatre* (Contributions to Drama and Theatre Studies, No. 27, Lives of the Theatre Series, Westport, CT, & London: Greenwood Press, 1997); and Peter Raby in *The Cambridge Companion to Harold Pinter*, edited by Peter Raby (Cambridge: Cambridge University Press, 2001). The website www.haroldpinter.org has been an invaluable resource, and we thank those who have maintained it.

Dr. Sally Brown and Dr. Chris Fletcher of the British Library Department of Manuscripts have been most helpful as was Dr. Alice Prochaska, formerly of the British Library and now at Yale University Library. We also thank Stuart Gillies, Information Services Manager, The British Library Newspaper Library, Colindale. Other librarians whose assistance has proved invaluable include Abby L. Yochelson at the Library of Congress, Washington, D.C., the librarians at the National Theatre Museum (London), the British Film Institute (London), The

Shakespeare Centre (Stratford-upon-Avon), Louise Ray, then archivist at the Royal National Theatre Archives (London), and Keith Feldman of the *Jewish Chronicle* Library (London). Thanks are also due to librarians at the Alexander Turnbull Library, Victoria University of Wellington, Wellington, New Zealand, the University Library, Massey University, Palmerston North, New Zealand, the Bodleian Library, Oxford, and the Cambridge University Library.

Marion Fallon and James Codd at the BBC Written Archives Centre, Caversham Park, Reading, have been most helpful. Special thanks are also due to Patrice S. Fox, John O. Kirkpatrick and Richard W. Oram at the Harry Ransom Humanities Research Center, the University of Texas at Austin, and Joel Silver at the Lilly Library, Indiana University, Bloomington, Indiana. G. Ronald Barshinger, Roberta Burk, and the staff at the Information Delivery Service (IDS) at Northern Illinois University Founders Memorial Library greatly helped with quickly obtaining books and articles. Also at Northern Illinois University Library, the Dean of Libraries, Dr. Arthur Young, and Mary Munroe, Associate Dean, proved most sympathetic to the needs of scholarship and research, as did Professor Jerrold H. Zar, former Associate Provost for Graduate Studies and Research and Dean of the Graduate School, Professor Frederick L. Kitterle, Dean of the College of Liberal Arts and Sciences, and respective Chairs of the Department of English. Gina Unger and Vicky Smith of the NIU Library performed wonders transforming unwieldy manuscript copy into a finished product. Gary VanderMeer at the NIU Law Library, Lynne Thomas, and Charles Larry of the NIU Library, are also to be thanked for securing valuable information. Professor Jitka Hurych of the University Libraries provided invaluable assistance with translating various languages into English. Thanks are due to Susan Oppenborn for careful proof-reading.

Individuals in publishing houses have been very helpful. They include the late Alan Clodd, who supplied much information about the Enitharmon Press and sold to William Baker many interesting Harold Pinter items including ephemera. His successor at the Enitharmon Press, Stephen Stuart-Smith, has been most helpful. Thanks are also due to: John Bodley, Jane Harrington, and Peggy Paterson at Faber and Faber (London); Amanda Smith, Editorial Director at Samuel French Inc. (London); Linda Kirkland at Samuel French Inc. (New York); Jean Rose at The Random House Group Archives and Library, Rushden, Wellingborough, Northants, UK (where Methuen files are now housed); Derrek Hines at the Cargo Press, Tregarne Manaccan, Cornwall; Alan Wilkinson of Brockhampton, Gloucestershire, and Anthony Astbury of The Greville Press, Leamington, Warwick.

Booksellers who have answered inquiries include Roger Duke of Kingston, Surrey, Rick Gekoski, Tim Guinnip of A to Zed Books, Curtis Faville, Compass Rose Books of Kensington, CA, Jeff Helman, Ted Hoffman, Bernard Quaritch Ltd, Julian Nagle and Julian Rota, amongst a host of others from whom William Baker has purchased Harold Pinter material for upwards of forty years. Over such a period many debts have been incurred, and we must apologize for inadvertent omission from these acknowledgements.

Thanks are due to Gerald Berkowitz, formerly of the Department of English, Northern Illinois University, who, upon retirement, sold William Baker his most interesting Harold Pinter collection. Thanks are also due to Charlotte Ainsworth, the *Guardian* newsroom; Elizabeth Bass of DeKalb, Illinois; Kirstie Blair of Glasgow University; Roy Copus of London; Dr. Richard Hansen, Middle Tennessee State University; Judy Daish, of Judy Daish Associates, Harold Pinter's agent; Hjordis Halvorson and Caroline Sietmann of the Newberry Library (Chicago); Dan Jacobson; Bernard Kops, another great Anglo-Jewish writer and a close personal friend of William Baker; Graham Law of Wasada University, Japan; Elizabeth Dyrud Lyman, Harvard University; Louis Marks; Craig Raine, editor of *Areté*; Peter Straus; Thelma Wax of ACTAC Theatrical and Cinematic; Professor Joseph Wiesenfarth of the University of Wisconsin, Madison; Laura Vorachek; Professor Ian Willison, of the University of London. We have wherever possible consulted with publishers when citing directly at any length, and thank in particular for permission and advice, Vanessa Coode, of the *London Review of Books* (www.lrb.co.uk).

This bibliographical tribute to greatness reflects personal engagement and passion on our part. Its genesis lies in a youthful William Baker's radio listening and theatre going. Powerful memories standing the test of time abide in his experiences of "A Slight Ache" (see *A12* and *W9*) broadcast on the BBC Third Programme on 29 July 1959 and of Pinter's "That's All," a short piece transmitted on 26 May 1960 on the Third Programme on Douglas Cleverdon's *Voices in the Air* (*A3*). Early in 1960 he went to the pre-London run of *The Caretaker* at the Theatre Royal, Brighton. Mick's smashing to pieces of Aston's Buddha remains one of the most frightening and powerful of theatrical moments witnessed by William Baker. It has haunted him and led to an obsession with Pinter's greatness, resulting in a monograph, *Harold Pinter* (written with S.E. Tabachnick) published in 1973 by Oliver & Boyd of Edinburgh and Barnes and Noble in New York and to various subsequent articles and reviews (see for instance "Metalingual Humor in Pinter's Early Plays," *English Studies*, 76 (May 1995), pp. 253–263, co-authored with Neil Norrick). Another consequence has been the amassing of a personal library of material by and about Harold Pinter which he has collected for over forty years.

The origins of the collaboration between the two bibliographical historians, William Baker and John C. Ross, is outlined in the "Acknowledgements" section of their *George Eliot: A Bibliographical History* (Oak Knoll, British Library, 2002), pp. xxv-xxvii. Living mostly in New Zealand, from 1965 to 1973 John C. Ross was based in London and getting to see as much theatre as he could afford. This included the first productions of *The Homecoming*, *Old Times,* and *Landscape*. He found the first especially memorable for conveying a sense of predatory beasts circling around and striking at one another. From *Old Times* he recalls the prolonged, yet precisely timed, pauses of the opening sequence and the quiet devastation of the ending, and from *Landscape* the delicate artistic control of the interweaving of the monologues of Beth and Duff. He has become increasingly aware of Pinter's artistic courage and imaginative integrity in pursuing his own diverse literary visions. In pursuing this project John Ross has gained equal respect for Pinter's political courage and articulateness in championing a multitude of humanitarian and radical political causes as reflected in his writings. Moreover, it has been fascinating to pursue his dramatic works through a range of drafts and through adaptations for different media. We dare to hope that the documentation provided here will do some justice to Pinter's manifold works and will help to make accessible something of this fascination.

Finally, special thanks are due to Mrs Diana Gurney of Camden Town and Rivka Baker of DeKalb, Illinois who provided generous hospitality to John Ross and Doreen D'Cruz in the winter of 2001–2002. Karen Baker and Sharon Baker-Davis provided generous hospitality to their father on his frequent London visits in pursuit of Harold Pinter. Emily Ross of Dunedin, New Zealand and Catherine Tuato'o Ross kindly checked out resources in local libraries. Our especial thanks to Professor Donald Hawes of London who has been wonderfully generous of his time and expertise in responding to numerous inquiries about vital details and double-checking information. Last, but not least, our heartfelt thanks to our wives, Rivka Baker and Doreen D'Cruz, for their love, support, and gracious patience.

William Baker
John C. Ross
October 2004

Abbreviations

BBC	British Broadcasting Corporation
BFI	British Film Institute, London
Billington	Michael Billington, *The Life and Work of Harold Pinter* (London: Faber and Faber, 1996)
CP&P	Harold Pinter, *Collected Poems and Prose* (London: Faber and Faber, 1991)
DF	Drama, foreign (in DLC registration numbers)
DLC	Library of Congress, Washington, District of Columbia
DP	Drama, published (i.e., in the USA; in DLC registration numbers)
DPS	Dramatists Play Service, New York
DU	Drama, unpublished (in DLC registration numbers)
Faber	Faber and Faber, publishers
Gale, *Sharp Cut*	*Sharp Cut: Harold Pinter's Screenplays and the Artistic Process* (Lexington, KY: University Press of Kentucky, 2003)
Gordon	Lois Gordon, "Selected Bibliography." In *Pinter at 70: A Casebook*, edited by Lois Gordon (New York and London: Routledge, 2001), pp. 291–331
ICA	Institute of Contemporary Arts, London
InU-L	Lilly Library, University of Indiana, Bloomington, Indiana
ISBN	International Standard Book Number
L	British Library, London
LCCN	Library of Congress Catalog Number
NSA	National Sound Archive, British Library
O	Bodleian Library, Oxford
p.	pence
PA	Pinter Archive, lodged in the Manuscripts Department, British Library
Page	*File on Pinter*, compiled by Malcolm Page (London: Methuen Drama, 1993)
P&P	Harold Pinter, *Poems and Prose 1949–1977* (London: Eyre Methuen, 1978)
pp.	pages
RNT	Royal National Theatre
RSC	Royal Shakespeare Company
RT	*Radio Times*
TPR	*The Pinter Review*
TxU-HRC	Harry Ransom Research Centre, University of Texas, Austin, Texas
VV	Harold Pinter, *Various Voices: Prose, Poetry, Politics 1948–1998* (London: Faber and Faber, 1998)
WAC	Written Archives Centre, BBC, Caversham Park, Reading

List of Illustrations

Colour illustrations of dust jackets for the following titles can be found after page xl.

Chronology

1930   10 October, born, the only child of Hyman (Jack) Pinter and Frances, *née* Mann, at 19 Thistlewaite Road, Hackney, London.

1939   Following the outbreak of war in September, evacuated to a castle, Caerhays, near Megavissey, in Cornwall. Returned home, late 1940; in 1941, evacuated again, for a time, to Reading, with his mother. In 1944, evacuated, for a time, to Norfolk. Otherwise, in London during most of the bombing.

1944–48   Attends Hackney Downs Grammar School. Plays football and cricket and goes in for sprinting and debating. Encouraged and inspired by the English teacher, Joseph Brearley. In 1946–48, has essays, poems, and debating speeches printed in issues of the *Hackney Downs School Magazine*. In 1947–48, acts the lead-roles in *Macbeth* and *Romeo and Juliet*.

1948   Attends (erratically) the Royal Academy of Dramatic Art, Gower Street, for two terms, to study acting.
In October, responds to National Service call-up by registering as a conscientious objector.

1949   Drops out of RADA. For refusing military service, twice arrested, tried, and fined. Living at home, reading, writing, work-seeking, through to 1951. Writes the short story, *Kullus*, and other short stories, some poetry.

1950   Four poems published in *Poetry London*. From late 1950, occasional work as a radio actor.

1951   January-July, at the Central School of Speech and Drama.
14 January, participates as an actor in a production by R. D. Smith for the BBC Third Programme of Shakespeare's *Henry VIII*.
Another poem in *Poetry London*.

1951–52   From September 1951 to Autumn 1952, with Anew McMaster's repertory company touring around Ireland. Writes some poetry.
In 1952, begins writing *The Dwarfs* as a novel (completed 1956; published 1990).

1953–57   Occasional acting work, casual jobs (waiter, dish-washer, bouncer, etc.), and writing. In early 1953, 3-month contract with Donald Wolfit's company, King's Theatre, Hammersmith; otherwise acting in provincial repertory companies. While with Wolfit's company, first encounters Vivien Merchant (her stage-name; born Ada Thomson) and also Alun Owen. In 1954, adopts stage-name "David Baron" (after September 1960, uses his own name).

1954–55   Writes *The Black and White* as short story.

1955   Writes *The Examination* as short story. Acting in Colchester Repertory, etc.

1956   14 September, marries actress Vivien Merchant in registry office marriage while both are acting in Bournemouth.

1957   15 and 16 May, first dramatic work, *The Room,* performed at the Drama Department of Bristol University, directed by Henry Woolf.

July, in Bristol, while on tour with the farce *Dear Charles,* meets Jimmy Wax (d.1983), who becomes his agent.

30 December, new production of *The Room* by the Bristol Old Vic Theatre School, directed by Duncan Ross, for the *Sunday Times* student drama competition, associated with the National Student Drama Festival in Bristol. Harold Hobson, the *Sunday Times* drama critic, one of the judges for the competition, writes in praise of the play, attracting the attention of the impresario Michael Codron.

Writes *The Birthday Party* and *The Dumb Waiter.* Living in a basement flat in Notting Hill Gate, London.

1958   29 January, son Daniel born (1975, changes name to Daniel Brand). Family moves to a first floor flat in Chiswick High Road.

28 April, *The Birthday Party* opens at the Arts Theatre, Cambridge; successful there and in Oxford, but in the Lyric Theatre, Hammersmith, opening 19 May, closes after one week.

Writes *A Slight Ache* (based upon an unproduced radio play, *Something in Common*) and *The Hothouse* (not submitted) as radio plays for the BBC.

1959   January, directs *The Birthday Party* in Birmingham.

28 February, *The Dumb Waiter* premièred in German in Frankfurt-am-Main.

11 May, *The Birthday Party* performed by the Tavistock Players at the Tower Theatre, Canonbury, Islington, which helps to rehabilitate the play.

Spring, early summer, writes *A Night Out* for radio.

15 July, *Trouble in the Works* and *The Black and White* (rewritten as sketch) premièred within Michael Codron's revue, *One to Another,* Lyric Theatre, Hammersmith.

29 July, *A Slight Ache* broadcast, BBC Third Programme.

23 September, *Request Stop, Last to Go,* and *Special Offer* premièred within Codron's revue, *Pieces of Eight,* Apollo Theatre.

During 1959 writes *The Caretaker.*

1960   21 January, double-bill, *The Room* and *The Dumb Waiter,* opens at the Hampstead Theatre Club; 8 March, transfers to the Royal Court Theatre.

1 March, *A Night Out* on radio, BBC Third Programme.

22 March, *The Birthday Party* on television, Associated Rediffusion TV.

24 April, *A Night Out* on television, ABC-TV (Pinter as Seeley).

27 April, *The Caretaker* opens at the Arts Theatre Club; 30 May, opens at the Duchess Theatre for a long run; wins *Evening Standard* award.

Summer, family moves to Fairmead Court, Kew.

21 July, *Night School* televised, networked by Associated Rediffusion.

27 July, first American production of *The Birthday Party* opens at the Actors' Workshop, San Francisco.

2 December, *The Dwarfs,* as radio play, on BBC Third Programme.

1961   18 January, *A Slight Ache* (as stage-play) opens, Arts Theatre Club, within a triple-bill, *Three.*

11 May, *The Collection* on television, Associated Rediffusion.

17 September, *A Night Out* (as stage play) opens, Gate Theatre, Dublin; 2 October, opens at the Comedy Theatre, within triple-bill, *Counterpoint.*

4 October, *The Caretaker* opens at the Lyceum Theatre on Broadway, New York, runs for five months (with two out of three actors from the London cast).

5 October, *The Room* televised, Granada.

1962   20 March, *The Caretaker* on BBC radio.

18 June, *The Collection* opens at the Aldwych Theatre, directed for the RSC by Peter Hall and Pinter.

9 November, *The Collection* on radio, BBC Third Programme.

November, *The Collection* staged off-Broadway, Cherry Lane Theatre.

December, shooting begins for film of *The Caretaker,* directed by Clive Donner.

Working on screenplay of *The Servant* with Joseph Losey (shooting begins January 1963) based on novel by Robin Maugham (first proposed by Losey, 27 April 1960).

Writes *The Lover* for television.

1963   28 March, *The Lover* broadcast on Associated Rediffusion Television [TV] (wins Prix Italia for Television Drama and several Guild of British Television Producers and Directors awards).

17 April, reads "Mac" on radio, BBC Third Programme.

18 September, *The Lover* (as stage-play) in double-bill with *The Dwarfs,* opens at the Arts Theatre Club, co-directed by Pinter and Guy Vaesen, produced by Codron.

14 November, film *The Servant* released, directed by Joseph Losey.

1 December, film of *The Caretaker* released (first screened in Berlin, 27 June; wins a Silver Bear award); released 20 January 1964 in USA as *The Guest*; film receives Screenwriters' Guild Award.

Writes *Tea Party* as short story; read by him on BBC Third Programme, 2 June 1964.

During 1963 family moves to 14 Ambrose Place, Worthing.

Writes screenplay of *The Pumpkin Eater,* from novel by Penelope Mortimer.

Writes *The Homecoming.*

1964   2 March, receives British Screenwriters' Guild Award for screenplay of *The Servant*; also, wins New York Film Critics' Award.

28 April, 12 May, 26 May, nine sketches directed by Michael Bakewell on BBC Third Programme.

18 June, *The Birthday Party,* revival by the RSC, opens at the Aldwych Theatre, directed by Pinter.

15 July, film *The Pumpkin Eater* released.

During 1964, family moves to Hanover Terrace, Regent's Park.

Writes *Tea Party* (as television play, for BBC-TV, European Broadcasting Union).

Writes first draft of screenplay of *The Go-Between,* by L. P. Hartley, for Joseph Losey.

1965   25 March, *Tea Party* broadcast on television (BBC-TV, etc.).

30 March, receives British Film Academy Award for screenplay of *The Pumpkin Eater.*

3 June, *The Homecoming* opens in London, Aldwych Theatre, directed by Peter Hall (opened in Cardiff, 25 March; Hall's production moves to Broadway, opens 3 January 1997; wins three awards).

During 1965 works on screenplay of *The Quiller Memorandum,* from novel by Elleston Trevor ("Adam Hall," *The Berlin Memorandum*).

1965–66   Working on screenplay of *Accident,* from novel by Nicholas Mosley; directed by Joseph Losey.

1966   June, created Commander of the Order of the British Empire (CBE).

25 September, *Night School* on radio, BBC Third Programme.

10 November, *The Quiller Memorandum* released.

During 1966 writes *The Basement* for BBC2 TV.

1967   6 February, *A Slight Ache* televised, BBC2.

9 February, film *Accident* released; wins Cannes Jury Prize.

13 February, *A Night Out* televised, BBC2.

20 February, *The Basement* broadcast on BBC2 TV, Theatre 625 series (Pinter as Stott).

27 July, directs Robert Shaw's *The Man in the Glass Booth*, St Martin's Theatre, London (in October 1968, directs Broadway production).

Autumn, writes *Landscape* for the RSC (Pinter refuses to accept cuts demanded by the Lord Chamberlain as censor of stage-plays).

1968   25 April, *Landscape* broadcast as radio play, BBC Third Programme. September, Theatres Act abolishes the censorship powers of the Lord Chamberlain (removes hindrance to stage-production of *Landscape*).

10 October, stage versions of *The Basement* and *Tea Party* open as double-bill, Eastside Playhouse, New York.

9 December, film version of *The Birthday Party* released in New York; released in London, February 1970; directed by William Friedkin. Writes *Silence*.

1969   9 April, sketch *Night* staged as part of an eight-sketch revue, *Mixed Doubles*, Comedy Theatre, London.

2 July, *Landscape* and *Silence* produced as double-bill, RSC at Aldwych.

2 August, *Silence* on radio, BBC Radio 3.

15 September, *Night* on radio, BBC Radio 3.

26 October, *The Lover* on radio, adaptation by Guy Vaesen, BBC Radio 4.

Writes revised screenplay for *The Go-Between* (shot during 1970). Television film *Pinter People*, NBC Experiment in TV.

1970   Spring, Shield Productions established as a company to produce new plays in London's West End with Pinter as one of the partners (with David Mercer, Christopher Morahan, Jimmy Wax, and Terence Baker), first production in May, David Mercer's *Flint*.

June, awarded German Shakespeare Prize of the Freiherr v. Stein Foundation, at Hamburg, gives acceptance speech.

17 September, *Tea Party* and *The Basement*, as double-bill, open at Duchess Theatre, London.

26 October, *The Servant*, radio adaptation by Guy Vaesen, on BBC Radio 4.

November-December, directs James Joyce's *Exiles* at Mermaid Theatre, London, as second production by Shield Productions.

1971   May, *The Go-Between* wins Grand Prix (Palm D'Or) at the Cannes Film Festival, and, later, Writers' Guild and BAFTA awards; released in July.

Directs Simon Gray's play *Butley*, in Oxford and the Criterion Theatre. Writing *Old Times*.

1 June, *Old Times* opens at the Aldwych Theatre, directed for the RSC by Peter Hall.

Autumn, writing film script of *Langrishe, Go Down,* by Aidan Higgins (filmed for TV in 1978; not filmed for cinema).

November, in New York, preparing *Old Times* for Broadway production.

Awarded Hon. D. Litt. by Birmingham University.

1972 Working with Joseph Losey and Barbara Bray on adapting Marcel Proust's *À la recherche du temps perdu* as screenplay (remains unfilmed, but published in 1978 as *The Proust Screenplay;* 1982, one section filmed and released as *Un Amour de Swann,* a box-office failure; December 1995, adapted by Michael Bakewell as a two-hour radio drama, broadcast by BBC Radio 3).

1973 February, becomes an associate director of the National Theatre, at Peter Hall's invitation; retains this position through to his resignation in mid-1983; participates in its shift from the Old Vic to the South Bank.

13 April, *Monologue* on television, BBC2-TV.

May, conflict with Luchino Visconti over Visconti's production of *Old Times* with the Teatro di Roma.

Directs Simon Gray's *Butley,* for BBC television.

Film *The Homecoming* released in USA (in UK in 1976), directed by Peter Hall for the American Film Theatre series.

Receives Austrian State Prize for European Literature.

Declares opposition to US-sponsored overthrow of democratic government of Chile.

1974 May, directs John Hopkins, *The Next of Kin,* for the Royal National Theatre.

Working on screenplay for *The Last Tycoon* from the uncompleted novel by Scott Fitzgerald.

Writes *No Man's Land;* completed in September; accepted for National Theatre.

Awarded honorary doctorates from Glasgow University and University of East Anglia.

1975 From January onward, develops a relationship with Lady Antonia Fraser, the wife of Hugh Fraser, MP, which leads to the break-up of his own marriage in late April, eventual divorce, and marriage to Antonia Fraser in October 1980.

23 April, *No Man's Land* opens at the Old Vic; 15 July, transfers to Wyndham's Theatre. Directs Simon Gray's *Otherwise Engaged,* first at Oxford, opens 28 July at the Queen's Theatre (and later, directs it in New York).

August, Pinter and Antonia Fraser return to London from a village near Burford, Oxfordshire; living in Launceston Place, South Kensington.

22 October, *Old Times* televised, BBC2.

3 December, *Monologue* on BBC Radio 3 (Pinter as The Man).

1976   February, *Old Times* on radio, BBC.

Directs Noel Coward's *Blithe Spirit,* for the National Theatre; opens 24 June.

October, directs William Archibald's *The Innocents,* and Gray's *Otherwise Engaged,* in New York.

10 November, film, *The Last Tycoon,* released in the USA; in 1977 in the UK; directed by Elia Kazan.

Directs *Butley* on television.

1977   July, film, *The Go-Between,* released.

August, moves to Antonia Fraser's family home in Holland Park.

Writes *Betrayal.*

1978   Directs Simon Gray's *The Rear Column,* at the Globe Theatre.

20 September, *Langrishe, Go Down* screened as television play, as BBC-2 Play of the Week.

3 October, *No Man's Land* on television, Granada.

15 November, *Betrayal* opens at the Lyttleton Theatre, South Bank, directed by Roger Hall for the RNT.

Begins writing screenplay of *The French Lieutenant's Woman* by John Fowles (first notes in 1970).

1979   September, participates in launching of the Greville Press at the Purcell Room, Royal Festival Hall (set up by Anthony Astbury, whom Pinter got to know in 1975, and Geoffrey Godbert; Pinter chairs the evening and compares readings by poets; Pinter will co-edit three anthologies of poetry for the Press and privately finance a number of its publications; in 1987, joins its board).

Directs Gray's *Close of Play,* at the Lyttleton Theatre, RNT, South Bank.

1980   24 April, *The Hothouse* (first written in 1958) opens at the Hampstead Theatre, directed by Pinter; 25 June, transfers to the Ambassadors Theatre.

27 October, legal marriage to Antonia Fraser.

Writes *Family Voices* for radio.

Directs Simon Gray's *The Rear Column* for television (BBC).

1981   22 January, *Family Voices* on radio, BBC Radio 3; 13 February, on stage ("platform performance"), RNT; wins Giles Cooper Award in 1982.

27 March, *The Hothouse* on television, BBC2, directed by Pinter.

25 June, "Players" on radio, BBC Radio 3: see *W20 (3)*.
The French Lieutenant's Woman released, directed by Karel Reisz for United British Artists.
Directs Gray's *Quartermaine's Terms,* at the Queen's Theatre.
Directs Robert East's *Incident at Tulse Hill,* at the Hampstead Theatre.
Presented with Common Wealth Award for Distinguished Service in Dramatic Arts, jointly with Tennessee Williams, in Shubert Theatre, New York.

1982   3 October, death of Vivien Merchant.
14 October, *Other Places* as a triple-bill, *A Kind of Alaska, Victoria Station, Family Voices,* opens at the Cottesloe Theatre, RNT, directed by Peter Hall.
Writes screenplay of Joseph Conrad's *Victory* (never filmed).
Wins David De Donatello Prize; awarded Hon. D. Litt. from Brown University.

1983   May, directs Jean Giraudoux's *The Trojan War Will Not Take Place* (*Le guerre de Troie n'aura pas lieu*), at the Lyttleton Theatre, RNT.
18 December, *Precisely,* a short sketch, directed by Pinter, premièred as part of an anti-nuclear show, *The Big One,* at the Apollo Victoria Theatre.
Film version of *Betrayal* released; directed by David Jones.

1984   13 March, *One for the Road* opens as part of a double-bill with *Victoria Station,* Lyric Theatre Studio, Hammersmith (Lunchtime Theatre).
Directs Simon Gray's *The Common Pursuit,* at the Lyric Theatre, Hammersmith.
Directs *Other Places* for Manhattan Theatre Club, New York, with *One for the Road* substituted for *Family Voices*; 7 March 1985, same triple-bill in Duchess Theatre, London.
16 December, *A Kind of Alaska* televised, Central Television.

1985   March, Pinter and Arthur Miller, on behalf of International PEN, as vice-presidents of the British and American branches of PEN, spend five days in Turkey, meeting intellectuals, dissidents, etc. Pinter continues thereafter to campaign on human rights abuses in Turkey.
Writes screenplay for Russell Hoban's *Turtle Diary,* produced and released this year.
23 July, *The Dumb Waiter* televised, BBC2-TV.
25 July, *One for the Road* televised, BBC2-TV.
July, directs Tennessee Williams' *Sweet Bird of Youth,* at the Theatre Royal, Haymarket.
Takes over role of Deeley in David Jones' production of *Old Times,* for American tour to St Louis and Los Angeles.
Film, *Turtle Diary,* released.

1986   June, directs Donald Freed's *Circe and Bravo,* Hampstead Theatre,
            later at Wyndhams Theatre
            20 June, Pinter and Antonia begin participating in regular meetings
            of a group of like-minded left-wing liberals, who come to be known
            as the June 20th Society (continued till 1992).

1987–89   Working on screenplay of Margaret Atwood's *The Handmaid's Tale;*
            it would be filmed and released in 1990 but with a script much worked
            on by other writers.

1987   February, takes part in public protest outside the American embassy
            against United States actions via the Contras in Nicaragua; later this
            year, launches Arts for Nicaragua Fund in the Royal Court Theatre;
            in December, writes article in the *Guardian* drawing attention to the
            condemnation by the International Court of Justice in June 1986 of
            United States actions in Nicaragua, and its overthrowing of democ-
            ratic governments in Guatemala in 1954, and in Chile in 1973.
            12 May, *The Dumb Waiter* televised, ABC Television.
            21 June, *The Birthday Party* televised, BBC2, in Theatre Night series
            (Pinter as Goldberg).
            26 December, *The Room* televised, ABC Television.

1988   20 October, *Mountain Language* opens, Lyttleton Theatre, RNT, as
            early-evening platform performance, directed by Pinter; 11
            December, televised on BBC2, directed by Pinter.
            Writes television adaptation of Elizabeth Bowen's *The Heat of the Day.*
            One of signatories, "Charter 88," a manifesto demanding a Bill of
            Rights and a written constitution for the UK.

1988–90   Writes screenplay of Fred Uhlman's novella *Reunion.*
            Writes screenplay of Ian McEwan's novel *The Comfort of Strangers.*
            In 1989, commissioned to write a film-script of Kafka's *The Trial,* for
            the Hungarian director Istvan Szabo, but the project does not get very
            far, at this time, because of incompatible visions.

1989   1 June, *The Birthday Party* televised, BBC2-TV.
            30 December, *The Heat of the Day* broadcast on television, Granada.

1990   6 February, delivers Salman Rushdie's Herbert Read Memorial
            Lecture, at Institute of Contemporary Arts (Rushdie was in hiding).
            Directs Jane Stanton Hitchcock's *Vanilla,* at the Lyric Theatre,
            Shaftesbury Avenue.
            October, *The Dwarfs* published, as a novel.
            9 October, *Betrayal* as a radio play, on BBC Radio 3.
            10 October, Pinter's sixtieth birthday: celebrated by four-hour pro-
            gramme on BBC Radio 3.
            Working on screenplay of Kazuo Ishiguro's novel *The Remains of the*

Day; much of the script would later be replaced with a new version by Ruth Prawer Jhabvala, but 7 or 8 scenes retained.

Film *The Comfort of Strangers* released; directed by Paul Schrader.

Film *The Handmaid's Tale* released; directed by Volker Schlöndorff.

Film *Reunion* released, directed by Jerry Schatzberg.

1991   Writing *Party Time.*

19–21 April, Pinter symposium at Ohio State University, Columbus, to honour Pinter's sixtieth birthday, included rehearsed reading of *Party Time,* and reading by Pinter of *The New World Order.*

Directs *The Caretaker,* opens 20 June at the Comedy Theatre.

June, participates in Nicaragua Solidarity Campaign appeal to the United States to comply with the World Court's ruling on Nicaragua.

19 July, sketch *The New World Order,* directed by Pinter, opens at Royal Court Theatre Upstairs.

26 October, *Old Times* televised, BBC2-TV.

31 October, *Party Time* opens at the Almeida Theatre; double-bill with *Mountain Language.*

1992   April, awarded insignia of Grand Officer, the Chilean Order of Merit, for his support for the restoration of democracy in Chile.

Revival of *No Man's Land,* at the Almeida Theatre, directed by David Leveaux, with Pinter playing Hirst (closes mid-December; re-opens at the Comedy Theatre, February 1993).

October, Pinter's mother dies.

17 November, *Party Time* as television play on Channel Four, directed by Pinter.

Writing screenplay of Franz Kafka's *The Trial,* for BBC Films.

1993   June, film *The Trial* released.

June, directs David Mamet's *Oleanna,* at the Royal Court Theatre; in September, transfers to the Duke of York's Theatre.

7 September, *Moonlight* opens at the Almeida Theatre; in November, transfers to the Comedy Theatre.

September, donates sixty boxes of manuscripts to the British Library; would become the Pinter Archive.

1994   May, first Pinter Festival, Gate Theatre, Dublin, with performances of three pairs of plays (short paired with long), over three weeks: *The Dumb Waiter* and *Betrayal; One for the Road* and *Old Times; Landscape* (directed by Pinter; this production later transferred to RNT) and *Moonlight.*

Working on a new screenplay of Vladimir Nabokov's novel *Lolita,* not used.

1995   March, awarded David Cohen British Literature Prize, for lifetime's achievement.

April, awarded honorary doctorate at Sofia University, Bulgaria; in acceptance speech foregrounds the downsides of Western democracies and corrupt usages of language.

Summer, directs Ronald Harwood's *Taking Sides*, Chichester Festival Theatre; transferred to Criterion Theatre.

Plays Roote in *The Hothouse,* Chichester Festival Theatre; transferred to Comedy Theatre.

21 October, *Landscape* televised, BBC2 (based on Gate Theatre production).

November, takes part in PEN protest condemning the Nigerian Government's hanging of Ken Saro-Wiwa and eight other Ogoni activists.

31 December, *The Proust Screenplay,* radio adaptation, on BBC Radio 3 (Pinter as the voice of the Screenplay).

1996   Directs Reginald Rose's *Twelve Angry Men,* Bristol Old Vic and Comedy Theatre.

12 September, *Ashes to Ashes* opens, Royal Court at the Ambassadors Theatre, directed by Pinter.

Receives Laurence Olivier Special Award for lifetime's achievement in theatre.

Film version of *Landscape* released.

December, "Pinter Autumn" festival at the Centro de Cultura Contemporània de Barcelona; see *G91.*

1997   Second Pinter Festival, Gate Theatre, Dublin: *The Collection* (with Pinter in role of Harry), *Ashes to Ashes* (directed by Pinter), *A Kind of Alaska* and *No Man's Land.*

Directs Simon Gray's *Life Support,* Aldwych Theatre.

Writes screenplay of *The Dreaming Child,* by Karen Blixen.

Received the Sunday Times Award for Excellence and a BAFTA Fellowship.

Received a Moliere d'Honneur in Paris.

1998   16 March, *Victoria Station* on radio, BBC Radio 4.

Publishes *Various Voices.*

Made a Companion of Literature by the Royal Society of Literature.

1999   Directs Simon Gray's *The Late Middle Classes,* Palace Theatre, Watford.

2000   16 March, *Celebration,* in double-bill with *The Room,* opens at the Almeida Theatre, both directed by Pinter.

18 April, awarded honorary degree, Aristotle University of Thessaloniki; see *E48.*

8 October, *Moonlight* as radio play, BBC Radio 3 (Pinter as Andy).

23 November, *Remembrance of Things Past* adapted as stage-play by

Di Trevis from *The Proust Screenplay,* opens at RNT.

Writes screenplay of *The Tragedy of King Lear* (not yet filmed).

Received The Critics' Circle Award for Distinguished Service to the Arts.

Awarded the Brianza Poetry Prize, Italy.

2001   16–29 July, Lincoln Center Festival 2001, New York, at Pinter Festival: productions from the Gate Theatre [4], Almeida Theatre [3] and Royal Court Theatre [2]: *A Kind of Alaska, One for the Road* (Pinter as Nicholas), *The Homecoming, Landscape, Monologue, The Room* (directed by Pinter), *Celebration* (directed by Pinter), *Mountain Language* and *Ashes to Ashes*; also "Symposia Series", with a talk by Michael Billington on Pinter, three symposia ("Playwrights on Pinter," "Actors on Pinter," "Directors on Pinter"), and "Pinter on Pinter" speaking with Mel Gussow (27 July), see *G112*; also, 21–31 July, screenings of ten films for which Pinter wrote the screenplays (including the television play *Langrishe, Go Down*).

10 September, awarded Laurea ad Honorem, University of Florence; see *E50*.

Received World Leaders Award, Toronto, Canada.

Received Hermann Kesten Medallion for outstanding commitment on behalf of persecuted and imprisoned writers, awarded by German PEN, Berlin.

Received S. T. Dupont Golden Pen Award, for a Lifetime's Distinguished Service to Literature.

Received "Premio Fiesole ai Maestri del Cinema," Italy.

Received the South Bank Show Award for Outstanding Achievement in the Arts.

2002   8, 11 February, two programmes of sketches at the RNT, including *Press Conference* (Pinter in role of The Minister) and *Tess* (also published as short story).

April, operation for cancer of the oesophagus, followed by chemotherapy.

August, created Companion of Honour (had declined offer of a knighthood).

25 August, appeared at the Edinburgh International Book Festival; see *G117*.

9 October, Barbican Screen: screening of *The Caretaker*; on-stage talk by Harold Pinter with Michael Billington about his life and work; 12 October: screening *The Basement, The Servant*; 13 October: screening *Langrishe, Go Down* and *The Go Between*.

From 26 October, for a fortnight, "Pinter at the BBC": BBC Two (TV): Arena series: two-part portrait by Nigel Williams; BBC Four (TV): season of Pinter's plays, films and talks; also items on BBC radio, BBC1.

October onward, involved in protests about the forthcoming invasion of Iraq; see *E52, E55, E56*.

27 November, awarded honorary degree, University of Turin; see *E54*.

2003 15 February, participated in massive Anti-Iraq War rally; see *E56*.

8 June, read poems from new collection *War*, at RNT; for on-stage conversation with Billington, see *G119*.

Continued involvement in Stop the War Coalition events. 13 October, one of group named as spearheading relevant cultural events, in programme of protest relating to President George W. Bush's visit to London *ca.* 20 November. One of the British signatories to the Cairo Declaration, relating to the International Campaign Against US Aggression in Iraq.

2004 Awarded Diploma "ad Honorem," Teatro Filmodrammatici, Milan, Italy.

18 May, reads three poems from *War* and three poems by Stephen Spender at "The Word Bites Like a Fish," Stephen Spender Memorial Trust Reading at the Queen Elizabeth Hall, London.

April–June, directing Simon Gray's *The Old Masters*, Birmingham Repertory Theatre, and later, Comedy Theatre, London.

June, takes part in Dublin Writers' Festival, awarded degree of Doctor of Literature, National University of Ireland.

4 August, given Wilfred Owen Award for Poetry, for his anti-war poems.

17 September, takes part in "Authors Take Side on Iraq" debate, Imperial War Museum.

14–17 October, participates in preliminary events of the Third European Forum, London, as one of the writers offering "Words of Resistance."

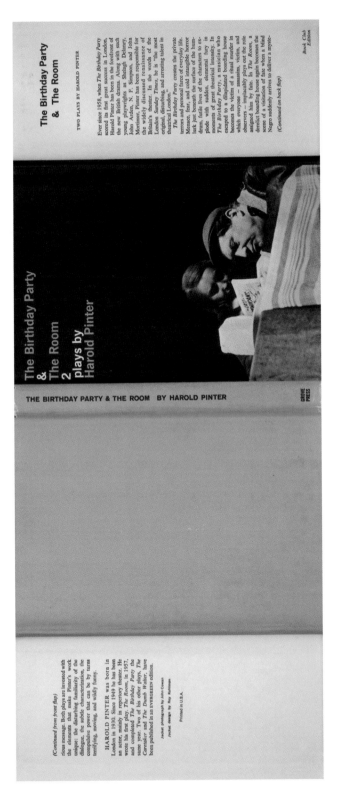

The Birthday Party & The Room

TWO PLAYS BY HAROLD PINTER

Ever since 1958, when *The Birthday Party* scored its first great success in London, Harold Pinter has been in the forefront of the new British drama. Along with such young playwrights as Shelagh Delaney, John Arden, N. F. Simpson, and John Mortimer, Pinter has been responsible for the widely discussed renaissance of Britain's theater. In the words of the London *Sunday Times*, he is "the most original, disturbing, and arresting talent in theatrical London."

The Birthday Party creates the private terrors and personal fears of everyday life. Menace, fear, and cold intangible horror lurk just beneath the surface of the humdrum, futile lives of the characters to explode with sudden, elemental fury. In *The Birthday Party*, a musician who escaped to a dilapidated boarding house becomes the victim of a ritual murder in which everyone — assassins, victim, and observers — implacably plays out the role assigned him by fate. In *The Room*, a derelict boarding house again becomes the scene of a visitation of fate when a blind Negro suddenly arrives to deliver a myste-

(Continued on back flap)

(Continued from front flap)
rious message. Both plays are invested with the elements that make Pinter's work unique: the disturbing familiarity of the dialogue, the subtle characterization, the compulsive power that can be by turns terrifying, moving, and wildly funny.

HAROLD PINTER was born in London in 1930. Since 1949 he has been an actor, mainly in repertory theatre. He wrote his first play, *The Room*, in 1957, and completed *The Birthday Party* the same year. Two of his other plays, *The Caretaker* and *The Dumb Waiter*, have been published in an EVERGREEN edition.

Jacket photograph by John Cowan
Jacket design by Roy Kuhlman

Printed in U.S.A.

The Birthday Party
&
The Room
2
plays by
Harold Pinter

THE BIRTHDAY PARTY & THE ROOM BY HAROLD PINTER

GROVE PRESS

A11b. *The Birthday Party & The Room*, Book Club Edition, 1961, dust jacket. Actual jacket size 21.3 x 51 cm.

A112a. *A Slight Ache and Other Plays*, Methuen, 1961. Actual jacket size 19 x 44·5 cm.

A28c. *Landscape and Silence*, Grove Press, 1970. Actual jacket size 20.7 x 47.5 cm.

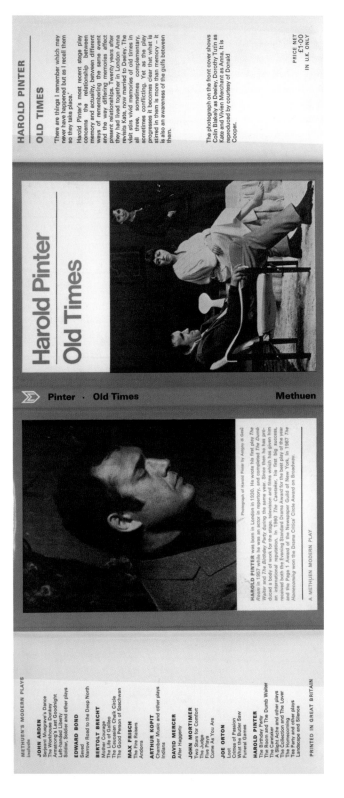

A34a. *Old Times*, Methuen, 1971. Actual jacket size 19 x 44.2 cm.

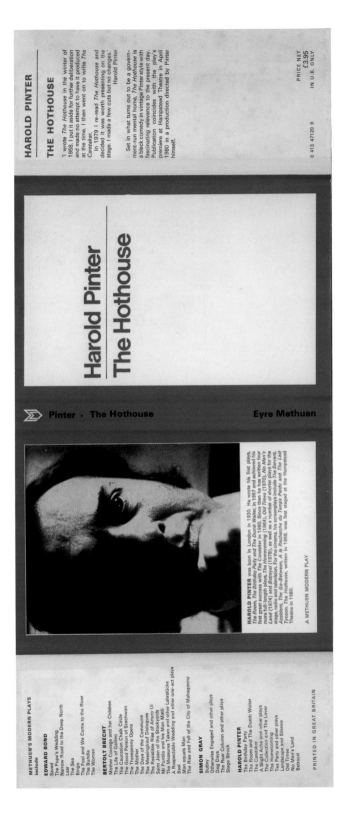

A39a. *The Hothouse*, Eyre Methuen, 1980. Actual jacket size 19.1 x 44.6 cm.

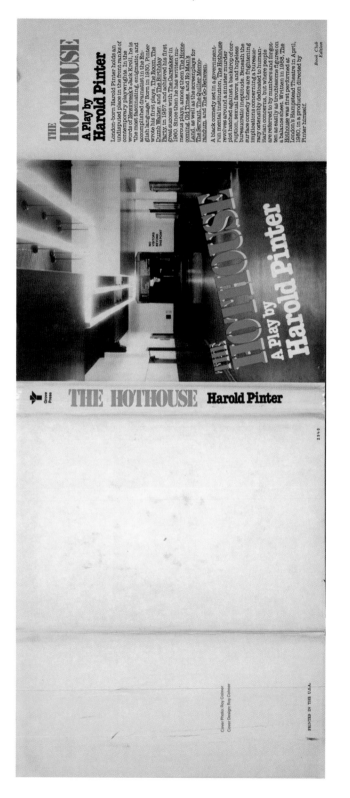

A39e. *The Hothouse*, Grove Press Book Club Edition, c. 1980. Actual jacket size 21.2 x 50.5 cm.

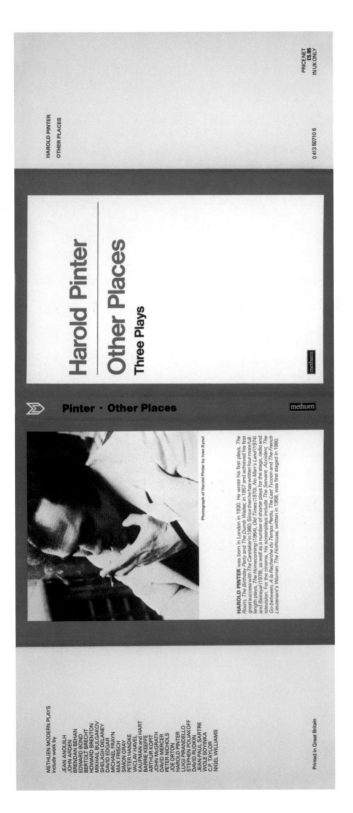

A41a. *Other Places, Three Plays*, Methuen, 1982. Actual jacket size 19.2 x 43.7 cm.

A45b. One for the Road, Methuen, 1985. Actual jacket size 25 × 56.4 cm.

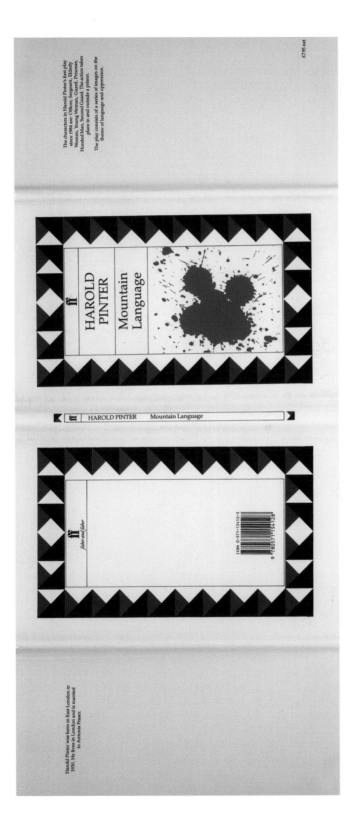

The characters in Harold Pinter's first play since 1984 are: Officer, Sergeant, Elderly Woman, Young Woman, Guard, Prisoner, Hooded Man, Second Guard. The action takes place in and outside a prison.

The play consists of a series of images on the theme of language and oppression.

£2.95 net

ff

HAROLD PINTER

Mountain Language

ff HAROLD PINTER   Mountain Language

ff
faber and faber

ISBN 0-571-15412-3

9 780571 154128

Harold Pinter was born in East London in 1930. He lives in London and is married to Antonia Fraser.

A47b. *Mountain Language*, Faber, 1988. Actual jacket size 20.3 x 46 cm.

$16.95

The world premiere of *Mountain Language,* Harold Pinter's first play in four years, occurred in London on October 20, 1988. In *The Times* (London) Irving Wardle wrote:

"In *Mountain Language,* there are no cunning verbal mechanisms to stand between the spectator and the brute spectacle of state-enforced oppression.

"Set in an unnamed country, it consists of four brief prison scenes. In the first, a group of women visitors wait outside all day to see their imprisoned menfolk, savaged by guard dogs and insulted by the military. We then move inside for more intimate glimpses of the inhuman regime: the prohibition of the prisoners' native language: a young wife catching sight of her battered husband; streams of bludgeoning insults like blows to the face; the final sight of an old woman who, finally permitted to speak the forbidden language, has nothing to say.

"[*Mountain Language*] is a scream of outrage, designed simply to point out yet again, and probably in vain, that such scenes are being enacted in prisons all over the world; that it is horrifyingly easy for human beings to start treating each other as an alien species; and that all this can take place in secrecy to an accompaniment of bland official disclaimers."

"[*Mountain Language*] effortlessly encapsulates the world.... If to want, to have, to use or abuse power over others is the essence of politics, then Pinter has been writing political plays since day one. No one but he could have written this one....This is a harsh, cruel, magisterial play, painful but compassionate."
—John Peter, *The Sunday Times* (London)

"What is astonishing is how much Pinter packs into a short space. He deals with the

(continued on back flap)

HAROLD PINTER

HAROLD PINTER   MOUNTAIN LANGUAGE

a play
MOUNTAIN LANGUAGE

GROVE PRESS

ISBN 0-8021-1157-2

(continued from front flap)

use of language as a repressive instrument, the arbitrary cruelty of military states which make up new rules as they go along, the brutish incompetence of totalitarian societies which shunt the wrong prisoners into the wrong place.... Pinter also makes his points—like late Beckett—through a series of resonant images.... [He] distills the daily barbarism of military societies with painterly precision. A masterly portrait of compressed suffering."
—Michael Billington, *The Guardian*

"A play of few words which adds up to an eloquent indictment of the banning of any human utterance.... Milan Kundera has written that the final barbarity of a totalitarian regime is that, by making its victims the butts of grim practical jokes, it even tries to deprive them of the tragic dignity which their suffering merits. In a succession of short, jabbing scenes, Pinter introduces us to such a world."
—Paul Taylor, *The Independent*

HAROLD PINTER is, in the words of *The New York Times,* "one of the most important playwrights of our day," the author of such classics of the modern stage as *The Birthday Party, The Homecoming,* and *The Caretaker.*

Jacket design by Lisdan Warwick Smith

GROVE PRESS

4/89 Printed in USA © 1989 Wheatland Corporation

A47d. *Mountain Language,* Grove Press, 1989. Actual jacket size 20.3 x 46 cm.

UK £12.99 net
Canada $19.99

Also available from
Faber and Faber

Harold Pinter's Collected Plays
Volumes 1–4
The Caretaker
The Birthday Party
Old Times
The Collection and The Lover
The Homecoming
The Hothouse
No Man's Land
Betrayal
The Room and The Dumb Waiter
One for the Road
Tea Party and Other Plays
Landscape and Silence
Other Places
A Slight Ache and Other Plays
Mountain Language
The Servant and Other Screenplays
The French Lieutenant's Woman
and other Screenplays
The Heat of the Day
The Comfort of Strangers
and Other Screenplays
Collected Poems and Prose
100 Poems by 100 Poets
The Dwarfs
The Trial
Party Time

ff

HAROLD
PINTER

Moonlight

HAROLD PINTER   Moonlight

ff
faber and faber

HAROLD PINTER
Moonlight

Moonlight is Harold Pinter's first
full-length play since Betrayal in
1978. The play was given its world
premiere at the Almeida Theatre,
London, in September 1993.

Jacket illustration by Andrzej Klimowski

ISBN 0-571-17085-4

9 780571 170852

Harold Pinter was born in
London in 1930. He is married to
Antonia Fraser.

A51a. *Moonlight*, Faber, 1993. Actual jacket size 20.5 × 44.5 cm.

A51b. *Moonlight*, Grove Press, 1994. Actual jacket size 21.5 x 50.5 cm.

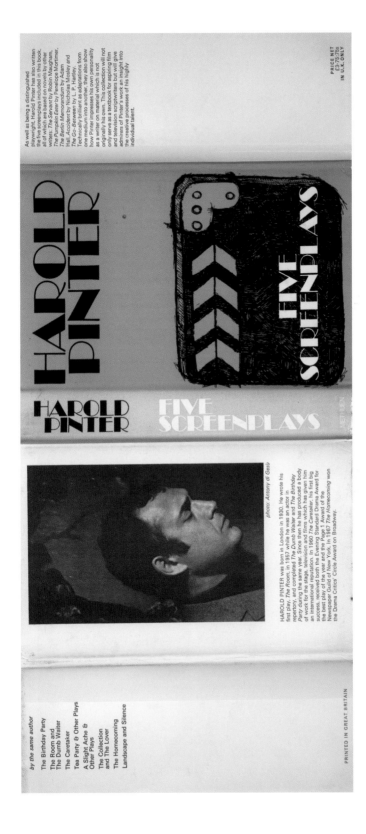

B2a¹. *Five Screenplays*, Methuen, 1971. Actual jacket size 22.1 x 49.3 cm.

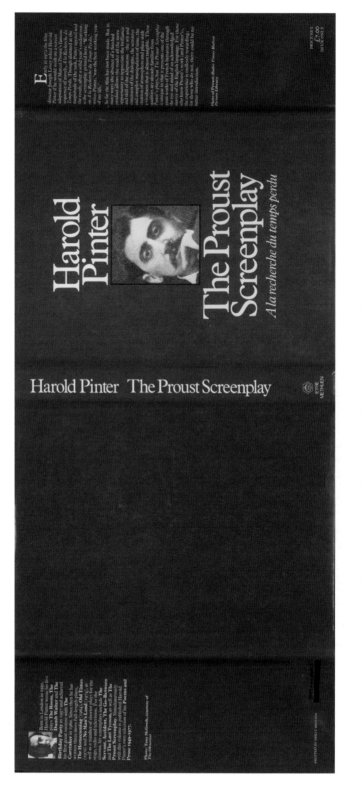

B3a¹. *The Proust Screenplay*, Eyre Methuen, 1978. Actual jacket size 25.1 x 58.6 cm.

B3c(A). *The Proust Screenplay*, Grove Press, 1977. Actual jacket size 23.8 x 52.5 cm.

B4a. *The Screenplay of The French Lieutenant's Woman*, Cape, 1981. Actual jacket size 22 x 48.6 cm.

$11.95

HAROLD PINTER

The
*French
Lieutenant's
Woman*
A SCREENPLAY

With a foreword by *John Fowles*

PINTER The *French Lieutenant's Woman* A SCREENPLAY

Little,
Brown

From left to right, Harold Pinter, John Fowles, and Karel Reisz, during the filming of *The French Lieutenant's Woman* in Lyme Regis.

ISBN 0-316-70851-8

Renowned playwright Harold Pinter has written a superb screenplay from John Fowles's best-selling novel of love and transgression in Victorian England, *The French Lieutenant's Woman*. Pinter's script is not "a mere 'version' of my novel," writes Fowles in his foreword, "but the blueprint . . . of a brilliant metaphor for it" that stands admirably on its own as a skillful, dramatic, and original work. Pinter's spare, evocative style, Fowles says, "can speak worlds in its smallest phrases, even in its silences."

Sarah is "poor Tragedy," the sad and secretive woman in black whom young Charles Smithson one day observes silently walking the lonely pier in Lyme Harbour, staring out to sea. The "French Lieutenant's Woman" he hears the townspeople mockingly call her, claiming she has gone quietly mad from endless months of waiting for the lover who jilted her to return and restore her good name. Strangely moved by pity and curiosity, Charles finds himself being drawn into the circle of her obsessively melancholy devotion, stirred by the power of her freedom and passion, and increasingly disenchanted with the more proper love for his own thoroughly conventional bride-to-be.

In adapting *The French Lieutenant's Woman* for the screen, Pinter was presented with a major dramatic challenge. Fowles narrates Charles's and Sarah's story from both a mid-nineteenth-century and a modern point of view, reflecting on the Victorian character, its repression and fierce propriety, as well as on contemporary problems of morality and sexuality. But Pinter takes an intriguing and boldly imaginative leap across the century by

ingeniously adding to the Victorian lovers' tale scenes from a contemporary affair between Mike and Anna, a movie actor and actress who are playing the novel's roles. Fowles's *The French Lieutenant's Woman* and the filming of it become deliberately intertwined, and the play-within-the-play allows the film also to have the novel's intriguing dual ending.

In his foreword, John Fowles relates the frustrating ten-year struggle to get the film of *The French Lieutenant's Woman* made. He decides that one reason he allows his books to be turned into movies is for the sheer delight in seeing daring re-creations such as Harold Pinter's, where "words, all those endless rows of algebra on a page, are literally become flesh, have provoked this very actual presence, skill with eye and ear. One has an odd sense of having come in for a moment from the cold."

Playwright Harold Pinter is the author of such modern classics as *The Homecoming, The Birthday Party, The Caretaker,* and *No Man's Land*. He also did screen adaptations for *The Last Tycoon, The Servant,* and *The Go-Between*. His screenplay of *The French Lieutenant's Woman* was filmed in 1980 by Karel Reisz, with stars Meryl Streep and Jeremy Irons.

John Fowles is the author of *The Collector, The French Lieutenant's Woman, The Ebony Tower, Daniel Martin,* and *The Magus*. He lives in England.

B4b. *The French Lieutenant's Woman, A Screenplay*, Little, Brown, 1981. Actual jacket size 21.2 x 50.3 cm.

THE HEAT OF THE DAY
Harold Pinter

London is at war: Robert and Stella are in love. But their idyll is disturbed by the appearance of the mysterious Harrison. Are his subtle approaches to Stella a continuance, or is he a professional undercover agent, as he implies? And if what he says is true, then what choice does Stella have, but to turn spy herself?

This is Harold Pinter's adaptation of Elizabeth Bowen's classic novel. *The Heat of the Day* is a feature for Granada Television, starring Michael Gambon and Patricia Hodge.

Jacket photo courtesy of Neil Macleod

£10.99 net

THE HEAT OF THE DAY Harold Pinter

ff
faber and faber

ISBN 0-571-14234-0

Faber Film

Woody Allen
Alan Bennett
John Boorman
Sergei Eisenstein
Peter Greenaway
Graham Greene
John Grierson
Trevor Griffiths
Christopher Hampton
David Hare
Derek Jarman
Neil Jordan
Hanif Kureishi
Akira Kurosawa
Louis Malle
Harold Pinter
Dennis Potter
Satyajit Ray
Martin Scorsese
Andrey Tarkovsky
Robert Towne
François Truffaut
Andrzej Wajda
Wim Wenders

B6(A). *The Heat of the Day*, Faber and Faber, 1989. Actual jacket size 22.3 x 50.5 cm.

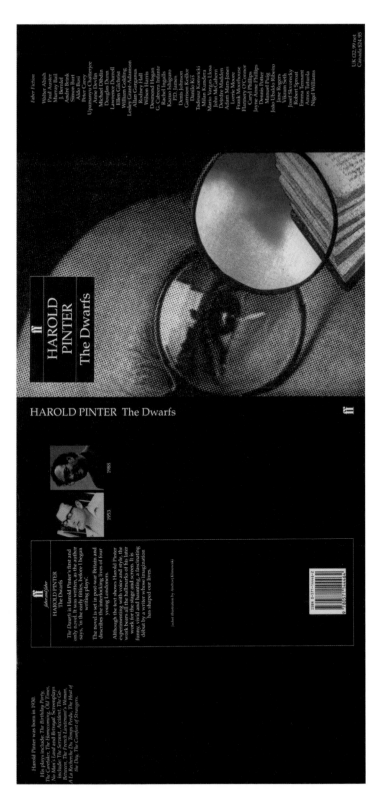

D8a. *The Dwarfs*, Faber and Faber, 1990. Actual jacket size 24 x 51 cm.

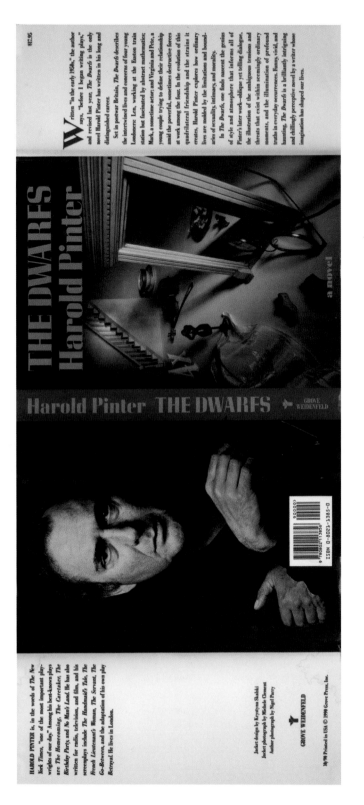

D8d. *The Dwarfs*, Grove Weidenfeld, 1990. Actual jacket size 21.5 x 49 cm.

The three editors of this latest *P.E.N. Anthology of Contemporary Poetry* have all figured as contributors to it in the past. Harold Pinter is, of course, now much better known in another field. From a submission of about ten thousand poems they have chosen fifty, the majority of them by new writers, though familiar names like Peter Porter, Hilary Corke, Gavin Ewart and Jon Stallworthy make their appearance. This is not an anthology with a programme. It succeeds in its intention of finding the best which is being written in the many different forms of poetry today. If there is one thing which unites these poets it is a feeling of depth and experience and a knowledge of the power of words and rhythms.

25s net
IN UK ONLY

1967
Edited by PINTER
HARM FULLEROVE
JOHN FULLER
PETER REDGE

NEW POEMS

NEW POEMS

A PENTHOLO OF

A PENTHOLOGY OF

MODERN POETRY

MODERN POETRY

NEW POEMS THE 1967 PEN ANTHOLOGY

HUTCHINSON

New poetry from Hutchinson

A SMALL DESPERATION
DANNIE ABSE

STOATS IN THE SUNLIGHT
STEWART CONN

LYRICS FOR THE DOG HOUR
MAUREEN DUFFY

THE BOY FROM THE GREEN CABARET TELLS OF HIS MOTHER
BARRY MACSWEENEY

THE STOPPED LANDSCAPE
ALAN RIDDELL

The P.E.N. Anthologies of Contemporary Poetry already Published by Hutchinson

NEW POEMS 1960

Edited by Anthony Cronin, Jon Silkin, Terence Tiller
WITH A FOREWORD BY ALAN PRYCE-JONES

NEW POEMS 1961

Edited by William Plomer, Anthony Thwaite, Hilary Corke
WITH AN INTRODUCTION BY THE EDITORS

NEW POEMS 1962

Edited by Patricia Beer, Ted Hughes, Vernon Scannell
WITH AN INTRODUCTION BY THE EDITORS

NEW POEMS 1963

Edited by Lawrence Durrell
WITH AN INTRODUCTION BY THE EDITOR

NEW POEMS 1965

Edited by C. V. Wedgwood
WITH AN INTRODUCTION BY THE EDITOR

The first seven P.E.N. anthologies were published by Michael Joseph, Ltd.
NEW POEMS 1952, 1953, 1954, 1955, 1956, 1957, 1958.

09 088510 9

Jacket Designed by Michael Brett.

Printed in Great Britain by
Fisher, Knight and Co., Ltd., St. Albans, Herts.

H3. *New Poems 1967 A P.E.N. Anthology of Modern Poetry*, Hutchinson, 1968. Actual jacket size 20.6 x 46.7 cm.

I3a². *Poems*, first edition, second issue, printed 1968, issued 1970. Actual jacket size 18.8 x 51.6 cm.

For this new edition of Harold Pinter's POEMS (first published in 1968) nine poems have been added, six of which are unpublished in any form.

£1.40

Harold Pinter

POEMS

Harold Pinter   Poems   Enitharmon

ENITHARMON PRESS POETRY

ROBIN SKELTON : Answers £2.25
BRENDA CHAMBERLAIN : Poems with Drawings £3.50
LEONARD CLARK : Walking with Trees £1.50
EDGELL RICKWORD : Fifty Poems £3.15
DAVID GASCOYNE : The Sun at Midnight £4.00
FRANCES BELLERBY : Selected Poems £2.10
HUGO MANNING : Encounter in Crete
£1.30 (cloth) 85p. (wrappers)

FORTHCOMING

PETER RUSSELL : Paysages Légendaires
RICHARD BURNS : Double Flute
JOHN HEATH-STUBBS : Artorius

I3b(i) *Poems*, second edition, Enitharmon, 1971. Actual jacket size 22.2 x 42.5 cm.

14a. *Poems and Prose 1949–1977*, Eyre Methuen, 1978. Actual jacket size 25.2 x 58.7 cm.

A

Plays and Sketches for the Stage, Radio, and Television

a. First edition (Encore) (1959):

The Birthday Party | [*thick rule*] | a play in three acts by Harold Pinter | ENCORE PUBLISHING CO. LTD. 25 HOWLAND STREET, LONDON, W.1

1 leaf, 57 pp. 20.2 × 13.8 cm. Paperback, white, stapled; on outside front: full-length photograph of Stanley, without his glasses, with, imposed below, in white lettering reversed out of black: "*The Birthday* | *Party* | HAROLD PINTER"; outside back blank; on inside front: "© *Copyright 1959 by Harold Pinter* | [*performing rights statement*] | [*details of first production*] | *First published in 1959* | *Printed in Great Britain by* | *Parnells the Printers Ltd., Reading, Berks.* | [*at left, level with following two lines:*] 5/- | [*to right:*] *Cover photograph of the Tavistock Repertory Co. production London, May, 1959 by* | *KENNETH JEPSON*"; on inside back, advertisement inviting subscriptions for Encore publications.

Published 1 December 1959 (L accession dated 7 JAN 60). 1,000 copies. The colophon is on the inside front of the wrapper, as above.

Contents: [i] title page; [ii] list of characters, list of acts, description of set; 1–57 text of play; [58] blank.

Notes: The speech prefixes are in capitals and lower case, and in bold, with "Stan." rather than "Stanley". The stage directions are in italic, with proper names in italic capitals, and are terse, often lacking articles or conjunctions. These and the set-description use "D.L.", "U.R.", etc. (for "downstage left", "upstage right", etc.). Encore was a London theatrical publisher. DLC copyright registration of unpublished play, 10 August 1959 (DU49518).

b. First Methuen edition, as single play, paperback (1963):

THE | BIRTHDAY PARTY | BY | Harold Pinter | LONDON | METHUEN & CO LTD | 36 ESSEX STREET WC2

91 pp., 2 blank leaves. 18.0 × 12.2 cm. Paperback; outside front blue: "[*in black:*] HAROLD PINTER | [*in white:*] The Birthday Party", below, production photo; outside back white: photo of Pinter, below: "[*in blue:*] HAROLD PINTER [*remaining text in black:*] [*7-line account of Pinter*] | [*below, to left:*] 2/6306/31

[*to right:*] PRICE | 4s 6d net | IN UK ONLY"; down spine: "[*in black:*] HAROLD PINTER [*in white:*] THE BIRTHDAY PARTY [*in black:*] METHUEN".

Published 25 July 1963 (L accession 17 JUL 63). 7500 copies. Price 4s. 6d. On verso of title-leaf: "TO VIVIEN | [*performing rights statement*] | Copyright © 1959 *and* 1960 *by Harold Pinter* | *Paperback edition first published* 1963 | *Printed in Great Britain by* | *John Dickens & Co Ltd* | *Northampton* | *Cat. No.* 2/6306/31".

Contents: [1–2] blank; [3] half-title, brief account of first performances and their reception, at foot: "*The photograph on the front cover shows a* | *scene from a production by the Tavistock* | *Repertory Company at the Tower Theatre,* | *Canonbury. It is reproduced by courtesy of* | *Ken Jepson. The photograph of Harold* | *Pinter on the back is by Roger Mayne.*"; [4] list, "*Methuen's Modern Plays* | EDITED BY JOHN CULLEN | *in paper covers*", 17 titles; [5] title page; [6] as above; [7] fly-title; [8] details of first production; [9]–91 text; [92–96] blank.

Notes: The first Methuen printing of the play had been within *The Birthday Party and Other Plays* (1960). The text pages in this edition are identical with the relevant pages within that volume, and were probably printed from the same litho plates.

c. *Second Methuen edition, revised (1965):*

THE | BIRTHDAY PARTY | BY | Harold Pinter | LONDON | METHUEN & CO LTD | 11 NEW FETTER LANE EC4

87 pp. Signed as [A]⁸ B-D⁸ E⁴ F⁸. 18.4 × 12.1 cm. Paperback, as for first Methuen, except, on outside back, at bottom left "02/6306/24", at bottom right "PRICE | 5s od net | IN UK ONLY".

Published 26 August 1965 (L accession 10 August 1965). Price 5s. 7500 copies; reprinted 14 June 1966, 16,000 copies (5s.); 17 September 1968; 1970 (37½p.); December 1972, 20,000 copies; May 1974 (60p.); 24 March 1976, 15,000 (95p.); 19 May 1976, 15,203 copies (95p.); 4 November 1976, 11,427 copies (£1.15). On verso of title leaf: "To VIVIEN | [*performing rights statement*] | 2.1 | *First published* 1960 | *Copyright* © 1959, 1960 *and* 1965 | *by Harold Pinter* | *Paperback Edition first published* 1963 | *Second edition, revised,* 1965 | *Printed in Great Britain by* | *John Dickens & Co Ltd* | *Cat. No.* 02/6306/24".

Contents: As for first Methuen, except: on [4], lists 26 titles; on [8], performance details include RSC at the Aldwych Theatre (from 18 June 1964), and time-setting of the three acts; [9]–87 text; [88] blank.

Notes: The signature-mode is, e.g., on p.17: "B.P.–B". While a substantial amount of local revision of the text took place, it is clear that as much as possible of the original typesetting was retained, presumably through cutting and pasting of litho plates. Consequently, several stage-directions have been retained which have been rendered meaningless by the cutting of preceding or following passages (e.g. on p.11: *"Vaguely."*; p.79: *"He exits with the chest expander."*; p.85, "GOLDBERG *puts the bowler hat on* STANLEY'S *head."*). See *Appendix Two*, A(1). The revisions evidently derived from Pinter's own production of the play at the Aldwych Theatre in 1964; see *Appendix Two*, B(2) for a brief description of its promptbook. Later reprints of this revised edition have some further local revision, with changes in lineation, and several small textual adjustments, correcting the previous retention of meaningless stage directions.

d. Faber edition (1991):

[*All within a single-rule frame:*] HAROLD PINTER | The Birthday Party | ff | *faber and faber* | LONDON • BOSTON

1 blank leaf, 87 pp., 3 blank leaves. 19.7 × 12.4 cm. Paperback, outside white; on outside front, standard Faber frame of black, grey, and white triangles, within it: within single-rule frame: "ff | [*rule*] | HAROLD | PINTER | [*rule*] | The Birthday | Party", partially coloured illustration of Stanley with drum on head; on outside back, at either side, border of triangles, within single-rule frame: "ff | *faber and faber* | HAROLD PINTER | The Birthday Party | [*9-line quotation and note on play*] | Cover illustration by Andrzej Klimowski | UK £4.99 net | Canada $12.95 | ISBN 0-571-16078-6 | [*bar-code*] | 9 780571 160785"; on spine: two overlapping triangles, below, within single-rule frame: "ff | [*rule*] | [*down spine:*] HAROLD PINTER The Birthday Party", below frame, two triangles.

Published 1991 (L accession 1 FEB 91). Reprinted 19 September 1993, 21 November 1995, 7 May 1996, 11 March 1997, 7 September 2000, totalling 59,634 copies printed. Price (of first printing) £4.99. On verso of title leaf: prior publication details, "This paperback edition first published in 1991 | by Faber and Faber Limited | 3 Queen Square London WC1N 3AU | Printed in England by Clays Ltd, St Ives plc", performing rights and conditions of sale statements, etc., "ISBN 0-571-16078-6".

Contents: Correspond to the revised Methuen, with blank leaves fore and aft.

Notes: The text is a reproduction of the revised form of the revised Methuen, with some further changes in lineation. The performance details on p.[7] include those for the BBC Television production, 28 June 1987, directed by Kenneth Ives. Later reprints omit places of publication in the title page, as in the Otago University (NZ) copy, which has a different colophon on the verso of the title leaf: "Printed and bound in Great Britain by | Makays [*sic*] of Chatham PLC, Chatham, Kent".

e. Methuen student edition (1981):

HAROLD PINTER | The Birthday Party | *With a Commentary and Chronology by* | PATRICIA HERN | *and Notes by* GLENDA LEEMING | Methuen Student Editions | EYRE METHUEN – LONDON

xxix [xxx], 97 pp. 18.6 × 11.7 cm. Paperback, front and back covers green, with white borders; on front cover, in white, reversed out of green: "HAROLD PINTER | The Birthday | Party | With commentary and notes | [*within white border, photo of Stanley, set at an angle*] | METHUEN STUDENT EDITIONS"; on back cover: "Methuen Student Editions | [*account of series, and list of titles published*] | [*at upper left, small photo of Pinter*] | [*at foot:*] Front cover photo: "Robert Shaw as Stanley in the film of | THE BIRTHDAY PARTY (EMI) | 0 413 39640 1"; spine white, lettered in black down spine: "PINTER THE BIRTHDAY PARTY METHUEN".

Published 1981 (L accession 8 FEB 82). Price £1.75. On verso of title leaf: "This Methuen Student Edition first published in 1981 by Eyre | Methuen Ltd, 11 New Fetter Lane, London EC4P 4EE | [. . .] | Commentary and notes copyright © 1981 by Eyre Methuen | Printed in Great Britain by Fakenham Press Ltd, Fakenham, Norfolk | ISBN 0 413 39640 1 | [*copyright and performing rights statements*] | *Thanks are due to James Gibbs, Malcolm Page and Non Worrall* | *for their help and advice in the preparation of this edition*".

Contents: [i] title page; [ii] as above; [iii] contents; [iv] blank; [v]–viii "Chronology", with lists of Pinter's plays, screenplays and directing; [ix]–xi "Plot"; [xii]–xxix "Commentary"; [xxx] "Suggestions for further reading"; [1–6] production photos; [7] fly-title; [8] performance details; [9]–87 text; [88]–97 "Notes".

Notes: The text corresponds to the further-revised form of the revised Methuen. A 1988 reprint has on the verso of the title leaf: "Reprinted 1983 and 1986 by Methuen London Ltd | Reprinted 1988 by Methuen Drama, Michelin House, | 81 Fulham Road, London SW3 6RB", also a performing rights statement. The retail price of this copy is given on a sticker as £3.99.

f. Faber educational edition (1993):

[*Within a single-rule frame:*] Harold Pinter | THE | BIRTHDAY | PARTY | *Educational Text* | Edited and with | an Introduction by | Margaret Rose | ff | *faber and faber* | LONDON • BOSTON

3 leaves, 137 pp. 19.7 × 12.5 cm. Cover same except outside is red; and on front cover, added: "[*rule*] | *Edited and with an introduction* | *by Dr Margaret Rose*"; on outside back, noted as "*Educational Edition*", with an account of this edition, "UK £3.99 non-net | Canada $9.99 | ISBN 0-571-16734-9 | [*bar-code*] | 9 780571 167340".

Published 8 March 1993 (L accession 21 JAN 93). On verso of title leaf, added: "This educational edition first published in 1993 | by Faber and Faber Limited | ... | Photoset by Parker Typesetting Service, Leicester | Printed by Clays Ltd., St Ives plc", impression numerals.

Contents: [1]–33 Introduction; [34] blank; [35–38] fly-title, first performance details; [39]–117 text; [118]–133 notes; [134]–137 bibliography; [138] blank.

Notes: The type-pages of the text correspond to that of the Faber paperback of 1991. Faber and Faber report (1.8.2001) having reprinted this edition on 19 July 1997 and 6 April 1999, totalling 6,422 copies.

g. Dutch educational edition, with notes (1967):

HAROLD PINTER | *The Birthday Party* | ANNOTATED BY | L. ANDRIESSEN | J. R. WOLTERS GRONINGEN | 1967

3 leaves, 80 pp., with, on pp.[1]–20, annotations in English and Dutch. In series Wikor Drama Library No. 17 (Wikor Theater Bibliothek), Unicorn Library. Published in conjunction with a series of Theatre Royal performances for schools.

h. Danish educational edition, with notes in English and Danish (1970):

ENGELSKLÆRERFORENINGENS UDGAVER | HAROLD PINTER | The Birthday Party | ANNOTATED | BY INGEBORG JØRGENSEN AND | ERNST NILSSON | GYLDENDAL

112 pp. 20 × 12 cm. Paperback, yellow; on outside front: "HAROLD | PINTER | THE [*in small font, in 4 lines:*] Annotated | by | Ingeborg Jørgenson | and Ernst Nilsson | BIRTHDAY | [*to left, two-thirds up:*] Gyldendal PARTY"; on outside back, within roughly rectangular border: publisher's emblem, "Engelsklærerforeningens udgaver", ISBN 87 00 75611 3; down spine: "Harold Pinter THE BIRTHDAY PARTY Gyldendal" (information partly from Dace).

Published 29 September 1970. 3000 copies. Price 18 kr. Reprinted as second edition, 14 March 1975, in 2000 copies. 22 kr. On verso of title leaf: British copyright information, "Bogen er sat med Intertype Baskerville | og trykt hos Nordisk Bogproduktion A.S. | Haslev. | Printed in Denmark 1970. | ISBN 87 00 75611 3".

Contents: [1] half title; [2] blank; [3] title page; [4] as above; [5] "Udgiverens forord"; [6] blank; 7–[14] introduction (in English); [15] cast and act lists; 16–[91] text; [92] abbreviation list; 93–112 notes.

i. Italian educational edition [ca. 1972 (?)]:

HAROLD PINTER | THE | BIRTHDAY PARTY | *Introduzione e note* | *di Emma Vendramin* | EDIZIONI CANOVA TREVISO

89 pp. Paperback, blue, white and maroon. In series: Autori inglezi e americani moderni e contemporanei. Arti Grafiche Longo e Zoppelli – Treviso. Prezzo L. 1500.

j. British acting edition, first edition (1965):

THE BIRTHDAY | PARTY | A Play in Three Acts | by | HAROLD PINTER | SAMUEL [*publisher's device*] FRENCH | LONDON

2 leaves, 75 pp. 21.1 × 13.5 cm. Paperback, blue, stapled; on outside front, at left, broad vertical band, in red, with, within it, in blue, reversed out of red: "[*publisher's device*] | French's | Acting | Edition"; to right, in red: "THE | BIRTHDAY | PARTY | A Play | HAROLD PINTER"; back cover blank; down spine, in red: "THE BIRTHDAY PARTY 6s net".

Published 16 March 1965 (L accession 30 MAR 65). Price 6s. First print-run 2000 copies; thereafter, reprinted in response to demand. On verso of title leaf: addresses of Samuel French companies in different countries, copyright statement, "MADE AND PRINTED IN GREAT BRITAIN BY | BUTLER & TANNER LTD. FROME AND LONDON | MADE IN ENGLAND".

Contents: [i] title page; [ii] as above; [iii] 1964 RSC performance details; [iv] within single-rule frame, French's performing rights statement; 1–69 text; [70] blank; [71] ground-plan; 72–73 "Furniture and Property List"; 74 "Lighting Plot"; 75 "Effects Plot"; [76] blank.

Notes: On p.25 (line 2), the stage direction at the end of Act I contains a typo, "*neckm*", where the second Methuen has "*neck,*"; this is still present in the 2001 reprint of the revised edition.

k. British acting edition, revised edition (1971):

THE BIRTHDAY PARTY | a Play in Three Acts | by | HAROLD PINTER | SAMUEL [*publisher's device*] FRENCH | LONDON | NEW YORK SYDNEY TORONTO HOLLYWOOD

2 leaves, 73, [3] pp. 21.5 × 13.5 cm. Paperback, white; front cover decorated, ruled and lettered in blue: "[*to left, three vertical rules*] [*upper left, publisher's device, partially overlapping rules*] [*two vertical rules*] The | Birthday | Party | A Play | HAROLD PINTER"; on outside back, within single-rule frame, advertisement for French's Theatre Bookshop, below, at bottom left: "ISBN 0 573 01042 0".

First published 1971. Price £6.00 (2001). On verso of title leaf: copyright statement, French's performing rights details, ISBN number.

Contents: As for first edition, with pp.74 and 75 unpaginated.

Notes: Seen in reprint of 2001.

l. American edition of French's acting edition [1968]:

The | *Birthday Party* | A PLAY IN THREE ACTS | *By Harold Pinter* | [*lion device*] | SAMUEL FRENCH, INC. | 25 WEST 45TH STREET NEW YORK 10036 | 7623 SUNSET BOULEVARD HOLLYWOOD 90046 | *LONDON TORONTO*

90 pp., 3 leaves (paginated #34–#39). 18.3 × 12.2 cm. Paperback, dull red; on front cover: "[*three vertical rules, of differing height, to right, and to left*] The | *Birthday Party* | A PLAY IN THREE ACTS | *By Harold Pinter* | [*lion device*] | Samuel French, Inc. | [*double rule*] | PRICE, $1.25 | [*rule*]"; on insides of front and back covers, and on outside of back cover, publisher's advertisements for plays.

Published 6 September 1968 (information from publisher; L accession 2 MAY 69). First print-run 2000 copies; further printings: 10 March 1970, 2000 copies; 7 October 1971, 2000 copies; 12 April 1974, 3000 copies. Price $1.25. On verso of title leaf: copyright, performing rights statements, mainly for USA and Canada, "PRINTED IN U. S. A.".

Contents: [1] title page; [2] as above; 3 performance details, for production directed by Alan Schneider, "at the Booth Theatre, | N.Y.C., October 3, 1967", American cast, timing of acts; [4] blank; 5–81 text; 82–88 property list; 89 costume plot; 90 groundplan; #34–#39 publisher's advertisements.

Note one: The text derives largely from the revised Methuen text, but retains some First Methuen readings.. On p.73 (corresponding to p.79 in the revised Methuen), it omits the repetition of Goldberg's "Come over here", with Lulu's first response "What's going to happen?" The stage-directions differ substantially from those in the London French edition, evidently reflecting the New York production.

Note two: The L copy has a small slip (8.2 × 3.2 cm.) pasted in, on p.5, the first page of the text, printed in red, warning "Anyone contemplating a production" that they should check with French's in London, as to whether the play is available for performance.

Note three: "The Birthday Party: a play in three acts" was given American copyright registration, at the Library of Congress, 17 April 1987 (RE-335-869); also, "*The Birthday Party*" was registered 17 November 1987 (RE-355-501).

m. In British anthology [extracts only] (1966):

Post-war Drama | [*rule, 9.5 cm.*] | *Extracts from eleven plays* | *edited with an introduction by* | JOHN HALE, M.A., F.S.A. | University of Warwick | FABER & FABER | 24 Russell Square London

222 pp. Paperback, outside upper quarter white, lower three-quarters red, with black lettering.

Published 1966 (reprinted 1967). On verso of title leaf, in copy seen (1967): "*First published in mcmlxvi by | Faber & Faber Limited | 24 Russell Square London WCI | Reprinted mcmlxvii | Printed in Great Britain by | Latimer Trend & Co Ltd Plymouth | All rights reserved | [at foot:] © John Hale 1966*".

Notes: An extract from the earlier part of Act II of *The Birthday Party* occupies pp.[108]–122, with a note on the play on p.[107]. Hale's introduction to the volume occupies pp.[7]–13.

n[1]. In American anthology, hardback (1962):

[*6 lines in open letters:*] SEVEN | PLAYS | OF | THE | MODERN | THEATER | *With an Introduction by Harold Clurman | Grove Press, Inc. New York*

xii, 548 pp., 1 leaf. 22.1 × 13.6 cm. Copy seen re-bound. Endpapers.

Hardback published 1962 (paperback 1967). On verso of title leaf, in copy seen: "COPYRIGHT © 1962 BY GROVE PRESS, INC. | All Rights Reserved | Copyright of individual plays is provided on the title | page of each play. | [*further copyright and performing rights statements*] | Library of Congress Catalog Card Number: 62-9779 | Second printing | Manufactured in the United States of America".

Contents: Clurman's introduction occupies pp.vii–xii. The plays in the anthology are: Samuel Beckett, *Waiting for Godot*; Brendan Behan, *The Quare Fellow*; Shelagh Delaney, *A Taste of Honey*; Jack Gelber, *The Connection*; Jean Genet, *The Balcony*; Eugene Ionesco, *Rhinoceros*; Harold Pinter, *The Birthday Party*. *The Birthday Party*, with the revised text, occupies pp. [473]–548 ([473] fly-title; 474 first British performance details, time of acts; 475 "To Vivien"; 476–548 text).

n[2]. American anthology, reprint, paperback (1967):

Title page as for 1962.

Paperback, outside front and spine purple, outside back white; on outside front: "*Seven plays of the modern theater* | [very thick horizontal rule, 8.8 cm.] | *with an introduction by Harold Clurman* | [*names and numbers in white, divided by a thick vertical rule, in black, 12.3 cm.:*] BeCkett 1 | gELbeR 2 | BeHaN 3 | deLaNEy 4 | PiNTEr 5 | GEnET 6 | IOnesCo 7 | [*in black:*] Text Edition"; on outside back, accounts of volume and of the seven plays; on spine: "SEVEN | PLAYS | OF | THE | MODERN | THEATER | [*thick rule, 2.3 cm.*] | [*names in white:*] BeCkett | gELbeR | BeHaN | deLaNEy | PiNTEr | GEnET | IOnesCo | [*remainder in black*] [*thick rule, 2.3 cm.*] | [*publisher's device*] | GROVE | PRESS".

Published 1967. On verso of title-leaf: as for 1962, except: "First Evergreen Edition 1967 | Third printing". That is, the plates for this play, apart from changes to pagination, are evidently as for that Evergreen Edition printing.

A2   THE CARETAKER   1960

a. First edition (Encore) (1960):

HAROLD | PINTER | [*title in graphic font, with letters of irregular height:*] The | Caretaker | A PLAY | IN THREE ACTS | ENCORE PUBLISHING CO. LTD. | 41 Great Russell St., London, W.C.1

1 leaf, 61, [1] pp. 21.0 × 13.1 cm. Paperback; front cover black, with lettering in white reversed out of black: "A PLAY | [*title in irregular-height graphic font:*] The | Care- | taker | BY | HAROLD | PINTER"; outside back off-white, lettering in black: "[*title in graphic font:*] The | Caretaker | ENCORE PUBLISHING COMPANY LIMITED | 41 GREAT RUSSELL STREET, LONDON, W.C.1"; inside of front cover: "5/-"; inside of back cover, invitation to subscribe to Encore.

Published [May?] 1960 (L accession 15 OCT 91). Price 5s.

Contents: [i] title page; [ii] blank; [1] "TO VIVIEN", descriptions of characters, list of acts, description of set; [2] copyright and performing rights statements, details of first presentation, 24 April 1960, "First published in 1960 | Cover design by | JOHN HARMER, L.S.I.A"; 3–61 text; [62] "Printed by | SUSAN TULLY LTD. | 9 Blenheim Street, | London, W.1."

b. First Methuen edition (1960):

THE CARETAKER | *a play by* | HAROLD PINTER | LONDON | METHUEN & CO LTD | 36 ESSEX STREET WC2

82 pp., 1 blank leaf. Signed as [A]⁸ B-D⁸ E¹⁰ (p.65 and p.67 are both signed "T.C.-E"). 18.4 × 12.2 cm. Hardback, black cloth; down spine, in gold: "Harold Pinter [*star*] THE CARETAKER [*star*] Methuen". Endpapers. Dust jacket blue on outside front and spine, white on outside back; on outside front: "[*in black:*] HAROLD PINTER | [*in white:*] The Caretaker | [*photo*]"; on outside back, photo of Pinter as Seeley at coffee stall, below, in white panel: "[*in blue:*] HAROLD PINTER [*in black:*] [*10-line biographical note*]"; down spine: "[*in black:*] HAROLD PINTER [*in white:*] THE CARETAKER [*in black:*] METHUEN"; on front flap, in black, title, 2 paragraphs about play, at foot: "2/6411/31 [*to right:*] 10s 6d net | in U. K. only"; on back flap, "PRINTED IN GREAT BRITAIN". Paperback: front cover as for dust jacket; back cover as for dust jacket, with at foot "2/6293/1 3s 6d"; spine as for dust jacket.

Published 21 July 1960 (paperback), 8 September 1960 (hardback) (hardback, L accession 26 AUG 60). Price 10s 6d. (hardback), 3s. 6d. (paperback). 7500 copies. On verso of title leaf: "To VIVIEN | [*copyright and performing rights statements*] | FIRST PUBLISHED IN 1960 | © 1960 BY THEATRE PROMOTIONS

LIMITED | CATALOGUE NO. 2/6293/1 (PAPERBACK) | 2/6411/1 (HARD COVER) | PRINTED IN GREAT BRITAIN BY | W. & J. MACKAY & CO LTD | CHATHAM".

Contents: [1] brief note about Pinter and this play, "*The illustration on the front of the cover shows* | *Donald Pleasence as Davies and Alan Bates as* | *Mick. It is reproduced by courtesy of* | *Michael Boys*"; [2] "*by the same author*", lists one title; [3] title page; [4] as above; [5] first presentation details, list of acts; [6] description of set; [7]–82 text; [83–84] blank.

Notes: DLC copyright registration, evidently of the paperback, 21 July 1960 (DF1366). A second printing was issued on 8 September 1960 (reported by Faber), evidently for the hardback. The photo on the outside back of the dust jacket of Pinter as Seeley in the A.B.C. Armchair Production of *A Night Out* broadcast 24 April 1960 was taken by David Sim.

c. Second Methuen edition, revised (1962):

Title page as first edition.

78 pp., 1 blank leaf. Signed [A]⁸ B-E⁸. 18.4 × 12.3 cm. Hardback binding as first edition. Endpapers. Dust jacket in blue and white; on front, upper sector blue: "[*in black:*] HAROLD PINTER | [*in white:*] The Caretaker", below, photo of Davies and Mick; on back, photo of Pinter, from *A Night Out*; down spine: "[*in black:*] HAROLD PINTER [*in white:*] THE CARETAKER [*in black:*] METHUEN"; on front flap, account of Pinter and of this play, at foot, to left, "2/6411/31", to right "10s 6d net | in U.K. only"; on back flap "PRINTED IN GREAT BRITAIN".

Published 23 August 1962 (L accession 9 AUG 62). 3000 copies (1000 cloth, 2000 paperback). Price 10s. 6d. (cloth), 4s. 6d. (paperback). On verso of title leaf: "TO VIVIEN | [*copyright and performing rights statements*] | FIRST PUBLISHED JULY 21 1960 | REPRINTED 1960 | SECOND EDITION, REVISED, 1962 | 2.1 | © 1960 BY THEATRE PROMOTIONS LIMITED | CATALOGUE NO. 2/6293/31 (PAPERBACK) | 2/6411/31 (HARD COVER) | PRINTED IN GREAT BRITAIN BY | W. & J. MACKAY & CO LTD | CHATHAM".

Contents: [1] as first edition; [2] "METHUEN'S MODERN PLAYS", two lists; [3] title page; [4] as above; [5] first presentation details, note of location, timing of acts; [6] set description; [7]–78 text; [79–80] blank.

Notes: There were four printings before 1966; the fifth was ordered in January 1966 (fifth for paperback, third for cloth: 13,500 copies paperback, 1,500 cloth), and the sixth in May 1966 (12,000 copies). Dace notes that the type was then worn out, hence resetting was needed. The 1963 reprint has on the verso of the title leaf "REPRINTED 1963 | 2.2" in place of "2.1"; and later reprintings doubtless correspond. Dace notes that an error occurred in the first printing: on p.12, lines 11–23 ("This is your house, then, is it?" to "Family of Indians live there"), a passage was retained that should have been deleted, when a substituted passage was inserted. It was cut for the May 1966 printing.

d. Revised Methuen, resetting, in hardback and paperback (1967):

THE CARETAKER | *a play by* | HAROLD PINTER | LONDON | 11 NEW FETTER LANE EC4

78 pp., 1 leaf. Signed as for second edition (leaf [A]2, bearing the title page, and colophon, appears to be a cancel). 18.4 × 12.0 cm. Price: £1.00 (hardback), 6s. 0d. (paperback). Hardback not seen. Paperback: on front cover, thick blue border, within white panel lettering in blue: "Harold Pinter [*rule, in black, 9.9 cm.*] | The Caretaker", below panel, production photo; on back cover, blue frame, photo of Pinter, below, in white panel, lettering in blue: "photo: Antony di Gesù | [*8-line biographical note*] | [*rule, in black, 10.0 cm.*] | A METHUEN MODERN PLAY 6s net in UK only"; on spine, at head, in white, Methuen device, lettering down spine, in black: "Pinter • The Caretaker Methuen".

Published 1967 in this new setting, in hardback and paperback (copy seen: paperback, reprint of 1970). On verso of title leaf (1970 reprint): "TO VIVIEN | [*performing rights statement*] | FIRST PUBLISHED JULY 21 1960 | REPRINTED 1960 | SECOND EDITION, REVISED, 1962 | REPRINTED FOUR TIMES | REPRINTED 1966 | RESET AND REPRINTED 1967 | REPRINTED 1968 TWICE | REPRINTED 1970 | 2·10 | © 1960 BY THEATRE PROMOTIONS LIMITED | SBN 416 62930 X (PAPERBACK) | SBN 416 64110 5 (HARD COVER) | PRINTED IN GREAT BRITAIN | COX & WYMAN LTD, | FAKENHAM NORFOLK", conditions of sale statement.

Contents: [1] as first edition; [2] list of other play-volumes "*by the same author*"; [3] title page; [4] as above; [5] details of first presentation, location and time of acts; [6] description of set; [7]–78 text of play; [79–80] publisher's lists.

Notes: Seen in 1970 paperback. Dace records that the 1967 resetting had errors on pp. 8, 41, 56, and 61; these were corrected for a printing *circa* February 1972. In 1970, the paperback price was 7s. 6d, or 37½p.

e. Faber edition (1991):

[*All within a single-rule frame:*] HAROLD PINTER | The Caretaker | ff | *faber and faber* | LONDON • BOSTON

78 pp., 1 blank leaf. 19.7 × 12.4 cm. Paperback, white, standard Faber design; on front cover, within single-rule frame: "ff | [*rule*] | HAROLD PINTER | [*rule*] | The Caretaker | [*illustration, showing Davies' head, behind hands*]"; outside

back, within frame: "ff | *faber and faber* | [*rule*] | HAROLD PINTER | The Caretaker | [*quotation from Daily Telegraph critique, brief account of play*] | Cover illustration by Andrzej Klimowski | UK £4.99 net | Canada $12.95 | ISBN 0-571-16079-4 | [*bar-code*] | 9 780571 160792".

Published 1991 (L accession 1 FEB 91). Reprintings on 7 October 1993, 31 March 1999, 17 April 2000, 25 September 2000, 23 November 2000, totalling 70,520 copies printed (to 1 August 2001). On verso of title leaf: "First published in this edition in 1991 | by Faber and Faber Limited | [. . . .] | Printed in England by Clays Ltd, St Ives plc | [. . . .] | ISBN 0-571-16079-4".

Contents: As for second (revised and re-set) Methuen.

Notes: Performance details include those for: Mermaid Theatre, 2 March 1972; Shaw Theatre, January 1976; National Theatre, November 1980; a broadcast by the BBC, March 1981. The text is a page-for-page reprint of the second Methuen text, to p. 55; but on p. 55, the repeated "There was a man holding the machine, you see, and he'd . . ." is not present; consequently, at the foot of the type-page an extra line of text is taken across from the top of p. 57.

f. Student edition with commentary and notes (1982):

HAROLD PINTER | The Caretaker | *With a Commentary and Notes by* | PATRICIA HERN | Methuen Student Editions | METHUEN – LONDON

xxxv [xxxvi], 92 pp. 18.6 × 12.0 cm. Paperback, front and back covers green with white borders; front cover lettered in white: "HAROLD PINTER | The Caretaker | With commentary and notes | [*photo, tilted, of Pleasence as Davies*] | METHUEN STUDENT EDITIONS"; on back cover, photo of Pinter, account of series, "ISBN 0 413 49280 X"; spine white, down spine in black: "THE CARE-TAKER HAROLD PINTER METHUEN".

Published 1982 (L accession 7 DEC 82). Price (on sticker, on back cover) £1.75. On verso of title leaf: "Methuen Student Edition first published in 1982 | [. . . .] | Printed in Great Britain by | Richard Clay | The Chaucer Press, Ltd, Bungay, Suffolk | ISBN 0 413 49280 X".

Contents: [i] title page; [ii] as above; [iii] contents; [iv] two production photos; [v]–viii Pinter chronology, publications; [ix]–xiii outline of plot and structure, with production photo on p.xiii; [xiv]–xxxv "Commentary"; [xxxvi] further reading; [1–2] photos from film; 3–80 text; 81–92 "Notes".

g. Faber Educational edition (1993):

[*All within single-rule frame:*] Harold Pinter | THE | CARETAKER | *Educational Text* | Edited and with an introduction by | Margaret Rose | ff | *faber and faber* | LONDON • BOSTON

3 leaves, 132 pp., 2 blank leaves. 19.7 × 12.4 cm. Paperback binding as for 1991 Faber, but outside red; on front cover, added lines: "[*rule*] | *Edited and with an introduction* | by Dr Margaret Rose"; on back cover, added account of this series, "UK £3.99 non-net Canada $9.99 | ISBN 0-571-16735-7 | [*bar-code*] | 9 78051 167357".

Published 1993 (L accession 21 JAN 93). Reprinted on 2 December 1997, 6 April 1999, totalling 13,583 copies printed (to 1 August 2001). Price £3.99. On verso of title leaf: "First published in 1993 by | Faber and Faber Limited | [. . . .] | Photoset by Parker Typesetting Service, Leicester | Printed by Clays Ltd, St Ives plc | [. . . .] | ISBN 0-571-16735-7", etc.

Contents: [i] accounts of Pinter and Dr Margaret Rose; [ii] list of titles "*by the same author*"; [iii] title page; [iv] as above; [v] contents; [6] blank; [1]–33 "Introduction"; [34] blank; [35–38] preliminaries; [39]–110 text; [111]–128 notes; [129]–132 bibliography.

Notes: The text is as for the 1991 Faber. Performance details on pp.[36–37] include those for the Comedy Theatre, June 1991.

h. Australian students' edition (1965):

THE CARETAKER | *by* | HAROLD PINTER | *with an Introduction by* | ALRENE SYKES | *Lecturer in English* | *at the University of Queensland* | HICKS SMITH & SONS PTY. LTD. | 301 KENT STREET, SYDNEY

xii, 75 pp. Hardback, white cloth; on outside front: "THE CARETAKER | Harold Pinter | [*rectangular pattern of rhythmical swirls in black, white, and orange-vermillion*] | The Gateway Library [*publisher's "G" device*]"; on outside back: "[*publisher's 'G' device*] The Gateway Library | [*same design as on front*] | Hicks, Smith and Sons"; down spine: "Harold Pinter [*in black in orange-vermillion panel:*] THE CARETAKER [*across spine, in white: publisher's 'G' device*]".

Published 1965. Price 12s 6d or A$1.25. Alrene Sykes' introduction occupies pp. v–ix. (Not seen; information from Dace.)

i. German students' edition (1969):

DIESTERWEGS NEUSPRACHLICHE BIBLIOTHEK | *The Caretaker* | A Play in Three Acts | by | HAROLD PINTER | Edited and annotated | by | GERHARD HORNUNG | VERLAG MORITZ DIESTERWEG | Frankfurt am Main • Berlin • München | 4150

84 pp. 17.9 cm. Paperback, white; on front cover, imposed on film still: "[*in white:*] Harold Pinter | [*in powder blue:*] THE CARETAKER | [*in white:*] Diesterweg"; on back cover: "Diesterweg 4150"; on inside of front cover: publisher's advertisements; on inside of back cover, last page of annotations; up spine: "Harold Pinter • The Caretaker".

Published 1969. Price DM 3,40. All in English, with an introduction before the text, and annotations following it, from p.75, extending to the inside back of the cover. (Not seen; information from Dace.)

j. Dutch educational edition (1980):

Harold Pinter | The Caretaker | Introduction by Karel van Muyden | Annotations by Wim van Houten | Wikor Dramatic Library No. 60 | 1980

142, [1] pp. 18.5 × 11.6 cm. Paperback, red and white, with black lettering.

Published 1980. On verso of title leaf: production details for a tour by the New Shakespeare Company of The Netherlands and Belgium, October-December 1980, "© 1962, H. Pinter Limited | © for this edition Stichting Wikor, 1980", conditions of sale, further copyright, and performing rights statements. Text occupies pp.26–137.

k. Japanese educational edition [date unknown]:

Harold Pinter | THE CARETAKER | *Edited with Introduction and Notes* | *by* | KENJI (BA | TSURUMI SHOTEN | TOKYO

88 pp. 18.3 × 12.5 cm. Introduction and notes in Japanese.

l. French's acting edition (1962):

THE CARETAKER | A Play in Three Acts | by | HAROLD PINTER | SAMUEL [*publisher's device*] | FRENCH | LONDON

2 leaves, 50 pp., 1 leaf. 21.2 × 13.8 cm. Paperback blue, lettered in Indian red; on front cover: "THE CARETAKER | A Play | HAROLD PINTER | FRENCH'S ACTING EDITION"; back cover blank; down spine: "THE CARETAKER 6s. *net*".

Published 13 June 1962 (L accession 3 JUL 62). Price 6s. 2000 copies printed, for first printing; thereafter, reprinted in response to demand. On verso of title leaf: publisher's addresses, copyright statement, "MADE AND PRINTED IN GREAT BRITAIN BY | LATIMER, TREND AND CO. LTD, PLYMOUTH | MADE IN ENGLAND".

Contents: [i] title page; [ii] as above; [iii] details of first presentation, and times of acts; [iv] French's performing rights statements; [1]–46 text; [47]–48 furniture and property list, headed with ground-plan; [49]–50 lighting plot; [51] effects plot; [52] blank.

Note one: In subsequent reprints of this edition, the text is same, but: p.[ii] French's statements; p.[iv] blank; and at the end, the effects plot and the lighting plot are in reverse order. More recent reprints have: ISBN 0 573 04002 8.

m. American acting edition [1963]:

[*To left, 8 vertical thick rules, 9.3 cm.*] | THE | CARETAKER | BY HAROLD PINTER | [*star*] | [*8 horizontal thick rules, 9.3 cm.*] | [*star*] | DRAMATISTS | PLAY SERVICE | INC. | [*to right, 8 vertical thick rules, 3.4 cm.*]

1 leaf, 68 pp., 1 leaf. 17 × 13 cm. Paperback, dull yellow, two staples; front cover lettered and ruled as for title page, except lengths of rules 12.8, 13.3, and 4.8 cm. respectively; on back cover, wavy borders above and below, list of DPS new titles; down spine: "THE CARETAKER – Pinter"; on inside of front cover, below thin rule, information about DPS, also, within single-rule frame, advertisement for Dr. Rudolph Liszt's *The Last Word in Make-Up: A Practical Illustrated Handbook;* on inside of back cover, within frame, single rules above and below, decorative at sides, list of DPS recent acquisitions.

Published 26 February 1963 (*Publishers' Weekly,* 1 April 1963, "Weekly Record": 63-1824); DLC copyright registration, 26 February 1963 (DP5007). 1000 copies, in first printing. Price $1.25. On verso of title leaf: "© COPYRIGHT, 1963, BY THEATRE PROMOTIONS LTD. (Acting Edition)", further copyright and performing rights statements, 3 paragraphs.

Contents: [i] blank; [ii] photo of set; [1] title page; [2] copyright and perform-
ing rights statements; [3] "Acting Edition Prepared by | CHARLES
FORSYTHE"; 4 first American performance details [Lyceum Theatre,
New York, 4 October 1962], list of scenes, further production per-
sonnel details; 5–60 text; 61 ground-plan of set; 62–64 "PROPERTY
PLOT"; 65 "OFF-STAGE PROPS" list, one sound-effect; 66–67
"SCENE CHANGES"; 68 "WARDROBE"; [69–70] DPS advertise-
ments for new plays, recent releases.

n. American anthology (extracts) (1962):

THE BEST PLAYS | OF 1961–1962 | EDITED BY HENRY HEWES | DODD, MEAD & COMPANY | NEW YORK • TORONTO | [*drawing, by Hirschfeld*]

Seen in reprint, 1975, by the Arno Press, a New York Times company. Original title page of 1962 reproduced, with, on facing verso, "THE | BURNS MANTLE | YEARBOOK". *The Caretaker,* in the form of extracts introduced and inter-
spersed with descriptive and narrative passages, occupies pp. 49–63. On p.258, details of first British production.

o. American anthology (1964):

THE NEW BRITISH DRAMA | [*rule*] | Edited and with an Introduction by | Henry Popkin | GROVE PRESS, INC./ NEW YORK

606 pp. 20.9 × 13.2 cm. Hardback, blue cloth; on spine, in silver: "*The* | *New* | *British* | Drama | [*short thick rule*] | H. POPKIN, EDITOR | GROVE | PRESS".

Published 1964. *The Caretaker* occupies pp. [470]–553; with Pinter's essay "WRITING FOR THE THEATRE" on pp. [574]–580. [In reprints, the volume's title was changed to: *Modern British Drama*.]

p. British anthology (1967):

TWELVE | MODERN DRAMATISTS | *by* | RAYMOND COWELL, B.A., Ph.D. | *Senior Lecturer in English, Trinity* | *and All Saints' Colleges, Leeds* | PERGAMON PRESS | OXFORD • LONDON • EDINBURGH • NEW YORK | TORONTO • SYDNEY • PARIS • BRAUNSCHWEIG

x, 143 pp. 19 × 11.8 cm.

Contents [relevant]: [134]–135 introduction to the play, and this extract; [136]–141 extract from Act II, following Mick's pursuing Davies with the vacuum cleaner, through to blackout; 141 "QUESTIONS AND DISCUSSION POINTS".

q. British anthology (1985):

LANDMARKS OF | MODERN BRITISH DRAMA | VOLUME ONE: | [*rule, 7.9 cm.*] | The Plays of | The Sixties | [*rule, 7.9 cm.*] | Arnold Wesker: Roots | John Arden: Serjeant Musgrave's Dance | Harold Pinter: The Caretaker | John Osborne: A Patriot for Me | Edward Bond: Saved | Joe Orton: Loot | Peter Barnes: The Ruling Class | *with introductions by* | Roger Cornish *and* Violet Ketels | [*below* "Roger Cornish":] *Rutgers University* [*below* "Violet Ketels":] *Temple University* | METHUEN • LONDON and NEW YORK

xxxvi, 732 pp. 19.7 × 12.3 cm. Published 1985. Price net £4.95, in UK only.

Contents [relevant]: [193]–200 introduction to Pinter's plays, and *The Caretaker*; [201] fly-title, and rights statement; [202] blank; [203] performance details; [204] description of set; [205]–276 text of play.

A3   THAT'S ALL [*also*] THE APPLICANT   1960

In: Informally published typescript [late May, 1960]:

VOICES IN THE AIR | Devised and Produced by Douglas Cleverdon. Introduced by Donald Cotton. BBC Third Programme, 26 May 1960.

1 leaf, 44 pp. The texts of a programme of short radio pieces; it includes also pieces by D. Cotton, N. F. Simpson, Michael Flanders and Donald Swann, Anthony Hopkins, Sandy Wilson, David Climie, John Betjeman, Piers Stephens, and Paul McDowell, with introductions and continuity by Cotton. Transmitted 26 May 1960, 21 June 1960. "That's All" is on pp.16–18, "The Applicant" on pp. 33–37. Copy seen owned by William Baker; copy also at TxU-HRC.

A4   THE BIRTHDAY PARTY AND OTHER PLAYS   1960

First edition (July, 1960):

THE | BIRTHDAY PARTY | AND OTHER PLAYS | BY | Harold Pinter | LONDON | METHUEN & CO LTD | 36 ESSEX STREET WC2

159 pp. 18.4 × 12.3 cm. Signed [A]⁸ B-K⁸ (e.g., p.17 signed at foot, left: "B.P.-B"). Hardback, black cloth ; lettered down spine in gold: "THE BIRTHDAY PARTY & other plays [*star*] HAROLD PINTER [*star*] Methuen". Endpapers. Dust jacket with front and spine blue, back and flaps white; on outside front: "[*in black*:] HAROLD PINTER | [2 *lines in white*:] The Birthday Party | AND OTHER PLAYS | [*photo of Rose and Bert, from* The Room]"; on outside back, photo of Pinter, below it, his name in blue capitals, a 9-line biographical note, in black, in italic; on front flap, in black, a brief account of these plays, and of Pinter, "*The photograph on the front cover of Michael | Brennan and Vivien Merchant in* The Room | *is reproduced by courtesy of John Cowan. The | portrait of Harold Pinter on the back is by | Roger Mayne.* | 2/6406/1 12s 6d net"; back flap blank.

Published 21 July 1960 (L accession 8 JUL 60). 3000 copies. On verso of title leaf: "TO VIVIEN | [*copyright and performing rights statements*] | *First published 1960* | *Copyright © 1959 and 1960* | *by Harold Pinter* | *Printed in Great Britain by* | *W. & J. Mackay & Co. Ltd* | *Chatham, Kent* | *Cat. No. 2/6406/1*".

Contents: [1] half-title; [2] "*by the same author* | [*star*] | THE CARETAKER"; [3] title page; [4] as above; [5] contents; [6] blank; [7] fly-title "The Birthday Party"; [8] first presentation details, times of acts; [9]–91 text; [92] blank; [93] fly-title "The Room"; [94] details of first professional production (Hampstead Theatre Club, 21 January 1960; transferred to the Royal Court Theatre, 8 March 1960, with four cast changes); [95]–120 text; [121] fly-title "The Dumb Waiter"; [122] first production details, as part of double bill with *The Room*, as above; [123]–159 text; [160] blank.

Note one: A proof copy bound in green light card, with, on the front cover, within a rectangular frame, "METHUEN | *Proof copy* | UNCORRECTED", and a description of the book as "Crown 8vo 160pp About 12s 6d net | Publication date July 1960", is owned by William Baker. On p.11, it has "Lady Mary Platt", as opposed to "Lady Mary Splatt" in the published edition.

Note two: A 1964 reprint (copy seen in Otago University, NZ) has on the verso of the title leaf: "1.3 | *First published 1960* | *Copyright © 1959 and 1960* | *by Harold Pinter* | *Reprinted 1962 and 1964* | *Printed in Great Britain by John Dickens & Co Ltd* | *Northampton*". On p.[2], there is a list for "*Methuen's Modern Plays* | EDITED BY JOHN CULLEN" ("*in paper covers*": 20 titles; "*in hard covers*": 8 titles).

Note three: The Dumb Waiter, first published in this volume, had received American copyright registration as an unpublished script at the Library of Congress on 7 April 1960 (DU50872).

A5   A SLIGHT ACHE   [1960]

a. As radio play; publication within periodical [1960]:

"'A SLIGHT ACHE' | Harold Pinter". *Tomorrow,* 4 [1960]: 17–32.

Note one: The dialogue begins directly below the title, with no introductory information, or scene-setting, nor is there any documentation of the play at the end of the text; but on the front cover, it is referred to as "'A SLIGHT ACHE' | a play for radio by | HAROLD PINTER". The text is in two columns, with speech-prefixes set to the left of each column, in full-size and small capitals. On p.3, in the "NOTES ON CONTRIBUTORS", that on Pinter is simply: "Plays: *The Room, The Dumb Waiter, The Birthday Party,* | *The Caretaker*". The radio play had been broadcast on the BBC's Third Programme on 29 July 1959. For the circumstances of this publishing, see W9(2). The text as reworked as a version for the stage would be published in *A Slight Ache and Other Plays* (1961).

Note two: The play received American copyright registration as an unpublished script at the Library of Congress on 16 November 1960 (DU52288).

b. British acting edition [1962?]:

A SLIGHT ACHE | A Play in One Act | by | HAROLD PINTER | SAMUEL [*publisher's device*] FRENCH | LONDON

2 leaves, 27, [1] pp. 18.0 × 12.3 cm. Paperback, blue; on outside front, in red: "A SLIGHT ACHE | A Play in One Act | by | HAROLD PINTER | 3s. net | FRENCH'S ACTING EDITION"; outside back blank; down spine, in red: "A SLIGHT ACHE".

Published 10 April 1962 (L accession 16 APR 62). 2000 copies (probably) in first print-run; thereafter, reprinted in response to demand. Price 3s. On verso of title leaf: "[*publisher's addresses*] | © 1961 BY HAROLD PINTER | [*copyright and performing rights statements*] | MADE AND PRINTED IN GREAT BRITAIN BY | LATIMER, TREND AND CO., LTD, PLYMOUTH | MADE IN ENGLAND".

Contents: [i] title page; [ii] as above; [iii] details of characters, setting, time; [iv] French's performing rights information; [1]–25 text; [26]–27 furniture and properties plot; [28] lighting plot.

Notes: Later reprints have the ISBN number 0 573 02249 6. Dace notes the text considerably differs from that in the Methuen volume *A Slight Ache and Other Plays,* in lines as well as in stage directions. It is the radio-play version.

c. In American anthology (1970):

A Treasury of the Theatre, edited by John Gassner and Bernard F. Dukore, 4ᵗʰ edition (New York: Simon & Schuster, 1970), Vol. 2: *From Henrik Ibsen to Robert Lowell.* Not seen. Pinter's play is not in earlier editions.

d. American anthology (1976):

[*Thick rule, curved down at left*] | CASEBOOK ON | EXISTENTIALISM 2 | William V. Spanos | State University of New York, | Binghampton | THOMAS Y. CROWELL COMPANY | Established 1834 New York | [*thick rule, curved up at right*].

xvi, 445, [1] pp. On verso of title leaf: copyright statement, 1966, 1976; copying restriction; note: "Published simultaneously in Canada by Fitzhenry & Whiteside, Ltd, | Toronto"; DLC cataloguing data, LCCN 75-44413, ISBN 0-690-00847-3, publisher's address, acknowledgements. *A Slight Ache* occupies pp.120-141.

e. American anthology (1977):

Drama through Performance | [*rule, 11.8 cm.*] | Mark S. Auburn | The Ohio State University | Katherine H. Burkman | The Ohio State University | Houghton Mifflin Company Boston | Atlanta Dallas Geneva, Illinois | Hopewell, New Jersey Palo Alto London

22.9 × 15 cm. Published 1977. The text of *A Slight Ache* (the stage version) occupies pp.712–736, with an introductory essay preceding it (pp.[709]–711) and "Action analysis and performance suggestions" following (pp.736–740).

f. American anthology (1977):

MODERNISM | IN | LITERATURE | TODD K. BENDER University of Wisconsin, Madison | NANCY ARMSTRONG Instituo de Estudos Norte-Americanos | Universities of Coimbro and Oporto, Portugal | SUE M. BRIGGUM University of Wisconsin, Madison | FRANK A. KNOBLOCH University of Wisconsin, Madison | HOLT, RINEHART AND WINSTON | New York Chicago San Francisco Atlanta | Dallas Montreal Toronto

22.7 × 13.4 cm. Published 1977. The text of *A Slight Ache* (the stage version) occupies pp.461–473.

g. German anthology (1979):

Modern | One-act Plays | Tom Stoppard • James Saunders | Harold Pinter | Edited by Horst Buss, Bruno von Lutz | and Kunibert Schäfer | Ernst Klett Schulbuchverlag | Stuttgart Düsseldorf Berlin Leipzig

A Slight Ache occupies pp.50–72, with biography and annotations on pp.73–77. The two other plays are Stoppard's *A Separate Peace* and Saunders' *A Slight Accident*.

A6   THE BLACK AND WHITE [*also*] TROUBLE IN THE WORKS   1960

a. In: *Sketches from One to Another, acting edition (1960)*:

SKETCHES | from | ONE TO ANOTHER | by | JOHN MORTIMER, N. F. SIMPSON | and HAROLD PINTER | SAMUEL [*publisher's device*] | FRENCH | LONDON

2 leaves, 31 pp. 21.6 × 13.9 cm. Paperback, orange; on front cover, lettered in red: "SKETCHES | from | ONE TO ANOTHER | by | JOHN MORTIMER, N. F. SIMPSON | & HAROLD PINTER | FRENCH'S ACTING EDITION".

Published 1960 (L accession 22 DEC 60). Price 5s. Number of copies in first print-run 2000; thereafter reprinted in response to demand. On verso of title leaf: publisher's addresses, copyright statements, "MADE AND PRINTED IN GREAT BRITAIN BY | LATIMER, TREND & CO. LTD, PLYMOUTH | MADE IN ENGLAND".

Contents: [i] title page; [ii] as above; [iii] first presentation details; [iv] performing rights statement; [1]–3 "Triangle" by Mortimer; [4]–9 "Gladly Otherwise" by Simpson; [10]–12 "The Black and White" by Pinter; [13]–15 "Trouble in the Works" by Pinter; [16]–18 "Cleaning up Justice" by Mortimer; [19]–22 "Collector's Piece" by Mortimer; [23]–26 "Conference" by Mortimer; [27]–31 "Can You Hear Me?" by Simpson.

Notes: DLC copyright registration, 20 December 1960 (DF1432). At TxU-HRC: a copy signed: "John Mortimer | Produced Lyric Hammersmith | & Apollo Theatre". Later reprints have the ISBN number 0 573 07021 0.

b. ("Trouble in the Works" only) *In: American anthology (1971)*:

CONTEMPORARY | AMERICAN SOCIETY | THROUGH LITERATURE | Munching | on | Existence | EDITED BY Robert Gliner | AND R. A. Raines | [*publisher's device*] The Free Press, New York

Published 1971. "Trouble in the Works" occupies pp.328–331. It occurs within a section on "occupational boredom," and a preliminary note on p.327 observes that the factory in which it is set *"might as well be an American one, in which scores of people busily dedicate their lives to the duplication of meaningless objects."*

c. ("The Black and White") only in: *Envoy Magazine* (May 1968): 42–43.

A7   THE ROOM   1961

a. British acting edition (1961):

THE ROOM | A Play in One Act | by | HAROLD PINTER | SAMUEL [*publisher's device*] FRENCH | LONDON

2 leaves, 24, [3] pp. Paperback, blue; on front cover, in red: "THE ROOM | A Play in One Act | by HAROLD PINTER | 3s. | FRENCH'S ACTING EDITION"; outside back blank; down spine, in red: "THE ROOM".

Published 3 January 1961 (L accession 5 JAN 61). Number of copies in first print-run 2000; thereafter, printed in response to demand. Price 3s. On verso of title leaf: "© 1960 BY HAROLD PINTER | [*publisher's addresses, copyright and performing rights statements*] | MADE AND PRINTED IN GREAT BRITAIN BY | LATIMER, TREND AND CO., LTD, PLYMOUTH | MADE IN ENGLAND".

Contents: [i] title page; [ii] as above; [iii] first professional production details, note of location, time; [iv] copyright and performing rights statements; [1]–24 text; [25] furniture and properties list; [26] lighting plot; [27] effects plot; [28] blank.

Notes: DLC copyright registration, 3 January 1961 (DF1407). Re-registered 5 January 1988 (RE-367-266). Later Samuel French reprints had the ISBN number 0 573 02236 4. A copy at TxU-HRC has on the title page, added to the imprint: "New York Toronto Sydney Hollywood"; verso of title leaf blank; at foot of p. [27]: "Printed in Great Britain | by Latimer Trend & Co Ltd | Whitstable".

A8   THE DUMB WAITER   1961

a. British acting edition (1961):

THE DUMB WAITER | A Play in One Act | by | HAROLD PINTER | SAMUEL [*publisher's device*] FRENCH | LONDON

2 leaves, 33 pp. 18.2 × 12.1 cm. Paperback, blue; on front cover, in red: "THE DUMB WAITER | A Play in One Act | by | HAROLD PINTER | 3s. net | FRENCH'S ACTING EDITION"; outside back blank; down spine: "THE DUMB WAITER".

Published 3 January 1961 (L accession 5 JAN 61). Number of copies in first print-run 2000; thereafter, reprinted in response to demand. Price 3s. On verso of title leaf: publisher's addresses, copyright statement, "MADE AND PRINTED IN GREAT BRITAIN BY | LATIMER, TREND AND CO. LTD, PLYMOUTH | MADE IN ENGLAND".

Contents: [i] title page; [ii] as above; [iii] first performance details; [iv] French's performing rights statement; [1]–29 text; [30] furniture and property plot; [31] lighting plot; [32]–33 effects plot; [34] blank.

Notes: Later reprints have the ISBN number 0 573 04210 1. Revised 1974. American copyright registration for the first edition, first printing: Library of Congress, 3 January 1961 (DF1408). Pre-publication: 7 April 1960 (Du 50872).

b. Dutch educational edition [1967?]:

ENGLISH OF ALL AGES | [*rule, 9.4 cm.*] | *HAROLD PINTER* | THE DUMB WAITER | ANNOTATED BY | B. JOHN MEYER | *English Master at* | *Leiden* | [*publisher's device*] | [*rule, 9.4 cm.*] | VAN GOOR ZONEN | DEN HAAG BRUSSEL

40 pp. 18.9 × 12.9 cm. 11-page word-list booklet inserted. Paperback, illustration on front cover and around spine of two gunmen.

Published in December 1967 or January 1968, and a second edition *ca.* January 1973 (Dace).

c. German students' edition (1975):

DIESTERWEGS NEUSPRACHLICHE BIBLIOTHEK | *The Dumb Waiter* | by | HAROLD PINTER | Edited and annotated | by | ERNST PALENBERG | VERLAG MORITZ DIESTERWEG | Frankfurt am Main • Berlin • München | 4038

47, [1] pp. 17 cm. Paperback, white, printed in shades of aqua: on outside front: "HAROLD PINTER | [*upper half of title* 'THE DUMB WAITER' *4 times*] | [*lower half of title 4 times*] | DIESTERWEG"; on outside back: aqua solid rectangle, "Diesterweg 4038"; spine blank.

Published 1975. Price DM. 3,80. [Not seen; information from Dace.]

Contents: [1] title page; [2] colophon, etc.; 3–11 introduction; 12–40 text; 41–[48] annotations.

d. Penguin anthology (1961):

NEW ENGLISH DRAMATISTS | 3 | INTRODUCED BY J. W. LAMBERT | EDITED BY TOM MASCHLER | THE LONG AND THE SHORT AND THE TALL | *Willis Hall* | LIVE LIKE PIGS | *John Arden* | THE DUMB WAITER | *Harold Pinter* | PENGUIN BOOKS

214, [1] pp. 18.1 × 11.1 cm. Paperback, outside with base-colour in blocks of darker green, pink, black, and lighter green; on front cover: "[*upper left, within white oval, publisher's device*] *Penguin Plays* | New English | Dramatists . 3 | The Long and the Short | and the Tall | WILLIS HALL | Live Like Pigs | JOHN

ARDEN | The Dumb Waiter | HAROLD PINTER | 2/6"; on outside back: "*Penguin Plays*", list of 4 other volumes in series; down spine: "[*in white, reversed out of green:*] *Penguin Plays* [*in black:*] New English Dramatists . 3 [*across spine, at foot:*] [*publisher's device*] | PL39".

Published 1961 (L accession 17 APR 61). On verso of title leaf: publisher's addresses, first publication and copyright details of 3 plays, "Made and printed in Great Britain | by C. Nicholls & Company Ltd".

Contents: [1] series half-title "PENGUIN PLAYS | PL39 | NEW ENGLISH DRAMATISTS | [*publisher's device*]"; [2] blank; [3] title page; [4] as above; [5] contents; [6] blank; 7–[10] introduction; [11]–91 [92] Hall play; [93]–184 Arden play; [185]–214 [215] Pinter play.

Notes: A later issue of this has, on the title page, below "EDITED BY TOM MASCHLER", a swelled rule, 1.6 cm.; leaf measure 17.7 × 10.2 cm.

e. Penguin anthology, new edition: Penguin Plays PL49 (1964):

The Long and the Short and the Tall | WILLIS HALL | [*small star*] | *The Dumb Waiter* | HAROLD PINTER | [*small star*] | *A Resounding Tinkle* | N. F. SIMPSON | PENGUIN BOOKS

190, [1] pp. Paperback, upper two-fifths brown, lower three fifths violet; on front cover, in upper two-fifths, in white dots "PENGUIN PLAYS", in lower three-fifths, in black: "WILLIS HALL | The Long and the Short | and the Tall | HAROLD PINTER | The Dumb Waiter | N. F. SIMPSON | A Resounding Tinkle | 3/6"; on back cover, brief descriptions of three plays, "*Cover design by Denise York* | Authors' photographs from right to left: Hall, Pinter, Simpson. | *For copyright reasons this edition is not for sale in the U.S.A.* | [*three photos*]"; on spine: "[*Penguin device, in white*] [*down spine, in black:*] HALL PINTER SIMPSON Plays [*across spine, at foot, in black:*] PL49".

Published 1964, reprinted 1965. On verso of title leaf: publisher's addresses, first publication and copyright details for each of the three plays, with dates of inclusion within this collection 1964, 1965, "Made and printed in Great Britain by | Cox & Wyman Ltd, London, Fakenham and Reading | Set in Monotype Bembo", conditions of sale statement.

Contents: [1] series half-title, with number as "PL49"; [2] blank; [3] title page; [4] as above; [5] contents; [6] blank; [7] fly-title for Hall play; [8] first performance details; 9–83 [84] text; [85] fly-title, Pinter play; [86] performance details; 87–113 [114] text; [115] fly-title, Simpson play; [116] performance details, character list; 117–190 [191] text; [120] blank.

Notes: The 1965 reprint has on the title page the Penguin device above "PENGUIN BOOKS". Its cover is coloured in three horizontal bands, blue, orange, and green; on the front cover, within the blue band, in white dots: "PENGUIN | PLAYS", within the green band, as for 1964, but authors' names in white; on back cover, lettering within blue band, authors' photos within orange and green bands.

f. American anthology (1966):

Twentieth Century | DRAMA: | *England, Ireland, the United States* | [*rule, 8.7 cm.*] | EDITED BY | RUBY COHN | AND | BERNARD F. DUKORE | *Queens College of The City University of New York* | [*publisher's device*] RANDOM HOUSE / *New York*

5 leaves, 692 pp., 1 blank leaf. 23.0 × 12.2 cm. Paperback, white; on front cover, design at head, of parts of three circles, with colours of US, French, and British flags, title in mauve, editors' names in red, list of playwrights in blue. The text of *The Dumb Waiter* occupies pp. [622]–647.

g. American anthology (1974):

The Theatre | of the Mind | [*wavy rule, 10.4 cm.*] | GEORGE SOULE | *Carleton College* | *Northfield, Minnesota* | PRENTICE-HALL, INC. | *Englewood Cliffs, New Jersey*

22.6 × 14.1 cm. Published 1974. ISBN 0-13-913020-9. *The Dumb Waiter* occupies pp. 634–662, and commentaries on it, pp. 662–665.

h. American anthology (1978):

[*rule, 13.8 cm.*] | SECOND EDITION | DRAMA AND DISCUSSION | [*rule, 13.8 cm.*] | *Edited by* | STANLEY A. CLAYES | *Loyola University of Chicago* | PRENTICE-HALL, INC., *Englewood Cliffs, New Jersey 07632*

Second edition published 1978 (date of first not ascertained). 23.7 × 16 cm. ISBN 0-13.219030-3. The text of *The Dumb Waiter* and an essay on "The Ironic Con Game" in this play occupy pp. 573–589.

i. American anthology (1978):

An Introductory Anthology | [*rule, 5.8 cm.*] | THIRTEEN PLAYS | *Edited by* | Otto Reinert | UNIVERSITY OF WASHINGTON, SEATTLE | Peter Arnott | Little, Brown and Company | BOSTON [*publisher's device*] TORONTO

xii, 762 pp., 12 blank leaves, 2 leaves. 21.3 × 13.2 cm. Paperback, green; on front cover, lettering (apart from "13") in white, rules in yellow: "[*in yellow:*] 13 | [*rule*] | THIRTEEN PLAYS | [*rule*] | An Introductory Anthology | [*rule*] | Otto Reinert / Peter Arnott | [*rule*]"; on back cover, in white, advertisement and list of contents for their larger anthology, *Twenty-three plays* (1978).

Published 1978. LCCN 78-50412. ISBN 0-316-73949-9. *The Dumb Waiter* occupies pp. 612–636, with a "FOREWORD" on pp. [611]–612, setting the scene, and an "AFTERWORD" on pp. 636–640, discussing the play.

Notes: The longer anthology has a similar title page but with "TWENTY-THREE | PLAYS". LCCN 78-50417. ISBN 0-316-739502. *The Dumb Waiter* occupies pp.1000-1024, with the foreword on pp. [999]–1000, and the afterword on pp.1024–1028. A note on the versos of the title pages indicates that both anthologies were simultaneously published in Canada through Little, Brown & Company (Canada) Limited.

A9   **A NIGHT OUT**   1961

a. Informally published radio script [1961]:

"A NIGHT OUT" | A new play for radio | by | Harold Pinter | Produced by Donald McWhinnie | First broadcast | by the Third Programme of the BBC on | Tuesday, 1st March 1960

Parallel title page, on facing verso: "UNE NUIT DE SORTIE" | Pièce nouvelle écrite pour le radio | par | Harold Pinter | Réalisation de Donald McWhinnie | Traduction française de Jacques Brunius (1) | Cette pièce a été radiodiffusé pour le première fois | par le Troisième Programme de la BBC le | 1er Mars 1960 | [*rule*] | (1) Cette traduction, aussi littérale que possible, n'est pas | destinée à la radio-diffusion sous sa forme actuelle. (N.d.T.)

1 blank leaf, 3 leaves, 50 leaves, 1 blank leaf. From p.[1], and the facing verso, parallel texts, with the French text on the left of the opening, and the English on the right, both numbered [1]–50 pp. Pale blue card covers, with a red plastic spiral binder; on the outside front, in red: "ITALIA PRIZE 1961 | BBC ENTRY | [*rule, 12.6 cm.*] | *A Night Out* | [*rule*] | By HAROLD PINTER | [*rule*] | *Produced by* DONALD MCWHINNIE *in the* | BBC THIRD PROGRAMME | *March 1, 1960*".

Contents: [i–iii] blank; [iv] title page in French; [v] title page in English; [vi] cast-list in French, at foot, below a rule, a footnote in French, numbered "(1)", about London late-night "coffee stalls" [there are no other footnotes]; [vii] cast-list in English; [viii]–"50" (verso) text in French; [1]–"50" (recto) text in English, texts corresponding page for page; verso of second p."50", blank. In duplicated typescript.

Notes: This publication was evidently produced in relation to the entry of the radio play, in English and French, for the Italia Prize in 1961. A loose leaf at the front of the volume has biographical notes about Donald McWhinnie and Harold Pinter, in English on the recto and in French on the verso. Within the text, stage-directions are underlined, not in italic. Those before or between speeches are in capitals; those following speech-prefixes or within dialogue passages are in capitals and lower case. The copy seen is owned by William Baker.

b. French's acting edition [1963]:

A NIGHT OUT | A Play | by | HAROLD PINTER | SAMUEL [*publisher's device*] FRENCH | LONDON

2 leaves, 52 pp. 18.5 × 12.3 cm. Paperback, pale blue; on front cover, in red: "A NIGHT OUT | A Play | by | HAROLD PINTER | FRENCH'S ACTING EDITION"; back cover blank; down spine: "A NIGHT OUT 2s 6d net".

Published 19 February 1963 (date from publisher; L accession date 23 FEB 63). Price 2s. 6d. Number of copies in first print-run 2000; thereafter reprinted in response to demand. On verso of title leaf: publisher's addresses, copyright statements ("© 1961"), "MADE AND PRINTED IN GREAT BRITAIN BY | LATIMER, TREND AND CO. LTD, PLYMOUTH | MADE IN ENGLAND".

Contents: [i] title page; [ii] as above; [iii] first presentation details, 2 October 1961, synopsis of scenes; [iv] French's performing rights statement; [1]–43 text; [44] blank; [45]–48 furniture and property list; [49]–50 lighting plot; [51]–52 effects plot.

Notes: Later reprints have a different cover and preliminaries. A copy at TxU-HRC has a mainly white cover with the front in blue and white, and on the back "HAROLD PINTER | A NIGHT OUT | GB 573 02176 7 [*within small blue circle, 2 lines in black*] 15p | net [*within a second small blue circle, 2 lines in black*] 3s | net". The imprint on the title page adds: "NEW YORK TORONTO SYDNEY HOLLYWOOD"; the verso of the title leaf is blank; and the printer's colophon is at the foot of p. 52. More recent printings have the ISBN number 0 573 02176 7.

c. In anthology (1972):

Conflict in Social Drama: Plays for Education, 2 vols. (London: Methuen, 1972); in Vol. 1: *The personal conflict.* Not seen.

A10   **THE CARETAKER AND THE DUMB WAITER**   1961

a. American first edition (1961):

THE CARETAKER | and | THE DUMB WAITER | *Two plays by* | *Harold Pinter* | GROVE PRESS, INC. NEW YORK

2 leaves, 121 pp., 1 blank leaf. 20.4 × 11.6 cm. (a) Hardback, pale vermillion cloth; down spine in gold: "THE CARETAKER and THE DUMB WAITER / *Pinter* [*across spine:*] GROVE | PRESS". Dust jacket not seen (presumably similar to paperback binding). (b) Paperback, white; on front cover: "[*in black:*]

The Caretaker | [*in orange*:] & The Dumb Waiter | [*in pale grey*:] two plays by | [*in black*:] Harold Pinter | [*orange-tinged production photo of Davies and Mick*] [*at lower right, lettered upward, in white*:] EVERGREEN ORIGINAL E-299. $1.75 [*small publisher's device*]"; on back cover: "[*in orange*:] EVERGREEN ORIGINAL [*publisher's device*] | [*in black*:] (E-299) – – $1.75 | [*large orange panel, 13.3 × 10.1 cm.; within panel*:] [*in white*:] THE CARETAKER | [*remaining lettering in black*:] & THE DUMB WAITER | TWO PLAYS BY HAROLD PINTER | [*account of Pinter and of the two plays*] | Cover photo by Michael Boys | Cover design by Roy Kuhlman | GROVE PRESS, INC., 64 University Place, New York 3, N. Y."; down spine in black: "THE CARETAKER & THE DUMB WAITER BY HAROLD PINTER [*across spine, at foot*] E-299".

Published *ca.* 15 May 1961. Price $3.50 (hardback), $1.75 (paperback). On verso of title leaf: copyright statement, "Library of Congress Catalog Card Number: 61-10903 | First Grove Press Edition 1961 | First Printing | [*performing rights statement*] | Manufactured in the United States of America".

Contents: [i] half-title; [ii] blank; [iii] title page; [iv] as above; [1] "*To Vivien*"; [2] blank; [3] fly-title "The Caretaker"; [4] blank; [5] first British presentation details, list of acts; [6] description of set; [7]–82 text; [83] fly-title "The Dumb Waiter"; [84] first presentation details; [85]–121 text; [122–124] blank.

Notes: By the fifth printing, pp. [122–124] were employed for the publisher's lists of titles. The relative priority of the first printings of Evergreen Press titles, even within the same year, is evident from their E numbers: this is E-299, whereas *The Birthday Party and The Room* is E-315.

b. Edition with revisions, from 9ᵗʰ printing (1965):

As for first version, but the verso of the title leaf has "Ninth Printing, Revised 1965". With cuts and other revisions to *The Caretaker,* the text ends on p.78, with pp. [79–82] being utilised for production photos, from the first British production (as presented in New York), two per page. At foot of p. [5]: "PHOTOGRAPHIC INSERT | Photos from the American production by | Sam Siegel". The paperback binding is the same, except: on the back cover, the publisher's address is given as: "80 University Place, New York, N.Y. 10003"; and to the right of the orange panel, in black: "ix"; on the spine the publisher's device and imprint are in lemon yellow rather than orange.

A11   **THE BIRTHDAY PARTY AND THE ROOM**   1961

a. First American edition (1961):

THE BIRTHDAY PARTY | and | THE ROOM | *Two plays by Harold Pinter* | GROVE PRESS, INC. NEW YORK

120 pp., 2 leaves. Hardback not seen. Paperback, black-and-white on outside front, yellowish-orange on spine, white on outside back; on front cover: full-length photo of Rose and Bert, from *The Room*, with imposed at upper left: "[*in orange*:] The Birthday Party | [*in white*:] & | [*in orange*:] The Room | [*in white*:] 2 | [*2 lines in orange*:] plays by | Harold Pinter", and to lower right, lettered upward, in orange: "EVERGREEN ORIGINAL E-315 $1.75 [*small device*]"; on back cover: "[in black:] EVERGREEN *ORIGINAL* [*Evergreen device*] E-315— $1.75 | [within large orange panel, in black, account of Pinter and the two plays, "Cover photograph by John Cowan / Cover design by Roy Kuhlman | GROVE PRESS, INC., 64 University Place, New York 3, N.Y."; down spine: "[*in black*:] THE BIRTHDAY PARTY [*in yellow*:] & [*in black*:] THE ROOM [*in yellow*:] BY HAROLD PINTER [*device*] [*across spine, in black*:] E-315 [*down spine in 2 lines, in yellow*:] GROVE | PRESS".

Published 21 September 1961. Prices: hardback: GP-257, $3.50; paperback $1.75. On verso of title leaf: copyright and performing rights statements, "Library of Congress Catalog Card Number: 61-11770 | First Grove Press Edition 1961 | First Printing | [. . . .] | Manufactured in the United States of America".

Contents: [1] half-title; [2] "*By the same author*", 2 titles; [3] title page; [4] as above; [5] contents; [6] "*To Vivien* | Acknowledgements: Photographs from *The Birthday* | *Party* © by Kenneth Jepson, taken for the produc- | tion by the Tavistock Repertory Company, Tower | Theatre, London; photographs from *The Room* by | John Cowan."; [7] fly-title "The Birthday Party"; [8] first presentation details, list of acts; [9]–91 text; [91a-d] 8 production photographs, 2 per page; [92] blank; [93] fly-title "The Room"; [94] first British production details; [95]–120 text; [121–124] 8 production photographs, 2 per page.

Notes: With the hardback not having been seen, it is uncertain whether it corresponds with the paperback (text to p.120) or to the Book Club edition (text to p.118). The hardback binding may be similar in style to that of *The Caretaker and The Dumb Waiter,* with a dust jacket similar to that for the Book Club edition. For the ninth printing, in paperback, on the front cover, the text in orange is, instead, in red; on the back cover, Grove Press's address is given as: "80 University Place, New York, N. Y. 10003".

b. Book club edition [1961]:

Title page as for standard trade edition.

118 pp., 1 blank leaf. 20.6 cm. Hardback: quarter-bound with orange-yellow cloth, boards bound in black paper; down spine, in red: "THE BIRTHDAY PARTY and THE ROOM / *Pinter* [*in two lines*:] GROVE | PRESS". Endpapers. Dust jacket: outside front similar to the front cover of the paperback, except: "plays by" in white, and Evergreen details and price absent; outside back orange-yellow,

blank; spine orange-yellow, down spine, in black: "THE BIRTHDAY PARTY
AND THE ROOM BY HAROLD PINTER [*across spine*] GROVE | PRESS";
flaps white; on front flap, in black: title, author, paragraphs about Pinter and the
two plays, continued on back flap; on front flap, at foot: "*Book Club | Edition*";
on back flap: "Jacket photograph by John Cowan | Jacket design by Roy
Kuhlman | Printed in U.S.A.".

On verso of title leaf: "*The Birthday Party* copyright © 1959 | by Harold Pinter
| *The Room* copyright © 1960 by Harold Pinter | [*further copyright and per-
forming rights statements*] | Printed in the United States of America".

Contents: [1] half-title; [2] blank; [3] title page; [4] as above; [5] contents; [6]
"To Vivien"; [7] fly-title "The Birthday Party"; [8] first presentation
details, list of acts; [9]–90 text; [91] fly-title "The Room"; [92] first
professional presentation details; [93]–118 text; [119–120] blank. At
foot of p.118: "J16". No photos.

Notes: The Book Club edition was printed with a different typesetting (or, at
least a different page make-up) from that used for the paperback, with a larger
type-page (p.11, in the Book Club edition: 17.2 (16.6) × 9.4 cm.; in the paperback: 16.2 (15.6) × 9.5 cm.).

c. Standard trade edition, revised version (1968):

Title page as for first edition.

116 pp., plus 12 unpaginated pages of production photographs interpolated.
Paperback, black on front cover and spine, white on back cover; on front cover:
"[*in white:*] The Birthday Party | [*in green:*] & | [*in white:*] The Room | [*2 lines
in green:*] 2 | plays by | [*in white:*] Harold Pinter", photograph, orange-tinged,
of Stanley and Meg [see *Note one*], to left of photo, lettered upward, in orange:
"[*publisher's device*] EVERGREEN E-315-K $1.75"; on back cover, no orange
panel, rules in green: "[*2 lines in black:*] EVERGREEN ORIGINAL E-315-K
$1.75 | The Birthday Party | [*in green:*] & | [*in black:*] The Room | [*in green:*] 2 |
[*in black*] plays by Harold Pinter | [*remaining lettering in black:*]; Eight pages of
photographs | [*rule*] | [*2 paragraphs about the play*] | [*rule*] | [*paragraph about
Pinter*] | [*rule*] | Cover photograph by Henry Grossman/Cover design by Roy
Kuhlman | Grove Press, Inc., 53 East 11th Street, New York, New York 10003 |
ISBN: 0-394-17232-9"; down spine: "[*in orange:*] THE BIRTHDAY PARTY [*in
green:*] & [*in orange:*] THE ROOM [*in grey:*] BY [*in green:*] HAROLD PINTER
[*across spine, at foot:*] [*small publisher's device*] | E-315-K | GROVE | PRESS".

Revised edition first published 1968. Price $1.75. On verso of title leaf: as for first
printing, except with the addition of: "Revised Edition 1968 | Nineteenth
Printing | [. . . .] | DISTRIBUTED BY RANDOM HOUSE, INC., NEW YORK
| Acknowledgements: Photographs from *The Birthday Party* by Henry |
Grossman; photographs from *The Room* by John Cowan."

Contents: [1] half-title; [2] "Previously Published" [copy seen lists 4 titles]; [3] title page; [4] as above; [5] contents; [6] "*To Vivien*"; [7] fly-title "The Birthday Party"; [8] first production details, British, and American [see *Notes*]; [9]–87 text; [88] blank; [89] fly-title "The Room"; [90] first production details; [91]–116 text. 12 pages (3 pairs of leaves) of photographs interpolated: after p.36 (end of *Birthday Party*, Act I): 4 pages; after p.66 (end of *Birthday Party*, Act II): 4 pages; after p.116 (end of *The Room*): 4 pages, with 2 photos per page.

Notes: The text and the photographs for *The Room* are unchanged. However, for *The Birthday Party,* whereas the text for the first printings corresponds to that of the first Methuen edition (1960), for the revised edition it follows that of the second Methuen edition (1965). The first performance details include those for the production at the Booth Theatre, New York, on October 3, 1968, directed by Alan Schneider; and all the photographs for this play, including that on the front cover, evidently derive from this production. A later copy seen, undated, possibly of the 29th printing, has yellow rather than orange tinging on the outside front, price as $6.95. A 1978 reprint has ISBN 03941723129 (Evergreen E-315).

d. Grove Weidenfeld reprintings (from 1968):

Title page as for first Grove printing, except imprint: "[*Evergreen device*] | GROVE WEIDENFELD | NEW YORK".

116 pp. 20.4 × 12.7 cm. Paperback binding as for 1968 revision, except price as $7.95, or (later) as $8.95, publisher as Grove Weidenfeld, no Evergreen number, colours of lettering vary, ISBN as below, bar-code number as 9 780802 151148.

On verso of title leaf: largely as for Grove 1968, with lineation differences; copyright, reproduction restriction and performing rights statements, publisher as Grove Weidenfeld, with address, ISBN 0-8021-5114-0, LCCN 61-11770, "This book is printed on acid-free paper.", no mention of Random House, numbers at foot indicating 31st printing, in copies seen.

Contents: As for 1968, with, on [2], Grove Weidenfeld's Pinter titles.

Notes: Of two copies seen, apparently of the same printing, one had the price given as $7.95 and the other as $8.95, on the top right of the back cover. A more recent printing has a blue cover with a red arrow, the author's name divided in 4 groups of 3 letters in black, and the title in yellow.

A12　　　　　　A SLIGHT ACHE AND OTHER PLAYS　　　　　　1961

a. First edition (1961):

A SLIGHT ACHE | AND OTHER PLAYS | BY | Harold Pinter | LONDON | METHUEN & CO LTD | 36 ESSEX STREET, W.C.2

134 pp., 1 blank leaf. Signed [A]⁸ B-H⁸ I⁴. 18.4 × 11.9 cm. Hardback, black cloth; down spine in gold: "Harold Pinter [*star*] A SLIGHT ACHE and other plays [*star*] Methuen". Endpapers. Dust jacket blue, with flaps white; on outside front: "[*in black:*] HAROLD PINTER | [*2 lines in white:*] A SLIGHT ACHE | AND OTHER PLAYS | [*photo, from A Night Out*]"; on outside back, photo of Pinter, below, in white panel, author's name in blue, 5-line biographical note in black; down spine: "[*in black:*] PINTER [*in white:*] A SLIGHT ACHE [*in black:*] METHUEN"; on front flap, title, brief account of plays, "*The photograph on the front cover is of Tom | Bell and Vivien Merchant in the A.B.C. | Television Armchair Theatre production of | A Night Out. The Portrait of Harold Pinter | at the back is by Mark Gerson.*", at foot: "2/6452/1 12s 6d net"; on back flap, notes on other titles by Pinter.

Published 1 June 1961 (L accession 30 MAY 61; DLC copyright registration 1 June 1961 [DF1968]). Price 12s. 6d. On verso of title leaf: "TO VIVIEN | [*copyright and performing rights statements*] | *First published 1961* | © *1961 by Harold Pinter* | *Printed in Great Britain by* | *W. & J. Mackay & Co Ltd,* | *Chatham* | *Cat. No. 2/6452/1*".

Contents: [1] half-title; [2] list of titles "*by the same author*"; | [3] title page; [4] as above; [5] contents; [6] blank; [7] fly-title "A Slight Ache"; [8] first and second presentation details, as radio play and as stage play; [9]–40 text (as stage play); [41] fly-title "A Night Out"; [42] first presentation details, radio and television; [43]–87 text (of television play); [88] blank; [89] fly-title "The Dwarfs"; [90] first presentation details, radio; [91]–116 text (as radio play); [117] fly-title "Revue Sketches" [5 titles]; [118] first performance details (*Last to Go* and *Request Stop* in *Pieces of Eight*, Apollo Theatre, 1959; *The Black and White* and *Trouble in the Works* in *One to Another*, Lyric Opera House and Apollo Theatre, 1959); [119]–121 text, "TROUBLE IN THE WORKS"; [122]–125 text, "THE BLACK AND WHITE"; 125–127 text, "REQUEST STOP"; 127–130 text, "LAST TO GO"; [131]–134 text, "APPLICANT"; [135–136] blank.

Note one: The texts of *A Slight Ache* and *A Night Out* remain unchanged in the second edition, but that of *A Slight Ache* appears with some corrections in the 1968 edition. *The Dwarfs* appears in three different versions. The first Methuen edition includes the radio play version, as broadcast on the BBC Third Programme, on 2 December 1960. The second Methuen edition (1966) includes the first stage version, as first presented on 18 September 1963. The second Methuen edition, revised (1968), includes the second stage version. These alterations were then followed in the successive Grove Press printings.

Note two: The 1963 reprint in hardback is as for 1961, but with the wording on the verso of the title leaf partly changed: "*First published 1961* | © *1961 by Harold Pinter* | *Reprinted 1963* | *Printed in Great Britain by* | *John Dickens &*

Co Ltd, | *Northampton* | *Cat. No.* 2/6452/31". The dust jacket is as for 1961, except, on the outside back, the biographical note on Pinter is extended to 13 lines, bringing it up to date; and on the front flap: at foot, left: "2/6452/31"; and at foot, right: "Price | 12s 6d net | in UK only".

b. Edition with revisions, hardback and paperback (1966):

Title page as for 1961, except publisher's address as "11 NEW FETTER LANE EC4".

136 pp. 17.7 × 11.1 cm. Hardback as for first printing. Dust jacket not seen. Paperback, as for first printing dust jacket, except on outside back: "Cat. No. 02/6452/24" and price 7s 6d.

Published 1966. On verso of title leaf: "TO VIVIEN | [*copyright and performing rights statements*] | *First published 1961* | *Copyright © 1961 by Harold Pinter* | *Paperback first published 1966* | *Printed in Great Britain by* | *John Dickens & Co Ltd,* | *Northampton*".

Contents: [1] half-title: "A Slight Ache | AND OTHER PLAYS | A collection of one-act plays, originally written for | radio and television, with, in addition, five revue sketches. | A SLIGHT ACHE was first presented on the stage at | the Arts Theatre, London, on January 18, 1961, | and subsequently at the Criterion Theatre. | *The photograph on the front cover is of Tom Bell and* | *Vivien Merchant in the A.B.C. Television Armchair* | *Theatre production of A NIGHT OUT.*"; [2] list of "*Methuen's Modern Plays*"; [3] title page; [4] as above; [5]–[88] as for 1961; [89] fly-title "The Dwarfs"; [90] first presentation details, radio and stage; [91]–118 text (stage version); [119] fly-title: "Revue Sketches [five titles]"; [120] first performance information for first four sketches; [121]–123 text, "TROUBLE IN THE WORKS"; [124]–127 text, "THE BLACK AND WHITE"; 127–129 text, "REQUEST STOP"; 129–132 text, "LAST TO GO"; [133]–136 text, "APPLICANT".

c. Hardback and paperback, reprint with corrections (1968):

A SLIGHT ACHE | AND OTHER PLAYS | BY | Harold Pinter | LONDON | METHUEN & CO LTD | 11 NEW FETTER LANE EC4

136 pp. 18.4 × 12.2 cm. Hardback: black cloth, lettering in gold down spine: "Harold Pinter [*star*] A SLIGHT ACHE and other plays [*star*] Methuen". Endpapers. Dust jacket: blue frame on outside front and back, and blue around spine; on outside front, within white panel, lettering in blue: "Harold Pinter | [*rule, in black, 10.0 cm.*] | A Slight Ache | and other plays | [*photo*]"; on outside back, lettering in blue: "[*photo of Pinter*] | photo: Anthony Digusu [*sic*] | [*account of Pinter, 10 lines*]"; on spine, Methuen device in white, down spine in

black: "Pinter • A Slight Ache and other plays Methuen". On front flap, lettering in black, account of plays and sketches, and of photos; on back flap, lettering in black and blue, account of other published volumes, headed: "[*in black*] Other Plays by | HAROLD PINTER". Paperback not seen.

Published 1968. Price (hardback) 18s – 90p. On verso of title leaf: "TO VIVIEN | [performing rights statement] | *First published 1961* | *Copyright* © *1961, 1966 and 1968 by Harold Pinter* | *Paperback edition first published 1966* | *Reprinted 1968 with corrections* | *Printed in Great Britain by* | *John Dickens & Co Ltd,* | *Northampton*", conditions of sale statement.

Contents: As for 1966, except *The Dwarfs* ends on p.117, with p.[118] blank (television version).

Notes: As Letitia Dace notes, the type-pages are identical with the 1966 issue through to p.97, with on p. 98 the omission of Len's "It's a mortuary without a corpse." following Mark's "What's the matter with Earl's Court?" Extensive rewriting begins on p.102. In the 1970 printing, a transposition of names in the cast list of *The Dwarfs* was corrected. In April 1973, the volume was assigned SBN 413 30950 9 (cloth), 413 30830 8 (paperback), and a fourth printing of 10,000 copies appeared in that year. The *Collected Edition* (see I1.a(ii), b(i), I2(a-b)) contains the stage version.

d. Faber edition (1991):

[*Within single-rule frame:*] HAROLD PINTER | A Slight Ache | *and Other Plays* | ff | *faber and faber* | LONDON • BOSTON

136 pp., 4 blank leaves. 19.7 × 12.4 cm. Paperback, white, with standard Faber design: outside front: "ff | [*rule*] | HAROLD | PINTER | [*rule*] | A Slight Ache | [*illustration*]"; outside back: publisher, author, title, account of plays, "Cover illustration by Andrzej Klimowski | UK £5.99 net | Canada $14.99 | ISBN 0-571-16093-X | [*bar-code*] | 9 780571 160938"; down spine: "HAROLD PINTER A Slight Ache".

Published 1991 (L accession 18 APR 91). Price £5.99. Verso of title leaf: publication details, "This edition first published in 1991 | [. . . .] | Printed in England by Clays Ltd, St Ives plc | [*copyright, performing rights, conditions of sale statements*] | ISBN 0-571-16093-X".

Notes: Faber and Faber report (1.8.2001) printings on 3 June 1991, 24 March 1998, totalling 2,955 copies printed.

A13   **THREE PLAYS**   1962

a. First printing (1962):

THREE PLAYS | BY | Harold Pinter | A SLIGHT ACHE | THE COLLECTION
| THE DWARFS | GROVE PRESS, INC. | NEW YORK

1 blank leaf, 3 leaves, 108 pp., 2 leaves (also, between p.[42] and p.[43], 2 unpaginated leaves, with production photos). 20.4 × 13.6 cm. Paperback, glossy white; on front cover: "[*in black:*] 3 | [*in turquoise:*] Three Plays | [*in black, rule, 5.6 cm.*] | [*in grey-green:*] A Slight Ache | [*in black, rule, 5.6 cm.*] | [*in dark prussian blue:*] The Collection | [*in black, rule, 5.6 cm.*] | [*in grey-green:*] The Dwarfs | [*in black, rule, 5.6 cm.*] | [*in black, 2 lines:*] Harold | Pinter | [*in black, rule, 5.6 cm.*] | [*in dark prussian blue:*] author of | [*in grey-green:*] The Caretaker | [*vertical, towards right edge, lettered upward, in dark prussian blue:*] EVERGREEN ORIGINAL E-350 $1.95 [*publisher's device*]"; on back cover: "[*in dark prussian blue:*] EVERGREEN ORIGINAL [*in black, publisher's device*] [*in black:*] (E-350)—$1.95", dark prussian blue panel, lettering within panel, in white: title, account of Pinter and the three plays, "Cover design by Roy Kuhlman | GROVE PRESS, INC., 64 University Place, New York 3, N.Y."; down spine: "[*in black:*] THREE PLAYS [*in grey-green:*] BY [*in dark prussian blue:*] HAROLD PINTER [*across spine, at foot:*] [*in black, publisher's device*] | [*in black:*] E-350 | [*in grey-green, 2 lines:*] GROVE | PRESS".

Published 20 December 1962 (DLC copyright registration: 20 December 1962 [DP5118]). Price $1.95. On verso of title leaf: copyright, performing rights statements, "Photographs by David Sim, London | Library of Congress Catalog Card Number: 62-19915 | First Printing | Manufactured in the United States of America".

Contents: [i–ii] blank; [iii] half-title; [iv] blank; [v] title page; [vi] as above; [vii] "TO VIVIEN"; [viii] blank; [1] fly-title "Three Plays"; [2] blank; [3] fly-title "A Slight Ache"; [4] blank; [5] first presentation details, radio and stage; [6–7] production photos, 2 per page; [8] blank; [9]–40 text (stage version); [41] fly-title "The Collection"; [42] blank; [42a] first presentation details, television and stage, details of stage-set; [42b–42c] production photos, 1 per page; [42d] blank; [43]–80 text (stage version); [81] fly-title "The Dwarfs"; [82] blank; [83] first radio presentation details; [84] blank; [85]–108 text (radio version); [109] blank; [110–114] Evergreen title list.

Notes: Dace notes that "at least *The Collection* was supposed to be offset from the Methuen edition."

b. Later printings:

Seen: Eleventh printing
Mainly as for first printing, but on back cover, at foot, in black "394-17240-X";

and the text of *The Dwarfs* is for the first stage version, as introduced for Methuen's 1966 paperback.

Contents: As for first printing, to p.[82]; [83] first presentation details for *The Dwarfs* include those for the British stage production premièred 18 September 1963; [84] blank; [85]–109 text (stage version); [110–114] blank.

Notes: Volker Strunk, in *Harold Pinter: Towards a Poetics of His Plays* (New York: Peter Lang, 1989), has shown that Grove Press retained the radio play version of *The Dwarfs* for the first to seventh printings, then used the first stage version for the eighth to thirteenth printings, and the second stage version from the fourteenth printing onward. However, no indication is given of the substitution of a different version (Strunk 125). The second stage version, from the fourteenth printing, is taken from Methuen's 1968 edition of *A Slight Ache and Other Plays* (see above).

A14   THE COLLECTION and THE LOVER   1963
                  [*also*, THE EXAMINATION]

a. First edition (1963):

THE COLLECTION | *and* | THE LOVER | BY | Harold Pinter | LONDON | METHUEN & CO LTD | 36 ESSEX STREET WC2

94 pp., 1 blank leaf. 18.4 × 12.4 cm. Hardback, black cloth; down spine in silver: "Harold Pinter [*star*] THE COLLECTION AND THE LOVER [*star*] Methuen". Endpapers. Dust jacket blue on outside front and spine, white on back and flaps; on outside front: "[*in black:*] HAROLD PINTER | [2 *lines in white:*] The Collection | and The Lover | [*photo, from* The Collection]"; on outside back, photo of Pinter, below, author's name in blue capitals, 10-line biographical note, in black, mainly in italics; down spine: "[*in black:*] PINTER [*in white:*] THE COLLECTION AND THE LOVER [*in black:*] METHUEN"; on front flap: title, account of contents, "*The photograph on the front of the jacket shows* | *John Ronane as Bill, and Kenneth Haigh as* | *James in* The Collection. *That on the back* | *shows Harold Pinter during a rehearsal of the* | *play. Both are reproduced by courtesy of David* | *Sim.* | [*at foot, left:*] 2/2675/31 [*at right:*] PRICE | 12s 6d net | IN U.K. ONLY"; on back flap, notes on other Pinter titles.

Published 25 April 1963 (L accession 9 APR 63; DLC copyright registration, 25 April 1963 [DF1970]). Price 12s. 6d. On verso of title leaf: copyright and performing rights statements, "*First published 1963* | © *1963 by H. Pinter Ltd* | *Printed in Great Britain by* | *W. & J. Mackay & Co Ltd* | *Chatham* | *Cat. No.* 2/2675/31".

Contents: [1] half-title "The Collection *and* The Lover"; [2] Methuen titles "*by the same author*", lists three; [3] title page; [4] as above; [5] "Contents", at foot of page: "My thanks are due to the editor of PROSPECT, in | which 'The Examination' first appeared. H.P."; [6] "TO VIVIEN | AND | PETER WILLES"; [7] fly-title "The Collection"; [8] details of first television and stage presentations, description of stage set; [9]–45 text (stage version); [46] blank; [47] fly-title "The Lover"; [48] details of first television presentation, note of season and locale of play; [49]–86 text (television version); [87] fly-title "The Examination"; [88] blank; [89]–94 text.

Notes: "The Examination", a short story, was first published in *Prospect* (Summer 1959): 21–25; see D1a.

b. Second edition (1964):

THE COLLECTION | *and* | THE LOVER | BY | HAROLD PINTER | LONDON | METHUEN & CO LTD | 11 NEW FETTER LANE EC4

92 pp., 2 blank leaves. Signed: [A]⁸ B-F⁸. 18.4 × 12.1–12.3 cm. Binding as for first edition.

Published 23 July 1964. 3,000 copies. Price 12s. 6d. On verso of title leaf: "*First published 1963 | Second edition 1964 | © 1963 and 1964 by H. Pinter Ltd | Printed in Great Britain by | W. & J. Mackay & Co Ltd | Chatham | Cat. No. 02/2675/24*".

Contents: To p.[47], as for first edition; [48] first presentation details for *The Lover* include those for the stage version presented at the Arts Theatre, 18 September 1963; [49]–84 text (stage version); [85] fly-title "The Examination"; [86] blank; [87]–92 text; [93–96] blank.

c. Paperback edition (1966):

Title page as for 1964 edition.

92 pp., 2 blank leaves. 18.3 × 11.9 cm. Paperback, front cover and spine blue, back cover white; on front cover: "[*in black:*] HAROLD PINTER | [2 *lines in white:*] The Collection | and The Lover | [*production photo for* The Collection]"; *on back cover:* "[*photo of Pinter*] | [*in blue:*] HAROLD PINTER [*in black:*] [*note on Pinter*] | PRICE 5s IN UK ONLY"; down spine: "[*in black:*] PINTER [*in white:*] THE COLLECTION AND THE LOVER [*in black:*] METHUEN".

Published 17 March 1966. 7,000 copies. Price 5s. On verso of title leaf: as for 1964, except includes: Cat. No. 02/2675/24. 416 63210 6. [1966 first printing not seen; details from Dace.]

Contents: As for 1964, except: [1] title, brief account of plays, and author, "*The photograph on the front cover shows John | Ronane as Bill and*

Kenneth Haigh as James in | *The Collection. It is reproduced by courtesy of* | *David Sim. The photograph of Harold Pinter* | *on the back cover is reproduced by courtesy of* | *Antony di Gesù.*"; [2] title list includes 7 titles; [4] changed colophon; [92–94] blank.

Notes: Reprinted 1968, 1970, 1971, 1973, 1976. In the reprint of 1971, pp. [92–94] bear Methuen's Modern Plays titles list. Binding differs: on front cover, within blue border, in white panel: "[*in blue:*] Harold Pinter | [*in black, rule*] | [*2 lines in blue:*] The Collection & | The Lover | [*photo*]"; on back cover, within blue border, photo, captioned in blue "Photograph of Harold Pinter by Antony di Gesù", in blue, 8-line biographical note, rule in black, "[*in blue:*] A METHUEN MODERN PLAY 40p net in U.K. only"; on spine, Methuen device in white, down spine in black: "Pinter • The Collection & The Lover Methuen". On verso of title leaf: copyright, performing rights and conditions of sale statements, "*First published 1961* | *Second edition 1964* | *Reprinted 1971* | *SBN 416 26750 5* | *2 . 2* | *Paperback edition first published 1966* | *Reprinted 1968, 1970 and 1971* | *SBN 416 63210 6* | *1 . 4* | © *1963 by H. Pinter Ltd* | *Printed Offset Litho and bound in Great Britain by* | *Cox & Wyman Ltd, Fakenham*". The 1976 reprint, for Eyre Methuen Ltd., has the SBN 413 30700 X, and price 95 p.

d. Faber edition (1991):

[*All within single-rule frame:*] HAROLD | PINTER | *The Collection* | and | *The Lover* | ff | faber and faber | LONDON • BOSTON

92 pp., 1 blank leaf. 18.9 × 10.4 cm. Binding standard Faber drama paperback design; on front cover: "ff | HAROLD | PINTER | *The Collection* | and *The Lover* | [*tinted illustration*];" on back cover: "ff | faber and faber | [*rule*] | HAROLD PINTER | *The Collection* and *The Lover* | [*five paragraphs about the two plays*] | Cover design by Andrzej Klimowski | UK £4.99 net | Canada $12.95 | ISBN 0-571-16083-2 | [*bar-code*] | 9 780571 160839"; *on spine:* "ff | [*rule*] | [down spine:] HAROLD PINTER *The Collection* and *The Lover*".

Publication 8 April 1991. Faber and Faber (1 August 2001) report reprinting of the paperback on 12 February 1993, 12 April 1994, 13 November 1995, and 1 January 1998, totalling 13,154 copies printed. On verso of title leaf: prior publication details, "This paperback edition first published in 1991 | [. . .] | Printed in England by Clays Ltd, St Ives plc | [*copyright, performing rights, conditions of sale and CIP record statements*] | ISBN 0-571-16083-2".

Contents: [i] half-title and note; [ii] Faber's Pinter titles; [1] title page; [2] as above; [3] contents, and note; [4] "TO | PETER WILLES"; [5] fly-title "The Collection"; [6] presentation details; [7] setting; [8] blank; [9]–92 as for 1966; [93–94] blank.

A15   DIALOGUE FOR THREE   1963

"Dialogue for Three." *Stand* (Newcastle upon Tyne), Vol. 6, No. 3 (1963–64): [4]–5.

This sketch can equally be regarded as a prose piece in dramatic form. The third piece of dialogue, a rambling reminiscence about a man called House Peters, had been employed as one of Roote's speeches in *The Hothouse* (written in 1958, though not performed till 1980).

A16   THE COLLECTION   [1963]

a. French's acting edition [1963]:

THE COLLECTION | A Play in One Act | by | HAROLD PINTER | SAMUEL [*publisher's device*] FRENCH | LONDON

2 leaves, 41 pp., 1 blank leaf. 18.5 × 12.3 cm. Paperback, blue; on front cover, to left, vertical red band, within it, in blue, reversed out of red: above, publisher's device, below, "French's | Acting | Edition"; to right, in red, "THE | COLLEC-TION | A Play | by | HAROLD PINTER | 3s. net"; back cover blank; down spine: "THE COLLECTION".

Published 17 December 1963 (L accession 1 JAN 64). Price 3s. Number of copies in first print-run 2000; thereafter reprinted in response to demand. On verso of title leaf: "[*publisher's addresses*] | © 1963 BY H. PINTER LTD | [. . . .] | MADE AND PRINTED IN GREAT BRITAIN BY | LATIMER, TREND AND CO., LTD, PLYMOUTH | MADE IN ENGLAND".

Contents: [i] title page; [ii] as above; [iii] details of first production, setting, time; [iv] French's performing rights information; [1]–34 text; [35]–36 furniture and property list; [37]–39 lighting plot; [40]–41 effects plot; [42] blank.

Notes: The L copy is rebound, with only the front cover preserved (the copy described is owned by William Baker). Later reprints have the ISBN number 0 573 02036 1, and are bound in white card, printed in bright blue.

b. German educational edition (1979):

DIESTERWEGS NEUSPRACHLICHE BIBLIOTHEK | *The Collection* | by | HAROLD PINTER | Edited and annotated | by | FRANK D. GILLAND | ADELINE GORBAHN | VERLAG MORITZ DIESTERWEG | [*at left:*] 4076 [*centred:*] Frankfurt am Main • Berlin • München

50 pp. 17.1 × 12.4 cm.

Published 1979. On verso of title leaf: series note, contents, "ISBN 3-425-04076-6", publication details, photos from Granada Television production. Text occupies pp.10–39.

c. American anthology (extracts) (1963):

THE BEST PLAYS | OF 1962–1963 | EDITED BY HENRY HEWES | [*drawing, captioned 'from "Oliver!"'*] | DODD, MEAD & COMPANY | NEW YORK • TORONTO

Contents [relevant]: 140–150 extracts of text, introduced and interspersed with
   descriptive and narrative passages; 320–321 production details for the
   New York production, Cherry Lane Theatre, opened 26 November
   1962, in a double bill with *The Dumb Waiter.* On verso facing title
   page: "THE | BURNS MANTLE | YEARBOOK", etc.

A17   THE LOVER   1964

a. French's acting edition [1964]:

THE LOVER | A Short Play | by | HAROLD PINTER | SAMUEL [*publisher's device*] FRENCH | LONDON | NEW YORK TORONTO SYDNEY HOLLY-WOOD

2 leaves, 34 pp., 1 leaf. 18.0 × 12.3 cm. Paperback, blue; front cover mainly blue, with vertical band of red near spine, and to right of it, thin vertical red line: " [*within red band, reversed out of red:*] [*towards head, publisher's device*] | [*towards foot:*] French's | Acting | Edition | [*within blue area, 3 lines in red*] THE LOVER | A Short Play | HAROLD PINTER "; back cover blank; down spine: "THE LOVER 3s. net".

Published May 1964. Price 3s. Number of copies in first print-run 2000; thereafter reprinted in response to demand. On verso of title leaf: "© 1963, 1964 by H. PINTER | LTD", copyright, performing rights and conditions of sale statements.

Contents: [i] title page; [ii] as above; [iii] first stage performance details; [iv]
   blank; [1]–30 text; [31]–32 furniture and properties plot; [33]–34
   lighting plot; [35] effects plot; on [36] "MADE AND PRINTED
   IN GREAT BRITAIN BY | LATIMER, TREND AND CO. LTD,
   PLYMOUTH | MADE IN ENGLAND".

Notes: On p.[1]: at head of text, greatly extended description of set; through-out, more extensive, more "theatrical" stage directions than in Methuen, using L, C, R, etc. A reprint pre-1966 has on the verso of the title leaf, below state-ments, "GB 573 02148 1"; on p.[36] a note about costume and wig hire, and the publisher's address given as "WHITSTABLE". The reprint of 1966 (L accession stamp 2 JUN 66) has on the verso of the title leaf: publisher's addresses, copyright statement, printer's colophon, as above, "ISBN 0 573 02148 1". Later publishings have a white cover. For the pre-1966 reprint, the front cover has to the left a vertical blue band, within which, mainly in white, reversed out of blue: French's device, at the head, and "French's | Acting | Edition", at the foot; to right, beyond a vertical rule in blue, lettering in black: "THE LOVER | *A Short Play* | HAROLD PINTER"; on back cover: "HAROLD PINTER | THE LOVER | GB 573 02148 [*within 2 blue circles, prices in black: obscured in copies seen*]"; down spine: "PINTER THE LOVER FRENCH".

b. American acting edition [1965]:

[*To left, 7 vertical thick rules, 9.3 cm.*] THE | LOVER | [*star*] | [*7 horizontal thick rules, 9.3 cm.*] [*within space within second rule:*] A PLAY IN ONE ACT | [*star*] | DRAMATISTS | PLAY SERVICE | INC. [*to right, 7 vertical thick rules, 3.5 cm.*]

1 leaf, 28 pp., 2 leaves. 18.9 × 12.9 cm. Paperback, pale yellow; front covered and ruled as for title page, except 8 rules in each position (12.8, 13.2, and 4.7 cm., respectively); down spine: "THE LOVER—PINTER".

Published 15 February 1965 (DLC copyright registration 15 February 1965 [DP5693]; re-registration 4 May 1993 [RE-617-050]; listed in *Publishers Weekly*, 29 March 1965, p.72). 1000 copies. Price $0.75. On verso of title leaf: "© Copyright, 1965, by HAROLD PINTER", further copyright and performing rights statements, note about sound effects available.

Contents: [i] blank; [ii] production photo, captioned "PHOTO BY ALIX JEFFRY"; [1] title page; [2] as above; [3] first American performance details, Cherry Lane Theatre, New York, 4 January 1964; [4] blank; 5–26 text; 27 "PROPERTY PLOT"; 28 "COSTUME PLOT"; [29–32] DPS advertisements, for new plays.

Notes: DLC Copyright Catalog No. 65-1883. In the copy seen (DePaul University Libraries, Lincoln Park Campus Library, Chicago) the insides of the front and back covers and the outside of the back cover are covered with reinforcing plain card, but may bear DPS advertisements listing new plays.

A18   THE BLACK AND WHITE [and] LAST TO GO   1965

a. British anthology (1965):

[*All within ornamental frame:*] THEATRE TODAY | *Edited by* | DAVID THOMPSON | [*publisher's device*] | LONGMANS

viii, 206 pp. "The Black and White" occupies pp. 200–202; "Last to Go," pp. 203–[206], with a fly-title to both on p.[197], an editor's note on pp.198–199. Volume within Longman's Heritage of Literature Series, Section B, No. 77.

b. German anthology (1980):

You and Others | Problems and possibilities in communication | edited by | Peter Jürgen Klein and Hans Jürgen Cremer | Leherausgabe | LENSING

Coursebook: Kursmaterialien Englisch Sekundarstufe II. Published 1980, Verlag Lambert Lensing GmbH, Dortmund. "The Black and White" occupies pp. 50–52, "Last to Go" pp. 57–59.

c. South African anthology ("Last to Go" only) (1984):

Modern Stage Directions | *a collection of short dramatic scripts* | *edited by* | *Stephen Gray and David Scalkwyk* | [publisher's device] | Maskew Miller Longman

Published 1984, Cape Town. ISBN 0 636 00317 5. *Last to Go* occupies pp. 137–141.

A19   THE CARETAKER AND THE BIRTHDAY PARTY   [1965?]

a. American edition [ca. 1965]:

TWO PLAYS BY | [*open letters:*] HAROLD PINTER | *The Caretaker* | [*rule, 4.7 cm.*] and [*rule, 6 cm.*] | *The Birthday* | *Party* | NELSON DOUBLEDAY, INC. GARDEN CITY, NEW YORK

2 leaves, 156 pp. 20.9 × 12.2 pp. Hardback, red cloth; down spine: "[*2 words in open letters, on two lines:*] HAROLD | PINTER [*on 1 line:*] The Caretaker The Birthday Party [*on 2 lines:*] NELSON | DOUBLEDAY". Dust jacket not seen.

Published *ca.*1965. On verso of title leaf: "*The Caretaker* Copyright © 1960 by Theatre Promotions Limited | *The Birthday Party* Copyright © 1959, 1960, 1965 by Harold Pinter | All Rights Reserved. | [*further copyright and performing rights statements*] | Published by Arrangement with Grove Press, Inc. | Manufactured in the United States of America".

Contents: [i] half-title; [ii] blank; [iii] title page; [iv] as above; [1] fly-title "*The Caretaker*"; [2] blank; [3] first British performance details, acts, "PHOTOGRAPHIC INSERT | Photos from the American production by | Sam Siegel" [not present in copy seen]; [4] description of set; [5]–77 text; [78] text; [79] fly-title "*The Birthday Party*"; [80] blank; [81] performance details, 1958, 1964; [82]–156 text.

b. Italian educational edition (1983):

HAROLD PINTER | the birthday | party | the caretaker | edited with an introduction and notes | by Donatella Abbate Badin | EDIZIONI [*2-line publisher's device*] | SCHOLASTICHE | BRUNO MONDADORI

206 pp. 21 × 13.6 cm. Paperback, light grey and white, with lettering, and sketch on front cover, in black. Introduction and bibliography occupy pp. 7–47, texts with annnotations thereafter.

A20   THE HOMECOMING   1965

a. First edition (1965):

THE HOMECOMING | Harold Pinter | LONDON | METHUEN & CO LTD | 11 NEW FETTER LANE EC4

83 pp. Signed [A]^8 B-D^8 E^{10} (i.e., E^8, with E4 + 1.2, with recto of first leaf of inserted bifolium signed as E*). 18.3 × 12.2 cm. Hardback, black cloth; down spine, in silver: "Harold Pinter [*star*] THE HOMECOMING [*star*] Methuen". Endpapers. Dust jacket in blue on outside front and spine, white on outside back and flaps; on outside front: "[*in black:*] HAROLD PINTER | [*in white:*] The Homecoming | [*production photo*]"; on outside back, as for *The Collection and The Lover*; down spine: "[*in black:*] PINTER THE HOMECOMING METHUEN"; on front flap, title, account of play and of Pinter, "*The photograph reproduced on the front of the | jacket shows Vivien Merchant as Ruth, Ian | Holm as Lenny and Michael Bryant as Teddy. | It is reproduced by courtesy of David Sim, | as is the photograph of Harold Pinter on the | back. |* [*at foot, right:*] PRICE | 12s 6d net | IN U.K. ONLY"; on back flap, list of other Pinter titles.

Published 10 June 1965 (L accession 14 JUN 65; DLC copyright registration 10 June 1965 [DF1969]). 4,000 copies in first printing. Price 12s. 6d. On verso of title leaf: performing rights and copyright statements, "*First published in 1965 | © 1965 by H. Pinter Ltd | Printed in Great Britain by | W. & J. Mackay & Co Ltd | Chatham*".

Contents: [1] half-title "The Homecoming"; [2] list of Methuen titles "*by the same author*"; [3] title page; [4] as above; [5] fly-title; [6] details of first production, and set-description; [7]–83 text; [84] blank.

b. Second edition, issued in hardback and in paperback (1966):

Title page as for first edition.

82 pp., 1 leaf (blank in hardback). Signed as for first edition. Hardback bound as for first edition, except lettering, etc., down spine in gold. Paperback: outside front as for dust jacket; outside back: as for dust jacket, except at foot: "PRICE 6s. NET IN UK ONLY"; spine as for dust jacket.

Published 17 March 1966 (hardback; L accession 15 APR 70), 19 May 1966 (paperback). First printing, 2,000 copies cloth, 5,000 paperback. Price 12s. 6d. (cloth), 6s. (paperback). On verso of title leaf: copyright and performing rights statements, *"First published in 1965 | Second edition 1966 | Paperback edition 1966 | © 1965 and 1966 by H. Pinter Ltd | Printed in Great Britain by W. & J. Mackay & Co Ltd | Chatham"*.

Contents: [1] a brief account of the play, a quotation from Penelope Gilliatt's critique in *The Observer:* "An exultant night . . . it offered the stirring spectacle | of a man in total command of his talent.", and, at foot, *"The photograph reproduced on the front shows Vivien | Merchant as Ruth, Paul Rogers as Max, John Normington | as Sam and Michael Bryant as Teddy. It is reproduced by | courtesy of David Sim, as is the photograph of Harold | Pinter on the back."*; [2] Methuen titles *"by the same author"*; [3] title page; [4] as above; [5] fly-title; [6] details of first production (listing Bryant as Teddy), time, set; [7]–82 text; [83–84] blank (in hardback; see *Notes* for paperback).

Notes: The cuts to the text mean that for Act I up to p.11, the text on each page is the same as for the corresponding page in the first edition, but thereafter it differs, with the same type-lines reimposed, with cutting and pasting of plates. The act ends on p.44 with only 11 lines of text (20 lines including blank lines), whereas in the first edition Act I had ended on the same page, but with 26 lines of text (about 43, counting blank lines). For Act II, the text on each page is the same, for pages 45 to 63, but differs thereafter, and the act ends on p.82, with in the hardback 10 lines of text, 19 counting blank lines. In the hardback the last leaf is blank; but in the paperback the final unpaginated leaf has Methuen's advertisements on recto and verso.

c¹. Paperback, second edition further revised (1967):

Paperback binding: as for dust jacket of hardback: on front cover: within blue border, panel in white, with lettering in blue: "Harold Pinter | [*rule, 9.3 cm., in black*] | The Homecoming"; below panel, production photograph (see *Notes*); on back, within blue border, photo of Pinter; spine blue, at head, small Methuen device in white, lettering down spine in black: "Pinter • The Homecoming Methuen".

Printed August 1967. First printing, 6,000 copies. Price 6s. On verso of title leaf: copyright statements, *"Printed in Great Britain by | Cox & Wyman Ltd, Fakenham, Norfolk"*.

Notes: The half-title has a brief description of the plot-situation, and the quotation from Gilliatt; and at foot: *"The photograph on the front cover shows Ian Holm as | Lenny and Paul Rogers as Max in the New York | production of* THE HOMECOMING. *It is reproduced by | courtesy of Friedman-Abeles, Inc. The photograph of | Harold Pinter on the back cover is reproduced by | courtesy of David Sim."*

On p. [6], the details of the first production include the added sentence: "The play was presented by the Royal Shakespeare Company | and Alexander H. Cohen at the Music Box Theatre, New | York, on 5 January, 1967 with one change in the cast: the | part of Teddy was played by Michael Craig."

Further cuts to the text result in Act II ending on p.82 with only 4 lines of text, 7 lines including blank lines. Dace notes from Methuen/Eyre Methuen records: Methuen: reprint in 1968 has further alteration (faulty) on p.74; reprint of 1970 has further alterations on pp. 58, 67, 74, 81; reprint in 1971 (fourth impression of cloth, sixth of paperback); reprint in 1973. Eyre Methuen: reprint in 1975 (cloth: ISBN 413 30450 7; paperback 413 30460 4; released 4 June; 15,000 copies), changes on pp. 29, 39, 47, 61, 71; reprinted 7 October 1976 (11,151 copies, at 95 p.). Reprinted 1977, 1979, 1980; thereafter Methuen London Ltd, reprinted 1982, 1983, 1986, etc.. The prices rose: 1971, cloth 63p., paperback 37½p.; 1973, cloth 80p., paperback 50p.; 1975, cloth £1.00, paperback 65p.

c². Second edition, later re-printing (1986):

HAROLD PINTER | The Homecoming | METHUEN • LONDON

2 leaves, 82 pp. Unsigned. 18.5 × 11.8 cm. Paperback; front cover occupied by a blue-tinged photo, with, towards the foot, within a plain blue frame (outer dimensions 5.4 × 6.0 cm.), a white panel, with lettering: "[2 *lines in black:*] Harold | Pinter | [2 *lines in blue:*] The | Homecoming", and below, imposed on a dark portion of the photo, within a thin, plain white frame, in white: "methuen"; on back cover, at top, within a plain blue frame (outer dimensions 5.3 × 6.0 cm.), a photo of Pinter, half-turned, and below it: "[*in black:*] Harold Pinter | [*in blue:*] The Homecoming | [*in blue, 6-line outline of the situation of the play; 7 lines providing citations of sentences from reviews*] | [*remaining text, etc., in black; at left:*] ISBN 0-413-41330-6 | [*bar-code*] | 9 780413 413307 | [*at right:*] PRICE NET | £3.95 | IN UK ONLY | A METHUEN PAPERBACK | MODERN PLAYS'. Spine blue, with, at head, in white, Methuen device; lettering down spine, in black: "Pinter • The Homecoming", at foot, within a small panel in black, with a thin white frame, in white (i.e., reversed out of black): "methuen".

Published 1986. Price £3.95. On verso of first leaf, facing title page: "A METHUEN PAPERBACK | *First published in 1965* | *Second edition 1966* | *Reprinted 1970* | *Paperback edition 1966* | *Reprinted six times* | *Reprinted 1975, 1977, 1979 and 1980* | *by Eyre Methuen* | *Reprinted 1982, 1983 by Methuen London, Ltd,* | *11 New Fetter Lane, London EC4P 4EE* | *Re-issued in this edition in 1986* | © *1965, 1966 and 1967 by H. Pinter Ltd* | *ISBN 0 413 41330 6*", performing rights statement, headed "CAUTION", with address of ACTAC, previously "16 Cadogan Lane, London, SW1", given as "c/o Judy Daish Associates, 83 Eastbourne | Mews, London W2 6LQ." The statement present in the first issue, "THIS BOOK IS AVAILABLE IN BOTH HARDBOUND | AND

PAPERBACK EDITIONS", is not present; the conditions of sale statement remains the same, in a smaller font and with differing lineation. At foot: *"Printed and bound in Great Britain by | Richard Clay (The Chaucer Press), Ltd, | Bungay, Suffolk"*.

Contents: [1] paragraphs about the play and about Pinter, at foot: *"The front cover photograph shows Paul Rogers* (Max), *Cyril Cusack* | (Lenny), *Terence Rigby* (seated, Joey) *and Vivien Merchant* (Ruth) | *in the film version of 'The Homecoming' (courtesy of American Express | films and National Film Archive). The back cover photograph of | Harold Pinter was taken by Ivan Kyncl.*"; [2] as above; [3] title page; [4] details of first production, and set; [7]–82 text.

Notes: This reprint lacks one leaf in the preliminaries (the previously-second page, bearing the list of other published volumes by Pinter, and the previously-fifth page, bearing the fly-title, are deleted, and the remaining pages reordered). It also lacks the unpaginated publisher's list leaf at the end and is unsigned. Otherwise, it presents the same typesettings of the pages with photographically slightly reduced type-page measures: on p.8 (the first paginated page), the type-page height (including the running title) is reduced from 15.2 cm. (for the 1986 printing) to 15.1 cm., and the width from 8.5 cm. to 8.3 cm.

d. Faber edition (1991):

[*All within single-rule frame:*] HAROLD | PINTER | The Homecoming | ff | *faber and faber* | LONDON • BOSTON

3 leaves, 82 pp., 4 blank leaves. 19.7 × 12.2 cm. Paperback, white, standard Faber design; on front cover: "ff | [*rule*] | HAROLD | PINTER | [*rule*] | [*illustration, male figure, coated, headless, standing outside a door*]"; on back cover: "ff | *faber and faber* | HAROLD PINTER | The Homecoming | [*quotation from critique, and outline of situation of play*] | Cover illustration by Andrzej Klimowski | UK £4.99 net | Canada $12.95 | ISBN 0-571-16080-8 | [*bar-code*] | 9 780571 16080 8".

Published 21 January 1991 (L accession 1 FEB 91). Price £4.99. On verso of title leaf: publication information, "Printed in England by Clays Ltd, St Ives plc", copyright, performing rights and conditions of sale statements, "ISBN 0-571-16080-8".

Notes: Faber and Faber report (1.8.2001) reprintings on 1 October 1993, 12 December 1994, 1 July 1996, 7 February 1997, 1 February 1998, 18 June 1999, totalling 61,714 copies printed.

e. British limited edition, illustrated and designed by Harold Cohen (1968):

[*On clear plastic leaf:*] THE HOMECOMING | HAROLD PINTER | IMAGES | HAROLD COHEN | KARNAC • CURWEN LONDON 1968

Unpaginated, [72] pp. [plus bound-in clear plastic leaves]. Book stitched in units of 6 normal leaves. 43.8 × 34.2 cm. Hard-bound in green terylene cloth; on front board, in black, at upper right, partial image of two hands; back board blank; down spine, in black: "THE HOMECOMING HAROLD PINTER HAROLD COHEN". Endpapers black. Slip-case bound in dark grey-green cloth.

Published October 1968 (L accession 31 OCT 68). 225 copies: 175 for sale at £84.25 with a duplicate set of lithographs, at £157.50; 25 'hors de commerce'.

Contents: [1–4] blank; clear plastic leaf, with half-title on recto: "THE HOME-COMING"; [5–7] blank; [8] page-size image of eye with eyebrow, brown on mauve; clear plastic leaf, with recto as title page; [9] image of eye with eyebrow, brown on mauve; [10] blank; [11] first presentation details, RSC at Aldwych and Music Box Theatre, New York; [12–13 opening] abstract image in reds and blues; [14] blank; [15–22] text; [23] image of Ruth's face, in pinks and reds; [24] blank; [25–32] text; [33] image of part of face, drinking from a glass; [34] blank; [35–39] text, to end of Act I; [40–42] "ACT TWO", text; [43] blank; [44] image of fingers holding hair, at side of face, in violet, orange and black; [45–48] text; [49] blank; [50] image of lips, etc., yellow and mauve; [51–54] text; [55] blank; [56] image of fingers, coming from above and from below; [57–62] text; [63] image of fingers, hair, clothing, in blues, black and white; [64] blank; [65–68] text; [69] abstract image in orange, red and blue; [71] note on this edition (see Note one); [72] blank.

Note one: On p.[71], all in bold italic: "This edition of 'The Homecoming' was designed entirely by | Harold Cohen and produced by the artist in collaboration with | Robert Simon, London, April 1967 – July 1968. The text used | was made available by Methuen & Co. Ltd. | Harold Pinter added amendments in March 1968. |
The book was printed at The Curwen Press, London, on | papers specially made for this edition by J. Barcham Green. | The nine lithographs and cover image were made by the artist | and the text set in a photographically modified version of | Bodoni Bold. |
The binding forms an integral part of the artist's design. | All copies have been bound in boards covered with a woven | Terylene, the colouring and processing of which have been | supervised by the artist. The binding and slip cases have been | made by Mansell, London. |
There have been 200 copies produced of this edition, each being | numbered and signed by the author and artist. Numbers 1–25 | contain an additional suite of the plates signed by the artist. | A further 25 copies 'hors de commerce' marked 'H.C.' and | numbered I–XXV, have been printed for those involved in the production of the book. | Published by H. Karnac (Books) Limited | 58 Gloucester Road, London, S.W.7".

Note two: The L copy has on p. [71], in pencil, holograph signatures of "Harold Pinter | Harold Cohen 1968 | 35/200". A copy owned by William Baker is similarly signed and numbered "171/200".

Note three: Images occupy the full surface of pages. The text occupies the right-hand portion of pages. Where the Methuen texts vary, this text usually has the later variant passage; in some instances, e.g. on p.[39], it has the first edition variant.

f. American standard edition (1967):

THE HOMECOMING | Harold Pinter | GROVE PRESS, INC. | NEW YORK

[3]–82 pp. 20.2 × 13.7 cm. Hardback, grey cloth [some copies in black cloth]; down spine in silver: "THE HOMECOMING HAROLD PINTER GROVE PRESS". Endpapers. Dust jacket, outside front and spine black, outside back and flaps white; on outside front: "[*in white:*] The Homecoming | [*in brownish red:*] a play by | [*in orange-red:*] Harold Pinter", above photo tinged in orange-red and yellow of Lenny and Max; on outside back, photo of Pinter, captioned at side: "Photo: Mark Gerson", yellow rule, biographical note about Pinter, yellow rule, "GROVE PRESS, INC., 80 University Place, New York, N. Y. 10003"; down spine: "[*in white:*] THE HOMECOMING [*in orange-red:*] BY [*in yellow:*] HAROLD PINTER [*in orange-red:*] GP-392 GROVE PRESS"; on front flap, price, account of play; on back flap, four quotations from "English Reviews of | The Homecoming", at foot, "DESIGN: KUHLMAN ASSOCIATES | Photo: David Sims".

Published 24 February 1967 (publisher's slip; GP-392). Price $3.95. On verso of title leaf: copyright and performing rights statements, "Library of Congress Catalog Card Number: 66-28734 | Manufactured in the United States of America".

Contents: [3] titlepage; [4] colophon; [5] fly-title "The Homecoming"; [6] details of first British presentation, and of set; [7]–82 text.

Notes: The front free endpaper is in effect pp. [1–2]. In copies seen, on the verso of the title page "First Printing" is not present, but later printings have, following the LCCN, e.g., "Fifth Printing". In the fifth printing, on p.[5]: instead of the fly-title, details of the first British production with an added note on the first American production, opened 5 January 1967, with the same cast, except for Michael Craig taking over the role of Teddy; on p.[6]: description of set. Dace notes the text is the same page-for-page as for the 1966 Methuen, so was possibly offset. The earliest paperback printing has not been seen, but its binding was doubtless similar in design to the hardback dust jacket and to that of later printings (its Evergreen number was presumably E-411).

g. Later Evergreen paperback printings:

A copy of the "Thirteenth Printing" [undated], in paperback, has the front cover the same as for the outside front of the dust jacket, with, at upper right, lettered downward, in red: "[*small publisher's device*] EVERGREEN E-411-T $1.95"; on the back cover, no photo of Pinter, otherwise similar to dust jacket's outside back, with, in black, Evergreen number and price, title in red, quotation from *The New Statesman* in black, rule in yellow, account of play in black, rule in yellow, "[*3 lines in black*:] Grove Press, Inc., 53 East 11th Street, New York, New York 10003 | 394-17251-5 | Photo: David Sims"; spine as for dust jacket spine, with altered number ("E-411-T").

h. Book Club edition [1967?]:

Title page: lettering as for trade edition, but in different settings.

92 pp., 2 blank leaves [2 inserted leaves of photos]. Quarter-bound in black cloth, with yellow on boards; down spine, lettering in gold, as for standard edition. Endpapers. Dust jacket not seen.

Published *ca.* 1967. On verso of title leaf: "Copyright © 1965 and 1966 by H. Pinter Ltd", further copyright and performing rights statements, "Photographs by courtesy of Friedman-Abeles | Printed in the United States of America".

Contents: [1] half-title; [2] blank; [3] title page; [4] blank; [5] first production details, and description of set; [6] blank; [7] fly-title "Act One"; [8] blank; [9]–24 (24a-b); 25–72 (72a-b); 73–92 text.

Notes: Four production photos facing pp. 24, 25, and 72, 73, that is, two leaves inserted, with full-page photos, with original British cast. Text as for standard edition, in different typesetting.

i. American collectors' edition (2000):

[*All within double-rule border, in red:*] | [*in red:*] THE HOMECOMING | [*rest of lettering in black:*] by | Harold Pinter | COLLECTOR'S EDITION | *Bound in Genuine Leather* | [*E/P device*] | [*in cursive script:*] *the Easton Press* | NORWALK, CONNECTICUT

92 pp. 22 × 14.7 cm. Binding in brown leather; front and back covers with elaborate gold tooling; on spine, in gilt: "[*tooled decorative device*] | [*rule*] | [*rule*] | [*down spine:*] THE HOMECOMING | [*rule*] | [*rule*] | [*down spine:*] Harold Pinter | [*rule*] | [*rule*] | [*E/P device*] | [*2 lines, within single-rule frame:*] SIGNED | EDITION | [*tooled decorative device*]". Endpapers.

Published June 2000. About 1500 copies printed (all copies signed by Harold Pinter). On verso of title leaf: copyright details, "The special contents of this edition | are copyright © 2000 by Easton Press (MBI, Inc.) | Norwalk, Connecticut.

| Photographs are courtesy of Friedman-Abeles.", reproduction restriction and performing rights details, "This book is printed on archival quality paper especially milled for this | Edition. It is acid-neutral", etc., "Printed and bound in the United States of America."

Contents: [1] within two borders, each of three rules: "[*Easton Press Signed Modern Classics device*] | This leather-bound edition of | *The Homecming* | is personally signed by | Harold Pinter. | [*short rule*] [*diamond*] [*short rule*] | [holograph signature "Harold Pinter"]; [2] blank; [3] title page; [4] as above; [5] fly-title; [6] blank; [7] cast; [8] blank; [9] fly-title for Act One; [10] blank; [11]–50 text; [51] fly-title for Act Two; [52] blank; [53]–92 text.

j. French's acting edition, first edition (1966):

THE HOMECOMING | A Play in Two Acts | by | HAROLD PINTER | SAMUEL [*publisher's device*] FRENCH | LONDON | NEW YORK TORONTO SYDNEY HOLLYWOOD

2 leaves, 50 pp., 1 leaf. 21.2 × 1.7 cm. Paperback, white; on front cover, to left, vivid-blue vertical band, and within it, at head, in white, publisher's device, at foot, white panel, with, within it, in blue: "French's | Acting | Edition"; to right, in black, "THE HOMECOMING | A Play | HAROLD PINTER"; on outside back, 3 production photos, and, within blue border, in black: "6s. | net"; down spine: "PINTER THE HOMECOMING FRENCH".

Published January 1966 (L accession 17 JAN 67). Price 6s. On verso of title leaf: "© 1965 BY H. PINTER LTD | [*copyright and performance rights statements*] | MADE AND PRINTED IN GREAT BRITAIN BY LATIMER, TREND & CO. LTD, PLYMOUTH | MADE IN ENGLAND".

Contents: [i] title page; [ii] as above; [iii] first performance details, synopsis of scenes; [iv] blank; [1]–43 text; [44]–46 furniture and property list; [47]–48 lighting plot; [49]–50 effects plot; [51] blank; [52] French's advertisement, and colophon (as on verso of title leaf).

Note one: After first publication in 1966, it appeared with a revised text in 1968, and was further revised in 1975, after the Lord Chamberlain's censorship function was abolished. The changes involve the restoration of the original stage-directions for the sequence in Act II in which Joey lies on top of Ruth on the sofa, and they then tumble to the floor with Joey still on top (on pp. 30–31 in the French edition). In the earlier French edition printings, they remain side-by-side on the sofa: "(JOEY *takes Ruth's arm, smiles at Lenny, sits with* RUTH *on the sofa,* | *embraces and kisses her.* LENNY *stands behind the sofa)*". The fall to the floor is omitted.

A series of letters between Pinter and the responsible employee of Samuel French Ltd., from 23 January to 24 February 1969, indicates that the person who had been responsible for the first Samuel French publication had unilaterally taken it upon himself to censor the text without consulting the author. Other unauthorised changes Pinter noticed (related to censorship by the Lord Chamberlain recently abolished) included: on p.2, the substitution of "stupid birk" for "stupid sod"; on p.24, the substitution of "lazy idle slug" for "lazy idle bugger"; on p.25, the cutting of Max's "Anyone could have you at the same time. You'd bend over for a half a dollar on Blackfriars Bridge." French's employee guaranteed that the original stage directions on pp. 30–31 would be restored in the reprint about to be issued; he asked that the other changes should be delayed until the following reprint because of the costs involved, and Pinter agreed to this. Also, an omission of two words needed correcting: on the first page of text, Max should say, "I was just looking <u>at it</u> in the kitchen." A further substitution, which Pinter did not draw attention to, was that of "a nice quiet bunk up" for "a nice quiet poke" (p.39). Curiously, this change did not later get reversed.

Note two: A somewhat later edition owned by William Baker, with a different cover and preliminaries, has the designation "GB 573 01555 4" on the verso of the title leaf and on the back cover. The printer's imprint is on p.[52]. It retains the bowdlerised stage-directions for the episode late in Act II. Later printings have the ISBN number: ISBN 0 573 01555 4.

k. American anthology (extracts) (1967):

[*3 lines within rectangular box of small circles:*] THE | BEST PLAYS | OF 1966–1967 | [*below box:*] EDITED BY OTIS L. GUERNSEY JR. | *Illustrated with photographs and* | *with drawings by* HIRSCHFELD | [*line of six circles*] | DODD, MEAD & COMPANY | NEW YORK • TORONTO

6 leaves, 498 pp. 23.2 × 15 cm. Binding red cloth, with black spine.

Published 1967. On verso of title leaf: "*Copyright © by Dodd, Mead & Company, Inc.* | *Library of Congress Catalog Card Number: 20-21432* | *Printed in the United States of America*", list of plays in anthology, with copyright and performing rights details, extending on to facing recto, with, at end, a "CAUTION" against violation of copyright or performing rights..

Contents [relevant]: The Homecoming occupies pp. 260–277, with a biographical note about Pinter and his plays on p.260; on p.261: "INTRODUCTION BY THE PLAYWRIGHT", with a footnote: "These comments were made during an interview on "The Pinter Puzzle," a television | program produced by WNDT, Channel 13, the Public Service Television Station in New York | City, and were designated by the author to introduce his play here." In this introduction, he begins with affirming: "As far as I'm concerned my play *The Homecoming* means exactly what it | says; exactly what it does; exactly what happens on the stage"; and he refers to a curious incident "on the very first night in New York." After Max hit Joey, and it was uncertain whether Joey, who was walking slowly towards him, would hit Max, "or what was going to happen, an ex- | traordinarily deep sound filled the theater. Everyone thought it a cunning | Royal Shakespeare Company theatrical effect. I was asked about its meaning | and purpose a number of times. | In fact, it was the Queen Mary, or something, in New York harbor. | HAROLD PINTER".

Notes: The text of *The Homecoming* is not complete, but a series of extracts, together with passages of discursive prose describing characters, commenting upon the action, or summarizing it. Following the last of the plays there is a section which contains information about the American productions of each of the plays, and brief plot summaries (for *The Homecoming,* on p.380). A later section on prizes and awards includes a record that this play received the Antoinette Perry (Tony) Award for Best Play for the season.

l. In American anthology (1993):

HBJ Anthology of Drama (Fort Worth, Texas: Harcourt Brace College Publishers, 1993).

On pp. 781–903, with an essay on the author and his work. New extended edition *ca.* 1996, with *The Homecoming* on pp. 1078–1099.

A21   THE DWARFS and EIGHT REVUE SKETCHES   1965

a. American acting edition, first version [1965]:

[*To upper left, 7 vertical thick rules, 9.2 cm.*] THE DWARFS | and | Eight Revue Sketches | BY HAROLD PINTER | [*star*] | [*7 horizontal thick rules, 9.2 cm., with second rule broken to left of centre, with, within this space, words* "PLAY IN ONE ACT"] | [*star*] | DRAMATISTS | PLAY SERVICE | INC. | [*to right, 7 vertical thick rules, 3.3 cm.*]

49 pp., 1 leaf. 19.6 × 13.3 cm. Paperback, darkish red; front cover lettered, ruled, etc., as for title page, except for having 8 rules in each position; on back cover, publisher's advertisement for new plays, borders above and below; on inside of front cover, information about DPS and, within single-rule frame, advertisement for Dr Rudolph Liszt's *The Last Word in Make-up*; on inside of back cover, within single-rule frame, list of DPS new plays; down spine: "THE DWARFS AND EIGHT REVUE SKETCHES — PINTER".

Published 18 October 1965. (L accession 15 DEC 70; DLC copyright registration 18 October 1965 [DP5851], renewed 4 May 1993 [RE-517-056]). 1000 copies in first printing. Price $1.25. On verso of title leaf: "© COPYRIGHT, 1965, BY

HAROLD PINTER | BRITISH EDITION © COPYRIGHT, 1961, BY HAROLD PINTER", further copyright, and performing rights statements, note on sound effects record, for door-bell.

Contents: [1] title page; [2] as above; 3 first performance details, for *The Dwarfs,* first British radio and stage productions; [4] blank; 5–24 text; 25 property plot; [26] blank; 27 fly-title: "REVUE SKETCHES', lists 8 titles; 28 first performance details (British), for first four sketches; 29–48 texts: 29–30 "TROUBLE IN THE WORKS"; 32–34 "THE BLACK AND WHITE"; 35–36 "REQUEST STOP"; 37–38 "LAST TO GO"; 39–41 "APPLICANT"; 42–44 "INTERVIEW"; 45–46 "THAT'S ALL"; 47–48 "THAT'S YOUR TROUBLE"; 49 property list; [50–52] DPS advertisements.

Notes: The L copy has an insert of two leaves, folded and held in place with a glide-clip, with typescript on the rectos only, headed "Revisions to printed text", with new passages for *The Dwarfs,* and notes as to where these should replace existing passages of text, on pp. 10, 13, 14, 15.

b. American acting edition, extended version [1999]:

[*To left, 8 vertical rules*] THE DWARFS | AND NINE REVUE SKETCHES | BY | HAROLD PINTER | [*star*] | [*8 horizontal rules*] | [*star*] | DRAMATISTS | PLAY SERVICE | INC. | [*to right, 8 vertical rules*]

52 pp. 19.7 × 13.2 cm. Paperback, pale red; front cover lettered, ruled, and decorated as for title page, except rules are thick; on back cover, within single-rule frame, account of *The Dwarfs,* and of each of the nine sketches, and at foot, left: "Also by Harold Pinter | THE CARETAKER | MOONLIGHT | THE LOVER | and many others | DRAMATISTS PLAY SERVICE, INC.", and at foot, left: "ISBN 0-8222-1733-3 | [*bar-code*] | 9 780822 217338", to right: "90000> | [*bar-code*]"; down spine: "THE DWARFS AND NINE REVUE SKETCHES — PINTER"; on inside of front cover, information about DPS; on inside of back cover, advertisements for 6 DPS publications.

Published 1999. On verso of title leaf: "THE DWARFS and NINE REVUE SKETCHES | Copyright © 1999, Harold Pinter | THE NEW WORLD ORDER | Copyright © 1991, Harold Pinter | THE DWARFS and EIGHT REVUE SKETCHES | Copyright © Renewed 1993, Harold Pinter | Copyright © 1965, Harold Pinter | British Edition © Copyright 1961, Harold Pinter | All rights reserved", further copyright and performing rights information, special note about the use of the author's name.

Contents: [1] title page; [2] as above; [3] first performance details for British radio and stage productions of *The Dwarfs;* [4] blank; 5–24 text, *The Dwarfs;* 25 "PROPERTY PLOT"; [26] blank; 27 fly-title: "REVUE SKETCHES", listing nine titles; 28 first performance details, first four sketches; 29–51 texts [as above, to 48; 49–51 "THE NEW WORLD ORDER"]; 52 property list.

A22   THE ROOM AND THE DUMB WAITER   1966

a¹. First British edition (1996):

THE ROOM | AND | THE DUMB WAITER | BY | Harold Pinter | LONDON | METHUEN & CO LTD | 11 NEW FETTER LANE EC4

71 pp. 17.4 × 11.5 cm. Paperback; front cover blue: "[*in black*:] HAROLD PINTER | [2 *lines in white*:] The Room and | The Dumb Waiter | [*photo of Rose and Hudd*]"; back cover white, with photo of Pinter, and below: "[*in blue*:] HAROLD PINTER [*in black, 9-line paragraph about him*] | [*in black*:] PRICE 5S IN UK ONLY"; spine blue, down spine in white: "PINTER THE ROOM AND THE DUMB WAITER METHUEN".

Published 12 May 1966. Price 5s. On verso of title leaf: "TO VIVIEN | [copyright and performing rights statements] | *First published* 1960 | *Copyright* © 1959 *and* 1960 | *by Harold Pinter* | *Paperback edition first published* 1966 | *Printed in Great Britain by* | *John Dickens & Co Ltd* | *Northampton*".

Contents: [1] brief accounts of the two plays, at foot: "*The photograph on the front cover showing Michael* | *Brennan and Vivien Merchant in* THE ROOM *is repro-* | *duced by courtesy of John Cowan. The portrait of* | *Harold Pinter on the back is by Mark Gerson.*"; [2] list of "*Methuen's Modern Plays*"; [3] title page; [4] as above; [5] contents; [6] first professional performance details, *The Room*; [7]–32 text; [33] fly-title, *The Dumb Waiter*; [34] first performance details; [35]–71 text; [72] blank.

Notes: A copy seen of the 1968 reprint is signed [A]⁴ B-E⁸. On the verso of the title leaf it has the same printer's colophon as the first printing, the SBN as below, and "1.2".

a². Third printing (1970):

Paperback binding: on front cover, within blue border, within white panel, lettering in blue: "Harold Pinter | [*rule, in black, 9.8 cm.*] | The Room and | The Dumb Waiter | [*below panel, photo of Rose and Hudd, in* The Room]"; on back cover, within blue border, photo of Pinter, below it, within white panel, lettered in blue: "photo: Antony di Gesù | [*account of Pinter*] | [*rule, in black, 10 cm.*] | A METHUEN MODERN PLAY 7s 6d/ 37½p. in U.K. only"; on spine, blue, at head, in white, publisher's device, down spine, in black: "Pinter • The Room and The Dumb Waiter Methuen".

Published 1970. Price 7s 6d, 37½p. On verso of title leaf: as above, except:

"*Reprinted* 1968 | *Reprinted* 1970 | *Printed in Great Britain by* | *Cox & Wyman Ltd* | *Fakenham Norfolk* | S.B.N. 416 63190 8 | 1.3", conditions of sale statement.

Contents: As for first printing, except, on [72], publisher's list, with a continuation of it printed on the facing recto, i.e., on the paste-down rear endpaper.

Notes: Reprinted in 1972. The following printings, from spring 1973 onward, were published by Eyre Methuen, SBN 413 30340 3: 1973 (twice), 1976 (twice), 1978, 1979, 1981, 1982; reprinted 1983 for Methuen London Ltd (publisher's lists pp. [72–79], with [80] blank). In 1973 the price was 50p., by 1975 60p.

b. Faber edition (1991):

[*All within single-rule frame:*] HAROLD | PINTER | The Room | *and* | The Dumb Waiter | ff | *faber and faber* | LONDON • BOSTON

1 blank leaf, 71 pp., 3 blank leaves. 19.8 × 12.5 cm. Paperback, white, with standard Faber design; on front cover: "ff | [*rule*] | HAROLD | PINTER | The Room | *and* | The Dumb Waiter | [*illustration*]"; on back cover: publisher, author, title, brief account of Pinter and the two plays, "Cover illustration by Andrzej Klimowski | UK £4.99 net | Canada $12.95 | [*bar-code*] | 9 780571 16083"; on spine: "ff | [*rule*] | [*down spine:*] HAROLD PINTER The Room *and* The Dumb Waiter".

Published 1991 (L accession 19 FEB 1991). On verso of title leaf: "First published by Eyre Methuen 1966; | paperback 1966 | Reprinted by Methuen London Ltd 1983 | This paperback edition first published in 1991 | [. . . .] Printed in England by Clays Ltd, St Ives plc | [*copyright, performing rights, conditions of sale statements*] | ISBN 0-571-16085-9".

Contents: [1] half-title; [2] Faber's Pinter titles; [3] title page; [4] as above; thereafter as for Methuen.

Notes: Faber and Faber report (1 August 2001) printings of 8 April 1991, 24 March 1998, 1 November 1998, 22 March 2000, totalling 21,636 copies printed.

A23   TEA PARTY AND OTHER PLAYS   1967

a. British first edition (1967):

TEA PARTY | *and other plays* | HAROLD PINTER | METHUEN & CO LTD | 11 NEW FETTER LANE LONDON EC4

115, [1] pp., 2 leaves. 18.6 × 12.1 cm. Hardback, black cloth; down spine in gold: "Harold Pinter [*star*] TEA PARTY and other plays [*star*] Methuen". Endpapers. Dust jacket in blue and white; on front cover, within blue border, white panel: "[*in blue:*] Harold Pinter | [*in black, short rule, 10.1 cm.*] | [2 *lines in blue:*] Tea

Party | and other plays", below, photo of Leo McKern as Disson; on back cover, within blue border, photo of Pinter, below, within white panel, in blue, 10-line biographical note, rule in black, "A METHUEN MODERN PLAY 18s net in U.K. only"; spine blue: "[*in white, Methuen device*] | [*down spine, in black:*] Pinter • Tea Party and other plays Methuen"; on front flap, account of plays, "*The photograph on the front cover shows Leo | McKern in a scene from the B.B.C. production | of* Tea Party *and is reproduced by courtesy of | the B.B.C.*", at foot "PRICE | 18s net | in U.K. only"; on back flap, list of Methuen Modern Plays titles, "PRINTED IN GREAT BRITAIN".

Published 15 June 1967 (DLC copyright registration 15 June 1967 [DF1945]). 4,000 copies. Price 18s 0d. On verso of title leaf: copyright and performing rights statements, "*First published 1967 | © 1967 by H. Pinter Ltd | Printed in Great Britain | by W. & J. Mackay & Co Ltd, Chatham, Kent*".

Contents: [1] half-title; [2] "*by the same author*", lists 6 other titles; [3] title page; [4] as above; [5] "*To my mother and father*"; [6] contents; [7] fly-title "*TEA PARTY*"; [8] first presentation details, BBC-TV; [9]–54 text; [55] fly-title "*THE BASEMENT*"; [56] first presentation details, BBC-TV; [57]–78 text; [79] fly-title "*NIGHT SCHOOL*"; [80] first presentation details, TV and radio; [81]–115 text; [116–119] publisher's advertisements; [120] blank.

Notes: A proof copy owned by Dr John Dawick has the leaf-measure as 18.4 × 12.4 cm. It is bound in plain brown light card; on front cover: 'TEA PARTY | and other plays | [*short double rule, thin, thick, 1.7 cm.*] | HAROLD PINTER | [*3 lines within decorated frame:*] Uncorrected | Proof copy from | Methuen & Co. Ltd | [*below frame:*] Crown 8vo. 128 pp. | To be published June 1967 | Approximate price: 18/- net'; back cover and spine blank. The text of *Tea Party* differs from the published text only in having: p [9]: above first line of text as published: "*An electric lift.*" (first line of published text, second of proof, starts "*An electric lift rising*"). And on p.14, letters at ends of last lines have got mixed with each other: so, l.33 ends "austere standards y,"(last word should be "up"); p.34 ends with "withof" (should be "within"), l.34 ends with "beaut in" (should be "beauty,"). The text of *The Basement* has on p. 73 a typo: a line ends: "bow ." (should be "bowl.")

b. Paperback edition (1970):

TEA PARTY | *and other plays* | HAROLD PINTER | METHUEN & CO LTD | 11 NEW FETTER LANE LONDON EC4

115, [1] pp., 2 leaves. Signed [A][8] B-H[8]. 18.3 × 12.6 cm. Paperback, blue and white; on front cover, as for dust jacket outside front; on back cover, photo of Pinter, below, in white panel, caption, in blue, "photo: Antony di Gesù", in blue, 9-line biographical note, in black, rule, "A METHUEN MODERN PLAY 7s 6d: 37½ p net in U.K. only"; spine as for dust jacket.

Published 4 June 1970. 14,000 copies. Price 7s 6d; 37½p. On verso of title leaf: copyright and performing rights statements, "*First published 1967 | Reprinted 1970 | Copyright © 1967 by H. Pinter (Screenplays) Ltd | Paperback edition first published 1970 | Printed in Great Britain by | Cox & Wyman Ltd Fakenham and London |* SBN 416 19130 4 *(hardback edition) |* 1.2 | SBN 416 19790 6 *(paperback edition) |* 1.1", conditions of sale statement.

Contents: [1] brief account of plays, "*The photograph on the front cover shows | Leo McKern in a scene from the B.B.C. | production of Tea Party and is reproduced | by courtesy of the B.B.C.*"; [2] "*by the same author*", lists 7 titles; [3] title page; [4] as above; [5]–115 as for first edition; [116–120] Methuen's lists of titles.

c. Second paperback edition, with addition of short story (1974):

Title page as for 1970, except publisher as "EYRE METHUEN LTD".

121 pp., 1 blank leaf. 18.6 cm. Paperback, white; front cover as for first edition dust jacket; back cover with photo of Pinter by Antony di Gesù, white panel with lettering in blue: caption, account of Pinter | [rule, in black, 9.9 cm.] | "A METHUEN MODERN PLAY 50p net in U.K. only"; on spine, M device, down spine in black: "Harold Pinter ▪ Tea Party and other plays Eyre Methuen".

Published 1974 (but see *Notes*). Price 50p. 9,941 copies. Verso of title leaf: "*First published 1967 Reprinted 1970 | Copyright © 1967 by Harold Pinter | Screenplays Ltd. | Paperback edition first published 1970 | Second edition with the addition of the short story, 'Tea Party', 1974 | [. . . .] | Printed in Great Britain by Cox and Wyman Ltd, Fakenham |* ISBN 0 413 31600 9 (paperback edition) | [*conditions of sale statement*]".

Contents: [1] account of plays, as above, with addition of short story, and of note on cover photo; [2]–115, as for first edition; [116]–121 story "Tea Party".

Notes: Dace states that despite the date 1974 on the verso of the title leaf, this impression was published on 3 April 1975. In later impressions the photo of Pinter on the outside back of the cover was replaced by one by Ivan Kyncl.

d. Faber re-publication (1991):

[*Within single-rule frame:*] HAROLD | PINTER | *Tea Party* | and Other Plays | ff | faber and faber | LONDON ▪ BOSTON

127 pp., 3 blank leaves. [A]⁸ B-G ⁸ [H]⁸. Binding standard Faber drama paperback design; on front cover: "ff | [*rule*] | HAROLD PINTER | Tea Party | and Other Plays | [*coloured illustration*] |"; on back cover: "ff | *faber and faber* | [*rule*] | HAROLD PINTER | Tea Party and Other Plays | *Tea Party, The Basement, Night School* | Three plays for television | [*one paragraph blurb about* Tea Party] |

Cover design by Andrzej Klimowski | UK £5.99 net | Canada $14.99 | ISBN 0-571-16094-8 | [*bar-code*] | 9 780571 160945"; on spine: "ff | [*rule*] | [*down spine:*] HAROLD PINTER Tea Party and Other Plays."

Contents: [1] half-title and note; [2] Faber's Pinter titles; [3] title-page; [4] as above; [5]–121 as for 1974; [122–124] blank.

Notes: Published 3 June 1991. 1519 copies printed. On verso of title leaf: "This paperback edition first published in 1991," etc., "Printed in England by Clays Ltd., St. Ives plc", copyright, performing rights, conditions of sale and CIP record statements, ISBN as above.

A24   THE LOVER, TEA PARTY, THE BASEMENT   1967

THE LOVER | TEA PARTY | THE BASEMENT | Two plays and a film script | by | Harold Pinter | Grove Press, Inc. | New York

112 pp. 20.2 × 13.4 cm. (A) Hardback binding, very dark navy blue cloth; down spine in gold: "THE LOVER, TEA PARTY, THE BASEMENT / PINTER Grove Press". Endpapers. Dust jacket black on outside front and spine, white on outside back and flaps; on outside front, to upper left: "[*in white:*] The Lover | [*2 lines in pale green:*] Tea Party | The Basement | [*2 lines in darker green:*] Two plays and | a film script by | [*in violet:*] Harold Pinter", to lower right: photo from *The Lover*; on outside back, rule in violet, 4 quotations from critics about Pinter, rule in violet, "[*in violet*] GROVE PRESS, INC. | 80 University Place, New York, N. Y. 10003"; down spine: "[*in pale green:*] THE LOVER, TEA PARTY, THE BASEMENT / [*in violet:*] PINTER [*in white:*] GP-458 [*across spine, at foot, 2 lines in white:*] GROVE | PRESS"; on front flap: "$3.95 | GP-458", titles and accounts of the three plays; on back flap, photo of Pinter, captioned down side: "Photo: Tom Blau. Copyright Camera Press Ltd.—Pix", brief biographical note about Pinter, below violet rule, in violet: "DESIGN: KUHLMAN ASSOCIATES | Cover photo: Miss Alix Jeffry".

(B) Paperback binding, black on front and spine, white on back; on front, as for front of dust jacket, but at lower right, Evergreen device, lettered up, in violet, "EVERGREEN E-432 $1.95"; on back cover: "[*in pale green:*] AN EVERGREEN BOOK E-432 $1.95 | [*in darker green, 4-line quotation about Pinter*] | [*in lighter green, rule*] | [*in black, 2 paragraphs about the plays, and Pinter*] | [*in light green, rule*] | [*in light green:*] GROVE PRESS, INC., 80 University Place, New York, N. Y. 10003 | [*vertical, to right, alongside second paragraph, about Pinter, in black:*] Cover photo: Miss Alix Jeffry".

Published 30 November 1967 (in paperback: Grove Press statement: "Pub. Date: November 30, 1967 | Price: $1.95"). Price $3.95 (hardback), $1.95 (paperback). On verso of title leaf: copyright and performing rights statements, "Library of Congress Catalog Card Number: 67-27884 | First Printing | Manufactured in the United States of America".

Contents: [1] title page; [2] as above; [3] fly-title "THE LOVER"; [4] first presentation details, Associated Rediffusion Television, 28 March 1963,
and Arts Theatre 18 September 1963; [5]–40 text; [41] fly-title "TEA
PARTY"; [42] first presentation details, BBC TV, 25 March 1965;
[43]–88 text; [89] fly-title "THE BASEMENT"; [90] first presentation
details, BBC TV, 1967; [91]–112 text.

Note one: The texts are as for the Methuen volumes, but on the first page of the
text for *Tea Party,* there is no drop-title, otherwise as for the text in Methuen's
Tea Party and Other Plays (but has at top of text "*An electric lift.*" as in proof
copy); *The Basement,* text as for this volume.

Note two: Listed in the *Publishers Weekly,* 18 March 1968, as published in
[1967]. DLC copyright 67-28884. The volume went through a number of reprintings. The sixth printing, *ca.* late 1974, in paperback, is similar, but is designated
E-432-T. The colours on the back cover differ: after the paragraph about Pinter,
"[*in darker green, rule*] | [*in pale green:*] Grove Press, Inc., 53 East 11ᵗʰ Street,
New York, New York 10003 | [*in black:*] 394-17263-9".

A25   SPECIAL OFFER   1967

In: Arnold P. Hinchliffe, *Harold Pinter,* Twayne's English Author Series (Boston,
MA: Twayne Publishers, a division of G. K. Hall & Co., 1967), 73–74.

Notes: Short sketch, a single speech of about 27 lines. From *Pieces of Eight*
(1959). Another Pinter sketch in this revue, "Getting Acquainted," has evidently
never been published, and according to Pinter in 1967 had been lost (see
Hinchliffe 73, 182).

A26   A NIGHT OUT, NIGHT SCHOOL, REVUE SKETCHES   1968

[*4 lines in open letters:*] A NIGHT OUT | NIGHT SCHOOL | REVUE
SKETCHES | [*rule, 6.7 cm.*] | Early Plays | [*rule, 6.7 cm.*] | by [*open letters:*]
Harold Pinter | [*normal letters:*] Grove Press, Inc., New York

2 leaves, 106 pp., 1 blank leaf. Hardback: 22 × 13.7 cm.; paperback: 20.3 × 13.6
cm. Bindings: (A) Hardback, yellow mottled cloth; down spine: "A NIGHT
OUT / NIGHT SCHOOL / REVUE SKETCHES Pinter Grove Press". Endpapers.
Dust jacket: outside front glossy black: "[*in light brown:*] A NIGHT OUT | [*in
light green:*] NIGHT SCHOOL | [*in grey-green:*] REVUE SKETCHES | [*in
lighter grey-green:*] EARLY PLAYS | [*in pale fawn:*] BY HAROLD
PINTER"; outside back white, headed: "Some comments on the work of Harold
Pinter" with 6 critics' comments, divided by yellow rules, with a green rule at
the bottom, preceding the publisher's address; down spine: "[*in yellow:*] A

NIGHT OUT [*in white:*] / [*in green:*] NIGHT SCHOOL [*in white:*] / [*in pale yellow:*] HAROLD PINTER [*3 lines across spine:*] GP-537 | GROVE | PRESS"; front flap green: "[*at top right:*] $3.95 | GP-537 | [*centred:*] [*in black:*] A NIGHT OUT | [*in pale yellow:*] NIGHT SCHOOL | [*in pale green:*] REVUE SKETCHES | [*in dark green:*] BY HAROLD PINTER", account of contents of volume; back flap green: note about qualities present in these earlier plays, photo of Pinter, captioned down right side: "Photo: Tom Blau", biographical note about Pinter, "DESIGN: KUHLMANN ASSOCIATES".

(B) Paperback, glossy black on outside; on front cover: as for outside front of dust jacket, except, at lower left, in green, lettered upward: "[*publisher's device*] EVERGREEN E-480 $1.95"; on back cover, at top right: "EVERGREEN ORIGINAL (E-480) $1.95 | [*Quotation: that Pinter is*] "quite possibly the best and most | important playwright now alive."– Jerry Talmer | [*light brown rule, 10.4 cm.*] | [*description of plays in this volume*] | [*light green rule*] | [*note about Pinter*] | [*yellow-fawn rule*] | GROVE PRESS, INC., 80 University Place, New York, N.Y. 10003".

Published 4 December 1968 (later reprint 4 December 1975). Price $3.95 (hardback), $1.95 (paperback). On verso of title leaf: "*A Night Out* and *Review Sketches* copyright © 1961 by Harold | Pinter | *Night School* copyright © 1967 by H. Pinter Ltd | [*further copyright and performing rights statements*] | Library of Congress Catalog Card Number : 68-54860 | First Printing | Manufactured in the United States of America".

Contents: [i] half-title; [ii] list of Pinter titles "Previously Published" by Grove; [iii] title page; [iv] as above; [1] fly-title "A NIGHT OUT"; [2] BBC and TV performance details; [3]–47 text; [48] blank; [49] fly-title "NIGHT SCHOOL"; [50] TV and radio performance details; [51]–88 text; [89] fly-title "REVUE SKETCHES"; [90] first performance details; [91]–93 text, "TROUBLE IN THE WORKS"; [94]–97 text, "THE BLACK AND WHITE"; 97–99 text, "REQUEST STOP"; 99–102 text, "LAST TO GO"; [103]–106 text, "APPLICANT"; [107–108] blank.

A27   LANDSCAPE   1968

a. First British edition (1968):

Landscape | HAROLD PINTER | [*double rule, thick and thin, 6.7 cm.*] | [*publisher's device: within brownish-green circular disc: in white, reversed out of green: dragon standing on pen*] | EMANUEL WAX | FOR PENDRAGON PRESS | 1968

45, [1] pp. 20.8 × 13.6 cm. Sewn as octavo, [A]–[B]⁸ [C]⁶. Hardback; (a) quarterbound with pink cloth, on boards: light-brown paper (colour varies: for some copies: pale grey or pale greenish-blue); down spine, in gold: "LANDSCAPE [*Maltese cross*] Pinter Pendragon Press"; (b) quarter-bound in rose-red cloth, on boards: off-white rope-textured cloth. Endpapers magnolia.

Published July 1968 (L accession 29 JUL 68). 2000 copies. Price £1.15s. On verso of title leaf: "© Harold Pinter | Library of Congress Catalogue card No. 68-9784 | [performing rights statement] | Designed and printed in Great Britain by | W. S. Cowell Ltd, 8 Butter Market, Ipswich".

Contents: [1] half-title; [2] blank; [3] title page; [4] as above; [5] first radio presentation details; 6 list of characters, set, note; 7–45 [46] text; [47] "This first edition is limited to 2,000 | copies of which 1,000 (numbered 1–1,000) are for sale in the British Isles | and 1,000 (1,001–2,000) in the United States of America.".

Notes: On p.[46], in the copies seen, facsimile of holograph signature of author. The paper is medium-thick, cream.

b. Reprinting in periodical (1969):

In: *Evergreen Review,* No. 68 (July 1969): 55–61.

On p.55: whole page tinted blue-grey: "[*in large open letters:*] LANDSCAPE | [*in normal letters thereafter:*] A Play by Harold Pinter | [2 *rules*] | The first U.S. production of a new play by the leading British play- | wright whose "The Birthday Party" was a recent Broadway success | [2 *rules*]", text in three columns, preceded at head of left column with: characters, setting, initial placing of characters, mainly in italic, two rules, note on characters not hearing one another, and being relaxed, in italic apart from heading; to left, lettered upward: "Copyright © Harold Pinter 1968, published by Emanuel Wax for Pendragon Press. Distributed in the U.S. by Grove Press, Inc."

Front cover of issue black: "[*in blue:*] evergreen | [*in white:*] EVERGREEN REVIEW NO 68 July 1969 / ONE DOLLAR | [2 *lines in blue:*] From Jean Genet's "Funeral Rites" / Complete Play by Pinter | Also : Seymour Krim, Leslie Garrett, John Lahr, Nat Hentoff | [*colour photograph of Pacific Island girl with necklace*]".

Notes: Three "illustrations" by Paul Davis, on pp. 56, 58, 60, showing the head and part of the shoulders of a fully dressed man, wearing a bowler hat, and behind him two nude women (on p.58, only one woman).

c. German educational anthology (1975):

Unterrichtsmodelle für die Sekundarstufe II – Reihe English | Herausgeber: Dr. Herbert Henss, Leiter der Fachdidaktischen Kommission Englisch | für die Sekundarstufe II des Landes Rheinland-Pfalz | READING MODERN DRAMA | E. Albee *The Zoo Story* | H. Pinter *Landscape* | S. Beckett *Krapp's Last Tape* |

Texte ausgewählt und kommentiert von Dr. Günter Reichert | Hirscggraben-Verlag • Frankfurt am Main | Bestell-Nr. 6605

44 pp. *Landscape* occupies pp. 21–30.

A28   LANDSCAPE AND SILENCE [*also* NIGHT]   1969

a¹. First edition:

LANDSCAPE | *and* | SILENCE | by | Harold Pinter | LONDON | METHUEN & CO LTD | 11 NEW FETTER LANE

61pp., 1 leaf. Signed [A]⁸ B-D⁸. 18.4 × 12.4 cm. Hardback, black cloth; down spine, in silver: "Harold Pinter [*star*] LANDSCAPE and SILENCE [*star*] Methuen". Endpapers. Dust jacket blue and white; on front, within blue border, large panel in white: "[*in blue*:] Harold Pinter | [*in black, rule, 8.9 cm.*] | [*in black, in open shadowed letters*:] LANDSCAPE | [*in black*:] and | [*in black, letters formed from 5 thin stripes*:] SILENCE"; on back, Antony di Gesù photo, 8-line biographical note, in blue, rule in black, in blue: "A METHUEN MODERN PLAY"; on spine, Methuen device in white, down spine in black: "Pinter • Landscape and Silence"; on front flap, account of plays, at foot "Price net | 15s=75p | in U.K. only"; on back flap, list of Methuen Modern Plays titles.

Published 24 July 1969 (L accession 18 AUG 69). 5000 copies. Price 15s. On verso of title leaf: "[*performing rights statement*] | *First published* 1969 | [*copyright statements*] | Printed in Great Britain by | COX & WYMAN LTD., | LONDON AND READING".

Contents: [1] half-title; [2] list of 7 other titles; [3] title page; [4] as above; [5] contents; [6] "To | VIVIEN"; [7] fly-title "Landscape"; [8] performance details, BBC 25 April 1968, RSC at Aldwych 2 July 1969; [9]–30 text; [31] fly-title "Silence"; [32] performance details, RSC at Aldwych 2 July 1969; [33]–51 text; [52] blank; [53] fly-title "Night"; [54] performance details, as part of *Mixed Doubles*, Comedy Theatre, 9 April 1969; [55]–61 text; [62–64] publisher's lists.

a². First edition, reprinted as paperback (1970):

Title page as for first edition.

61 pp., 1 leaf. Signed as first edition. 18.5 × 12.0 cm. Paperback, blue and white; on front cover, within blue border, white panel: "[*in blue*:] Harold Pinter | [*in black, rule, 10 cm.*] | [*in blue*:] Landscape and | Silence", below, photo from *Silence*; back as for first edition dust jacket, price as "7s 6d: 37½p net in U.K. only"; spine as for dust jacket.

Published 18 June 1970. 7,500 copies. Price 7s 6d, 37½p. On verso of title leaf: "*First published 1969 | First published as a paperback edition 1970 | [. . . .] | SBN 416 15100 0 (Hardback) | SBN 416 65260 3 (Paperback)*", conditions of sale, performing rights statements.

Contents: [1] brief note of plays, "*The photograph on the front cover shows Norman | Rodway, Frances Cuka and Anthony Bate in Silence. | It is reproduced by courtesy of Zoë Dominic. The | photograph of Harold Pinter on the back cover is | reproduced by courtesy of Antony di Gesù.*"; [2]–[64] as for first printing, with changes on p.[4].

Notes: The text contains some alterations deriving from the first stage-productions, on pp. 17, 44, 45, 71. With Eyre Methuen coming into being, the paperback was assigned SBN 0413 30090 0. A reprint followed in 1972/73 of 5,000 copies, and another in 1974/75 of 5,000 copies.

b. Faber edition (1991):

[*Within single-rule frame:*] HAROLD PINTER | Landscape | *and* | Silence | ff | *faber and faber* | LONDON • BOSTON

1 leaf, 61 pp. 19.7 × 12.5 cm. Paperback, white, standard Faber design; on front cover: "ff | [*rule*] | HAROLD | PINTER | [*rule*] | Landscape *and* | Silence | [*illustration*]"; on back cover: publisher, author, titles, brief accounts of plays, "Cover illustration by Andrzej Klimowski | UK £4.99 net | Canada $12.99 | ISBN 0-571-16087-5 | [*bar-code*] | 9 780571 160877"; on spine: "ff | [*rule*] | [*down spine:*] HAROLD PINTER Landscape *and* Silence".

Published 8 July 1991 (L accession 21 MAY 91). 1536 copies printed, in first printing. On verso of title leaf: publication information, "Printed in England by Clays Ltd, St Ives plc", copyright, performing right, conditions of sale state-ments, "ISBN 0-571-16087-5".

Contents: As for Methuen, but performance details include BBC 2 presentation; consequently, the description of characters, set, initial situation, note that characters don't appear to hear each other, etc., is on the facing recto, on an extra preliminaries leaf, with its verso blank. No publisher's lists.

c. American first edition (1970):

LANDSCAPE | *and* | SILENCE | by | Harold Pinter | GROVE PRESS, INC. | NEW YORK

61 pp. 20.3 × 13.2 cm. (hardback), 20.1 × 13.2 cm. (paperback). Bindings: (A) Hardback, pale blue cloth; down spine: "Harold Pinter LANDSCAPE *and* SILENCE GROVE PRESS". Endpapers. Dust jacket: outside front, within white border, dark green: "[*in blue, white, etc., colour photo of Rodway as Bates, in*

Silence] | [*in green:*] Landscape | [*in blue:*] & [*in green:*] Silence | [*in white:*] Harold Pinter"; outside back white: "[*green-tinged photo of Pinter*] | [*to lower right of photo, lettered upward:*] Photograph by Tom Blau | [*at foot of photo:*] Grove Press, Inc., 214 Mercer Street, New York, N. Y. 10012"; spine white, down spine: "[*in black:*] LANDSCAPE & SILENCE [*in green:*] HAROLD PINTER [*in black:*] GP 634 GROVE PRESS"; on front and back flaps: at top right (front flap) "$3.95 | GP-634", centred, below heading, account of plays, and of Pinter, at foot (back flap): "DESIGN: KUHLMAN ASSOCIATES | Cover photo by Zoë Dominic | from the Royal Shakespeare Co. production". (B) Paperback, white on spine and back; on front cover: full-length colour-photo, green-tinged, of Rodway as Bates in *Silence*, with, imposed on lower area of photo: "[*in green:*] Landscape | [*in blue:*] & [*in green:*] Silence | [*in white:*] Harold Pinter | [*at bottom left, lettered upward, in blue:*] [*small publisher's device*] EVERGREEN E-555 $1.95"; on back cover: "[*in black, at top right:*] EVERGREEN ORIGINAL (E-555) $1.95 | [*in black:*] Landscape | [*in green:*] & [*in black:*] Silence | [*in blue:*] Harold Pinter | [*in green, rule*] | [*in black, 3 paragraphs about the plays*] | [*in blue, rule*] | [*in black, paragraph about Pinter*] | [*in green, rule*] | [*2 lines in black:*] Grove Press, Inc., 214 Mercer Street, New York, N. Y. 10012 | Cover photo by Zoë Dominic from the Royal Shakespeare Co. production"; down spine: " [*in black:*] LANDSCAPE & SILENCE [*in blue:*] HAROLD PINTER [*in black:*] [*small publisher's device*] E-555 GROVE PRESS".

Published 3 November 1970. Prices $3.95 (hardback), $1.95 (paperback). Initial print-run 1000 copies. On verso of title leaf: "To | Vivien | © *Landscape*, 1968, by H. Pinter Ltd | © *Silence* and *Night*, 1969, by H. Pinter Ltd | All Rights Reserved | Originally published by Methuen & Co Ltd, London | [*further copyright and performing rights statements*] | Library of Congress Catalog Card Number: 79-101386 | First Grove Press Edition, 1970 | First Printing | Manufactured in the United States of America".

Contents: [1] half-title; [2] list of other Grove Press Pinter titles; [3] title page; [4] as above; [5] contents; [6] photo, captioned "*Landscape*. Duff and Beth. American production."; [7–8] first presentation details, including those for the American production, 2 April 1970, at The Repertory Theatre of Lincoln Center, New York, "*Photographs from the American production | by Martha Swope*"; [9]–30 text, *Landscape*; [31] first presentation details for *Silence*, RSC, and American, in double bill with *Landscape*, photos by Martha Swope; [32] photo, captioned "*Silence*. Rumsey, Ellen, Bates (foreground). American production."; [33]–50, 52 text; [51] 2 photos, captioned, American production; [53] fly-title "Night"; [54] first performance details, as part of *Mixed Doubles*; [55]–61 text; [62] blank.

A29   THE BASEMENT   1969

[*To left, 7 vertical thick rules, 9.2 cm.*] THE | BASEMENT | A PLAY | BY
HAROLD PINTER | [*star*] | [*7 horizontal thick rules, 9.3 cm.*] | [*star*] | DRAMA-
TISTS | PLAY SERVICE | INC. | [*to right, 7 vertical thick rules, 3.3 cm.*]

21, [1] pp. 19.4 × 13.0 cm. Paperback, gray; on front cover, as for title page, except
with 8 rules rather than 7, in each place, 12.8, 13.5, and 4.7 cm. respectively;
on back cover: within single-rule border, list of new titles; down back cover,
adjacent to spine: "THE BASEMENT—PINTER"; on inside of front and back
covers, information about Dramatists Play Service, and advertisements.

Published 3 September 1969. DLC copyright registration 3 September 1969
(DP7129), re-entered 12 December 1997 (RE-766-702), with additions and
revisions to text. First printing 1000 copies. On verso of title leaf: "© COPY-
RIGHT, 1969, BY H. PINTER LTD. (ACTING EDITION) | © COPYRIGHT,
1967, BY H. PINTER LTD", copyright and performing rights statements, and
note that a doorbell sound effect can be purchased from Dramatists Play Service.

Contents: [1] title page; [2] as above; [3] first American performance details: in
double bill with *Tea Party,* New York, 15 October 1968; [3] list of
characters; 5–15 text; 16–19 property list; 20–21 costume plot;
[22–24] advertisements for DPS titles.

A30   TEA PARTY   1969

[*To left, 7 vertical thick rules, 9.2 cm.*] | TEA PARTY | A PLAY | BY HAROLD
PINTER | [*star*] | [*7 horizontal thick rules, 9.2 cm.*] | [*star*] DRAMATISTS |
PLAY SERVICE | INC. | [*to right, 7 vertical thick rules, 3.3 cm.*]

43, [1] pp. 19.1 × 11.5 cm. Paperback, olive-yellow; on front cover: as for title
page, except 8 rules in each of three positions, 12.5, 13.2, and 4.9 cm. respectively;
on back cover, and insides of front and back covers: Dramatists Play Service
advertisements; down outside back, adjacent to spine: "TEA PARTY – PINTER".

Published 2 October 1969. DLC copyright registration 2 October 1969 (DP7131);
re-entered 12 December 1997 (RE-766-703), with additions and revisions to the
text. 1,000 copies. Price 75 cents. On verso of title leaf: "© COPYRIGHT, 1969,
BY H. PINTER (SCREENPLAYS) LTD. | (ACTING EDITION) | © COPY-
RIGHT, 1967, BY H. PINTER (SCREENPLAYS) LTD.", further copyright and
performing rights statements, sound effects note.

Contents: [1] title page; [2] as above; 3 American stage performance details,
New York, opened 15 October 1968 (double bill with *The Basement*);
4 character-list; 5–35 text; 36–40 property-list; 41–43 costume-plot;
[44] DPS advertisement.

A31   TEA PARTY AND THE BASEMENT   1969

[7 *vertical thick rules*] TEA PARTY | and | THE BASEMENT | TWO PLAYS | BY HAROLD PINTER | [*star*] | [7 *horizontal thick rules*] | [*star*] | DRAMATISTS | PLAY SERVICE | INC. | [7 *vertical thick rules*]

65, [1] pp., 2 leaves. 19.4 × 13 cm. Paperback, yellowish; on front cover, as for title page, except 8 rules in each position; on back cover, and insides of front and back covers, information about DPS and advertisements; spine concealed in copy seen.

Published 1969 (re-registration at DLC in 12 December 1997 (RE-766-703), with additions and revisions to the text of *Tea Party*). On verso of title leaf: "© Copyright, 1969, by H. Pinter (Screenplays) Ltd. | (Acting Edition) | TEA PARTY – © Copyright, 1967, by H. Pinter | (Screenplays) Ltd. | THE BASEMENT – © Copyright, 1967, by H. Pinter Ltd", further copyright and performing rights statements, note on sound effects records.

Contents: [1] title page; [2] as above; 3 contents; [4] fly-title "TEA PARTY"; 5 first American stage performance details, as above; 6 character-list; 7–37 text; 38–42 property-list; 43–45; costume plot; [46] fly-title "THE BASEMENT"; 47 first American stage performance details, as above; 48 character-list; 49–60 text; 61–63 property plot; 64–65 costume plot; 66–68 DPS advertisements for new plays.

Notes: The copy reported is a recent reprint, ISBN 0-8222-1115-7.

A32   NIGHT   1970

a. In Methuen anthology (1970):

Mixed Doubles | AN ENTERTAINMENT ON MARRIAGE BY | *Alan Ayckbourn* | *John Bowen* | *Lyndon Brook* | *David Campton* | *George Melly* | *Alun Owen* | *Harold Pinter* | *James Saunders* | *Fay Weldon* | METHUEN & CO LTD | 11 NEW FETTER LANE • LONDON EC4

90 pp., 2 leaves. 18.5 × 12.4 cm. Hardback, black cloth; lettered down spine, in silver: "MIXED DOUBLES Methuen". Endpapers. Dust jacket in white and blue, with lettering in blue and black; on outside front: within blue border, white, with names of playwrights in blue, at varied angles; on outside back, white, list of playwrights, etc., in black.

Published 1970 (L accession 2 JUL 70). Price net 18s, 90p. On verso of title page leaf: "*First published in 1970 by Methuen and Co Ltd.* | *Printed in Great Britain by* | *Cox & Wyman Ltd, Fakenham, Norfolk* | SBN 416 16169 X", copyright and performing rights statements for each of the plays.

Contents: [1] title page; [2] as above; [3] contents; [4] blank; [5–6] details of presentation; [7] fly-title *"Part One"*; [8] blank; [9]–44 texts of 8 sketches; [45] fly-title *"Part Two"*; [46] blank; [47]–84 texts of 8 sketches; [85] fly-title *"Appendix"*; [86] blank; [87]–90 texts of 2 sketches; [91–94] publisher's lists.

Notes: Pinter's *Night* occupies pp. [41]–44. The account of the production on pp. [5–6] notes that it was first presented at the Hampstead Theatre Club on 6 February 1969, with the title *We Who Are About To . . .*, and in its final version with the new title at the Comedy Theatre on 9 April 1969.

b. In same anthology, British acting edition (1977):

Title page as for above, except imprint: "SAMUEL FRENCH Ltd | LONDON".

2 leaves, 90 pp., 2 leaves. Paperback, white, with lettering, decorative vertical band, and French's device in blue.

Published 1977. On verso of title leaf: "First published in Great Britain | by Methuen & Co Ltd 1970 | This edition reprinted by arrangement | with Eyre Methuen 1977", copyright and performing rights information, "ISBN 0 573 01584 8". *Night* again on pp. [41]–44.

A33   LANDSCAPE AND SILENCE [*without* NIGHT]   1971

American acting edition [1971]:

LANDSCAPE | and | SILENCE | By Harold Pinter | [publisher's device] | SAMUEL FRENCH, INC. | 25 WEST 45TH STREET NEW YORK 10036 | 7623 SUNSET BOULEVARD HOLLYWOOD 90046 LONDON TORONTO

37, [1] pp., 1 leaf. 18.5 cm. Paperback, gold; on front cover: within border formed with groups of three rules, to left and right, of uneven height, ascending inward, and at foot, two rules, thick and thin: *"LANDSCAPE | and | SILENCE | By Harold Pinter | [publisher's device] | Samuel French, Inc. | PRICE, $1.50 | [rule]"*; on inside of front and back covers, and outside of back cover: publisher's advertisements; down spine: "LANDSCAPE and SILENCE".

Published 27 January 1971 (information from publisher). 2000 copies. On verso of title leaf: copyright and performing rights information.

Contents: [1] title page; [2] as above; 3–18 *Landscape* text; 19 property plot; 20 costume plot; 21 scene design; 23–35 *Silence* text; 36 costume plot; 37 scene design; [38]–40 publisher's advertisements.

A34   OLD TIMES   1971

a. First edition (1971):

OLD TIMES | by | HAROLD PINTER | LONDON | METHUEN & CO LTD | 11 NEW FETTER LANE

75 pp., 1 blank leaf. Signed [A]⁸ B-D⁸. 18.4 × 12.2 cm. Hardback, black cloth; down spine, in gold: "Harold Pinter [*star*] OLD TIMES [*star*] Methuen". Endpapers. Dust jacket in blue and white; on outside front, within blue border, in white panel: "[*in blue*:] Harold Pinter | [*in black, rule, 9.9 cm.*] | [*in blue*:] Old Times", below, photo of Deeley, Kate, and Anna; on outside back, within blue border, photo, captioned in blue:"Photograph of Harold Pinter by Antony di Gesù", in blue, 8-line biographical note, rule in black, in blue: "A METHUEN MODERN PLAY"; spine blue: in white, Methuen device, down spine in black: "Pinter • Old Times Methuen"; on front flap, title, brief account of play, "The photograph on the front cover shows | Colin Blakely as Deeley, Dorothy Tutin as | Kate and Vivien Merchant as Anna. It is | reproduced by courtesy of Donald | Cooper. | [*at foot, right*:] PRICE NET | £1.00 | IN U.K. ONLY"; on back flap, list of Methuen's Modern Plays titles.

Published 17 June 1971 (L accession 9 JUL 71; DLC copyright registration 17 June 1971 [DF2089]). 7,000 copies. Price £1.00. On verso of title leaf: "First published 1971 | © 1971 by H. Pinter Limited | All rights reserved | SBN 416 18650 5 | Printed in Great Britain | by Cox & Wyman Ltd | Fakenham, Norfolk", performing rights statement, acknowledgements for extracts from songs.

Contents: [1] half-title "Old Times"; [2] list of titles "*by the same author*"; [3] title page; [4] as above; [5] "To Peter Hall"; [6] details of first presentation, RSC, 1 June 1971, and of set, and of time of acts; 7–75 text; [76–78] blank.

b. Specially bound Karnac issue (1971):

OLD TIMES | by | HAROLD PINTER | LONDON | H. KARNAC (BOOKS) LTD | 56/58 GLOUCESTER ROAD LONDON SW7

75 pp., 2 blank leaves. Hardbound, quarter-bound in black cloth (extending around spine to about 4.7 cm. of the width of each board), remaining two-thirds of boards in orange-vermillion cloth; at the junction, on the black cloth, a thick vertical line in gold; down spine, in gold: "HAROLD PINTER Old Times Karnac". Black endpapers. Glasserine dust jacket.

Contents: As for the Methuen edition, except on p.[1], instead of the half-title: "This limited, specially bound edition | is published by arrangement with Methuen and Co Ltd | and appears simultaneously with their first edition. | One hundred and fifty copies have been | numbered and *signed by the author.* | *This is number"* [A copy owned by William Baker is numbered "87." and signed.].

c. Revised Methuen edition, paperback [1972]:

Title page, etc., as for first Methuen printing. Paperback; as for dust jacket, except at foot of back cover, price.

Published 27 July 1972 (reprinted 1973, 1976, 1977, 1978, 1979, 1981, 1983). 7,500 copies in first printing. Price 50p. On verso of title leaf: copyright statements, "ISBN 0 416 18650 5 (Hardback) | ISBN 0 413 29360 2 (Paperback) | Set, printed and bound in Great Britain by | Fakenham Press Limited, Fakenham, Norfolk", "ACKNOWLEDGEMENTS" for use of extracts from songs.

Notes: Text as for first edition, except on p.73: "He was bemused, aghast, resisted with force."

d. Re-publication of revised edition, Faber (1991):

[*Within single-rule frame:*] HAROLD | PINTER | Old Times | ff | *faber and faber* | LONDON • BOSTON

1 leaf, 75 pp., 1 blank leaf. 19.7 × 12.4 cm. Paperback, standard Faber design; on outside front: "ff | HAROLD | PINTER | [*rule*] | Old Times | [*illustration*]"; outside back: publisher, author, title, brief account of play, "Cover illustration by Andrzej Klimowski | UK £4.99 net | Canada $12.95 | ISBN 0-571-16081-6 | [*bar-code*] | 9 780571 160815"; on spine: "ff | [*rule*] | [*down spine:*] HAROLD PINTER Old Times".

Published 1991 (L accession 4 FEB 1991). Price £4.99. 5,085 copies printed. On verso of title leaf: "First published in this edition in 1971 [*sic, for 1991*] | by Faber and Faber Limited | [. . .] | Reprinted in England by Clays Ltd, St Ives plc", statements re: copyright, performing rights, acknowledgements for songs, conditions of sale, "ISBN 0-571-16081-6".

Contents: As for first Methuen, except, on p. [5], details of first presentations include those for the television production, in October 1975, and at the Theatre Royal, Haymarket, April 1985; consequently, the set-description is displaced to p. [6].

e. American Book Club edition, large print [1971?]:

OLD TIMES | by | Harold Pinter | GROVE PRESS, INC. | NEW YORK

1 leaf, 82 pp. Hardback, black cloth; down spine in gold: "Harold Pinter OLD TIMES GROVE PRESS". Endpapers. Dust jacket not seen.

Published 1971 (?). Verso of title leaf: as for standard edition, except Library of Congress catalogue, edition, and printing data not present.

Contents: [i] half-title; [ii] blank; [1] title page; [2] as above; [3] "To Peter Hall"; [4] blank; [5] acknowledgements, for songs; [6] blank; [7] fly-title; [8] blank; [9] first British performance details; [10] blank; [11] set, time of action; [12] blank; [13] "ACT ONE"; [14] blank; [15]–48 text, Act One; [49] "ACT TWO"; [50] blank; [51]–82 text, Act Two.

Notes: Text in larger font and more widely spaced than for the standard edition (with dust jacket not seen, no indication this is the book club edition, but presumed to be).

f¹. American standard edition (1971):

Title page as for large print edition, but smaller font-sizes for first three lines, larger for imprint.

1 leaf, 75 pp. 18.3 × 12.6 cm. Hardback, black cloth; down spine, in silver: "Harold Pinter OLD TIMES GROVE PRESS". Endpapers. Dust jacket: on outside front, dark yellow: "[*rule*] | [*in white:*] Old Times a play by Harold Pinter | [*inverted commas in white, rest in black:*] "The finest play of a master dramatist" | [*rule, 19 cm.*] Clive Barnes, *The New York Times* [*rule, 19 cm.*] | [*tinted photo, unframed, of Kate, Deeley and Anna*]"; outside back dark yellow, with photo of Pinter; spine pale yellow, down spine: "[*in black:*] Old Times [*in white:*] by Harold Pinter [*across spine, in black:*] GROVE | PRESS"; on front and back flaps, accounts of the play and of Pinter, divided by white rules.

Published 1971. Price hardback $4.50, paperback $1.95. On verso of title leaf: "Copyright © 1971 by Harold Pinter Limited | All Rights Reserved | Originally published by Methuen & Co Ltd, London, England | [*further copyright and performing rights statements*] | Library of Congress Catalog Card Number: 72-182581 | First Grove Press Edition, 1971 | First Printing | Manufactured in the United States of America".

Contents: [i] half-title; [ii] list of Grove's Pinter titles; [1] title page; [2] as above; [3] "To Peter Hall"; [4] acknowledgements, for songs; [5] first British performance details; [6] set, time of action; [7]–75 text; [76] blank.

Notes: According to Dace, the first paperback issue of this edition was in the Black Cat series, B-354, at $1.95. Not seen. Dace notes this edition was probably offset from the Methuen edition.

f³. American reprint, Evergreen Press (1973)

OLD TIMES | by | Harold Pinter | GROVE PRESS, INC. | NEW YORK

1 blank leaf, 1 leaf, 75 pp., 1 leaf. 20.4 × 12.9 cm. Paperback, blue-mauve; on front cover: "[*in pink, rule, 11.4 cm.*] | [*in white:*] Old Times a play by Harold Pinter | [*in black:*] "The finest play of a master dramatist" | [*in pink, rule, 2.4 cm.*] [*in black:*] Clive Barnes, *The New York Times* [*in pink, rule, 2.4 cm.*] | [*unframed*

photo, with Kate tinted pink, Deeley, standing behind, untinted, Anna tinted blue] | [*at lower left, lettered upward, in black:*] [*small publisher's device*] EVER-GREEN E-606 $1.95"; on back cover: lettering in black, rules, 10 cm., in pink: "AN EVERGREEN BOOK (E-606) $1.95 | *Old Times* is Harold Pinter's first full-length | play since *The Homecoming* | [*rule*] | [*paragraph about the play*] | [*rule*] | [*quoted passage, about the play*] | [*rule*] | [*paragraph about Pinter*] | [*rule*] | 394-17761-4"; down spine: "[*in black:*] OLD TIMES [*in white:*] BY HAROLD PINTER [*in black:*] [*small publisher's device*] E-606 GROVE PRESS".

Published 1973. Price $1.95. On verso of title leaf: as above, but "First Grove Press Edition, 1971" followed by: "First Evergreen Edition 1973 | First Printing | Manufactured in the United States of America | Distributed by Random House, Inc., New York".

Contents: As for first edition, but in the fifth printing, p.[76] is not blank, bears a selected list of titles.

Notes: The fifth printing has additionally on the verso of the title leaf: "ISBN: 0-394-17761-4 | Grove Press ISBN: 0-8021-4143-9".

g. Evergreen paperback, second edition [n.d.]:

OLD TIMES | by | Harold Pinter | [*publisher's device*] | GROVE PRESS | NEW YORK

75 pp. 20.4 × 12.1 cm. Paperback; front cover silver, with four horizontal black bands, with lettering mainly within the bands, mainly in silver, as reversed out of black: "HAROLD [*with A in red*] | PINTER [*with T in red*] | [*in red:*] "The finest play of a master dramatist" – Clive Barnes, *The New York Times* | OLD | TIMES [*with T in red*]"; on outside back, mainly silver, with lettering in red, but with a black band, within which lettering is in white, lettering providing information and critical comments about the play and its author; with below, at left, "Cover design by Rick Pracher | Grove Press | 841 Broadway | New York, NY 10003 | Printed in the USA 11930795", and at right, within white panel, in black, bar-code and numerals "9 780802 150295 [*above, right:*] 9000 | [*below:*] ISBN 0-8021-5029-2"; spine black, down spine in white: "HAROLD PINTER OLD TIMES GROVE PRESS".

Notes: Generally, this edition appears to be of the same typesetting as before, but with the point-size increased.

h. American anthology (extracts) (1972):

[*3 lines within frame of small circles:*] THE | BEST PLAYS | OF 1971–1972 | [*below frame:*] EDITED BY OTIS L. GUERNSEY JR. | *Illustrated with photographs and* | *with drawings by* HIRSCHFELD | [*line of 6 small circles*] | DODD, MEAD & COMPANY | NEW YORK • TORONTO

23.2 × 15.3 cm. On the verso facing the title page: "THE | BURNS MANTLE | YEARBOOK". *Old Times*, in the form of extracts introduced and interspersed with passages of description and plot-summary, and preceded by an account of Pinter, occupies pp. [221]–231; on p.324, details of the first American production.

A35 MONOLOGUE 1973

a¹. First edition, standard issue (1973):

monologue | harold pinter

12 leaves, unpaginated. 20.1 × 13.4 cm. Hardback, chrome-yellow cloth; on front cover, in gold: single-rule border, within it: "[*at upper right:*] monologue | [*in centre, stamped, unframed illustration of seated figure facing empty chair*] | [*at bottom right:*] harold pinter"; back cover blank; down spine, in gold: "MONOLOGUE HAROLD PINTER". Endpapers. Dust jacket mid-brown; on outside front and spine, lettering and decoration as for binding, except in dark brown; on front flap, title, note on the play.

Published 1973 (L accession 2 FEB 74). 1,900 standard-edition copies at £1.75; 100 limited-edition copies at £15.50 (see below). On verso of title leaf: "First published in 1973 | by Covent Garden Press Limited | 80 Long Acre London WC2E 9NG | © H Pinter Ltd, 1973 | Printed and made in Great Britain".

Contents: [1] half-title "monologue"; [2] blank; [3] title page; [4] as above; [5] "To Daniel"; [6] blank; [7] "Man alone in a chair. | He refers to another chair, which is empty."; [8] blank; [9–19] text; [20] blank; [21] "Monologue was produced by BBC Television in April 1973, | directed by Christopher Morahan and played by Henry Woolf. | Designed by Peter Juerges | Published and Printed by | Covent Garden Press Limited | 80 Long Acre London WC2E 9NG" [*to left of imprint, publisher's device*: "CGP"]; [22–24] blank.

a². Limited edition (1973):

Title page and text as for standard edition, but printed in dark brown ink on light brown paper, on folded leaves, so that each recto and verso are on two conjunct leaves, with the fold at the outer edge. Following p. [20] there is an additional pair of folded leaves, with, on the recto of the first: "This edition consists of 100 copies | signed and numbered by the author. | Bound in quality calfskin with slipcase. | Printed on Strathmore Artlaid 120gsm. | Typeset in 11pt Press Roman. | This is number................." [A copy owned by William Baker has the number in ink "71", and below it the holograph signature "Harold Pinter".] The corresponding verso is blank. The following recto is as for the ordinary edition, p. [21], with the verso blank. The binding is in tan calfskin, with the front cover and spine ruled, decorated and lettered as for the ordinary copies, but in dark brown (back cover blank). The slip-case is covered in pale chrome-yellow cloth.

A36   NO MAN'S LAND   1975

a. First edition (1975):

No Man's Land | by | Harold Pinter | [*small device*] | EYRE METHUEN | LONDON

95, [1] pp. 18.6 × 12.2 cm. Hardback, black cloth; down spine in silver: "Harold Pinter [*star*] NO MAN'S LAND [*star*] Eyre Methuen". Endpapers. Dust jacket in blue and white; on outside front: within blue border, large white panel: "[*in blue:*] Harold Pinter | [*in black, rule, 9.9 cm.*] | [*in blue, 3 lines in open, shadowed letters:*] NO | MAN'S | LAND"; on outside back, within blue border, photo of Pinter, captioned, in blue: "Photograph of Harold Pinter by Antony di Gesú", in blue, 9-line biographical note, rule in black, in blue: "A METHUEN MODERN PLAY"; spine blue, on spine, in white, publisher's device, down spine, in black: "Pinter • No Man's Land Eyre Methuen"; on inside flap, author, title, account of play, at foot: "PRICE NET | £2.00 | IN U.K. ONLY"; on back flap, list of other Methuen Modern Plays titles.

Published 3 April 1975. 6,000 copies. Price £2.00. On verso of title leaf: "*First published 1975 by Eyre Methuen Ltd | 11 New Fetter Lane, London EC4P 4EE | Copyright © 1975 by H. Pinter Limited | Printed in Great Britain by | Cox & Wyman Ltd, Fakenham, Norfolk | ISBN 0 413 34220 4*", performing rights statement.

Contents: [1] half-title; [2] "*by the same author*", lists 14 titles; [3] title page; [4] as above; [5] "To Jimmy Wax"; [6] blank; [7] cast details, etc., for first performance, 23 April 1975; [8] blank; [9] brief description of set; [10] blank; [11] "Act One"; [12] blank; [13] Summer. | Night."; [14] blank; [15]–53 text of Act One; [54] blank; [55] "Act Two"; [56] blank; [57] "Morning"; [58] blank; [59]–95 text of Act Two; [96] publisher's notice.

Note one: Peter Hall, at that time the artistic director at the National Theatre, recorded in his diary for 11 September 1974 that Pinter rang him to say he had finished writing the play, and on 13 September he first read it with surprise and enthusiasm, planning to direct it himself. Rehearsals began on 10 February 1975, with John Gielgud and Ralph Richardson in the lead-roles. On 3 April, Pinter invited the associates to consider one of Spooner's lines: "The present is truly unscrupulous. I am a poet. I am interested in where I am eternally present and active." Pinter responded to their disquiet with "unscrupulous", but it was not till a breakfast with Hall on 8 April that "after interminable conversation we came up with the line 'The present will not be distorted'" (*The Peter Hall Diaries*

[London: Hamish Hamilton, 1983], pp. 118, 147, 156–57). On 5 November 1976, Hall flew to Washington to work on the production before it re-opened in the USA at the Eisenhower Theater 10 November (Hall 268–69). On 19 January 1978, he commenced work on the television production, which Pinter decided to keep uncut, with "the bad language" retained, and Granada Television supported this decision (Hall 332–33).

Note two: On the outside back of the dust jacket, in copies seen, the name "Gesu" is spelled with an acute accent rather than the grave accent which is used in the standard form of the name.

b. Specially bound Karnac issue (1975):

No Man's Land | by | Harold Pinter | H. KARNAC (BOOKS) LTD | 56/58 GLOUCESTER ROAD LONDON SW7 4QY

95, [1] pp. 18.5 cm. Binding as for Karnac *Old Times*, except, on spine: "HAROLD PINTER No Man's Land Karnac".

Contents: As for Eyre Methuen first, except, on p.[1], instead of half-title: "*This limited, specially bound edition | is published by arrangement with Eyre Methuen Ltd | and appears simultaneously with their first edition. | One hundred and fifty copies have been | numbered and signed by the author. | This is number*" [A copy owned by William Baker is numbered "49." and signed].

Notes: A copy of this first edition, inscribed to Ralph Richardson by Harold Pinter ("with deep gratitude and admiration") and dated for the opening night of the first production in London, "April 23.75", was listed for sale as item 98 in Bernard Quaritch Ltd's catalogue no. 1296 (2002), for £1250.

c. Revised edition, paperback (1975):

No Man's Land | by | Harold Pinter | [*small publisher's device*] | EYRE METHUEN | LONDON

95, [1] pp. 18.7 × 12.0 cm. Paperback; on front cover, within thick blue border, panel in white, lettering in blue: "Harold Pinter | [*rule in black, 9.8 cm.*] | No Man's Land", below panel, photo; on back cover, thick blue border, photo of Pinter, below it, within a white panel, with lettering in blue: "[*brief account of Pinter's life and career, 9 lines*] | [*rule in black, 9.3 cm.*] | A METHUEN MODERN PLAY 80p net in U.K. only"; spine blue: "[*publisher's device*] | [*down spine:*] Pinter • No Man's Land Eyre Methuen".

Published 1975. Price 80p. On verso of title leaf: copyright statement, "*First printed in 1975 by Eyre Methuen Ltd | [. . . .] | Revised paperback edition 1975 | Printed in Great Britain by | Cox & Wyman Ltd, Fakenham, Norfolk | ISBN 0 413 34640 4 (Paperback)*", performing rights and conditions of sale statements.

Contents: [1] half-title, 8-line account of play, three brief passages from critiques, at foot: "*The photograph on the front cover shows John Gielgud and Ralph | Richardson in the National Theatre production, directed by Peter | Hall. The photo is by Anthony Crickmay and is reproduced with | permission. The photograph of Harold Pinter on the back cover is | by Tony McGrath and is reproduced by courtesy of* The Observer."; [2] list of works "*by the same author*", 10 titles; [3] title page, as for first; [4] as above; [5–6] as for first; [7] details of first presentation, as for first, but adding: "The play was subsequently presented at Wyndham's Theatre, | London, from 15 July 1975, with the same cast."; [8]–[96] as for first Methuen.

Notes: Revised text on pp. 20, 30, 33, 76, and 79 (Dace). Reprinted 1977 and 1979; reprinted 1984 by Methuen London Ltd; reprinted 1988 by Methuen Drama. Price in 1988: £4.50.

d. *Faber (1991):*

[*Within single-rule frame:*] HAROLD PINTER | No Man's Land | ff | *faber and faber* | LONDON • BOSTON

95 pp. 19.8 × 12.5 cm. Paperback, standard Faber design; on front cover: "ff | [*rule*] | HAROLD | PINTER | [*rule*] | No Man's Land | [*illustration*]; on back cover: publisher, author, title, account of play, "Cover illustration by Andrzej Klimowski | UK £4.99 | US $9.95 | ISBN 0-571-16088-3 | [*bar-code*] | 9 780571 160884"; down spine: "HAROLD PINTER No Man's Land".

Published 8 July 1991 (L accession 21 MAY 91). On verso of title leaf: "First published in this edition 1991 | [. . .] | Printed by Clays Ltd, St Ives plc", copyright, performing rights, conditions of sale statements, "ISBN 0-571-16088-3".

Notes: The text pages are as for Methuen's *Plays 4* (See I1a(iv)). Faber and Faber report (1.8.2001) reprintings on 13 November 1992, 1 March 1993, 19 January 1994, 24 March 1998, totalling 9,646 copies printed.

e¹. *American standard edition (1975):*

NO MAN'S LAND | by Harold Pinter | GROVE PRESS, INC., NEW YORK

95, [1] pp., 1 blank leaf. 21.1 × 13.2 cm. (hardback), 20.2 × 12.9 cm. (paperback). Binding: (A) Hardback, black cloth; down spine in gold: "Harold Pinter NO MAN'S LAND GROVE PRESS". Dust jacket blue: on outside front: to left, 3 lines, in white: "No | Man's | Land", to right, 4 lines, in yellow: "A | Play | by | Harold | Pinter", photo; outside back: photo, captioned "*Harold Pinter*", at foot, in white: "GROVE PRESS, INC., 53 East 11th Street, New York, N.Y. 10003 0-394-49931-X"; down spine: "[*in white:*] NO MAN'S LAND [*in yellow:*] HAROLD PINTER [*at foot, across spine, in white:*] [*publisher's device*] |

GP-769 | GROVE | PRESS"; on front flap: "[*at top right:*] GP-768 $6.95 | [*to left, in 3 lines:*] No | Man's | Land | [*to right, in 4 lines, in dark blue:*] A | Play by | Harold | Pinter | [*centred:*] [*rule, dark blue*] | [*account of play, in black*] | [*rule, dark blue*]"; on back flap: "[*rule, dark blue*] | [*continuation of account of play*] | [*rule, dark blue*] | [*brief account of Pinter*] | [*rule, dark blue*] | Cover Photo: Anthony Crickmay | Design: Kenneth R. Deardoff".

(B) Paperback, turquoise on outside front and spine, white on back; on front cover, to left, 3 lines in white: "No | Man's | Land", to right, 4 lines in orange: "A | Play by | Harold | Pinter", photo, below it, at left foot, in white: "[*small publisher's device*] EVERGREEN E-663 $1.95"; on back cover: "[*in black:*] AN EVERGREEN BOOK (E-663) $1.95 | [*title in black and in turquoise*] | [*in turquoise, rule*] | [*in black, two paragraphs about the play*] | [*in turquoise, rule*] | [*in black, paragraph about Pinter*] | [*in turquoise, rule*] | [*in black:*] GROVE PRESS, INC., 53 East 11th Street, New York, N.Y. 10003 0-394-17885-8"; down spine: "[*in white:*] NO MAN'S LAND [*in orange:*] HAROLD PINTER [*in white:*] [*small publisher's device*] E-663 GROVE PRESS".

Published 22 September 1975. Price $6.95 (hardback), $1.95 (paperback). On verso of title leaf: (a) hardback: copyright and performing rights statements, "ISBN: 0-394-49931-X | Grove Press ISBN: 0-8021-0101-1 | Library of Congress Catalog Card Number: 75-13555 | First Printing | Manufactured in the United States of America | Distributed by Random House, Inc., New York | GROVE PRESS, INC., 53 East 11th Street, N.Y., N.Y. 10003"; (b) paperback: copyright and performing rights statements, "ISBN 0-394-17885-8 | Grove Press ISBN: 0-8021-0102-X", otherwise as for hardback, but adds in new line above "First Printing", "First Evergreen Edition".

Contents: [1] half-title; [2] list of 10 Pinter titles; [3] title page; [4] as above; [5] "To Jimmy Wax"; [6] blank; [7] first presentation details; [8] blank; [9] description of set; [10] blank; [11] "Act One"; [12] blank; [13] "Summer. | Night."; [14] blank; [15]–95 text; [96] selected list of Grove titles; [97–98] blank.

e^2. *Fifth printing (Grove Weidenfeld):*

Title page as for first Grove printing, except imprint: "[*publisher's device*] | GROVE WEIDENFELD | NEW YORK".

95 pp., 1 blank leaf. 20.7 × 13.1 cm. Paperback, as for first Evergreen, except: front cover as for hardback dust jacket; on back cover, price as $8.95, at foot, publisher as Grove Weidenfeld, two bar-codes, with ISBN as 0-8021-5187-6; spine as for dust jacket, except, at foot, down spine, publisher as "GROVE WEIDENFELD".

On verso of title leaf: numerals "10 9 8 7 6 5" identify copy as of fifth printing; publisher as Grove Weidenfeld, ISBN as 0-8021-5187-6 (pbk).

f. American book club edition [1975?]:

Title page as for standard edition, but in smaller and different-face fonts.

5 leaves, 86 pp. Hardback, yellow cloth, lettered down spine as for standard edition, in blue. Endpapers. Dust jacket not seen.

Published [1975?]. On verso of title leaf: copyright and performing rights statements, "Manufactured in the United States of America | GROVE PRESS, INC., 53 East 11th Street, N.Y., N.Y. 10003". Text in smaller font.

g. German educational edition (1977):

DIESTERWEGS NEUSPRACHLICHE BIBLIOTHEK | No Man's Land | by | HAROLD PINTER | Edited and annotated | by | FRANK D. GILLAND | VERLAG MORITZ DIESTERWEG | [*at left:*] 4024 [*centred:*] Frankfurt am Main • Berlin • München

ISBN 3-425-04024-3. Text occupies pp. 13–49.

A37   BETRAYAL   1978

a. First edition (1978):

Betrayal | by | Harold Pinter | [*small publisher's device*] | EYRE METHUEN | LONDON

138 pp., 1 blank leaf, 2 leaves. 18.6 × 12.1 cm. Hardback, black cloth; down spine in silver: "Harold Pinter [*star device*] BETRAYAL [*star device*] Eyre Methuen". Dust jacket blue, with large white panels, flaps white; on outside front: blue border, white panel: "[*in blue:*] Harold Pinter | [*rule, in black*] | Betrayal"; on outside back: blue border, photo of Pinter, below it in white panel, in blue, 9-line biographical note, rule in black, "A METHUEN MODERN PLAY"; on spine: in white, publisher's device, down spine in black: "Pinter • Betrayal Eyre Methuen"; on front flap, lettering mainly in blue, rule in black: "HAROLD PINTER | [*rule*] | BETRAYAL | [*note on play*] | [*at foot, left, in black:*] 0 413 39620 7 [*at foot, right, in black:*] PRICE NET | £3.50 | IN U.K. ONLY"; on back flap: "[*2 lines in blue:*] METHUEN'S MODERN PLAYS | include | [*in black, selected list*] | [*in blue:*] PRINTED IN GREAT BRITAIN".

Published 16 November 1978. On verso of title page: "*First published 1978 by Eyre Methuen Ltd | 11 New Fetter Lane, London EC4P 4EE | Copyright © 1978 by H. Pinter Limited | Printed in Great Britain by | Cox & Wyman Ltd, Fakenham, Norfolk | ISBN 0 413 39620 7*", performing rights statement.

Contents: [1] half-title "Betrayal"; [2] list of titles "*by the same author*"; [3] title page; [4] as above; [5] "To Simon Gray"; [6] blank; [7] characters list, with ages in 1977; [8] cast details, etc., for first performance, 15

November 1978, with note below: "*Betrayal* can be performed without an interval, or with an interval after Scene Four."; [9] fly-title "1977"; [10] blank; [11]–138 text [each of the nine scenes is preceded by a leaf with the date on the recto, and the verso blank]; [139–140] blank; [141–143] Methuen's advertisements; [144] blank.

Notes: Pinter delivered the completed play to Hall on 27 January 1978, rehearsals began on 3 October, and it opened on 15 November in the midst of threats of strikes by the stage staff (Hall, pp. 334, 378, 390–91). On 15 November 1979, Hall began working in New York with an American cast on a production which opened on 5 January 1980 (Hall, pp. 473, 481).

b. Specially bound Karnac edition (1978):

Betrayal | Harold Pinter | H. KARNAC (BOOKS) LTD | 56/58 GLOUCESTER ROAD LONDON SW7 4QY

Binding as for Karnac *Old Times,* except down spine: "HAROLD PINTER Betrayal Karnac".

Contents: As for Eyre Methuen edition, except on p.[1]: "*This limited, specially bound edition* | *is published by arrangement with Eyre Methuen Ltd* | *and appears simultaneously with their first edition.* | *One hundred and fifty copies have been numbered and signed by the author.* | *This is number*" [A copy owned by William Baker is numbered "147." and signed].

Notes: A "Hors de commercé" copy inscribed by Harold Pinter, to the actor Ralph Richardson, "To Ralph with my love, Harold", was listed for sale as item 99 in Bernard Quaritch Ltd's catalogue no. 1296 (2002), for £400.

c¹. Revised paperback edition (1980):

Betrayal | by | Harold Pinter | [*small publisher's device*] | EYRE METHUEN | LONDON

138 pp., 3 leaves. 18.6 × 12 cm. Paperback, blue and white; on front cover, within blue border, white panel: "[*in blue:*] Harold Pinter | [*in black, rule, 9.9 cm.*] | [*in blue:*] Betrayal | [*photo of Emma, with a male hand holding her elbow*]"; on back cover, within blue border, photo of Pinter, below it, in blue, 8-line biographical note, "A METHUEN MODERN PLAY price net £1.95 in U.K. only | 0 413 47070 9"; on spine, in white, Methuen device, down spine in black: "Pinter • Betrayal Eyre Methuen".

Published 1980. Price £1.95. On verso of title leaf: "*First published 1978* . . . | *Revised paperback edition first published in 1980*", copyright information, "*Set, printed and bound in Great Britain by* | *Fakenham Press Limited, Fakenham, Norfolk* | ISBN 0 413 47070 9", performing rights statement.

Contents: [1] title, extracts from three critiques, "*The photo on the front cover, showing Penelope Wilton as Emma | in the National Theatre production, is by Sally Fear.*"; [2] list of Pinter titles; [3] title page; [4] as above; [5]–138 as for first edition; [139–143] Methuen's title lists; [144] blank.

c². Reprint (1986):

Harold Pinter | BETRAYAL | METHUEN • LONDON

138 pp., 3 leaves. 18.5 × 11.8 cm. Paperback; on front cover, photo, blue-tinted, with at upper left, within blue frame, a white panel: "[*2 words in black:*] Harold | Pinter | [*in blue:*] Betrayal"; on back cover, within a blue frame, photo of Pinter, below, title of play, brief account of play, at foot, to left: "ISBN 0-413-47070-9 | [*bar-code*] | 9 780413 470706", to right "PRICE NET | £3.95 | IN U K ONLY | A METHUEN PAPERBACK | MODERN PLAYS".

Reprint of 1986 (L accession 26 AUG 87). On verso of title leaf: "*First published in 1978 by Eyre Methuen Ltd | 11 New Fetter Lane, London EC4P 4EE | Revised paperback edition first published in 1980 | Reprinted 1984, 1986 by Methuen London Ltd | © 1978, 1980 by H. Pinter Limited | ISBN 0 413 47070 9 | [copyright and performing rights statements] | Printed in Great Britain by | Richard Clay (The Chaucer Press) Ltd | Bungay, Suffolk*".

Contents: [1] as for 1980, but adds: "*The photo of Harold Pinter on the back cover is by Ivan | Kyncl.*"; [2] list of Pinter titles; [3] title page; [4] as above; [5]–[144] as for 1980.

d. Faber edition (1991):

[*All within single-rule frame:*] HAROLD | PINTER | Betrayal | ff | *faber and faber* | LONDON • BOSTON

138 pp., 3 blank leaves. 19.7 × 12.5 cm. Paperback, white, standard Faber design; on front cover: "ff | [*rule*] | HAROLD PINTER | [*rule*] | Betrayal | [*illustration: two spread hands touching*]"; on back cover: "ff | *faber and faber* | [*rule*] | HAROLD PINTER | Betrayal | [*brief account of play*] | Cover illustration by Andrzej Klimowski | UK £5.99 net Canada $14.95 | ISBN 0-571-16082-4 | [*bar-code*] | 9 780571 16082"; on spine: "ff | [*rule*] | [*down spine:*] HAROLD PINTER Betrayal".

Published 21 January 1991 (L accession 8 FEB 91). Price £5.99. 17,849 copies printed. On verso of title leaf: publication information, "Printed in England by Clays Ltd, St Ives plc", copyright, performing rights and conditions of sale statements, "ISBN 0-571-16082-4".

Contents: As for Methuen, with appropriate variation in the preliminaries.

e¹. American edition (1979):

HAROLD PINTER | [*graphic font*] BETRAYAL | GROVE PRESS, INC. | NEW YORK

138 pp., 3 leaves. 20.3 × 13.0 cm. (paperback). Hardback not seen. Paperback, glossy white; on front cover: within a single-rule border, with rules over-running, and dots, at corners: "[*in black:*] Betrayal | [*in open letters, in black:*] a play by | [*2 lines in red:*] Harold | Pinter | [*at lower right, within border, in black:*] [*publisher's device*] | E-724 | $3.95"; on back cover, within same style of border, in black, 4 paragraphs about Pinter and this play, at lower left: "Cover design: Charlotte Staub | GROVE PRESS, INC. | 196 West Houston St. | New York, N.Y. 10014", at lower right: "[*in red, small publisher's device*] | [*2 lines in black:*] E-724 | $3.95", below border, to right, in black: "0-394-17084-9"; on spine: "[*in red:*] [*small publisher's device*] | [*2 lines in black:*] GROVE | PRESS | [*down spine:*] [*in black:*] Betrayal [*in red:*] Harold Pinter [*across spine, at foot, in black:*] E-724".

Published late 1979 (listed in *Publishers Weekly*, 22 January 1980, p.118, in Grove Press "Spring List": Cloth $7.95 | 0-394-50525-5; Evergreen paperbound $2.95 | 0-394-17084-9). Copy seen: Second Printing, 1980. Price $3.95. On verso of title leaf (in copy seen): copyright and performing rights statements, "First Edition 1979 | Second Printing, 1980 | ISBN: 0-394-50525-5 | Grove Press ISBN: 0-8021-0175-5 | Library of Congress Catalog Card Number: 78-65251 | First Evergreen Edition 1979 | First Printing 1979 | ISBN: 0-394-17084-9 | Grove Press ISBN: 0-8021-4236-2", same LC number, etc.

Contents: [1] half-title; [2] Grove's other Pinter titles (paperback); [3] title page; [4] as above; [5]–138 as for British edition; [139–144] Grove Press title list.

e². Sixteenth printing [post-1998]:

HAROLD PINTER | BETRAYAL | [*Grove device*] GROVE PRESS | NEW YORK

138 pp., 4 blank leaves. 20.3 × 13.7 cm. Paperback, binding similar, except: on outside front, Evergreen number and price not present; on outside back, at top right: "$12.50"; at foot, left: "Grove Press books are | distributed by Publishers | Group West | Cover design: Charlotte Staub | [*publisher's device, in red, to right of it, in black, in 2 lines:*] PUBLISHED BY | GROVE PRESS"; at foot, right: "[*bar-code*] | 9 780802 30808 | ISBN 0-8021-3080-1", to right, second bar-code, with above, "1250"; down spine: "[*in black:*] BETRAYAL [*in red:*] Harold Pinter [*across spine, in red, publisher's device*] [*down spine, in black:*] GROVE PRESS".

Published post-1998. On verso of title leaf: copyright, restriction and performing rights statements, "*Printed in the United States of America*", cataloging data, "Grove Press | 841 Broadway | 00 01 02 03 20 19 18 17 16".

f. Book club edition [1979?]:

Title page as for standard edition.

3 leaves, 119 pp., 2 blank leaves. 20.7 × 13.7 cm. Hardback, red cloth; down spine in black: "HAROLD PINTER [*in graphic font*] BETRAYAL [*across spine:*] GROVE | PRESS". Dust jacket not seen.

On verso of title leaf: copyright (1978), reproduction restriction and performing rights statements, "Printed in the United States of America".

Contents: [i] half-title; [ii] blank; [iii] title page; [iv] as above; [v] "To Simon Gray"; [vi] blank; [1] character-list; [2] first performance details, and note signed "H.P."; [3] fly-title for first scene "1977"; [4]–119 text; [120–124] blank.

g. American acting edition [1980]:

[*To left, 7 vertical thick rules*] | BETRAYAL | BY HAROLD PINTER | [*star*] | [*7 horizontal thick rules*] | [*star*] | DRAMATISTS | PLAY SERVICE | INC. | [*to right, 7 vertical thick rules*]

41, [1] pp., 3 leaves. 18.2 × 8.7 cm. Paperback, stapled, light blue; on front cover, as for title page, except 8 rules in each position; on back cover, with wavy borders above and below, list of 12 new titles; down spine: "BETRAYAL—PINTER"; on insides of front and back covers, information about Dramatists Play Service, and DPS advertisements.

Published 1 April 1980 (date from DLC copyright registration, 8 April 1980 [PA-64–262]; claimant Neabar Investments, Ltd.). On verso of title leaf: "© COPYRIGHT, 1980, BY| NEABAR INVESTMENTS LIMITED (REVISED) | © COPYRIGHT, 1978, BY H. PINTER LIMITED", copyright and performing rights statements.

Contents: [1] title page; [2] as above; [3] "TO SIMON GRAY"; [4] list of characters; [5] details of first British and American performances, also list of scenes, with note signed "H.P."; [6] blank; 7–40 text; 41 property plot; [42]–[48] DPS advertisements.

h. American anthology (extracts) (1980):

[*3 lines within frame of small circles:*] THE | BEST PLAYS | OF 1979–1980 | [*below frame:*] EDITED BY OTIS L. GUERNSEY JR. | *Illustrated with photographs and* | *with drawings by* HIRSCHFELD | [*line of 6 small circles*] | DODD, MEAD & COMPANY | NEW YORK • TORONTO

23.2 × 15 cm. On verso facing title page: "THE | BURNS MANTLE | YEAR-BOOK". *Betrayal,* in the form of extracts of text introduced by and interspersed with passages of description and plot summary and with an initial account of Pinter, occupies pp. [153]–163; on pp. 378–379, details of the first American production, Trafalgar Theatre, opened 5 January 1980.

A38   THE EXAMINATION   1979

In anthology (1979):

Ambiance | Almost Free Playscripts 3 | TEN OF THE BEST | BRITISH SHORT PLAYS | Edited by Ed Berman | Inter-Action Imprint | London 1979

xv, 209 pp. "The Examination" occupies pp. 200–205, with an introductory note on p.199, and a production photo of Derek Godfrey as performer.

Published 1979. On verso of title leaf: copyright details, "ISBN 0 904571 16 5 Hardback | ISBN 0 904571 17 3 Paperback | Typeset by T & R Filmsetters Limited, | 77 Salisbury Road, London NW6 6NH | Printed and bound by Billing & Sons Limited | Walnut Tree Close, Guildford, Surrey, U. K."

Notes: On p.199: "The first stage presentation of *The Examination* was at the Ambiance Lunch-Hour Theatre Club at the Almost Free Theatre, London W1, on the 12 March 1978, spoken by: Derek Godfrey. An Inter-Action Production designed by Norman Coates and directed by Jack Emery". Berman's introduction to the volume mentions a policy of "finding pieces of writing that have never been done as plays and making them work on stage. . . . Pinter's remarkable short story . . . when spoken on stage directly, without pauses except for breathing, . . . produced an electric shock during our Rights and Campaigns season in 1978" (xiii).

A39   THE HOTHOUSE   1980

a. First British edition (1980):

The Hothouse | by | Harold Pinter | [*small publisher's device*] | EYRE METHUEN | LONDON

154 pp., 3 leaves. 18.6 × 12.3 cm. Hardback, black cloth; down spine in silver: "Harold Pinter [*star*] THE HOTHOUSE [*star*] Eyre Methuen". Endpapers. Dust jacket blue and white, with flaps white; on outside front: within blue border, large white panel, within panel: "[*in blue:*] Harold Pinter | [*in black, thin rule, 10 cm.*] | [*in blue:*] The Hothouse"; on outside back, photo of Pinter, below, in white panel, in blue, 9-line biographical note, "A METHUEN MODERN PLAY"; on spine, in white, Methuen device, lettered down spine in black: "Pinter • The Hothouse Eyre Methuen"; on front flap: in blue, author's name, title; in black, notes about the play, at foot, left, ISBN number "0 413 47120 9", at right: "PRICE NET | £3.95 | IN U.K. ONLY"; on back flap, list of Methuen's Modern Plays titles, "PRINTED IN GREAT BRITAIN".

Published 24 April 1980. On verso of title leaf: publication and copyright state-
ments, "*Set, printed and bound in Great Britain by* | *Fakenham Press Limited,
Fakenham, Norfolk* | ISBN 0 413 47120 9", performing rights statement.

Contents: [1] half-title; [2] list of Pinter titles; [3] title page; [4] as above; [5] "To
Henry Woolf"; [6] "Author's Note | I wrote *The Hothouse* in the
winter of 1958. I put it aside for | further deliberation and made no
attempt to have it produced | at the time. I then went on to write *The
Caretaker.* | In 1979 I re-read *The Hothouse* and decided it was worth
| presenting on the stage. I made a few cuts but no changes. |
HAROLD PINTER"; [7] character-list; [8] first performance details;
[9] locations-list; [10] blank; [11] "Act One"; [12] blank; [13]–154
text; [155–160] Methuen title lists, and notice.

Notes: As written in 1958, this was originally conceived of as a radio play. It
drew its initial idea from Pinter's experience as a voluntary subject ("guinea-
pig") for a psychological research experiment in the Maudsley Hospital in
London in 1954, when he needed the small fee that was paid (Billington 102).
The episode in which Lamb is interrogated by Miss Cutts would give rise to the
sketch *The Applicant.*

b. Revised paperback edition (1982):

The Hothouse | by | Harold Pinter | METHUEN • LONDON

154 pp., 3 leaves. 18.6 × 11.9 cm. Paperback, blue and white; on front cover,
within blue border, in white panel: [*in blue:*] Harold Pinter | [*in black, rule, 8.4
cm.*] | [*in blue:*] The Hothouse | [*photo of Roote, Gibbs and Lush*]"; on back
cover, within blue border, photo of Pinter, in white panel: "[*in black:*] Photograph
of Pinter by Ivan Kyncl | [*in blue, biographical note*] | [*in black, rule, 10.1 cm.*] |
[*in blue:*] A METHUEN MODERN PLAY £2.50 in U.K. only | 0 413 47950 1";
on spine, in white, Methuen device, down spine: "Pinter • The Hothouse Methuen".

Published 1982. On verso of title leaf: "*First published in hardback 1980 by Eyre
Methuen Ltd* | [. . .] | *This revised paperback edition first published* | *1982 by
Methuen London Ltd* | *Copyright © by Neabar Investments Limited* | *Made and
printed in Great Britain by* | *Richard Clay (The Chaucer Press) Ltd* | *Bungay,
Suffolk* | ISBN 0 413 47950 1", performing rights and conditions of sale state-
ments.

Contents: As for first edition, except: [1] half-title, with notes about this printing and the play, and three brief citations from reviews, and at foot:
"*The photo on the front cover is by John Haynes and shows Derek* |
*Newark as Roote, James Grant as Gibbs and Robert East as Lush, in
the* | *1980 Hampstead Theatre production*"; [6] lineation of author's
note differs, and the last sentence reads: "I made a few changes
during rehearsal, | mainly cuts."

c. Faber paperback edition (1991):

[*Within single-rule frame:*] HAROLD PINTER | The Hothouse | ff | *faber and faber* | LONDON • BOSTON

154 pp., 3 blank leaves. Paperback, standard Faber design; details not recorded.

Published 8 February 1991. On verso of title leaf: "First published in 1980 by Eyre Methuen Ltd | Revised paperback edition published in 1982 | by Methuen London Ltd | This paperback edition first published in 1991 | [. . .] | Printed in England by Clays Ltd, St Ives plc | All rights reserved | © Neabar Investments Limited 1980, 1982 | [*performing rights, conditions of sale and CIP statements*] | ISBN 0-571-16082-7."

Contents: As for the revised paperback.

Notes: Faber reports (1.8.2001) reprinting on 30 October 1995, totalling 5,074 copies printed.

d. First American standard edition (1980):

[*In inline font:*] THE HOTHOUSE | [*in normal letters thereafter:*] A PLAY BY | HAROLD PINTER | Grove Press, Inc. | New York

154 pp., 3 leaves. 20.3 × 13.0 cm. (A) Hardback not seen. (B) Paperback, white on back cover and spine; on front cover: full-length photo of an empty institutional room, imposed on photo at top right, in red: "[*small publisher's device*] | E-764 | $4.95", lower, slightly angled up, from left to right, "[*2 lines in red, with letters shadowed in yellow:*] THE | HOTHOUSE | [*2 lines in white:*] A Play by | Harold Pinter"; on back cover: "[*at top right, in black:*] [*small publisher's device*] | E-764 | $4.95 | [*below, 2 lines in red:*] THE | HOTHOUSE | [*2 lines in black:*] A Play by | Harold Pinter | [*in black, paragraphs about the play, and about Pinter*] | [*bottom left, 7 lines in red:*] Cover Photo: Roy Colmer | Cover Design: Roy Colmer | An Evergreen Book | Published by Grove Press, Inc. | 196 West Houston Street | New York, N.Y. 10014 | ISBN: 0-394-17675-8"; on spine: "[*in black:*] [*small publisher's device*] | Grove | Press | [*down spine:*] [*in red:*] THE HOTHOUSE [*in black:*] Harold Pinter [*across spine, at foot, in black:*] E-764".

Published 1980 (listed in Grove Press "Fall 1980" list, in *Publishers Weekly*, 29 August 1980, p.112: cloth $12.50, 0-394-51395-9; Evergreen paperbound $4.95, 0-394-17675-8). On verso of title leaf: copyright and performing rights statements, "First Edition 1980 | First Printing 1980 | ISBN: 0-394-51395-9 | Grove Press ISBN: 0-8021-0203-4 | Library of Congress Catalog Card Number: 80-996 | First Evergreen Edition 1980 | First Printing 1980 | ISBN: 0-394-17675-8 | Grove Press ISBN: 0-8021-4134-8", etc.

Contents: [1] half-title; [2] list of other Pinter titles; [3] title page; [4] as above; [5] "To Henry Woolf"; [6] "Author's Note"; [7] character-list; [8]

details of first performances; [9] "Locations" of scenes; [10] blank; [11] "Act One"; [12] blank; [13]–154 text; [155–160] list of Grove Press titles.

Notes: Subsequent DLC copyright registration 8 April 1981 (PA-111-784), for printing published 21 February 1981, claimant Neabar Investments, Ltd., © notice 1980.

e. Grove Press Book Club edition [ca. 1980]:

Title page as for standard edition.

4 leaves, 120 pp., with 4 unpaginated pages of photos. 20.8 × 13.5 cm. Hardback: red cloth; on spine: "*[publisher's device]* | GROVE | PRESS *[down spine:]* THE HOTHOUSE Harold Pinter". Endpapers. Dust jacket: on outside front, as for paperback; outside back cream, blank, bottom right in black type "2940"; on spine: "*[publisher's device]* | Grove | Press | *[down spine, in red:]* THE HOT-HOUSE Harold Pinter"; on front flap, title [in red; remainder in black], author, one paragraph about Pinter, one about the play, with titles underlined, and at foot, right: "*Book Club | Edition*"; on back flap: "Cover Photo: Roy Colmer | Cover Design: Roy Colmer | PRINTED IN THE U.S.A".

On verso of title leaf: "To Henry Woolf | Copyright © 1980 by Neabar Investments Limited | *[further copyright and performing rights statements]* | Photographs by Constance Brown | Manufactured in the United States of America | Distributed by Random House, Inc., New York | GROVE PRESS, INC., 196 West Houston Street, New York, N. Y. 10014".

Contents: [i] half-title; [ii] blank; [iii] title page; [iv] as above; [v] characters; [vi] brief first British performance details; [vii] locations; [viii] author's note; [1]–120 text; between 56 and 57, 2-leaf insert, with 4 photos, one per page, captioned with passages of dialogue, on [56a] "PHOTOS BY CONSTANCE BROWN"; Act One ends on 57, with [58] blank, 59 fly-title for "Act Two", [60] blank; [61]–120 text.

f. American acting edition [1982]:

[To left, 7 vertical thick rules] THE | HOTHOUSE | A PLAY BY | HAROLD PINTER | *[star]* | *[7 horizontal thick rules]* | *[star]* | DRAMATISTS | PLAY SERVICE | INC. | *[to right, 7 vertical thick rules]*

68 pp., 2 leaves. 19 × 13 cm. Paperback, light lime green; on front cover, lettering and rules as for title page, except 8 rules in each position; on back cover, within box with plain rules above and below, decorative sides, advertisement for DPS recent acquisitions; down spine: "THE HOTHOUSE – PINTER"; on insides of front and back covers, information about DPS, and DPS advertisements.

Publication 1982. On verso of title leaf: "© Copyright, 1980, by Neabar Investments Limited", further copyright and performing rights statements.

Contents: [1] title page; [2] as above; [3] "TO HENRY WOOLFE" [*sic*]; [4] "AUTHOR'S NOTE", unsigned; [5] "CHARACTERS"; [6] brief details for first British performance, more extensive details for first American production, Playhouse Theatre, New York, 6 May 1982, also, times of the two acts; [7] "LOCATIONS"; [8] blank; 9–66 text; 67–68 "Property List"; [69–72] advertisements for DPS, within boxes, or between borders above and below.

A40   FAMILY VOICES   1981

a. First edition (1981):

HAROLD PINTER | FAMILY VOICES | A PLAY | FOR RADIO | WITH 7 PAINTINGS | BY GUY VAESEN | [2 *lines within round device:*] NEXT | EDITIONS | IN ASSOCIATION WITH FABER & FABER

26 pp., 8 leaves. 22.8 × 15.9 cm. Light card covers, with plastic-coated wire spiral binding ("wiro"); front cover black (to depth 10.3 cm.) and green: within black area: "[2 *lines in white:*] HAROLD PINTER | FAMILY VOICES", imposed below, coloured picture of seated figure in room, within white border, outer measure 15.8 × 12.9 cm.; back cover white, in black: "[*black band*] | FAMILY VOICES | is Harold Pinter's | new play, written | for radio and first | broadcast in | January 1981 | [*within circle:*] 2 [2 *lines within circle:*] NEXT | EDITIONS [*within circle:*] £2.95 | [*black band*]"; the inside front and back are mottled black on white, as are the facing free end-papers.

Published 1981. Price £2.95. 4,732 copies printed [source: Faber]. On verso of title leaf: "First published in 1981 | by Next Editions Limited | 21 Colville Terrace, London W11 | in association with | Faber and Faber | Distributed by Faber and Faber, | 3 Queen's Street, | London, WC1N 3AU | Editor: Emma Tennant Book Design: Julian Rothenstein | Printed in England by Villiers Publications Limited | ISBN 0 907147 03 8 | © Harold Pinter 1981 | *Family Voices* will appear in a collection of Harold Pinter's | plays out from Eyre and Methuen in the Autumn 1981| All rights reserved. No part of this publication | may be reproduced in any form or by any means without | prior permission in writing from Next Editions Limited".

Contents: [1–2] leaf as front endpaper, mottled on recto, blank on verso; [3–4] plain blue leaf; [5] title page; [6] as above; [7] blank; [8] "VOICE 1: a young man | VOICE 2: a woman | VOICE 3: a man"; 9–26 text; [27–28] blank leaf; [29–39] coloured reproductions of 6 paintings by Vaesen; [40] device: within circle: "NEXT | EDITIONS", list of four other titles forthcoming, three already published; [41–42] back free endpaper, recto blank, verso with mottled design to match inside of back cover.

Notes: An American edition was announced in Grove Press's "Fall 1981" list, in the *Publishers Weekly,* as Evergreen paperbound $7.95, ISBN 0-394-17938-2, but either this was never published or else it was a re-publication of the British edition. There are a series of silk screen prints designed and signed by Guy Vaesen and countersigned by Harold Pinter in a limited edition of forty, each signed and numbered in pencil by Pinter and Vaesen. They measure 55 × 38.5 cms. Presumably these were issued at the same time as the publication of *Family Voices* by "Next Editions."

b. British acting edition [1984]:

Family Voices | (from *Other Places*) | A Play | Harold Pinter | [*at foot, to left:*] *Samuel French – London* | *New York – Sydney – Toronto – Hollywood* | [*to right, publisher's device*]

3 leaves, 12 pp., 2 leaves, 1 blank leaf. 17.8 × 12 cm. Paperback, white: front cover decorated, ruled and lettered in red: to left, two pairs of vertical rules, overlapping them, near top, publisher's device, to right: "*Family* | *Voices* | (from *Other Places*) | A Play | Harold Pinter"; back cover: in red, account of play, "ISBN 0 573 12067 6 0000 1 8511"; to right, adjacent to spine, vertical, "PINTER FAMILY VOICES FRENCH".

Published 1984 (L accession 16 DEC 85). Price £1.10. Number of copies in first print-run 2000; thereafter reprinted in response to demand. On verso of title leaf: "© 1981 BY HAROLD PINTER", performing rights information, "ISBN 0 573 12067 6".

Contents: [1]–12 text; [13] furniture and property list; [14] lighting plot; [15] effects plot, at foot, "MADE AND PRINTED IN GREAT BRITAIN BY | LATIMER TREND & COMPANY LTD PLYMOUTH | MADE IN ENGLAND".

c. British anthology (1982):

BEST RADIO | PLAYS OF 1981 | The Giles Cooper Award Winners | Peter Barnes: The Jumping Mimuses of Byzantium | Don Haworth: Talk of Love and War | Harold Pinter: Family Voices | David Pownall: Beef | John P. Rooney: The Dead Image | Paul Thain: The Biggest Sandcastle in the World | METHUEN LONDON / BBC PUBLICATIONS

Published 1982. On verso of title leaf: first publication details for this collection (1982) and for Barnes's play, "Set in IBM 10pt Journal by [*AT symbol*] Tek-Art, Croydon, Surrey | Printed in Great Britain by Richard Clay (The Chaucer Press) Ltd, | Bungay, Suffolk. | ISBN 0 413 50290 2", copyright and performing rights details for each of the plays.

Contents [relevant]: [51] fly-title for *Family Voices*, with note at foot about Pinter; [52] first presentation details, BBC Radio 3, 22 January 1981; [52]–61 text.

A41   OTHER PLACES: THREE PLAYS   1982

a. First British edition (1982):

Other Places | Three Plays | by | HAROLD PINTER | METHUEN • LONDON

4 leaves, 83 pp., 2 leaves. 18.6 × 12.2 cm. (hardback); 17.8 × 11.3 cm. (paperback). Bindings: (A) Hardback, black cloth; down spine in silver: "Pinter ▪ Other Places [*silver rectangular panel, with* "methuen" *reversed out of silver*]". Endpapers. Dust jacket in white and blue; outside front white, with blue border: "[*in blue:*] Harold Pinter | [*in black, rule, 9.8 cm.*] | [*in blue:*] Other Places | [*in black:*] Three Plays", at foot, left, small black rectangle, with "methuen" in white, reversed out of black; on outside back, within blue border, photo, captioned in blue: "Photograph of Harold Pinter by Ivan Kyncl", 8-line biographical note, in blue; spine blue: "[*publisher's device*] | Pinter ▪ Other Places", at foot, within black panel, in white reversed out of black: "methuen"; on front flap, title in blue, at foot, in black, to left "o 413 50710 6", to right "PRICE NET | £5.95 | IN U.K. ONLY"; on back flap, list of Methuen Modern Plays playwrights.

(B) Paperback: on front cover: as for dust jacket; on back cover: as for dust jacket, except at foot, left: "PRICE NET | £2.95 | IN UK ONLY", at foot, right: "A METHUEN PAPERBACK | METHUEN MODERN PLAYS | o 413 50720 3"; spine as for dust jacket.

Published 1982. Price hardback £5.95, paperback £2.95. On verso of title leaf: "*This collection first published in Great Britain as a Methuen | Paperback and simultaneously in Hardback in 1982 by Methuen | London Ltd, 11 New Fetter Lane, London EC4P 4EE |* [first publication statement for *Family Voices*; copyright statements for the three plays] | *Filmset by Northumberland Press Ltd, | Gateshead, Tyne and Wear | Printed in Great Britain by | Richard Clay (The Chaucer Press) Ltd, | Bungay, Suffolk |* ISBN o 413 50710 6 (Hardback) | o 413 50720 3 (Paperback)", performing rights and conditions of sale statements.

Contents: [i] title, account of the three plays; [ii] list of titles "*by the same author*"; [iii] title page; [iv] as above; [v] "To Mick Goldstein"; [vi] blank; [vii] first performance details of triple bill; [viii] blank; [1] fly-title "A Kind of Alaska"; [2] blank; [3] author's acknowledgement that the play owed its inspiration to Oliver Sacks's book *Awakenings*; [4] list of characters; [5]–40 text; [41] fly-title "Victoria Station"; [42] blank; [43] character-list; [44] blank; [45]–62 text; [63] fly-title "Family Voices"; [64] blank; [65] character-list; [66] first performance details, radio and stage ("platform performance"); [67]–83 text; [84] blank; [85–88] Methuen's Modern Plays titles list.

Notes: See *A46* for the American acting edition of *Other Places: Four Plays* (with the addition of *One for the Road*).

b. Faber edition (1991):

[*All within single-rule frame:*] HAROLD PINTER | Other Places | *Three Plays* | ff | *faber and faber* | LONDON . BOSTON

4 leaves, 83 pp., 2 blank leaves. 19.7 × 12.5 cm. Paperback, standard Faber design; on front cover: "ff | [*rule*] | HAROLD | PINTER | Other Places | [*illustration: overlapping partial images of girl in bed, one with eye shut, the other with eye open*]"; on back cover: "ff | [*rule*] | HAROLD PINTER | Other Places | [brief description, with *Guardian* quotation re *A Kind of Alaska*] | Cover illustration by Andrzej Klimowski | UK £4.99 | Canada $12.99 | ISBN 0-571-16089-1 | [*barcode*] | 780571 160891".

Published 8 July 1991 (O accession 23 MAY 1991). Price £4.99. 1420 copies printed. On verso of title leaf: previous publication and copyright information; "Printed in England by Clays Ltd, St Ives plc"; performing rights and conditions of sale statements, "ISBN 0-571-16089-1".

Contents: As for Methuen, except final leaves blank, and on [vii], added performance information, for a revival, March 1985, Duchess Theatre: *Victoria Station, A Kind of Alaska, One for the Road.*

c. American edition (1983):

Other Places | Three Plays | by | HAROLD PINTER | GROVE PRESS, INC., NEW YORK

4 leaves, 83 pp., 2 leaves [see *Contents*]. 20.3 × 12.8 cm. (A) Hardback, black cloth; on spine, in silver: "[*publisher's device*] [*down spine, in 2 lines:*] Grove | Press [*in 1 line:*] Other Places Harold Pinter". Dust jacket: outside front black: "[*in yellow:*] Other | [*in red:*] Places | [*in grey:*] By Harold Pinter | [*3 lines in white:*] A Kind of Alaska | Victoria Station | Family Voices | [*within yellow and black rims, photo of Judi Dench*]"; on outside back, white: "[*black-rimmed photo of Pinter*] | [*paragraph about Pinter*] | [*at foot, left:*] Photograph of Harold Pinter by Ivan Kyncl [*at foot, right:*] ISBN: 0-394-53131-0"; on spine, black: "[*in white, publisher's device*] | [*down spine, in 2 lines, in grey:*] Grove | Press | [*in 1 line:*] [*in yellow:*] Other [*in red:*] Places [*in grey:*] Harold Pinter GP-866"; on front flap: "[*at top, right, in black:*] [*publisher's device*] | GP-866 | $15.00 | [*centred:*] [*in yellow:*] Other | [*in red:*] Places | [*in grey:*] By Harold Pinter | [*remainder in black:*] A Kind of Alaska | Victoria Station | Family Voices | [*3 paragraphs about the plays*]"; on back flap, at foot: "Jacket Photo of Judy Dench

in | A Kind of Alaska by Laurence Burns | Jacket Design: David Johnson | Published by Grove Press, Inc. | 196 West Houston Street | New York, N.Y. 10014".

(B) Paperback, front cover as for dust jacket; on back cover, white: [at top, right:] [publisher's device] | E-849 | $4.95 | [centred:] [in yellow:] Other | [in red:] Places | [in grey:] By Harold Pinter | [remainder in black:] A Kind of Alaska | Victoria Station | Family Voices | [paragraphs about the three plays, and about Pinter] | Cover Photo of Judy Dench in A Kind of Alaska by Laurence Burns | Cover Design: David Johnson | An Evergreen Book Published by Grove Press, Inc. | 196 West Houston Street, New York, N.Y. 10014 ISBN 0-394-62449-1"; spine as for dust jacket.

Published 1983. On verso of title leaf: copyright, rights reserved, reproduction restriction and performing rights statements, "First Hardcover Edition published in 1983 | First Evergreen Edition published in 1983", cataloging data, ISBN numbers, as above, "Manufactured in the United States of America", Grove address, "83 84 85 86 8 7 6 5 4 3 2 1".

Contents: [i] half-title; [ii] Grove's Pinter titles; [iii] title page; [iv] as above; [v]–[84] as for Methuen; [in paperback only] [85–88] list of Grove Press drama and theater paperbacks [in hardback, 2 leaves blank].

Notes: Included in Grove Press list of new publications for March 1983, in its list for Spring 1983, in Publishers Weekly, 4 February 1983, p.93. Cloth $15.00, 0-394-53131-0. Evergreen paperbound $6.95, 0-394-62449-1. The Book Club edition (apart from any differences to the dust jacket, not seen) is distinguished from the hardback by having on the verso of the title leaf only the copyright, rights reserved, reproduction restriction and performing rights statements, and "Manufactured in the United States of America".

d. Grove Weidenfeld paperback:

Title page as for Grove, except imprint as: "[publisher's device] | GROVE WEIDENFELD | NEW YORK".

4 leaves, 83 pp., 1 leaf, 1 blank leaf. 20.4 cm. Paperback, as for Grove, except: on front cover: lettering in orange, red, grey, and white; on back cover: no publisher's device at top, price as $6.95, title and author in orange, red, and grey, and at bottom left imprint as "[publisher's device] | AN EVERGREEN BOOK | Published by Grove Weidenfeld", at bottom right, two bar-codes, "ISBN 0-8021-5189-2"; down spine, "[in orange:] Other [in red:] Places [in grey:] Harold Pinter [across spine, publisher's device] [down spine, 2 lines, in grey:] Grove | Weidenfeld".

First publication date not known. On verso of title leaf: as for Grove, except "Published by Grove Weidenfeld" with address, added ISBN 0-8021-5189-2,

"Printed on acid-free paper | First Grove Press Edition 1983 | First Evergreen Edition 1983 | 8 7 6 5 4 3 2".

Contents: As for Grove, except: [ii] Grove Weidenfeld's Pinter titles; [85–86] list of plays and screeenplays available from Grove Weidenfeld; [87–88] blank.

A42   **A KIND OF ALASKA**   **1982**

British acting edition [1982]:

A Kind of Alaska | (from Other Places) | A Play | Harold Pinter | [*at foot, to left:*] *Samuel French – London* | *New York – Sydney – Toronto – Hollywood* | [*to right, publisher's device*]

3 leaves, 19, [3] pp. 18.4 × 12.1 cm. Paperback, white; front cover decorated, ruled and lettered in blue: to left, two pairs of vertical rules, overlapping them, near top, publisher's device; to right: "*A Kind* | *of Alaska* | (from *Other Places*) | A Play | Harold Pinter"; on back cover: account of play, "ISBN 0 573 1219 X 0000 18511", down right edge, "PINTER A KIND OF ALASKA FRENCH".

Published December 1982 (L accession 16 DEC 85). Price £1.10. Number of copies in first print-run 2000, thereafter reprinted in response to demand. On verso of title leaf: copyright, performing rights information, "ISBN 0 573 12129 X".

Contents: [1]–19 text; [20] furniture and property list; [21] lighting plot; [22] effects plot, at foot, "MADE AND PRINTED IN GREAT BRITAIN BY | LATIMER TREND & COMPANY PLYMOUTH | MADE IN ENGLAND".

Notes: On [v], a note specifies that companies performing the play must acknowledge its having been "inspired by *Awakenings* by Oliver Sacks MD." Before Deborah's long speech, "Oh yes. The most crushing spaces. . . . until . . .", a stage-direction is added: "*During the following, Pauline enters*".

A43   **VICTORIA STATION**   **1984**

British acting edition [1984]:

Victoria Station | (from *Other Places*) | A Play | Harold Pinter | [*at foot to left:*] *Samuel French – London* | *New York – Sydney – Toronto – Hollywood* | [*at foot to right: publisher's device*]

2 leaves, 9, [3] pp. 18.5 × 12.3 cm. Paperback, white; front cover decorated, ruled and lettered in green: "[*to left, two pairs of vertical rules, overlapping them, towards top, publisher's device*] [*to right:*] Victoria | Station | (*from Other Places*) | A Play | Harold Pinter"; on back cover: account of play, with two quotations

from critiques, "ISBN 0 573 04225 X 0000 18511", and down right edge: "PINTER VICTORIA STATION FRENCH".

Published 1984 (L accession 16 DEC 85). Price £1.10. Number of copies in first print-run 2000; thereafter, reprinted in response to demand. On verso of title leaf: copyright and performing rights information, "ISBN 0 573 04225 X".

Contents:[1]–9 text; [10] furniture and property list; [11] lighting plot; [12] effects plot, at foot, "MADE AND PRINTED IN GREAT BRITAIN BY | LATIMER TREND & COMPANY PLYMOUTH | MADE IN ENGLAND".

Notes: The opening and closing stage directions, and the numerals "274," etc., are in more extended form than in the standard edition [A41A]:
p. [1] "The Lights come up on an office. The Controller is sitting at a | microphone".
Controller. Two-seven-four? Where are you?
The Lights come up on the Driver in his car
p. 9: The Lights go out in the office. The Driver sits still. The Lights go | out in the car.

A44   **PRECISELY**   1984

a. Within an anthology (1984):

THE BIG ONE | An anthology of original sketches, | poems, cartoons and songs on the theme of peace | Edited by | Susannah York and Bruce Bachle | METHUEN

3 leaves, 90 pp. (2 illustration leaves bound in between pp. 42 and 43). 19.8 × 13.0 cm. Paperback, outside multi-coloured; on front cover: illustration of a grotesque ape against a multi-coloured background, lettered above: "[2 lines in red:] THE | BIG ONE | [3 lines in white:] An anthology of original sketches, | poems, cartoons and songs on the | theme of peace", below: "[2 lines in white:] EDITED BY | SUSANNAH YORK AND BILL BACHLE | [within black panel, in white:] methuen"; on back cover: "[2 lines in red:] THE | BIG ONE | [remainder of lettering in white:] A peace-ful anthology of original sketches, poems and songs | intended to restore some sense – and sense of humour – to a | world apparently poised on the brink of nuclear holocaust. | Edited by Susannah York and Bill Bachle. The Big One | features contributions specially commissioned from | [lists 16 writers] | with original cartoons by | [lists 8 cartoonists] | ROYALTIES FROM THIS BOOK GO TO THE PEACE MOVEMENT | [at foot, to left:] PRICE NET | £2.95 | IN UK ONLY | [at foot, right:] A METHUEN PAPERBACK | HUMOUR ANTHOLOGY | FRONT COVER: GERALD SCARFE | 0 413 55910 6"; down spine: "[in red:] SUSANNAH YORK AND BILL BACHLE [in white:] THE BIG ONE [foot obscured in copy seen]".

Published 1984.

Contents: [i] half-title, with biographical notes about editors; [ii] dedication and small cartoon; [iii] title page; [iv] copyright details, etc.; [v] contents; [vi] cartoon; 1–2 "Introduction" signed on p.2: "Susannah York | Bill Bachle | 1984", about the show and this book; 3–82 texts of sketches and poems, cartoons; 83 fly-title "*Music*"; 84–90 songs with scores.

Notes: Precisely was written and directed by Pinter for the five-hour anti-nuclear gala, *The Big One,* which opened at the Apollo Victoria Theatre, London, on 18 December 1983. In this subsequent volume it occupies pp. 32–35. Cf. W47.

b. First American publication (1985):

[Sketch] | PRECISELY. *Harper's Magazine,* 270 (May 1985): 37.

Below the title: "*By Harold Pinter. Pinter read this sketch at New* | *York University in December upon receiving the* | *Elmer Holmes Bobst Award in Arts and Letters.*"

A45   **ONE FOR THE ROAD**   **1984**

a. First British edition (1984):

[*Two lines in stencil-style font:*] ONE FOR THE ROAD | HAROLD PINTER | A Methuen New Theatrescript | Methuen • London

24 pp. 20.9 × 14.7 cm. Paperback, semi-gloss black, lettered in white (unless otherwise stated); on front cover: "[*2 lines in shadowed capitals:*] ONE FOR | THE ROAD | A Play by | Harold Pinter | [*within small white panel, in black:*] methuen | METHUEN'S NEW THEATRESCRIPTS"; on back cover: brief accounts of the play and its author; at foot, left: "PRICE NET | £1.25 | IN UK ONLY"; at foot, right: "A METHUEN PAPERBACK | THEATRESCRIPT (SECOND SERIES) No. 27 | 0 413 56060 0"; at right edge, lettered downward: "ONE FOR THE ROAD PINTER [*within small white panel, in black:*] methuen". In one copy seen, on the back cover, at left foot, a sticker gives the price as £1.50.

Published 1984. Price £1.25. On verso of title leaf: "A METHUEN PAPERBACK | First published as a Methuen Paperback original | in 1984 by Methuen London Ltd | [. . .] | Copyright © 1984 by Harold Pinter | [. . .] | ISBN 0-413-56060-0 | Printed in Great Britain by Expression Printers Ltd, London N7", performing rights and conditions of sale statements.

Contents: [1] half-title and note: "One for the Road | *One for the Road* is a chilling story of power and powerlessness. The play is | published to coincide with the premiere production, directed by Harold | Pinter at the Lyric Theatre, Hammersmith, in spring 1984."; [2] list of other titles "*by the same author*"; [3] title page; [4] as above; [5] details of first performance, and setting; [6] blank; 7–24 text.

b. Second British edition, revised and reset, with photos and interview (1985):

[*thick rule, 6.3 cm.*] One | for the | Road | HAROLD | PINTER | With production photos | by Ivan Kyncl | and an interview on | the play and its politics | Methuen • London | [*thick rule, 6.3 cm.*].

80 pp. 23.7 × 18.1 cm. (A) Hardback, dark azure blue cloth; spine ruled and lettered in gold: "[*rule*] | [*down spine:*] One for the Road | [*rule*] | [*down spine:*] HAROLD PINTER | [*rule*] | [*down spine:*] METHUEN". Endpapers pale blue. Dust jacket dark azure blue; on outside front: "[*2 lines in white:*] Harold | Pinter | [*photo, 6.6 × 9.8 cm., of Nicholas and Victor*] | [*2 lines in very pale blue-grey:*] One for | the Road | [*2 lines in white:*] With production photos by Ivan Kyncl | and an interview on the play and its politics"; outside back blank; down spine: "[*in white:*] Harold Pinter [*in pale blue:*] One for the Road [*in white, within black panel with white border:*] methuen"; on front flap, in white, 3 paragraphs about the play, at foot, left, within white panel, in black: "ISBN 0-413-58950-1 | [*bar-code*] | 9 780413 589507", at right, in white: "PRICE NET | £8.95 | IN UK ONLY"; on back flap, biographical note about Pinter, "PRINTED IN GREAT BRITAIN".

(B) Paperback, glossy dark azure blue, with lettering mainly in white; on front cover: as for outside front of dust jacket; on back cover, in white, notes on the play, this edition of it, and Pinter's career, and at foot, at left, within panel in white, "ISBN 0-413-58370-8 | [*bar-code*] | 9 780413 583703", and, at right, "PRICE NET | £3.95 | IN UK ONLY"; spine as for dust jacket.

Published 3 October 1985. Prices: hardback £8.95; paperback £3.95. On verso of title leaf: "*One for the Road* first published | by Methuen London in 1984 | This revised and reset edition | with illustrations and introduction | first published in simultaneous | hardback and paperback in | Great Britain in 1985 | by Methuen London Ltd, | 11 New Fetter Lane, London, EC4P 4EE | [*copyright statements*] | Printed in Great Britain by | Fletcher & Son Ltd, Norwich | ISBN 0 413 58950 1 (Hardback) | 0 413 58370 8 (Paperback) | [*performing rights statements*]."

Contents: [1] half-title; [2] list of Methuen titles "By the same author"; [3] title page; [4] as above; 5 fly-title "[*thick rule, 6.3 cm.*] A Play and its Politics | A conversation | between Harold Pinter | and Nicholas Hern"; 6 blank except for page number; 7–23 text of conversation, dated on 23 "February 1985"; 24 "POSTSCRIPT", 16 lines of text, signed at bottom "H P : May 1985"; 25 fly-title "[*thick rule, 6.3 cm.*] | One for the Road"; 26 information as to other countries where the play had been produced, or productions were planned; 27 details of first British performances, and BBC-TV production; 28 blank except for page number; 29 [setting for first scene]: "[*thick rule, 6.3 cm.*] | A *room. Morning.*"; 30–80 photos and text, with thick rules above and sometimes below. Photos on pp. 30, 31, 32, 35, 36, 39, 41, 42, 44, 45, 49, 51, 54, 56–57, 60, 63, 65, 70, 72–73, 76, 79. Cf. G57.

Notes: The "Postscript" related to Pinter's time in Turkey with Arthur Miller in March 1985, "on | behalf of International Pen. We met over a hundred | writers, academics and Trade Unionists. Most of these people | had spent some time in military prison and the majority | had been tortured." Many "had been imprisoned for their ideas; they had committed | no concrete act against the state." They had never been brought to trial, and yet in many cases their lives, and those of their relations, had been ruined. "This state of affairs | is supported by the USA, in its fight to keep the world | clean for democracy."

c. Faber edition (1991):

ONE FOR THE ROAD | Harold Pinter | ff | *faber and faber* | LONDON • BOSTON

3 leaves, 53 pp., 2 blank leaves. 19.7 × 12.4 cm. Paperback, standard Faber design: on front cover: "ff | [*rule*] | HAROLD PINTER | [*rule*] | One for the Road | [*illustration, half-coloured, with fist above lower half of face, with upper part of chest*]"; on back cover: publisher, author, brief account of play, "Cover illustration by Andrzej Klimowski | UK £4.99 net | Canada $12.99 | ISBN 0-571-16092-1 | [*bar-code*] | 9 780571 160921"; spine: not recorded.

Published 3 June 1991 (L accession 13 NOV 91). 2,064 copies printed.

Contents: [i] half-title; [ii] list of Pinter titles; [iii] title page; [iv] colophon; [v] performance details, 1984 and 1985; [vi] blank; 1–53 [text and pagination on rectos only].

d. American edition, with photos and interview, first (Grove Press) printing (1986):

[*Thick rule, 6.3 cm.*] One | for the | Road | HAROLD | PINTER | With production photos | by Ivan Kyncl | and an interview on | the play and its politics | Grove Press, Inc.| New York | [*thick rule, 6.3 cm.*].

80 pp. 23.5 × 17.7 cm. Paperback, dark azure blue; on front cover, as for Methuen edition, except, at top right, in white: "[*publisher's device*] | E-975 | $7.95"; on back cover, in white: "Harold Pinter | [*rule, 7 cm.*] | One for the Road [*level with these two lines, at right, with letters and numerals in small font:*] [*publisher's device*] | E-975 | $7.95 | [*centred, below main heading, three paragraphs about the play; rule, 10.7 cm.; quoted statement by Pinter, about the prevalence of torture; rule, 10.7 cm.*] | "A violent, disturbing, enthralling short play." –

Financial | *Times* | [*at foot, to left*:] Cover Photo: Ivan Kyncl | An Evergreen Book | Published by Grove Press. Inc. | 196 West Houston Street | New York. N.Y.10014 | ISBN: 0-394-54575-3"; on spine, in white: "[*publisher's device*] | Grove | Press | [*down spine*:] Harold Pinter One for the Road".

Published May 1986. On verso of title leaf: "*One for the Road* copyright © 1984, 1985 by Harold Pinter | Photographs copyright © 1985 by Ivan Kyncl | Interview—'A play and its politics'—copyright © by Harold Pinter and Nicholas Hern | All rights reserved | [*conditions of sale statement*] | First published in 1984 by Methuen London | [*copyright and performing rights statements*] | First Grove Press Edition 1986 | First Printing 1986 | ISBN: 0-394-54575-3 | Library of Congress Catalog Card Number: 86-4662 | First Evergreen Edition 1986 | First Printing 1986 | ISBN: 0-394-62363-0 | Library of Congress Catalog Card Number: 86-4662 | [*DLC cataloging data*] | Printed in the United States of America | GROVE PRESS. INC., 196 West Houston Street, New York. N.Y. 10014 | 5 4 3 2 1".

Contents: As for Methuen edition, except p.[2] headed "Other Works by Harold Pinter | Published by Grove Press", and list is of Grove titles.

e. American edition, with photos, second (Grove Weidenfeld) printing (1986):

Title page as for Grove issue, except imprint: "[*small publisher's device*] | Grove Weidenfeld | New York".

Pagination as for Grove. Paperback: front cover as for Methuen (i.e., does not have Evergreen device, number, or price at top right); back cover as for Grove, except, at top right: "$7.95" (i.e., does not have Evergreen device or number), and at foot, to left: "Cover Photo: Ivan Kyncl | [*2-line publisher's device*] AN EVERGREEN BOOK | Published by Grove Weidenfeld", to right, within white panel, in black: "[*two bar-codes*] | [*below left-hand bar-code*:] 9 780802 151889 | [*above right-hand bar-code*:] 90000 | [*below both*:] ISBN 0-8021-5188-4".

On verso of title page: "[*initial copyright data, as above*] | All rights reserved | [*conditions of sale statement*] | Published by Grove Weidenfeld | A division of Wheatland Corporation | 841 Broadway | Nwc [*sic*] York, NY 10003-4793 | [*copyright and performing rights statements*] | First published in 1984 by Methuen London | [*DLC cataloging data*] | ISBN 0-8021-5188-4 | Manufactured in the United States of America | Printed on acid-free paper | First Grove Press Edition 1986 | First Evergreen Edition 1986 | 6 5 4 3 2".

f. British acting edition (1984):

One for | the Road | (from *Other Places*) | A play | Harold Pinter | *Samuel French* – London | *New York* – *Sydney* – *Toronto* – *Hollywood* [*to right, publisher's device*]

2 leaves, 13, [2] pp. Paperback, cream, lettered in pink: on front cover: to upper

left, publisher's device, two vertical rules, "*One for | the Road |* (from *Other Places)* | A play | Harold Pinter".

Published December 1984. Price 60p. Number of copies in first print-run 2000; thereafter, reprinted in response to demand. On verso of title leaf: copyright, performing rights and professional rights statements, "ISBN 0 573 12184 2".

Contents: [i] title page; [ii] as above; [iii] first performance details, performing rights warning; [iv] blank; [1]–13 text; [14] furniture and property list; [15] lighting plot; [16] blank.

A46   OTHER PLACES: FOUR PLAYS   1984

American acting edition (1984):

[*To left, 7 vertical rules, 9.3 cm.*] OTHER | PLACES | FOUR PLAYS | BY | HAROLD PINTER | [*star*] | [*7 horizontal rules, 9.25 cm.*] | [*star*] | DRAMATISTS | PLAY | SERVICE | INC. [*to right, 7 vertical rules, 3.4 cm.*]

1 leaf, 57, [5] pp. 19.8 × 13.2 cm. Paperback, yellow; front cover as for title page, except rules 5.1, 13 and 5.1 cm., and lineation differs: "OTHER PLACES | FOUR PLAYS | BY HAROLD PINTER"; on inside of front cover and outside of back cover, DPS advertisements.

Published 1984. On verso of title leaf: copyright and performing rights statements, for the USA and Canada.

Contents: [i] blank; [ii] photo, captioned: 'PHOTO BY GERRY GOODSTEIN | Henderson Forsythe and Dianne Wiest in a scene from the | Manhattan Theatre Club production of "A Kind of Alaska" from | "Other Places." Set design by John Lee Beatty.'; [1] title page; [2] as above; [3] "To Mick Goldstein"; 4 notes about the plays; 5 British first performance details; 6 performance details, Manhattan Theatre Club, 17 April 1984; 7 contents; [8] blank; [9] fly-title "A KIND OF ALASKA"; 10 notes; 11–22 text; 23 fly-title "VICTORIA STATION"; 24 characters; 25–30 text; 31 fly-title "FAMILY VOICES"; 32 characters, British radio and stage presentation details; 33–45 text; [46] blank; 47 fly-title "ONE FOR THE ROAD"; 48 characters; 49–56 text; 57 property lists; [58–62] DPS advertisements.

Notes: The notes on p. 4 are as for the British edition but with the addition: "In the New York production, by the Manhattan Theatre Club, | *Family Voices* was replaced by *One for the Road*. Groups produc- | ing *Other Places* are free to use either combination of plays. (Or, if they wish, all four plays on one program.) | Please note, however, that when *A Kind of Alaska* is licensed for | separate production, with a companion piece, the companion | piece *must* be another play by Harold Pinter or a play approved | by Mr. Pinter. In the latter situation, requests should be made | in writing to the Play Service well in advance of projected pro- | duction dates."

A47   **MOUNTAIN LANGUAGE**   1988

a. Publication in periodical (1988):

Mountain Language. Times Literary Supplement (7–13 October 1988) 1110–1111.

b. First edition, hardback and paperback (1988):

MOUNTAIN LANGUAGE | [*rule, 7.5 cm.*] | Harold Pinter | ff | *faber and faber* | LONDON • BOSTON

47 pp. 19.7 × 12.5 cm. (A) Hardback, black cloth; spine ruled and lettered in white: "[*rule*] | ff | [*rule*] | [*down spine:*] HAROLD PINTER Mountain Language [*across spine, rule*]". Endpapers. Dust jacket glossy white, with standard Faber design, in black, grey and white; on outside front: "ff | [*rule*] | HAROLD PINTER | [*rule*] | Mountain Language | [*rule*] | [*in red, splash of blood*]"; on outside back: "ff | *faber and faber* | [*at foot:*] ISBN 0-571-15412-3 | [*bar-code*] | 9 780571 154128"; on spine: "ff | [*rule*] | [*down spine:*] HAROLD PINTER Mountain Language"; on front flap, brief note about the play, at foot, right: "£7.95 net"; on back flap, brief note about Pinter.

(B) Paperback, standard Faber design; front cover as for outside front of dust jacket; back cover: "ff | *faber and faber* | [*10 lines, brief accounts of play, and of Pinter*] | ISBN 0-571-15413-1 | [*bar-code*] | 9 780571 154135"; spine as for dust jacket.

Published 10 October 1988 (paperback), 17 October 1988 (hardback) (L accession 17 OCT 88). Prices: hardback £7.95, paperback not known. Hardback: 750 copies printed. On verso of title leaf: publication information, "Printed in Great Britain by | Richard Clay Ltd, Bungay, Suffolk", copyright, performing rights and conditions of sale statements, "ISBN 0-571-15412-3 | ISBN 0-571-15413-1 Pbk".

Contents: [1] half-title "MOUNTAIN LANGUAGE"; [2] blank; [3] title page; [4] as above; [5] "To Antonia"; [6] blank; [7] fly-title "MOUNTAIN LANGUAGE"; [8] details of first performance, the National Theatre, 20 October 1988, with names of cast, "*Designed by Michael Taylor | Directed by Harold Pinter*"; [9] "CHARACTERS"; [10] blank; 11–47 text (on rectos only, with versos unpaginated and blank); [48] blank.

Notes: Fabers report (1 August 2001) reprinting on 6 April 1990, 14 July 1992, totalling 7,709 copies printed of the paperback.

c. In American periodical (1989):

MOUNTAIN LANGUAGE. In: *Harper's Magazine* (February 1989) 44–46.

Within section "Forum: Talk of the Times" (pp. 37–39, 42–46), with an introduction on p. [37], and passages from David Hare's *The Secret Rapture* and David Mamet's *Dodge*.

d. American edition (1989):

MOUNTAIN LANGUAGE | [*short rule, 25 cm.*] | HAROLD PINTER | [*publisher's device*] | GROVE PRESS | *New York*

47 pp., 1 blank leaf. 28 × 13.6 cm. Hardback, quarter-bound in black cloth, with boards in off-white cloth; lettered down spine, in white: "MOUNTAIN LANGUAGE (HAROLD PINTER [*small publisher's device*] GROVE PRESS". Dust jacket, outside front mainly white: "HAROLD PINTER | [*red bloodsplash*] | [*black block, with wavy upper edge, suggesting mountains; within this block, lettering in white:*] [*level with upper part of large, bold initial* "M":] a play | MOUNTAIN | LANGUAGE"; outside back white, with at foot, centre: "[*bar-code*] | 9 780802 111579 [*to right:*] 90000 | [*second bar-code*] | ISBN 0-8021-1157-2"; down spine: "HAROLD PINTER MOUNTAIN LANGUAGE [*across spine, publisher's device*] [*down spine:*] GROVE PRESS"; on front flap: at top right: "$16.95", centred: account of play, with cited passages from reviews by Irving Wardle, John Peter, Michael Billington, latter continued; on back flap: continuation of cited passage from Billington, cited passage from Paul Taylor's review, brief biographical note about Pinter, "Jacket design by Liadain Warwick Smith | [*publisher's device*] | GROVE PRESS | 4/89 Printed in USA © Wheatland Corporation".

Published March 1989. Price $16.95. On verso of title leaf: "Copyright © 1988 by Harold Pinter | All rights reserved | [*further copyright, performing rights, and publisher's registration statements*] | Published by Grove Press | a division of Wheatland Corporation | 841 Broadway | New York, N.Y. 10003 | [*cataloging data*] | Manufactured in the United States of America | This book is printed on acid-free paper | First Edition 1989 | 10 9 8 7 6 5 4 3 2 1".

Contents: [1] half-title; [2] blank; [3] title page; [4] as above; [5] "To | Antonia"; [6] blank; [7] fly-title; [8] first-performance details; [9] characters; [10] blank; 11–47 text (on rectos only, with versos blank and unpaginated); [48–50] blank.

Notes: Given that the type-page measure (13.0 × 7.5 cm.; page measured, p.23) is identical with that of the Faber first edition (1988), the Grove edition may have been printed from Faber's litho plates. A signed copy, owned by William Baker, has in black ink on the title page: "To Joel | from | Harold | Pinter". "Joel" was Joel Helman of Framingham, MA.

e. British acting edition [1988]:

Mountain Language | A play | Harold Pinter | [*lower left:*] *Samuel French – London* | *New York – Sydney – Toronto – Hollywood* | [*lower right: publisher's device*]

3 leaves, 14 pp. 18.4 × 12.3 cm. Paperback, white; on front cover, in purple: "Mountain | Language | A PLAY BY | HAROLD PINTER | SAMUEL FRENCH LTD"; on back cover: brief account of play, "[*lower left:*] ISBN o 573 12163 X [*lower right:*] oooo 1 8907 | [*vertical, down right edge:*] PINTER MOUNTAIN LANGUAGE FRENCH".

Published December 1988. Price £1.50. [2001 reprint: £3.25.] Number of copies printed in first print-run 1000; thereafter reprinted in response to demand. On verso of title leaf: copyright and performing rights statements, "ISBN o 573 12163 X".

Contents: [i] title page; [ii] as above; [iii] "To Antonia"; [iv] first performance details, 20 October 1988; [v] list of characters; [vi] copyright information; [1]–11 text; [12] furniture and property list; [13]–14 lighting plot; 14 effects plot.

f. American acting edition [1989?]:

[*To left, 7 vertical thick rules*] MOUNTAIN LANGUAGE | BY HAROLD PINTER | [*star*] | [*7 horizontal thick rules*] | [*star*] | DRAMATISTS | PLAY SERVICE | INC. | [*to right, 7 vertical thick rules*]

1 leaf, 15, [1] pp., 3 leaves. 19.5 × 13.1 cm. Paperback, off-white; front cover lettered and ruled as for title page, except for having 8 rules in each position; on back cover: with borders above and below, list of DPS's new plays, also, below lower border, bar-code, and ISBN number: "3 0711 11462 4578"; down spine: "MOUNTAIN LANGUAGE — PINTER"; on insides of front and back covers, information about DPS and advertisements.

Published 1989(?). On verso of title leaf: "© Copyright, 1988, by Harold Pinter", further copyright and performing rights statements.

Contents: [i] blank; [ii] production photo, with "PHOTO BY TOM CHARGIN", and caption; [1] title page; [2] as above; 3 "To Antonia"; 4 performance details for first British production, and first American production (Classic Stage Company, New York, 31 October 1989); 5 "CHARACTERS"; [6] blank; 7–14 text; 15 "PROPERTY LIST"; [16–22] DPS advertisements.

A48   THE NEW WORLD ORDER   1991

a. American acting edition (1991):

THE NEW WORLD ORDER | by | Harold Pinter

2 leaves, 9 leaves paginated on rectos only 1–9. Unbound, 11 leaves stapled.

Published 1991. On [iii]: "(c) Copyright, 1991, by Harold Pinter", further copyright and performing rights statements.

Contents: [i] title page; [ii] blank; [iii] as above; [iv] blank; 1–9 text.

Notes: The title page is printed; otherwise, this is in typescript, and appears to be mimeographed. At the end of the text are three small stars, and the date "April 1991". Copy seen: Irwin Library, Butler University.

b. In periodical (1991):

"THE NEW WORLD ORDER". *Granta,* No. 37 (Autumn 1991): 251–254.

Title on p.[249] as fly-title; on p. [250], a photo of a naked man in a room, with apparatus for torture. Reprinted in: *The Pinter Review: Annual Essays 1991,* 5 (1991): 1–3.

c. In American periodical (1991):

"*The* | NEW | ["O" as clouded globe] WORLD | ORDER | *A Sketch by* | HAROLD PINTER". *American Theatre,* 8. 8 (November 1991): 28–30.

Note on p.28: "The New World Order | *opened at the Theatre Upstairs | of the Royal Court on July 19 | and moved to the main stage | on Oct. 31. The Potomac | Theatre Project of Wash- | ington, D.C. presented the | American premiere July 27– | Aug. 11.*"

A49   PARTY TIME   1991

a. Stage version (1991):

PARTY TIME | Harold Pinter | [*facsimile of signature*] | ff | *faber and faber* | LONDON • BOSTON

5 leaves, 38 pp. 19.2 × 12.5 cm. Hardback not seen. Paperback, white, standard Faber design; on front cover: "ff | [*rule*] | HAROLD | PINTER | [*rule*] | Party Time | [*coloured illustration*]"; on back cover: publisher, author, title, two short paragraphs on the play, "Cover illustration by Andrzej Klimowski | UK £3.99 net | Canada $8.99 | ISBN 0-571-16585-0 | [*bar-code*] | 9 780571 165858"; down spine: "HAROLD PINTER Party Time".

Published (hardback and paperback) 4 November 1991. 801 copies (hardback), 5034 (paperback) (as reported 1 August 2001). Price £3.99 paperback On verso of title leaf: publication information, "Photoset by Parker Typesetting Service, Leicester | Printed in England by Clays Ltd, St Ives plc", copyright, performing rights, and conditions of sale statements, "ISBN 0-571-16584-2 | 0-571-16585-0 (pbk)".

Contents: [i] half-title, with brief note about the author; [ii–iii] list of other Pinter titles; [iv] blank; [v] title page; [vi] as above; [vii] "To Antonia"; [viii] blank; [ix] character-list; [x] first stage-performance details, white slip pasted over original cast-list [see *Notes*]; 1–38 text.

Notes: A slip pasted over the original performance information for the Almeida Theatre production, premièred 31 October 1991, gives one change in the cast-list: the role of Terry was played by Peter Howitt; as originally printed, it had been played by Colin Firth.

b. Television version [1994]:

PARTY TIME | *a screenplay* | HAROLD PINTER | ff | *faber and faber* | LONDON • BOSTON

5 leaves, 47 pp. 19.3 × 12.5 cm. Paperback, white, standard Faber design; on front cover: "ff | [*rule*] | HAROLD | PINTER | [*rule*] | Party Time | [*coloured photo, of formally dressed man and woman*]"; on back cover: publisher, author, title, account of play as television version, "Cover photo © Andy Strickland/Graham Attwood | UK £5.99 net | Canada $12.99 | ISBN 0-571-17005-6 | [*bar-code*] | 9 780571 170050"; down spine: "HAROLD PINTER Party Time".

Published 10 April 1994 (from Faber records). 6,422 copies. Price £5.99. On verso of title leaf: as for stage version, except "ISBN 0-571-17005-6".

Contents: [i] half-title; [ii–iii] Faber's Pinter titles; [iv] blank; [v] title page; [vi] as above; [vii] "To Antonia"; [viii] stage presentation details; [ix] television production details; [x] characters; 1–47 text; [48–54] blank.

A50   PARTY TIME AND THE NEW WORLD ORDER   1993

American edition (1993):

PARTY TIME | *and* | THE NEW | WORLD ORDER | Two Plays by Harold Pinter | [*publisher's device*] | Grove Press | *New York*

7 leaves, 60 pp. 20.1 × 12.5 cm. Paperback, black: on front cover: "[*3 lines in white:*] "The most fascinating, enigmatic, and | accomplished dramatist in the English language." | –Jack Kroll, *Newsweek* | [*within red quadrilateral panel, in black:*] Party Time | [*in grey:*] and | [*within blue quadrilateral panel, 2 lines in black:*] The New | World Order | [*in white:*] Two Plays by | [*in grey:*] Harold Pinter | [*small, yellow, quadrilateral panel, within it a plain cross, in black*]"; on back cover, in grey (mainly): "DRAMA $10", 4 paragraphs about Pinter, and about the two plays, with, at end of second paragraph, 2 lines in red, and at end of third paragraph, 3 lines in yellow, "[*at foot, left, 7 lines in blue:*] Cover design by Nancy Silva | • | Grove Press | 841 Broadway | New York, NY 10003 | • | Printed

in the USA 0194 | [*at foot, right, within white panel:*] [*bar-code*] | 9 780802 133526 | ISBN 0-8021-3352-5 | [*to right, above second bar-code*] 90000>"; down spine: "[*in yellow:*] Harold Pinter [*small quadrilateral panel, in grey, within it, cross, in black*] [*in red:*] Party Time [*in white:*] *and* [*in blue:*] The New World Order [*across spine, in grey: publisher's device*]".

Published 1993. Price $10. On verso of title leaf: "Copyright © 1993 by Harold Pinter | [*further copyright statements, first British publication details*] | First Grove Press edition published in October 1993 | *Printed in the United States of America* | FIRST EDITION", DLC cataloguing data, publisher's address, impression numerals.

Contents: [i] half-title; [ii–iii] Grove Pinter titles; [iv] blank; [v] title page; [vi] as above; [vii] "To Antonia"; [viii] blank; [ix] fly-title "PARTY TIME"; [x] blank; [xi] first British stage performance details; [xii] blank; [xiii] first British television production details; [xiv] characters; 1–47 text; [48] blank; [49] fly-title "THE NEW WORLD ORDER"; [50] blank; 51 first British performance details; [52] blank; 53–60 text; [61–62] blank.

Notes: Both plays have generous spacing between speeches, and between dialogue and stage directions.

A51   MOONLIGHT   1993

a. First edition (1993):

HAROLD PINTER | Moonlight | ff | *faber and faber* | LONDON • BOSTON

1 blank leaf, 5 leaves, 1–80 pp., 2 blank leaves. 19.7 × 12.5 cm. Hardback, bluish-black cloth; on spine, in white: [*rule*] | ff | [*rule*] | [*down spine:*] HAROLD PINTER Moonlight | [*across spine, rule*]". Endpapers off-white. Dust jacket white, standard Faber design; on outside front: "ff | [*rule*] | HAROLD | PINTER | [*rule*] | Moonlight | [*coloured illustration*]"; on outside back: publisher, author, title, brief note about play, "Jacket illustration by Andrzej Klimowski", at foot, "ISBN 0-571-17085-4 | [*bar-code*] | 9 780571 170852"; on spine: "ff | [*down spine:*] HAROLD PINTER Moonlight"; on front flap, other Pinter titles, at foot, right: "UK £12.99 net | Canada $19.99"; on back flap, brief note about Pinter. Paperback not seen.

Published 6 September 1993 (O accession 5 AUG 1993). Prices: hardback £12.99, paperback £5.99. Copies printed: hardback 710, paperback (with reprints of 15 July 1994, 16 July 1997) 5,034 copies (as of 1 August 2001). On verso of title leaf: "First published in Great Britain in 1993 | by Faber and Faber Limited | 3 Queen Square London WC1N 3AU | Photoset by Parker Typesetting Service, Leicester | Printed by Clays Ltd, St Ives plc | [*copyright and performing rights statements*] | ISBN 0-571-17085-4 (cased) | 0-571-17086-2 (pbk)".

Contents: [i] half-title; [ii–iii] list of Faber's Pinter titles; [iv] blank; [v] title page; [vi] as above; [vii] "*To Antonia | with my love*"; [viii] blank; [ix] list of characters and of main playing areas; [x] first performance details, Almeida Theatre, 7 September 1993; 1–80 text; [81–84] blank.

Notes: On the half-title leaf in the hardback copy seen is pasted a small erratum slip: "ERRATUM | Page 1 line 1 should read: | I can't sleep. There's no moon. It's so dark. I". Faber reports reprints on 15 July 1994, 16 July 1997.

b. American edition (1994):

HAROLD PINTER | Moonlight | [*small publisher's device*] | GROVE PRESS | NEW YORK

1 blank leaf, 5 leaves, 80 pp., 2 blank leaves. 20.9 × 13.8 cm. (A) Hardback, bound with red paper; down spine, in gold: "MOONLIGHT HAROLD PINTER [*small publisher's device*] GROVE PRESS". Endpapers. Dust jacket: on outside front, red with black circles: "[*2 lines black on red, or red on black:*] HAR | OLD | [*in yellow:*] Moonlight | [*2 lines black on red or red on black:*] PIN | TER"; outside back blue, with, at bottom right, within small white rectangle, in black: "11197"; spine yellow, down spine: "[*in blue:*] MOONLIGHT [*in black:*] HAROLD PINTER [*small publisher's device*] [*in red:*] GROVE PRESS"; on back and front flaps, account of the play, and of Harold Pinter, also, on back flap "Cover design by Evelyn Kim".

(B) Paperback: front cover as for outside front of dust jacket; back cover blue, lettered in black with red initial letters for first words of paragraphs: "Drama $12 | [*accounts of play and of Pinter*] | Cover design by Evelyn Kim | [*at foot, left:*] Grove Press | 841 Broadway | New York,, NY 10003 | Printed in the USA 0794 | [*at foot, right, within white panel:*] "[*bar-code*] | 9 780802 133939 | ISBN 0-8021-3393-2 | [*to right:*] 90000> | [*bar-code*]"; spine as for dust jacket.

Published 1994. On verso of title leaf: copyright and performing rights statements, "First Grove Press edition, July 1994 | [. . . .] | ISBN: 0-8021-3393-2 | Grove Press | 841 Broadway | New York, NY 10003", impression numerals. Paperback has also: "Library of Congress Catalog Card Number: 94-76461 | FIRST AMERICAN EDITION".

Contents: [i–ii] blank; [iii] half-title; [iv–v] list of Grove's Pinter titles; [vi] blank; [vii] title page; [viii] as above; [ix]–[84] as for British edition.

c. American acting edition [1996]:

[*To left, 7 vertical thick rules*] MOONLIGHT | BY HAROLD PINTER | [*star*] | [*7 horizontal thick rules*] | [*star*] | DRAMATISTS | PLAY SERVICE | INC. [*to right, 7 vertical thick rules*]

1 leaf, 37, [1] pp. 19.6 × 13.2 cm. Paperback, light blue; front cover as for title page, except 8 rules in each position; on back cover: within 2-rule box, account of *Moonlight*, and list of other Pinter plays, also, below box, at left: "ISBN: 0-8222-1481-4", at right: "Catalogue No.: 6107"; down spine: "MOONLIGHT – PINTER"; on insides of front and back covers: information about DPS, advertisements.

Published 23 January 1996 (DLC copyright registration 20 February 1996 [PA-785-832]). On verso of title leaf: "© Copyright 1996, by Harold Pinter | © Copyright 1993, by Harold Pinter | [*further copyright and performing rights statements*] | Originally produced in the United States by | Roundabout Theatre Company, 1995. | Todd Haimes, Artistic Director."

Contents: [i] blank; [ii] production photo from British production, "Photo by Ivan Kyncl" and caption; [1] title page; 2 as above; 3 "*To Antonia | with my love*"; 4 first performance details for first British production and first American production (Roundabout Theatre Company, New York, 27 September 1995); 5 "CHARACTERS" and account of "THREE MAIN ACTING AREAS"; [6] blank; 7–35 text; 36 "PROPERTY LIST"; 37 "SOUND EFFECTS"; [38] within single-rule box, list of DPS new plays.

A52   ASHES TO ASHES   1996

a. British edition (1996):

HAROLD PINTER | Ashes to Ashes | ff | *faber and faber* | LONDON • BOSTON

4 leaves, 85 pp., 1 blank leaf. 19.8 × 12.2 cm. Paperback, glossy dark grey; on front cover: "ff | PLAYS | Harold Pinter | Ashes to Ashes | [*coloured illustration*]"; on back cover: photo of Pinter, with caption "© Jill Furmanovsky", publisher, brief quotation and information about play, at foot to left, within white panel, "UK £6.99 RRP | Canada $12.99 | [*vertical:*] ISBN 0-571-19027-8 | [*bar-code*] | 9 780571 190270] | [*to right:*] Cover illustration by Andrzej Klimowski"; on spine: "ff | [*down spine:*] Harold Pinter Ashes to Ashes".

Published 1996 (L accession 20 SEP 96). 260 copies printed. Verso of title leaf: "First published in 1996 | by Faber and Faber Limited | [. . .] | Photoset by Parker Typesetting Service, Leicester | Printed by Mackays of Chatham PLC, Chatham, Kent | [*copyright, performing rights, conditions of sale, and CIP record statements*] | ISBN 0-571-19027-8", impression numerals.

Contents: [i] half-title; [ii] list of Faber titles "*by the same author*"; [iii] title page; [iv] as above; [v] "To Antonia"; [vi] blank; [vii] first performance details, for Royal Court production, 12 September 1996, directed by Pinter; [viii] blank; 1–85 text, on rectos only, with versos blank; [86–88] blank.

b. American edition (1997):

HAROLD PINTER | Ashes to Ashes | [*small publisher's device*] | Grove Press | New York

5 leaves, 85 pp. (A) Hardback, black cloth; down spine, in gold: "HAROLD PINTER ASHES TO ASHES [*small publisher's device*] GROVE PRESS". Endpapers. Dust jacket black and grey design on outside front, black on outside back and spine; on outside front, design similar to that for Grove's *Moonlight,* but in black and grey, midway down, in red, "ASHES TO ASHES", above it, to right, vertical, in white, lettered upward: "HAROLD PINTER"; outside back plain, except at lower right, within small white rectangle, in black: "15678", to right, within white panel, in black: bar-code, "9 780802 135 100 | ISBN: 0-8021-3510-2"; down spine: "[*in white:*] HAROLD PINTER [*in red:*] ASHES TO ASHES [*across spine, in white: publisher's device*] [*down spine, in white:*] GROVE PRESS"; on front and back flaps, brief account of play, and of Pinter.

(B) Paperback: front cover as for dust jacket; back cover black, lettered in white: "Drama $10 | [*accounts of the play and of Pinter*] | [*at foot, left:*] Grove Press books | are distributed by | Publishers Group West | Printed in the U.S.A. 0497 | [*at foot, right: within white panel, bar-code and numerals as on dust jacket, plus additional bar-code, to right, and above it:*] 51000"; down spine, in white: "ASHES TO ASHES PINTER".

Published April 1997. On verso of title leaf: (hardback): "Copyright © 1996 by Harold Pinter | [*further copyright and performing rights statements*] | Printed in the United States of America | ISBN 0-8021-3510-2"; (paperback): additional: "First Grove Press edition, April 1997", DLC cataloguing data, "FIRST AMERICAN EDITION", publisher's address, impression numerals.

Contents: [i] Grove Press device; [ii] blank; [iii] biographical note about Pinter; [iv] list of Grove's Pinter titles; [v] title page; [vi] as above; [vii] "To Antonia"; [viii] first performance details; [ix] character-list, time of action; [x] blank; 1–85 setting, and text [on rectos only, versos blank]; [86] blank.

A53   CELEBRATION & THE ROOM   2000

a. British edition (2000):

HAROLD PINTER | Celebration | & | THE ROOM | ff | *faber and faber*

4 leaves, 135 pp. 19.2 × 12.6 cm. Paperback, glossy grey; on front cover: lettering in white: "ff | PLAYS | Harold Pinter | Celebration | & The Room | [*coloured illustration: hand holding wineglass, tray*]"; on back cover, mainly in white: brief accounts of two plays, small photo of Pinter, "Cover design by Pentagram

| Cover illustration by Andrzej Klimowski | Author photo © Jill Furmanovsky | [*within white panel, in black, to left:*] £6.99 RRP | Canada $18.99 [*to centre:*] ISBN 0-571-20497-X | [*bar-code*] | 9 780571 204977 | [*to right:*] 90100 | [*barcode*]", at foot, to far left, "ff".

Published 20 March 2000. Price £6.99. 2,406 copies printed (Faber records, as of 2002). On verso of title leaf: "First published in 2000 | by Faber and Faber Limited | [. . .] | Typeset by Country Setting, Kingsdown, Kent CT14 8ES | Printed in England by Mackays of Chatham plc, Chatham, Kent | [*rights reservation, copyright, first publication, authorship, performing rights, conditions of sale and CIP record statements*] | 0-571-20497-X | 2 4 6 8 10 9 7 5 3 1".

Contents: [i] half-title, with note about Pinter; [ii] Faber titles "*by the same author*"; [iii] title page; [iv] as above; [v] contents; [vi–vii] performance details, double bill, Almeida Theatre, 16 March 2000; [viii] blank; [1] fly-title "CELEBRATION"; [2] blank; 3–72 text; [73–74] blank; [75] fly-title "THE ROOM"; [76–77] first performances details; [78] blank; 79–135 text; [136] blank.

b. American edition (1999):

HAROLD PINTER | Celebration | and | The Room | [*publisher's device*] | Grove Press | New York

8 leaves, 125 pp., 1 blank leaf. 21 × 13.3 cm. Paperback, yellow and pale brown vertical bands; on front cover: "[*in red:*] HAROLD | [*vertical, in red:*] PINTER | [*horizontal, between 'E' and 'R', in black*] "One of the most influential British theatrical careers of the century." —John Lahr, *The New Yorker* | [*thick rule*] | CELEBRATION [*vertical, between short vertical thick rules:*] AND [*horizontal:*] THE ROOM | [*4 thick rules, second and third shorter*] [*at right, parallel with second and third rules:*] 2 [*vertical thick rule*] PLAYS"; on back cover: at top left "Drama", at top right: "USA $13.00 | Can $20.00 | [*rule*] | [*critical praise of* Celebration *by Lahr*] | [*account of the two plays, in bold, and two critiques of* Celebration] | [*thick rule*] | [*red panel, within it:*] Cover design by Rodrigo Corral | Grove Press books | are distributed by Publishers Group West | Printed in the USA | [*to right, within white panel, to left:*] ISBN 0-8021-3708-3 | [*bar-code*] | 9 780802 137081 | [*to right:*] 51300 | [*bar-code*]"; down spine: "[*in red:*] HAROLD [*in black:*] PINTER [*in red:*] CELEBRATION [*across spine, in black:*] AND [*down spine, in red:*] THE ROOM [*across spine, in black, thick rule*] [*red panel, within it, in white, publisher's device*]".

Published June 2000. Price $13. On verso of title leaf: "*Celebration* copyright © 1999 Harold Pinter | *The Room* copyright © 1960 Harold Pinter and Neabar Investments | [*further copyright and performing rights statements*] | Printed in the United States of America | [*DLC cataloging data*] | Grove Press | 841 Broadway | New York, NY 10003", impression numerals.

Contents: [i–ii] blank; [iii] publisher's device; [iv] blank; [v] half-title; [vi–vii] titles "*by the same author*"; [viii] blank; [ix] title page; [x] colophon, etc.; [xi] "To Antonia"; [x] blank; [xi] contents; [xii] blank; [xiii] contents; [xiv] blank; [xv] fly-title; [xvi] blank; [1] fly-title "CELEBRATION"; 2 characters; 3 first performance details; [4] blank; [5]–67 text; [68] blank; [69] fly-title "THE ROOM"; 70 characters; 71–72 performance details, including 16 March 2000, Almeida Theatre; 73–123 text; [124] blank; 125 biographical note on Pinter; [126–128] blank.

A54   REMEMBRANCE OF THINGS PAST   2000

Remembrance | of | Things Past | BY MARCEL PROUST | *adapted by* | Harold Pinter & Di Trevis | ff | *faber and faber*

3 leaves, 138 pp. Paperback, glossy grey, lettering mainly in white: on front cover: "ff | PLAYS | Remembrance of Things Past | by Marcel Proust | adapted by Harold Pinter & Di Trevis | [*colour illustration*]"; on back cover: 3 short paragraphs about the novel, screenplay, and stage-play, small photo captioned "Harold Pinter", at foot, left: "ff", at foot, right: "Cover design by Pentagram | Cover illustration by Andrzej Klimowski | Author photo © Jill Furmanovsky | [*within white panel, in black:*] [*to left:*] £7.99 RRP [*centre:*] ISBN 0-571-20750-X | [*bar-code*] | 9 780571 207602 [*to right:*] 90100 | [*bar-code*]"; down spine: "Marcel Proust Remembrance of Things Past Harold Pinter & Di Trevis [*across spine:*] ff".

Published 2000. On verso of title leaf: "First published in 2000 | by Faber and Faber Limited | [. . .] | Typeset by Country Setting, Kingsdown, Kent CT14 8ES | Printed in England by Mackays of Chatham plc, Chatham, Kent | [*copyright, performing rights, conditions of sale and CIP record statements*] | 0-571-20760-X | 2 4 6 8 10 9 7 5 3 1".

Contents: [i] paragraphs about Proust, Pinter, and Trevis; [ii] list of Faber's Pinter titles; [iii] title page; [iv] as above; [v–vi] first performance details; [1] fly-title; [2] blank; 3–138 text.

Notes: This was an adaptation for live theatre of *The Proust Screenplay*; see *B3*.

A55   MOUNTAIN LANGUAGE & ASHES TO ASHES   2001

HAROLD PINTER | Mountain Language | & | Ashes to Ashes | ff | *faber and faber*

8 leaves, 69 pp., 5 blank leaves. 19.7 × 12.4 cm. Paperback, black; on front cover:

photo showing a blurred figure running past a wall, below, in white: "ff | PLAYS | Harold Pinter | Mountain Language & | Ashes to Ashes"; on back cover, in white, 3 brief comments on the plays by critics, a note about the Royal Court double-bill, at foot, left: "ff", at right: "Cover photograph by CACAO", white panel, within it, in black: "[to left:] UK £7.99 RRP [in centre:] ISBN 0-571-21237-9 | [bar-code] | 9 780571 212378 [to right:] 90100 | [bar-code]"; down spine, in white: "Harold Pinter Mountain Language & Ashes to Ashes [at foot, across spine] ff".

Published 21 May 2001. Price £7.99. 7,709 copies printed. On verso of title leaf: publication data, "Typeset by Country Setting, Kingsdown, Kent CT14 8ES | Printed in England by Mackays of Chatham plc, Chatham, Kent", copyright, performing rights and conditions of sale statements, "ISBN 0-571-21237-9 | 2 4 6 8 10 9 7 5 3 1".

Contents: [i–xii] reproduction in black and white of the Royal Court Theatre programme, for the production of the double-bill in the Jerwood Theatre Downstairs, first presented 21 June 2001; [xiii] title page; [xiv] as above; [xv] contents; [xiv] blank; [1] fly-title "MOUNTAIN LANGUAGE"; [2] blank; [3] character-list; [4] details of first production; 5–22 text; [23] fly-title "ASHES TO ASHES"; [24] blank; [25] character-list; [26] details of first production; 27 setting; [28] blank; 29–69 text; [70–80] blank.

Notes: Peggy Paterson of Faber and Faber notes that the plays were "put . . . together" in this volume because of the imminent presentation of the double-bill (communication to William Baker, 24 July 2001). The first page of the programme bears the information that the Royal Court production was also being presented "as part of the Lincoln Center Festival of Harold Pinter's plays in New York, July 2001."

A56   PRESS CONFERENCE   2002

HAROLD PINTER | [thick rule, 9.9 cm.] | Press Conference | ff | faber and faber

[16] pp. 21.6 × 13.6 cm. Paperback, red, blank. Wrapper buff; on outside front: "HAROLD PINTER | [thick rule, 9.5 cm.] | ff"; on outside back, towards foot: "ISBN 0-571-21607-2 | [bar-code] | 08 780571 216079 [to right:] 90100 | [bar-code]"; on front flap, at head: "Harold Pinter can sketch a world in | a few lines which reveal the power | of his vision focussed on the horrors | that have been and that are to | come."; on back flap, at head: "Harold Pinter was born in London | in 1930. He is married to Antonia | Fraser. In 1995 he won the David | Cohen British Literature Prize, | awarded for a lifetime's achieve- | ment in literature. In 1996 he was | given the Laurence Olivier Award | for a lifetime's achievement in | theatre."

Published 2002. On verso of title leaf: "First published in 2002 | by Faber and Faber Limited | [. . .] | Typeset by Faber and Faber | Printed in England by Character Print and Design Ltd | All rights reserved | © Harold Pinter, 2002 | [*copyright, performing rights, conditions of sale and CIP record statements*] | ISBN 0-571-21607-2 | 2 4 6 8 10 9 7 5 3 1".

Contents: [1] half-title "PRESS CONFERENCE"; [2] blank; [3] title page; [4] as above; [5] fly-title "Press Conference"; [6] blank; [7] details of first performances, 8 and 11 February 2002; [8] blank; [9]–[13] text; [14] blank; [15] other Faber titles "*by the same author*"; [16] blank.

A57   **CELEBRATION**   2002

Acting edition (2002):

CELEBRATION | Harold Pinter | [*lion device*] | SAMUEL FRENCH, INC. | [to left] 45 West 25th Street | NEW YORK 10010 | *LONDON* | 7623 Sunset Boulevard | HOLLYWOOD 90046 | *TORONTO*

38 [39–40] pp. Binding orange light card, with two staples; on outside front, within partial frame of rules (groups of three rules of differing height, to left, and right, two rules at foot): "CELEBRATION | Harold Pinter | [*lion device*] | SAMUEL FRENCH, INC."; on outside back: within border of three rules (thin, thick, thin), advertisement for Samuel French Theater Bookshops, with a male figure in a tophat and dress-suit; below border, to left "ISBN 0 573 62828 9", to right "#5870"; down spine (at extreme right of outside back): "CELEBRATION HAROLD PINTER Samuel French, Inc."; on inside front, within a two-rule border (thin, thick): "Modern classics by | HAROLD PINTER | The Birthday Party | The Homecoming | Landscape and Silence | Night | Available from | Samuel French, Inc."; on inside back, within a two-rule border: "REVIEWERS' PRAISE FOR | *CELEBRATION*", three citations.

Published May 2002 (information from publisher). Price US$6.25. Initial print-run 1000 copies. On verso of title page leaf: "Copyright © 1999, 2002 by Harold Pinter | *ALL RIGHTS RESERVED* | [*performing rights statements*] | ISBN 0 573 62828 9 Printed in USA #5870"

Contents: [1] title page; [2] copyright and performing rights statements, etc.; [3] copyright and perfoming rights restrictions and conditions; [4] within two-rule border (thick, thin): first performance details, at the Almeida Theatre, 16 March 2000; [5] list of characters; [6] blank; [7]–38 text; [39] blank; [40] "ABOUT THE AUTHOR" [five-line biographical note].

B

Screenplays

The organisational principle of citing British editions first and American second is maintained, although in the case of *The Proust Screenplay*, the American first edition appeared earlier than the British one. *The Compartment* is included here, despite being only "informally published," because of its special interest as the first of Harold Pinter's works to be initially composed as a screenplay, as opposed to the four plays for other media which he adapted for cinema. Conversely, the television version of *Party Time,* despite being designated on its title page as a screenplay, is included in *Section A* rather than in this section, as an adaptation of a work initially composed for the stage.

B1   **THE COMPARTMENT**   [1965]

Distributed typescript [1965]:

1 leaf, 27 pp. (type and pagination on rectos only).

Written in 1963–65 as a screenplay for a film never made, planned as part of a triple-bill, *Project I,* promoted by the Grove Press, New York, with Samuel Beckett's *Film* and Eugene Ionesco's *The Hard-Boiled Egg.* Of the three, only *Film* would be produced, being released in 1965. Pinter would later substantially re-write his piece for television, as *The Basement* (Billington 191). Manuscripts and typescripts for "The Compartment" (the longest of them 23 pages plus the title leaf) are in *PA Box 2.* See also S. Gale, *Sharp Cut,* pp. 148–152.

"The Compartment" received copyright registration at the Library of Congress as "A Play for the screen" (unpublished, 27. 1 pp.; DU62438) on 4 March 1965, registered to Evergreen Theatre Inc. and Four-Star Television. A copy of the typescript is in the Manuscripts Division of the Library of Congress, Washington (information from Ms Abby Yochelson).

A full copy of *Project I* is at TxU-HRC, as 82 loose leaves (28 × 21.6 cm.), type-script on rectos only, in a folder, inscribed "Anne Myerson, Inc. | Typing and Mimeographing, | 101 Park Avenue - Room 514 | New York – N. Y." In a slip-case, which bears date 1964. This copy is signed on its title page "Samuel Beckett". "The Compartment" occupies 27 leaves.

B2   FIVE SCREENPLAYS   1971

a¹. First Methuen edition, hardback (1971):

Five Screenplays | by HAROLD PINTER | THE SERVANT | THE PUMPKIN EATER | THE QUILLER MEMORANDUM | ACCIDENT | THE GO-BETWEEN | Methuen & Co Ltd

3 leaves, 367 pp., 1 blank leaf. 21.6 × 13.8 cm. Hardback, dark green cloth, on spine, three panels of brighter green; lettering down spine, in gold; within first panel, in two lines: "HAROLD | PINTER"; within second panel: "Five Screenplays"; within third panel: "METHUEN". Endpapers cream. Dust jacket orange and red, with flaps white; on outside front, upper half orange, in black: "HAROLD | PINTER", lower half red, with design in orange and black, of film box with clapper above it, and within box, in white: "FIVE | SCREENPLAYS"; on outside back (orange): photo of Pinter, by "Antony di Gesù", below it 10-line biographical note; down spine (orange): "[*in 2 lines, in black, shunted:*] HAROLD | PINTER [*in 2 lines, in white:*] FIVE | SCREENPLAYS [*across spine, in white:*] METHUEN"; on front flap: account of Pinter, at foot: "PRICE NET £3.75 | IN UK ONLY"; on back flap: list of 8 Pinter titles, "PRINTED IN GREAT BRITAIN".

Published 18 March 1971 (L accession 22 FEB 71). 3,500 copies. Price £3.75. On verso of title leaf: "*First published 1971*", copyright statements for the original works and for the screenplays, "*Printed in Great Britain | by W. & J. Mackay & Co Ltd* | SBN 416 14370 9".

Contents: [i] half-title "Five Screenplays"; [ii] "*Plays by Harold Pinter*" [lists 9 Methuen titles]; [iii] title page; [iv] as above; [v] contents; [vi] dedication, "To Joseph Losey, Jack Clayton, | Michael Anderson | and Pamela Davies"; [1] fly-title "The Servant"; [2] first presentation details; [3]–60 text; [61] fly-title "The Pumpkin Eater"; [62] first presentation details; [63]–135 text; [136] blank; [137] fly-title "The Quiller Memorandum"; [138] first presentation details; [139]–216 text; [217] fly-title "Accident"; [218] first presentation details; [219]–284 text; [285] fly-title "The Go-Between"; [286] details of film, with note "*At the time of going to press, the date of first show-| ing was not yet fixed*"; [287]–367 text; [368–370] blank.

Notes: The five films were released in 1963, 1964, 1966, 1967, and 1969 respectively. A second impression of the hardback was issued in 1973 for Eyre Methuen (new ISBN number 0 413 30520 1). Adam Hall's novel was published in Britain as *The Berlin Memorandum*, in USA as *The Quiller Memorandum*. For textual differences between the two, see S. Gale, *Sharp Cut*, pp. 431–432.

a^2. *Second impression re-issued in paperback (1976):*

Title page: As for first impression, except imprint: "[*small publisher's device*] | Eyre Methuen Ltd".

Pagination as for first impression. 20.2 × 13.1 cm. Paperback, outside lime green; on front cover: "HAROLD | PINTER | [*design in black resembling a clapper above a film-case, with, in lower portion, in green, reversed out of black:*] FIVE | SCREENPLAYS". (L copy re-bound; back cover and spine not seen.)

Published 2 September 1976 (L accession 26 AUG 76). 1000 copies. Price £2.75. On verso of title leaf: "*First published 1971 | Reprinted 1973*", copyright statements for the novels and for the screenplays, "*Printed in Great Britain | by Lowe & Brydon (Printers) Ltd | Haverhill Suffolk*", and on a pasted-in sticker, "*This paperback edition | first published 1976 | ISBN 0 413 35000 2*".

Notes: Dace notes that this paperback was created in 1976 by binding 1,000 existing sets of sheets from the second hardback impression.

b. Karnac edition (1971):

Five Screenplays | by HAROLD PINTER | THE SERVANT | THE PUMPKIN EATER | THE QUILLER MEMORANDUM | ACCIDENT | THE GO-BETWEEN | H. Karnac (Books) Ltd | 56/58 Gloucester Road, London SW7

Pagination as for Methuen. 21.5 × 13.8 cm. Hardback, quarter-bound with black cloth, extending 5.3 cm. across front and back boards, remaining area of boards covered with dark vermillion cloth, width 8.1 cm., separated by a narrow vertical gilt band, width 3 mm.; down spine, in gilt: "[*in 2 lines:*] HAROLD | PINTER [*in single line:*] Five Screenplays Karnac". Endpapers vermillion.

Published March 1971 (L accession 3 MAR 71). 150 copies. Price £10.50. Verso of title leaf: as for first Methuen.

Contents: As for Methuen, but on p.[i], in place of half-title: "*This limited, specially bound edition | is published by arrangement with Methuen & Co Ltd | and appears simultaneously with their | first edition. One hundred and fifty copies | have been numbered and signed by the author. | This is number*" [in copy seen, added in black ink: "IX | [cursive script] *Hors de commerce* | Harold Pinter"].

c. Faber edition (1991):

[*All within single-rule frame:*] THE SERVANT | AND | OTHER SCREEN-PLAYS | HAROLD PINTER | The Servant | The Pumpkin Eater | The Quiller Memorandum | Accident | The Go-Between | ff | *faber and faber* | LONDON · BOSTON

5 leaves, 367 pp., 3 blank leaves. 21.6 × 12.9 cm. Paperback, outside glossy black; on front cover, design and lettering in white: within single-rule frame, with striped clapper above: "ff | [*rule*] | HAROLD | PINTER | The Servant | and Other | Screenplays"; frame partially overlapping photo, a still from *The Servant*, with Dirk Bogarde and James Fox; back cover ruled and lettered in white: title, etc., and brief information about volume, "Cover photo courtesy of BFI Stills | UK £8.99 net Canada $19.95", white panel with, in black: "ISBN 0-571-16084-0 | [*bar-code*] 9 780571 160846"; on spine, in white, within single-rule frame: "[*across spine*:] ff | [*rule*] | [*down spine, in 2 lines*:] HAROLD PINTER | The Servant and Other Screenplays".

Published 1991 (O accession 28 FEB 1991). Price £8.99 net, Canada $19.95. On verso of title leaf: 'This edition first published in 1991", publisher's name and address, "Printed in Great Britain by Clays Ltd, St Ives plc", copyright (for original works and screenplays), performing rights, conditions of sale and CIP record statements, "ISBN 0-571-16084-0".

Contents: [i] half-title, note about Pinter; [ii] blank; [iii] list of Faber's Pinter titles; [iv] blank; [v] title page; [vi] as above; [vii] "In memory of Joe Losey"; [viii] blank; [ix] contents; [x] blank; thereafter as for Methuen.

d¹. American edition, hardback [1973]:

Five Screenplays | by HAROLD PINTER | THE SERVANT | THE PUMPKIN EATER | THE QUILLER MEMORANDUM | ACCIDENT | THE GO-BETWEEN | Grove Press, Inc.   New York

1 blank leaf, 5 leaves, 367 pp., 4 blank leaves. 20.2 × 13.5 cm. Hardback, black cloth with purplish tinge, lettered down spine, in silver: "FIVE SCREENPLAYS Harold Pinter [*5 mauve horizontal rules: 3 shorter alternating with 2 longer*] *Grove Press*". Endpapers. Dust jacket silver on front and spine, back and flaps white; on outside front, rules in black: "[*rule*] | [*2 lines in purple:*] HAROLD | PINTER | [*2 lines in black:*] FIVE | SCREENPLAYS | [*rectangular grid of rules, within it, in black, titles of screenplays numbered, as:*] 1. The Servant | [. . .] | 5. The Go-Between"; on outside back, photo of Pinter "by R. Jones" (caption vertical), paragraph about Pinter, ISBN number; on spine: "[*down spine:*] [*in black:*] FIVE SCREENPLAYS [*in purple:*] BY HAROLD PINTER | [*at foot, across spine, in black:*] G-719 | GROVE | PRESS"; on front flap, lettering in black: "G-719 $10.00", title, author, with underlining in purple, account of screenplays; on back flap, beneath purple rule, account continued.

Published September 1973. Price $10. On verso of title leaf: copyright statements for the original novels and for the screenplays, details of first USA publication of the novels, "ISBN: 0-394-48821-0 | Library of Congress Catalog Card Number: 73-6219 | First Printing | Manufactured in the United States of America | Distributed by Random House, Inc."

Contents: [i–ii] blank; [iii] half-title; [iv] blank; [v] *"Other works by Harold Pinter Published by Grove Press"* [lists 9 titles]; [vi] verso blank; [vii] title page; [viii] as above; [ix] contents; [x] blank; [xi] dedication; [xii] blank; thereafter, as for Methuen, with 3 additional blank leaves at the end.

d². American edition, Evergreen paperback (1973):

Title page as for hardback, except imprint: "Grove Press New York".

[Seen in fifth printing] Pagination as for hardback. 21 × 13.6 cm. Paperback, front cover and spine silver, back cover white; front cover lettered and ruled as for front of dust jacket; on back cover, no photo, lettered and ruled in black, publisher's device, bar-code with numerals; down spine: "FIVE SCREENPLAYS HAROLD PINTER".

Published 1973. Price $3.95. On verso of title leaf: mainly as for hardback, except: additional reproduction restriction and Grove Press name statements, Grove address, "ISBN 0-8021-5119-1", LCCN 73-6220, "First Evergreen Edition 1973", issue numerals.

Notes: In the copy seen (fifth printing), on the outside back of the binding, the top right corner is obscured with a sticker, but presumably bears the Evergreen number E-617, and the price $3.95 (first printing) or $7.95 (later printings); the foot of the spine is also obscured but may bear "GROVE PRESS".

B3   THE PROUST SCREENPLAY   1977

a¹. First British edition, first issue, in hardback (1978):

À la Recherche du Temps Perdu | The Proust Screenplay | [*short curving double-rule device, 3.2 cm.*] | by HAROLD PINTER | *with the collaboration of* | Joseph Losey and Barbara Bray | Eyre Methuen, London | in association with | Chatto & Windus, London

viii, 165, [1] pp., 1 blank leaf. 24.5 × 18.5 cm. Hardback, mid-green cloth; most lettering down spine, rules across spine, in gilt: "[*ornamental double rule, 1.3 cm.*] The Proust Screenplay [*rule, 1.2 cm.*] HAROLD PINTER [*ornamental double rule, 1.3 cm.*] [*across spine:*] Eyre | Methuen". Dust jacket dark green; on outside front: "[*2 lines in white:*] Harold | Pinter | [*within thin black frame, photo of Proust, 6.9 × 6 cm.*] | [*3 lines in pale greenish yellow:*] The Proust | Screenplay | A la recherche du temps perdu"; outside back blank; down spine: "[*in white:*] Harold Pinter [*in pale greenish yellow:*] The Proust Screenplay [*across spine:*] [*publisher's device*] | EYRE | METHUEN"; on front flap, in white, blurb about screenplay, "Photo of Proust: *Radio Times Hulton | Picture Library*", price as £7; on back flap, small photo of Pinter, in white, note about Pinter, "Photo: Tony

McGrath, courtesy of | *The Observer* | [*to left:*] PRINTED IN GREAT BRITAIN [*to right, in black:*] ISBN 0 413 38960X | [*thick rule, 3.2 cm.*]".

Published 1978. Price £7. On verso of title leaf: "First published in Great Britain in 1978 by Eyre Methuen Ltd, | 11 New Fetter Lane, London EC4P 4EE | Copyright © 1978 by H. Pinter Ltd | Printed in Great Britain | by W & J Mackay Limited, Chatham | ISBN 0 413 38960 X", copyright protection notice.

Contents: [i] half-title "The Proust Screenplay"; [ii] lists of Pinter titles published by Eyre Methuen, and Proust titles published by Chatto & Windus, along with *Marcel Proust: A Biography*, by George D. Painter; [iii] titlepage; [iv] as above; [v] dedication: "*To Joe and Barbara*"; [vi] blank; vii–viii "*Introduction*", signed on viii, "Harold Pinter"; [1] fly-title; [2] blank; 3–165 [166] text; [167–168] blank.

Note: Unusually, the first British edition was published later than the first American edition. An uncorrected proof copy of this volume is at TxU-HRC, in off-red paper wrappers [PN 1997.3 P567 1978p] (for typescripts at TxU-HRC, see W32(2). The Random House Archives, in Northampton, have a variant copy of the dust jacket, with lettering in white and yellow. The screenplay was written in 1972, but has never been filmed, because funding could not be secured. It has however been adapted for a successful two-hour radio play by Michael Bakewell, 1995 (Billington 267), and, in 2000, a stage-play version, *Remembrance of Things Past,* adapted by Pinter and Di Trevis, was premièred and published. A copy inscribed by Harold Pinter to "Ralph [Richardson] & Moo [Meriel] with my love, Harold" listed for sale as item 100 in Bernard Quaritch Ltd, catalogue, no. 1296 (2000) for £250.

a². First edition, second issue, in paperback (1980):

Title page as for first issue.

viii, 165, [1] pp., 1 blank leaf. 23.8 × 18 cm. Paperback, outside dark olive-green; on outside front: "[*two words in white:*] Harold | Pinter | [*within square frame, framed by a thin black line: detail of photograph: face of Marcel Proust*] | [*three lines in lighter olive-green*] The Proust | Screenplay | À la recherche du temps perdu"; on outside back, in light green, with titles in white and bold, account of the screenplay, with seven citations of critical praise, and at foot, to left, "0 413 47200 0", to right "PRICE NET | £2.95 | IN UK ONLY"; down spine: "[*in white:*] Harold Pinter [*in light green:*] The Proust Screenplay [*across spine:*] EYRE | METHUEN".

Published 1980. Price £2.95. On verso of title leaf, as for 1978, except small white slip pasted below copyright protection notice: "Re-issued in paperback in 1980 | ISBN 0 413 47200 0".

b. Faber edition (1991):

[*All within single-rule frame:*] THE PROUST | SCREENPLAY | *A la recherche du temps perdu* | HAROLD PINTER | With the collaboration of | Joseph Losey and Barbara Bray | ff | *faber and faber* | LONDON · BOSTON

viii, 165, [1] pp., 1 blank leaf. Paperback, outside black; on outside front, in white, design of box with clapper above, within box, in white: "ff | [*rule*] | HAROLD | PINTER | [*rule*] | THE | PROUST | SCREENPLAY | *A la recherche du temps perdu* | [*rule*] | `A masterpiece of wit and understanding.' *TLS* | [*below box, at an angle, coloured reproduction of painting of a French town across a river*]"; on outside back, within white single-rule frame, in white: "ff | *faber and faber* | [*rule*] | HAROLD PINTER | The Proust Screenplay | *A la recherche du temps perdu* | [*note on play, critical citation*] | [*price details, concealed in copy seen*] | [*within white panel, in black*] ISBN 0-571-16097-2 | [*bar-code*] | 9 780571 160976"; on spine, with lettering and rules in white on a black background: "ff | [*down spine, within single-rule frame:*] HAROLD PINTER The Proust Screenplay".

Published 1991. On verso of title leaf: first publication details, "This paperback edition first published in 1991", Faber and Faber address, "Printed by Clays Ltd, St Ives plc", copyright, conditions of sale and CIP record statements, "ISBN 0-571-16097-2".

c. American first edition, hardback and paperback (1977):

À LA RECHERCHE DU TEMPS PERDU | THE | PROUST | SCREENPLAY | BY | HAROLD | PINTER | WITH | THE | COLLABORATION | OF | JOSEPH LOSEY | AND | BARBARA BRAY | GROVE PRESS, INC., NEW YORK

1 blank leaf, x, 176, [1] pp., two blank leaves. Bindings: (A) hardback: on boards, mottled white and grey cloth; on spine, light brown cloth, lettered in gold: "[*down spine, in 2 lines:*] HAROLD PINTER | THE PROUST SCREENPLAY [*at foot, across spine:*] GROVE | PRESS". Dust jacket: outside dark ochre, lettered and ruled in white; on outside front: "[*rule*] | À la Recherche du Temps Perdu | THE PROUST | SCREENPLAY | [*rule*] | [*roundel design, with stylised lions, light brown on black background*] | [*rule*] | HAROLD | PINTER | [*at foot, adjacent to spine, lettered upward:*] GP - 794"; outside back plain, at foot "ISBN 0-394-42202-3"; on spine: "[*publisher's device*] | Grove | Press | [*down spine:*] THE PROUST SCREENPLAY · HAROLD PINTER"; front flap: "THE PROUST | SCREENPLAY | À La Recherche du Temps Perdu | HAROLD | PINTER", account of screenplay; back flap: continuation of account, black and white photo of Pinter, brief account of Pinter, at foot: "Cover Design: Kenneth R. Deardoff | Published by Grove Press, Inc. | 196 West Houston Street, New York, N.Y. 10014".

(B) Paperback, outside dark ochre, lettered in white; on outside front, as for dust jacket, except at top right: "E-690 [*publisher's device*] $2.95"; on outside back: at top left:"The Proust Screenplay | by Harold Pinter | À la Recherche du Temps

Perdu", at top right: "*[publisher's device]* | E-690 | $2.95", centred, in two columns, account of screenplay, note on Pinter, at foot of right column: "Cover design: Kenneth R. Deardoff | An Evergreen Book | Published by Grove Press, Inc. | 196 West Houston Street | New York, N.Y. 10014 | ISBN: 0-394-17018-0"; on spine: "*[publisher's device]* | Grove Press | *[down spine:]* The Proust Screenplay   Harold Pinter".

Published 30 September 1977 (DLC registration 30 October 1976 [PA 17–328]) On verso of title leaf: "Copyright © 1977 by H. Pinter Limited | All Rights Reserved | *[conditions of sale statement]* | First Edition 1977 | First Printing 1977 | ISBN: 0-394-42202-3 | Grove Press ISBN: 0-8021-0138-0 | Library of Congress Catalog Card Number: 77-72676 | First Evergreen Edition 1977 | First Printing 1977 | ISBN: 0-394-17018-0 | Grove Press ISBN: 0-8021-4083-1 | Library of Congress Catalog Card Number: 77-72676 | Manufactured in the United States of America | Distributed by Random House, Inc., New York | GROVE PRESS, INC., 196 West Houston Street, New York, N.Y. 10014".

Contents: 1 blank leaf; [i] blank; [ii] list of Grove's Pinter titles; [iii] half-title "THE | PROUST | SCREENPLAY"; [iv] blank; [v] title page; [vi] as above; [vii] "To Joe and Barbara"; [viii] blank; ix–x "INTRODUC-TION"; [1] fly-title "THE | PROUST | SCREENPLAY"; [2] blank; 3–176 [177] text; [178–182] blank (in hardback; see note).

Notes: In the paperback, pp. [177–180] bear the publisher's lists of titles, and the final blank leaf, pp. [181–182], is absent. Re-published 2000, ISBN 080213646X.

B4   THE FRENCH LIEUTENANT'S WOMAN   1981

a. First British edition (1981):

HAROLD PINTER | *The Screenplay of* | THE FRENCH | LIEUTENANT'S | WOMAN | based on the novel by John Fowles | *[decorative rule, 4.2 cm.]* | with a Foreword | by John Fowles | JONATHAN CAPE | in association with | EYRE METHUEN

1 blank leaf, xvi, 104 pp., 1 blank leaf. 21.5 × 13.7 cm. Hardback, black cloth; down spine, in gold: "*[in 2 lines:]* The Screenplay of THE FRENCH | LIEUTENANT'S WOMAN *[in 2 lines:]* HAROLD | PINTER", at foot, across spine: publisher's device of Jonathan Cape. Dust jacket: outside, very pale olive; on outside front: "*[within thin white border, colour photograph, 6.9 × 10.6 cm.]* | *[shallow ornament, in white]* | *[in 2 lines, in white:]* HAROLD PINTER | The Screenplay of | *[in 3 lines, open letters, in black:]* THE FRENCH | LIEUTENANT'S *[with letters L and S extended below base-line]* | WOMAN | *[in white:]* with a Foreword by John Fowles"; outside back: "*[2 rules, thin and thick, 5.6 cm.]* The portrait is of Meryl Streep | as Sarah Woodruff in the film

of | *The French Lieutenant's Woman* | [*2 rules, thick and thin, 5.6 cm.*]"; down spine: "[*in 2 lines, in white:*] HAROLD | PINTER [*2 lines:*] [*in white:*] The Screenplay of [*remainder in black, in open letters:*] THE FRENCH | LIEUTENANT'S WOMAN", at foot, across spine: device of Jonathan Cape; on front flap, blurb for Fowles' novel and Pinter's screenplay, at foot: "£5.50 net | [*rule, 1.6 cm.*] | IN UK ONLY"; on back flap, brief biography of Pinter, "ISBN 0 224 01983 X | Jacket design by Mon Mohan | © Jonathan Cape Ltd 1981".

Published 1981. Price £5.50 net. On verso of title leaf: "First published 1981 | Copyright © 1981 by United Artists Corporation | Foreword © 1981 by J. R. Fowles Ltd | Jonathan Cape Ltd, 30 Bedford Square, London WC1 | [*cataloging data*] | ISBN 0 224 01983 X | Typeset by Computape (Pickering) Ltd and | printed in Great Britain at The Camelot Press Ltd, Southampton".

Contents: 1 blank leaf; [i] half-title "*The Screenplay of* | THE FRENCH | LIEUTENANT'S | WOMAN"; [ii] lists of "*Other works by Harold Pinter*" and "*Other works by John Fowles*"; [iii] title page; [iv] as above; [v] contents; [vi] blank; vii–xv "*Foreword*", signed at end "*January 1981* JOHN FOWLES"; xvi note by Pinter: "The writing of this screenplay took over a year. This is the final | version with which we began shooting. Inevitably a number of | scenes were cut and some structural changes made during | the course of production. | *March 1981* HAROLD PINTER"; 1–104 text, divided into 245 shots; [105–106] blank.

Notes: The initial and final blank leaves are not added free endpapers but are conjunct with the first and last gatherings. The film was first presented in Britain by United Artists in 1981, directed by Karel Reisz. "Uncorrected Proof" copy at TxU-HRC: in red wrappers, "Trimmed page size 216 × 138 mm | Extent: 120 pages | Provisional publication date: 3 September 1981 | Provisional published price: £5.50".

b. American trade edition (1981):

[*On left page of opening:*] [*4 lines in semi-cursive italic:*] The | French | Lieutenant's | Woman | [*in normal italic:*] A SCREENPLAY || [*on right page of opening:*] BY | HAROLD PINTER | With a foreword by [*in larger font, in semi-cursive italic:*] John Fowles | Little, Brown and Company   Boston - Toronto

1 blank leaf, 2 leaves, xv [xvi–xvii], 104 pp. 20.7 × 14 cm. Quarter-bound with grey cloth, boards dark red; lettered down spine, in red: "*PINTER* [*2 lines, semi-cursive italic:*] The | French Lieutenant's Woman [*single line, italic:*] A SCREENPLAY [*2 lines, across spine:*] Little, | Brown". Endpapers. Dust jacket: outside grey; on outside front: "[*in black:*] HAROLD PINTER | [*4 lines in semi-cursive italic, in reddish-brown:*] The | French | Lieutenant's | Woman | [*in normal italic, in black:*] A SCREENPLAY | [*to right, photo of Sarah Woodruff standing on the beach*] |

[*at foot:*] *Foreword by* [*larger font, semi-cursive:*] *John Fowles"*; on outside back: black and white photo, with, below it, caption: "From left to right, Harold Pinter, John Fowles, and Karel Reisz, during the | filming of *The French Lieutenant's Woman* in Lyme Regis."; down spine: as for book, in black; on front flap, and part of back flap: account of screenplay, and notes about Pinter, the film, and Fowles; on back flap, at top right, "$11.95", below, notes continued, "Jacket design by Marjorie Anderson | Front photo Copyright © Juniper Films 1981. All | rights reserved."

Published September 1981. Price $11.95. On verso of leaf bearing some title page material on recto: "COPYRIGHT © 1981 by United Artists Corporation | Foreword COPYRIGHT © 1981 by J. R. Fowles Ltd. | [*conditions of sale statement*] | LIBRARY OF CONGRESS CATALOG CARD NO. 81-87032 | FIRST EDITION | MV | PRINTED IN THE UNITED STATES OF AMERICA". ISBN 0-316-70851-8.

Contents: [a–b] blank; [c] half-title; [d] other Pinter titles; [e] other Fowles titles; [f]–[i] title page material; [ii] as above; [iii] Pinter's note; [iv] details of film; [v] contents; [vi] blank; vii–xv foreword; [xvi] blank; [xvii] fly-title; [xviii] blank; 1–104 text.

c. American special edition (1981):

As for trade edition, but bound in black cloth; on outside front, pasted-on cream label: "[*within single-rule frame:*] [*4 lines in green:*] The | French | Lieutenant's | Woman | [*3 lines in black:*] A SCREENPLAY | BY | HAROLD PINTER"; on spine, lettering as for trade edition, in gold. Endpapers green. In slip-case.

LCCN 81-83031. On inserted leaf, preceding half-title, limitation statement: "*This special edition of | the screenplay of | THE FRENCH LIEUTENANT'S WOMAN | is limited to 360 copies signed by HAROLD PINTER and JOHN FOWLES | 350 numbered copies are for sale | and 10 roman numeral copies are | reserved for the use of the publisher. | This is copy ____.* " [A copy owned by William Baker is numbered "269" and signed by both Harold Pinter and John Fowles.]

B5   **THE FRENCH LIEUTENANT'S WOMAN,**   1982
AND OTHER SCREENPLAYS

a. First edition (1982):

THE FRENCH | LIEUTENANT'S | WOMAN | *and other screenplays* | by HAROLD PINTER | [*short decorative rule, 4.2 cm.*] | *The French Lieutenant's Woman* | (published in association with Jonathan Cape) | *Langrishe , Go Down* | *The Last Tycoon* | [*short decorative rule, 4.2 cm.*] | A Methuen Paperback | Methuen . London

4 leaves, 277 pp., 1 blank leaf. 21.4 × 13.4 cm. Off-white, light card binding; dark olive on outside, lettering off-white, reversed out of dark olive; on outside front: "HAROLD | PINTER | [*decorative rule, 7.3 cm.*] | THE FRENCH | LIEUTENANT'S | WOMAN | AND OTHER | SCREENPLAYS | [*decorative rule, 7.4 cm.*] | The Last Tycoon . Langrishe, Go Down | The French Lieutenant's Woman | [*within single-rule box:*] methuen"; on outside back: summary account of the three screenplays (15 lines), lists also *Five Screenplays* and *The Proust Screenplay*; at foot to left "PRICE NET | £4.95 | IN UK ONLY"; at foot to right "A METHUEN PAPERBACK | CINEMA/PLAYS | 0 413 48680 X"; down spine "[*large font:*] PINTER [*smaller font, in two lines:*] THE FRENCH LIEUTENANT'S WOMAN | AND OTHER SCREENPLAYS | [*across spine, in single-rule box:*] methuen".

Published 1982. On verso of title leaf: copyright statements, details of first publication of novels, "Printed in Great Britain by | Richard Clay (The Chaucer Press) Ltd, Bungay, Suffolk | Filmset in Monophoto Bembo by | Northumberland Press Ltd, Gateshead".

Contents: [i] half-title, with brief account of author; [ii] list of other titles; [iii] title page; [iv] as above; [v] contents; [vi] blank; [vii] fly-title "THE FRENCH | LIEUTENANT'S | WOMAN"; [viii] first presentation details; 1–104 text; [105–106] blank; [107] fly-title "LANGRISHE, GO DOWN"; [108] blank; [109–110] first presentation details, etc.; 111–190 text; [191] fly-title "THE LAST TYCOON"; [192] first presentation details; 193–277 text; [278–280] blank.

Notes: The Last Tycoon was first presented in Britain by CIC in 1977; directed by Elia Kazan.

Langrishe, Go Down was first presented on BBC-2 television on 20 September 1978; directed by David Jones. On p.[107], the fly-title page for *Langrishe, Go Down* bears: "*Note.* The camera directions in this screenplay are | particularly detailed as I originally wrote it with | the intention of directing it myself. | Obviously, David Jones did not observe every | direction in the shooting of the film. The structure | of the film, however, remained the structure as | written. | HAROLD PINTER".

b. Faber edition (1991):

[*All within single-rule box:*] THE FRENCH | LIEUTENANT'S WOMAN | AND OTHER SCREENPLAYS | HAROLD PINTER | The French Lieutenant's Woman | Langrishe, Go Down | The Last Tycoon | ff | *faber and faber* | LONDON · BOSTON

Pagination as for Methuen. 21.5 × 13.3 cm. Paperback, outside glossy black; on outside front: clapper design, within single-rule box in white, lettering and rules in white: "ff | [*rule*] | HAROLD | PINTER | The French | Lieutenant's | Woman and | Other Screenplays", below and partly behind title panel, illustration, slanted, showing Sarah with a shawl over her head; on outside back, in white, within single-rule box, publisher, author, title, brief account of volume, "Cover photo courtesy of United International Pictures | UK £8.99 net | [*within white panel, in black:*] ISBN 0-571-16096-4 | [*bar-code*] | 9 780571 160969"; on spine, in white, within single-rule box: "ff | [*rule*] | [*down spine, in 2 lines:*] HAROLD PINTER | The French Lieutenant's Woman and Other Screenplays".

Published 1991 (L accession 15 MAY 91). On verso of title leaf: publication information, "Printed in England by Clays Ltd St Ives plc", copyright statements for screenplays and novels, conditions of sale statement, "ISBN 0-571-16096-4".

Contents: As for Methuen.

B6   THE HEAT OF THE DAY   1989

THE HEAT | OF THE DAY | [*short rule, 8.0 cm.*] | Harold Pinter | *adapted from the novel* | *by Elizabeth Bowen* | ff | *faber and faber* | LONDON · BOSTON

3 leaves, 103 pp., 1 blank leaf. 22.1 × 13.4 cm. (hardback) 21.5 × 13.4 cm. (paperback). (A) Hardback, black cloth; on spine in white: "ff | [*rule*] | [*down spine:*] THE HEAT OF THE DAY Harold Pinter [*across spine, rule*]". Endpapers. Dust jacket glossy black, lettered and ruled mainly in white; on outside front: clapper design, above single-rule white frame, within it: "ff | [*rule*] | THE HEAT | OF THE DAY | [*rule*] | Harold | Pinter", below frame, set at an angle, within a white border (outer measure 12.2 × 8.0 cm.) colour photo of the character Stella (Patricia Hodge), in a railway compartment; on outside back: "ff | *faber and faber* | [*colour photo of Michael York as Robert, Patricia Hodge as Stella*] | [*within small white panel in black:*] ISBN 0-571-14254-0 | [*bar-code*] | 9 780571 142545"; on spine, single-rule frame, in white, lettered and ruled in white: "ff | [*rule*] | [*down spine:*] THE HEAT OF THE DAY Harold Pinter"; on front flap: title, author, 14-line account of screenplay, "Jacket photos courtesy of Neil Morland", at foot, right: "£10.99 net"; on back flap: "Faber Film", list of 25 screenplay authors.

(B) Paperback, glossy black: front cover as for outside front of dust jacket; on outside back, single-rule white frame, within it, lettered and ruled in white: "ff | *faber and faber* | [*rule*] | THE HEAT OF THE DAY | Harold Pinter | [*14-line account of the situation of the screenplay, and of its status, as the script for* "a feature for | Granada Television, starring Michael | Gambon and Patricia Hodge."] | Cover photo courtesy of Neil Marland | UK £4.99 net | Canada $12.95 | [*white panel, within it, in black:*] "ISBN 0-571-14072-6 | [*bar-code*] | 9 780571 140725"; spine as for dust jacket, except lettering within single-rule frame.

Published 1989. Prices UK hardback £10.99; paperback £4.99, Canada $12.95. On verso of title leaf: "First published in 1989 | by Faber and Faber Limited | 3 Queen Square London WC1 3AU | Printed in Great Britain by | Richard Clay

Ltd. Bungay, Suffolk | All rights reserved | © Harold Pinter, 1989 | This screenplay is based on the novel | *The Heat of the Day* by Elizabeth Bowen, | published by Jonathan Cape | Phototypeset by Input Typesetting Ltd, London | [*conditions of sale and CIP data statements*] | ISBN 0-571-14072-6".

Contents: [i] half-title, with note on Pinter; [ii] "*by the same author*", 1 title; [iii] title page; [iv] as above; [v] production details; [vi] blank; 1–103 text; [104–106] blank.

Notes: The film was produced by Granada Television in 1989; directed by Christopher Morahan. Another copy of the hardback copy has on verso of title page a pasted slip over the original ISBN. It contains "ISBN 0-571-14254-0" as the revised ISBN.

B7 THE COMFORT OF STRANGERS AND OTHER SCREENPLAYS 1990

THE COMFORT OF | STRANGERS | REUNION | TURTLE DIARY | VICTORY | Harold Pinter | ff | *faber and faber* | LONDON · BOSTON

1 blank leaf, 3 leaves, 226 pp., 3 blank leaves. 21.5 × 13.4 cm. (A) Hardback, black cloth; on spine, in white: "[*all within single-rule frame:*] ff | [*rule*] | [*down spine, in two lines:*] HAROLD PINTER | The Comfort of Strangers and Other Screenplays". Endpapers. Dust jacket, glossy black; on outside front, in white: "[*clapper design above single-rule frame; within frame:*] ff | [*rule*] | HAROLD | PINTER | [*rule*] | The Comfort | of Strangers | and Other | Screenplays | [*below frame, within a white border: colour photo of a man in a white suit*]"; on outside back: at top, in white: "ff | *faber and faber*", toward foot: "[*within white panel, in black:*] ISBN 0-571-14419-5 | [*bar-code*] | 9 780571 144198"; on spine, as for spine of book; on front flap, in white: author, title, blurb about contents, "Jacket photo © Deborah Beer", at foot: "UK £14.99 net"; on back flap: "*Faber Film*", list of authors.

(B) Paperback, glossy black: front cover as for outside front of dust jacket; on back cover, all within single-rule frame within white panel, in black: headed as for outside back of dust jacket, rule, text as for front flap, with: "Cover photo © Deborah Beer | UK £7.99 net | [*within white single-rule frame:*] ISBN 0-571-14420-9 | [*bar-code*] | 9 780571-144204"; spine as for dust jacket.

Published 17 September 1990. Prices: hardback £14.99; paperback £7.99. On verso of title leaf: "First published in 1990 | [. . .] | Photoset by Wilmaset Birkenhead Wirral | Printed in Great Britain by | Richard Clay Ltd Bungay Suffolk", copyright, author-identification, acknowledgement of original works, conditions of sale, and CIP record statements, "ISBN 0-571-14419-5 | ISBN 0-571-14420-9 (PBK)".

Contents: [i–ii] blank; [iii] note on Pinter; [iv] Faber titles "*by the same author*"; [v] title page; [vi] as above; [vii] contents; [viii] blank; [1] fly-title "The Comfort of Strangers"; [2] production details; 3–51 text; [52]

blank; [53] fly-title "Reunion"; [54] production details; 55–99 text; [100] blank; [101] fly-title "Turtle Diary"; [102] production details; 103–163 text; [164] blank; [165] fly-title "Victory"; [166] "AUTHOR'S NOTE | I wrote *Victory* in 1982, working with the director, Richard | Lester. The finance for the film was never found. | Harold Pinter"; 167–226 text; 3 blank leaves.

B8	**THE TRIAL**	1993

THE TRIAL | adapted from the novel by Franz Kafka | Harold Pinter | ff | *faber and faber* | LONDON · BOSTON

4 leaves, 166 pp., 3 blank leaves. 21.5 × 13.3 cm. Paperback, outside glossy black; on outside front, in white within single-rule box, with clapper above: "ff | [*rule*] | HAROLD | PINTER | [*rule*] | The Trial | [*below box, within white border, colour photograph*]"; outside back: in white, all within single-rule box: "ff | *faber and faber* | [*rule*] | HAROLD PINTER | *The Trial* | [*brief account of work*] | Cover photo of Kyle MacLachlan as Joseph K. | by Simon Mein | UK £8.99 net | Canada $14.99 | [*within white panel, in black:*] ISBN 0-571-16876-0 | [*bar-code*] | 9 780571 168767"; on spine, in white, within single-rule frame: "ff | [*rule*] | [*down spine:*] HAROLD PINTER The Trial". Endpapers.

Published 1993 (O accession 8 JUL 1993). Price UK £8.99 Canada $14.99. On verso of title leaf: publication, copyright, and conditions of sale statements, "Photoset by Parker Typesetting Service, Leicester | Printed in England by Clays Ltd, St Ives plc". ISBN 0-371-16876-0

Contents: [i] half-title, with note on Pinter; [ii] Faber's Pinter titles; [iii] title page; [iv] as above; [v] "To David Jones and Louis Marks"; [vi] blank; [vii] production details; [viii] "Author's Note | This screenplay was shot in its entirety. During the editing of the film | however, a number of scenes were cut. These cuts were made with my approval. | HP"; 1–66 text; [67–72] blank. Production photos, half- or quarter-page, on pp. 13, 17, 21, 40, 55, 61, 66.

B9	**COLLECTED SCREENPLAYS**	2000

Vol. I:

HAROLD PINTER | Collected Screenplays One | *The Servant* | *The Pumpkin Eater* | *The Quiller Memorandum* | *Accident* | *The Last Tycoon* | *Langrishe, Go Down* | Introduced by the author | ff | *faber and faber*

xi, 660 pp. 19.6 × 12.4 cm. Paperback, outside glossy black; on outside front, to left, part of still; to right, below clapper design, lettering in white: "Collected Screenplays 1 | The Servant | The Pumpkin Eater | The Quiller Memorandum |

Accident | The Last Tycoon | Langrishe, Go Down | Harold Pinter"; on outside back, in white: critiques of films, brief notes about Pinter as adaptor, "Each volume contains a new introduction by the author", small photo of Pinter with caption, "Cover design by Pentagram | Cover photograph © BFI Stills, Posters and Designs | Author photograph © Jill Furmanosky | [*within white panel: to left:*] UK £20.00 [*in centre:*] ISN 0-571-20319-1 | [*bar-code*] | 9 780571 203192 [*to right:*] 90100 | [*bar-code*]", at foot, left: "ff www.faber.co.uk"; down spine, in white, clapper bar, "Collected Screenplays 1 Harold Pinter [*at foot, across spine:*] ff".

Published 2000 (L accession 23 OCT 00). Price £20. On verso of title leaf: "First published in this collection in 2000 | [. . .] | Photoset by Parker Typesetting Service, Leicester | Printed in England by Mackays of Chatham plc, Chatham, Kent", statements of copyright in films and in the original novels, of conditions of sale, of Pinter's right as author, ISBN as above.

Contents: [i] half-title; [ii] other Faber titles "*by the same author*"; [iii] title page; [iv] as above; [v] rights statement; [vi] blank; [vii] contents; [viii] blank; ix–xi introduction, dated "13 September, 2000"; [xii] blank; [1] fly-title "The Servant"; [2] production details; 3–91 text; [92] blank; [93] fly-title "The Pumpkin Eater"; [94] production details; 95–215 text; [216] blank; [217] fly-title "The Quiller Memorandum"; [218] production details; 219–341 text; [342] blank; [343] fly-title "Accident"; [344] production details; 345–444 text; [445] fly-title "The Last Tycoon"; [446] production details; 447–556 text; [557] fly-title "Langrishe, Go Down", with "Note" on camera-directions; [558] production details; [559] note on "main action of this film", and ages of characters; [560] blank; 561–660 text.

Vol. II:

HAROLD PINTER | Collected Screenplays Two | *The Go-Between* | *The Proust Screenplay* | *Victory* | *Turtle Diary* | *Reunion* | Introduced by the author | ff | *faber and faber*

ix, 609 pp., 2 blank leaves. 19.7 × 12.5 cm. Paperback; on outside front, left-hand third, colour photo (detail; side-view of woman), right-hand two-thirds green, clapper-board design and lettering in white: "Collected Screenplays 2 | The Go-Between | The Proust Screenplay | Victory | Turtle Diary | Reunion | Harold Pinter | [*in light green:*] ff"; outside back black, lettering in white, 5 paragraphs describing contents, otherwise as for Vol. I, with "ISBN 0-571-20324-8 | [*bar-code*] | 9 780571 203246"; down spine, in white: "[*clapper strip*] Collected Screenplays 2 Harold Pinter [*at foot, across spine:*] ff".

Published 2000 (L accession 30 OCT 00). Price $20. On verso of title leaf: "First published in this collection in 2000 | [. . .] | Photoset by Parker Typesetting Service, Leicester | Printed in England by Mackays of Chatham plc", copyright statements, including those for the original novels, first publication details for latter; author's right, performing rights, conditions of sale, and CIP record statements; ISBN as above; impression numerals.

Contents: [i] half-title, with paragraph about author; [ii] list of Faber titles "*by the same author*"; [iii] title page; [iv] as above; [v] contents; [vi] blank; vii–ix introduction, signed "Harold Pinter | 13 September, 2000"; [x] blank; [1] fly-title "The Go-Between"; [2] production details; 3–119 text; [120] blank; [121] fly-title "The Proust Screenplay"; [122] blank; 123–310 text; [311] fly-title "Victory"; [312] "AUTHOR'S NOTE"; 313–413 text; [414] blank; [415] fly-title "Turtle Diary"; [416] production details; 417–531 text; [532] blank; [533] fly-title "Reunion"; [534] production details; 535–609 text; [610–614] blank.

Vol. III:

HAROLD PINTER | Collected Screenplays Three | *The French Lieutenant's Woman* | *The Heat of the Day* | *The Comfort of Strangers* | *The Trial* | *The Dreaming Child* | Introduced by the author | ff | *faber and faber*

viii, 551 pp. 19.6 × 12.3 cm. Paperback; on outside front, to left, collage of colour stills, from *The French Lieutenant's Woman*, to right, navy blue base-colour, lettering in white: "[*clapper design*] | Collected Screenplays 3 | The French Lieutenant's Woman | The Heat of the Day | The Comfort of Strangers | The Trial | The Dreaming Child | Harold Pinter"; outside back blue, lettered in white: account of Pinter as screenwriter, otherwise as for Vol. I, with "ISBN 0-571-20733-2 | [*bar-code*] | 9 780571 207336"; down spine, diagonally striped strip, in white: "Collected Screenplays 3 Harold Pinter [*across spine:*] ff".

Published first in this collection 2000 (L accession 23 OCT 00). Price £20. On verso of title leaf: statements as for Vol. I. Copyright for the screenplay of *The Trial*, "© 1992 Harold Pinter"; for *The Dreaming Child*, "© 2000 Fox Searchlight Pictures Inc."; the author of the latter, "Isak Dinesen", is identified as Karen Blixen-Finecke; ISBN as above; impression numerals.

Contents: [i] half-title, with brief account of Pinter; [ii] Faber titles "*by the same author*"; [iii] title page; [iv] as above; [v] contents; [vi] blank; vii–viii introduction, signed "Harold Pinter | 13 September, 2000"; [1] fly-title, *The French Lieutenant's Woman,* with a footnote by Pinter, that some cuts and structural changes made during the production postdate this form of the screenplay; [2] production details; 3–138 text; [139] fly-title, *The Heat of the Day;* [140] production details; 141–242 text; [243] fly-title, *The Comfort of Strangers;* [244] production details; 245–328 text; [329] fly-title, *The Trial;* [330] production details; [331] author's note; [332] blank; 333–440 text; [441] fly-title, *The Dreaming Child;* [442] blank; 443–551 text; [552] blank.

C

Poetry

This section deals with publishings of individual poems first published separately. Collections of poems are covered in Section I, subsection 2. They include: *Poems* (1968), *Poems,* second edition, extended (1971), *Poems and Prose 1949–1977* (1978), *I Know the Place* (1979), *Collected Poems and Prose* (Methuen edition of 1986 and Faber editions of 1991 and 1996), *Ten Early Poems* (1992), *Various Voices* (1998), and *War* (2003) (for some of these, there is a corresponding American edition). In all but the latest of these collections, some poems were published for the first time; for identification of them, see the entries for these volumes.

The entries refer to sites of first publication, and these may include more than one poem, where at least one of them is published for the first time. The entry may also cover subsequent significant printings of the same poem. Textual differences are noted where they have been observed, but these have not been systematically checked for. Dates of composition as indicated at the foot of later reprintings of the poems are noted only when they are discrepant with the dates of first publication. Some more recent poems have also appeared on the website www.haroldpinter.org, but only one of those listed here has so far appeared only on that site, and such appearances are not normally noted.

C1   Dawn. *Hackney Downs School Magazine,* 161 (Spring 1947) 27.

C2   O beloved maiden. *Hackney Downs School Magazine,* 162 (Summer 1947) 14.

C3   New Year in the Midlands [*also*] Chandeliers and Shadows. *Poetry London,* 5: 19 (August 1950) 8–10.
Author's name given as "Harold Pinter." The latter portions of the two poems have been interchanged. The first 20 lines of "New Year in the Midlands" are followed by the last 18 lines of the other poem. The first 14 lines of "Chandeliers and Shadows" are followed by the last 12 lines of "New Year". The second poem has its *Duchess of Malfi* epigraph.

C4   NEW YEAR IN THE MIDLANDS [*also*] RURAL IDYLL [*also*] EUROPEAN REVELS. *Poetry London,* 5: 20 (November 1950) 8–9.
Author's name given as "Harold Pinta." "New Year in the Midlands" is reprinted correctly on p.8, with the editors' note, at the foot of p. 8:
"The Editors regret that owing to a typographical error which could not be corrected in time the | concluding lines of Mr Harold Pinta's two poems, "New Year in the Midlands" and "Chandeliers | and Shadows," printed in the last issue, became interchanged. We tender our apologies

to the | author, and re-print the first of these very interesting poems in the correct form."

"Rural Idyll" has 19 lines in 3 clearly indicated stanzas, but a page division after line 6 creates uncertainty as to whether there is meant to be a further stanza division here.

C5   So, This Morning of Marvels. *Poetry Quarterly*, 13: 1 (Spring 1951) 7.

Author's name given as "Harold Pinta."

C6   The Second Visit. *The Window*, 2 [*ca*. April 1951] 13.

Author's name given as "Harold Pinta." L accession 14 APR 51. *The Window*, edited by John Sunkey, was published by Villiers Publications, 290 West End Lane, London NW6.

C7   ONE A STORY, TWO A DEATH. *Poetry London*, 6: 22 (Summer 1951) 22–23.

Author's name given as "HAROLD PINTA". 3 sections (each divided into stanzas) numbered *I*, *II*, and *III*. Accompanying illustration of a desperate young man, looking around, beside an open coffin with a woman's body in it, outdoors.

C8   I shall Tear Off my Terrible Cap. *Poetry Quarterly*, 13: 2 (Summer 1951) 59.

Author's name as "Harold Pinta." In line 13, this text has "With his vicious cut he [i.e., Time] shall close my trap"; the text in *Poems* (1968) and later printings reads "With this vicious cut he shall close my trap". Either reading fits the context.

C9   You in the Night. *The Glass*, 7 [*ca*. January 1953] [27].

Author's name given as "Harold Pinta." L accession 31 JAN 53. *The Glass*, edited by Anthony Borrow, was published in Lowestoft.

C10   THE ERROR OF ALARM. In: *New Poems 1957*, edited by Kathleen Nott, C. Day Lewis, and Thomas Blackburn (London: Michael Joseph, 1957) 98.

Undated here. In *VV*, dated 1956.

C11   Afternoon. *Twentieth Century*, 169: 1008 (February 1961) 218.

In *P&P*, dated 1957.

C12   The Error of Alarm [*also*] The Table [*also*] Afternoon. *Poetry Northwest*, VIII: 1 (Spring 1967) 3–5.

On p. 47, the note on Pinter in "*About Our Contributors*" reads: "HAROLD PINTER is probably the best and most influential playwright in the | English-speaking world. Of his own poetry, he says, 'I've written many poems | in the past but there are only about three that I think are any good.' These | are the three." In *P&P*, etc., "The Table" is dated 1963, and "Afternoon" 1957. The texts are invariant, but "Afternoon" appears here in three stanzas, whereas in *P&P* its second stanza is divided into two, after "Their articles of faith."

C13   THE ISLANDS OF ARAN SEEN FROM | THE MOHER CLIFFS. [1968] Small broadsheet, 25.4 × 18.8 cm. At foot of text: "From *Poems* (1968) | Number   ".

A copy owned by William Baker is numbered in ink "xiii", and signed "Harold Pinter". It is tucked into a copy of *Alan Clodd and the Enitharmon Press*.

C14   All of That. *Times Literary Supplement*, LXIX: 3589 (11 December 1970) 1436.
Reprinted in: *Vogue*, 158 (July 1971) 98.

C15   Poem ("they kissed I turned they stared"). *New York Times Magazine* (5 December 1971) 135.
Printed in association with Mel Gussow, "A Conversation [Pause] with Harold Pinter," see *G37*.

C16   Poem ("and all the others"). *Aquarius*, 7 (1974) 9.

C17   "Later". *The New Review*, 2: 23 (February 1976) 26.
In *P&P*, dated 1974.

C18   Message [*also*] The Doing So. *The New Review*, 4: 39/40 (June/July 1977) 26.

C19   Paris [*also*] I Know the Place. *Bananas*, 9 (Winter 1977) 35.
Both dated 1975. Also printed on this page, "New Year in the Midlands", dated 1950. *Bananas* was published in London.

C20   Poem ("The lights glow"). *Times Literary Supplement*, 4076 (15 May 1981) 531.

C21   The Ventriloquists. *London Magazine*, n.s., 22: 1 and 2 (April/ May 1982) 36–37.
In *CP&P*, dated 1981.

C22   Ghost. *Times Literary Supplement*, 4205 (4 November 1983) 1204.

C23   Before They Fall. *Observer* (22 January 1984) 52.
In *CP&P*, dated 1983.

C24   Partners ("The Russians and Americans love each other"). *Only Poetry*, Vol. 8 (Summer 1986) [iv].
In pamphlet form, unpaginated, [32] pp. Published from Emscote Lawn, Warwick.

C25   Joseph Brearley 1909–1977 [*also*] Poem ("I saw Len Hutton in his prime"). *Soho Square*, II (1989) 182.
In *CP&P*, dated 1977 and 1986, respectively. *Soho Square* was edited by Ian Hamilton.

C26   Restaurant. *Daily Telegraph*, 1989.
In *CP&P*, etc., dated 1989. No more specific date of first publication given.

C27a   It Is Here. *Times Literary Supplement*, 4531 (2–8 February 1990) 113.
Below the title, "(for A)".

C27b   It Is Here. [*At foot of leaf:*] *Published by Bernard Stone and Raymond Danowski. The Turret Bookshop London May 1993.*
Published as a single printed leaf, on white paper. One of a series of such publications of single poems by Stone and Danowski. The copy listed in the British Library catalogue is missing, but there is a copy in *PA* Box 61, which also contains holograph and typescript drafts, and a proof (with the title in capitals) for this printing.

C28   Poem ("This man has a nose and two eyes"). *Independent* (16 February 1991), Weekend Books section: 29.
Typescript drafts and offprint in *PA* Box 61.

C29a American Football | (Reflection on the Gulf War). *BOMB*, XXXVIII (Winter 1992) 82.
Despite the ostensible date, this issue was published in the first week of December 1991 (information from Daniel Grossman, BOMB office, West Village, New York). Prior to this publishing, the poem, written in August 1991, had been rejected by the *London Review of Books,* the *Guardian,* the *Observer,* the *Independent* and the *New York Review of Books.*

C29b American Football. *The Pinter Review V: Annual Essays for 1991* (1991) 41.
This volume has on the verso of its titlepage "copyright © 1991", and was published in December 1991. The poem is here dated August 1991.

C29c American Football – A Reflection on the Gulf War. *Socialist* (15–28 January 1992).
This fortnightly newspaper had been launched in London in 1989, by Hilary Wainwright and others, who subsequently closed it down, to launch instead the monthly magazine *Red Pepper.* From its inception, Pinter had given it significant support.

C29d [Reprintings within articles that surveyed its troubled quest for publication] E. B., "Harold Pinter: le poème interdit," *Actes de la Recherche en Sciences Sociales* (10 June 1992): 32 (based upon a previous article by Lucas Ligtenberg in *Dagbladunie* [27 Fevrier 1992], not traced). "Blowing up the Media," *Index on Censorship* 21: 5 (May 1992): 2–3 (conversation with A. Graham-Yooll; see *E30*). Also, in *Handelsblad* (a Dutch newspaper; article referred to in *TPR,* but not traced).

C29e [Further significant reprintings, in:] Billington 329. *Red Pepper,* 61 (June 1999), [birthday supplement:] 3. *101 Poems Against War,* edited by Matthew Harris and Paul Keegan, with an afterword by Andrew Motion (London: Faber and Faber, 2003) 80. *War* [19]. Also published in Bulgaria, Greece, and Finland.

C30   God. *Times Literary Supplement,* 4734 (24 December 1993) 21.
The use of hotel writing paper for holograph drafts in *PA* Box 61 (which also contains typescript drafts and proofs of it) indicates Pinter began working on this poem in Dublin.

C31   Justin Falkus (about to depart for Japan) [dated 1993]. On website www.haroldpinter.org/cricket.
Falkus played for the Gaieties cricket team.

C32   Poem ("Don't look."). *Guardian* (17 January 1995), Section 2, Features: 7.
Here dated 12 January 1995. Reprinted, *Evening Standard* (18 January 1995). In Billington, text printed (from a draft), and referred to as "Chokepit" (363–364).

C33   Cricket at Night. *Guardian* (3 June 1995), Guardian Features: 29.
Holograph and typescript drafts (dated May 1995) and offprint in *PA* Box 61.

C34   The Other Guy. *Guardian* (15 July 1995), Guardian Features: T6.
Holograph and typescript drafts (dated June 1995) and offprints in *PA* Box 61.

C35   Order. *Guardian* (12 September 1996), Guardian Features: 29.
Holograph and typescript drafts and proofs in *PA* Box 65.

C36   The Old Days. *Observer* (29 September 1996), Observer Review section: 18.

C37   Death (Births and Deaths Registration Act 1953). *Times Literary Supplement*, 4932 (10 October 1997) 11.
Holograph and typescript drafts and offprints in *PA* Box 61. Written at the time of his father's death. Reprinted in: *War* [21], under the title "Death."

C38   The Disappeared 1998. *Sunday Times* (16 August 1998), Features: 6.

C39   Requiem for 1945. *Sunday Times* (30 May 1999), Books section: 4.

C40   Cancer Cells. *Guardian* (14 March 2002), G2: 5.
Headed, below the title, "Harold Pinter has been diagnosed with cancer of the oesophagus. 'Cancer cells are those which have forgotten how to die' – nurse, Royal Marsden hospital." Also printed alongside article by Nigel Reynolds, "Pinter writes poem on his cancer fight," *Daily Telegraph* (15 March 2002), seen on *Telegraph* website. Poem reprinted in: *New York Review of Books* (23 May 2002) 14 (at foot of poem, "Copyright © 2002 by Harold Pinter and © 2002 by Guardian Newspapers Limited.").

C41   Meeting. *Guardian* (28 August 2002), G2: 4.
Printed in association with an interview with Ramona Koval, at the Edinburgh Festival, pp.2–4 (the poem "Cancer Cells" is also reprinted here). See *G117*. Reprinted in: *War* [9].

C42   After Lunch. *Guardian* (5 October 2002) 37.
As "The Saturday Poem." Dated September 2002. Reprinted in: *War* [10].

C43   God Bless America. *Guardian* (22 January 2003), G2: 4.
See also: Mark Steyn. "Stanza to Reason." *Daily Telegraph* (filed 25 February 2003; seen on website www.telegraph.co.uk), a satiric account of a (possibly wholly imaginary) recording of this poem, at the Abbey Road studio, London. Poem reprinted in: *War* [11].

C44   The Bombs. *Independent* (15 February 2003).
Spoken as part of Pinter's speech at the No War in Iraq Rally, Hyde Park, 15 February 2003 (see *E56*). Reprinted in: *War* [12].

C45   To A. ("What was that sound that comes in on the dark?").
Spoken by Pinter at the Arvon Foundation's "Promises to Keep" event, Duke of York's Theatre, London, 3 March 2003, along with readings of other poets' poems by him and by other speakers. Four lines quoted in: "Pinter the performer outdoes Pinter the poet: Lloyd Evans reviews the

Pinter reading at the Duke of York's." *Daily Telegraph,* filed 4 March 2003, seen on website www.telegraph.co.uk. The event was mounted to raise funds for The Hurst, a Shropshire estate, where young poets can stay and receive mentoring.

C46   Democracy. *Spectator* (15 March 2003) 13.

Also printed as A4-sized broadsheet, and placed as a broadside poster outside the Tricycle Theatre, April-May 2003, during the first production of Kerry Lee Crabbe's *The Dwarfs,* adapted from Pinter's novel. Reprinted in: *War* [13], dated February 2003. See *D8,* for *The Dwarfs* as a novel and *A12,* for the earliest publication of Pinter's own play, also, relevant entries in *Appendix One.*

C47   Weather Forecast ("The day will get off to a cloudy start."). *Guardian* (20 March 2003). G2:2.

Dated in *Guardian* "19 March 2003". Reprinted in *War* [14].

C48   To my wife. *Guardian* (22 July 2004), G2:4.

C49   The "special relationship." *Guardian* (9 September 2004), G2:4.

D

Fiction

A few of the items in this section have a sufficiently complex history to also be given separate notice in *Appendix One*. One item, the novel *The Dwarfs*, merits a full-scale entry here. The short fiction pieces have been included in a series of collections (see the headnote for the previous section), with only the first of these being noted. The items would also have appeared in the American publications of these collections.

D1a   The Examination. *Prospect* (Summer 1959) 21–25.
D1b   The Examination. *Encounter*, 96 (September 1961) 9–11.
       Reprinted in: *The Collection and The Lover* (1963) [89]–94; *P&P* 61–66 (dated 1955), etc.
D2a   The Black and White. *The Spectator*, 203 (1 July 1960): 16.
D2b   THE BLACK & WHITE | An unpublished text by | HAROLD PINTER. *Flourish*, 4 (Summer 1965) 4.
       Flourish was the "Royal Shakespeare Club Newspaper". On this page, there is also a portrait-photo of Pinter, a production-photo of Lenny (Ian Holm) and Teddy (Michael Bryant) from *The Homecoming*, and a poem by Nicki Tester, "Silence Please: Written after seeing *The Homecoming* at the Theatre Royal, Brighton". Cutting in *PA* Box 67. Reprinted in: *Transatlantic Review*, 21 (Summer 1966): 51–52; *P&P* 57–58 (dated 1954–55), etc.
D3a   Tea Party. *Playboy* (January 1965) 124.
       Cutting in *PA* Box 67. Reprinted in: *P&P* 69–73 (dated 1963), etc. It was commissioned by *Playboy* in late 1963, although it would not be printed till over a year later. It was read, by Pinter, as a short story, on the BBC Third Programme, on 28 April 1964 (recorded 23 April). It formed the basis for a play for television, see A21, W22(2).
D3b   [Tea Party.] GORGONA 8 1965 | HAROLD PINTER [Private edition, published in Zagreb, Yugoslavia, by Josip Vanista.]
       Unpaginated, 4 leaves. 21 cm. Bound in white paper covers, printed in olive and gold; on outside front: "GORGONA"; on inside back: "EXAMPLE | [3 rules] | PRIVATE EDITION | JOSIP VANISTA | ZAGREB – JUGOSLAVIA". 250 copies printed in English. Also, a translation into Serbo-Croat by Vlatista Nakloba was published with the same format and cover, in 280 copies.
D3c   Tea Party. In: Joan Kahn, ed. *The Edge of the Chair*. London: Arlington Books: 1968

ix, 562 pp. Hardback "Tea Party" is on pp.120–123. In the "Biographical Notes" on p. 120, relating to Pinter: "He lists his recreation as drinking." The editor states on p. 2 that the "over-all theme of this collection is suspense." The book was also published in the same year in New York by Harper and Row.

D4   Kullus. In: *Poems* (London: Enitharmon Press, 1968) 22–24. Dated 1949. Reprinted in *P&P* 51–54, etc.

D5   The Coast. *Transatlantic Review* 56/56 (May 1976) 5. Reprinted in *P&P* 93, etc., dated 1975.

D6   LOLA / HAROLD PINTER. *The New Review,* 3. 36 (March 1977) 7. Reprinted in *P&P* 101–[102], etc.

D7   Problem. *Transatlantic Review,* 60 (June 1977) 30–31. Reprinted in *P&P* 97, etc., dated 1976.

D8   **THE DWARFS**   1990

a. British standard edition (1990):

The Dwarfs | A *Novel* | HAROLD PINTER | [*short rule, 2.8 cm.*] | ff | *faber and faber* | LONDON · BOSTON

3 leaves, 183 pp., 1 blank leaf. 23.3 × 15.1 cm. Binding black cloth; down spine in silver: "HAROLD PINTER The Dwarfs [*across spine, at foot:*] ff". Endpapers. Dust jacket black; on outside front, picture of part of face, with spectacles, one lens showing one eye, the other lens a circle of sky, together with the edges of an open book; at upper left, within a blue panel, ruled and lettered in white: "ff | [*rule*] | HAROLD | PINTER | [*rule*] | The Dwarfs"; on outside back, to left, within white single-rule frame, publisher, author, title, brief account of novel, "Jacket illustration by Andrzej Klimowski", within white panel, in black: "ISBN 0-571-14446-2 | [*bar-code*] | 9 780571 144464", to right, two photos of the author, dated 1953 and 1988; down spine, in white: "HAROLD PINTER The Dwarfs [*across spine, at foot:*] ff"; on front flap, in white, list of authors of "*Faber Fiction*", at foot: "UK £12.99 net | Canada $24.95"; on back flap, brief list of Pinter's plays and screenplays.

Published *ca.* 10 October 1990 [date on proof copy]. Price £12.99. On verso of title leaf: "First published in 1990 | [. . .] | Photoset by Parker Typesetting Service, Leicester | Printed in Great Britain by | Richard Clay Ltd Bungay Suffolk", copyright statements, CIP record notice, ISBN number (as above).

Contents: [i] half-title "The Dwarfs"; [ii] list of other titles "*by the same author*"; [iii] title page; [iv] as above; [v] "To Judy Daish"; [vi] "AUTHOR'S NOTE"; [1] fly-title for Part One, "I"; [2] blank; 3–183 text; on 183, below text: "1952–1956 Revised 1989"; [184–186] blank.

Note one: A proof copy of this edition, bound in pale blue light card, with the Faber and Faber "ff" design on the outside, has on its front cover, within a single-rule box, in black: "ff | *faber and faber* | [*rule*] | The Dwarfs | Harold Pinter | Probable publication date: | 10 October 1990 | Probable price £11.99 | Uncorrected advance proofs"; down spine: "The Dwarfs   Harold Pinter". 5 leaves (includes 2 copies of title leaf), 183 pp. (pp. [1–2] as blank leaf). Leaf-measure 21.5 × 13.6 cm. (typesetting corresponds to published edition, but printed in smaller font). [Copy owned by William Baker.]

Note two: In the "AUTHOR'S NOTE" Pinter records that he wrote this "in the early fifties," then in 1960 "extracted some elements" for a short play, and in 1989 decided upon some reworking, mainly involving cuts, to render the novel publishable. "Despite this reshaping, the text is fundamentally that written | over the period 1952–1956." Prior to the publication of the novel, chapters from it had been published in *TPR*, 1: 1 (1987): 4–6, and in 2:1 (1988): 5–7. For *The Dwarfs* as a radio play (1960), and as a stage-play (1963), see *A12*, and *Appendix One*.

b. Paperback edition (1990):

Title page as for hardback, but short rule measures 1.6 cm., imprint "LONDON . BOSTON".

3 leaves, 183 pp. 19.7 × 12.5 cm. Paperback, outside front, back and spine as for dust jacket of hardback, except, on outside back, price given as "UK £5.99 net | Canada $12.99", and within the other white panel: "ISBN 0 - 571 - 16417 - X | [*bar-code*] | 9 780571 164172".

c. "Limited Edition" (1990):

Title page as for standard hardback.

5 leaves, 183 pp., 1 blank leaf. 23.4 × 15.1 cm. Hardback, quarter-bound in brown cloth (extending 3.7 cm. across width of each board), boards bound with marbled paper; at junction of paper and cloth, on the cloth, a vertical line in gilt; on spine, within a double rule frame in gilt, ruled and lettered in gilt: "Harold | Pinter | [*star*] | The | Dwarfs | [*star*] | [*rule*] | LONDON | LIMITED | EDITIONS". Endpapers. Grease-proof paper dust jacket.

Contents: As for standard edition, except for extended preliminaries: [i] "HAROLD PINTER | THE DWARFS | [*at foot of page, within a double-rule frame:*] LONDON | [*rule*] | LIMITED | [*rule*] | EDITIONS"; [ii] blank; [iii] "One of 150 numbered copies of the | First Edition of | *The Dwarfs* | signed by the author and | specially bound | No." [Copy owned by William Baker numbered "53" and signed in black ink "Harold Pinter"; TxU-HRC copy numbered "63" and signed.]

d. American edition (1990):

The Dwarfs | A Novel | HAROLD PINTER | [*short rule*] | [*small publisher's device*] | Grove Weidenfeld | NEW YORK

4 leaves, 183 pp. 21.2 × 13.7 cm. Hardback, quarter bound with pale green cloth extending 3.2 cm. across width of boards, boards bound with grey paper; down spine in silver: "Harold Pinter THE DWARFS [*small publisher's device*] [*in two lines:*] GROVE | WEIDENFELD". Endpapers. Dust jacket green-tinged, on front wrapper schematic design of elements of domestic interior spread with personal possessions, above: "[*in green:*] THE DWARFS | [*in grey:*] Harold Pinter", at foot: "[*in grey:*] a novel"; on back, large photo of Pinter, small panel at foot in white, with bar-code, "9 780802 113856 | ISBN 0-8021-1385-0", to right, second bar-code, with above it: "90000>"; lettered down spine, in grey, as for spine of book; on front flap, price "$17.95", and account of novel; on back flap, brief biographical note about Pinter, "Jacket design by Krystyna Skalski | Jacket photograph by Michele Clement | [*Grove device*] | GROVE WEIDENFELD | 10/90 Printed in USA © 1990 Grove Press Inc."

Published November 1990 (*Publishers Weekly*, 6 February 1991, p.78). Price $17.95. On verso of title leaf: "Copyright © 1990 by Harold Pinter | All rights reserved | [*conditions of sale statement*] | Published by Grove Weidenfeld | A division of Grove Press, Inc. | 841 Broadway | New York, New York 10003-4793 | First published in Great Britain in 1990 by Faber and Faber Limited, London | [*DLC cataloging data*] | Manufactured in the United States of America | Printed on acid-free paper | First American Edition 1990 | 10 9 8 7 6 5 4 3 2 1".

Contents: As for Methuen edition.

D9   Short Story. *London Magazine*, n.s., 35. 7 & 8 (October/November 1995) [3].
Begins: "There was another daughter who died." Reprinted in: VV 96.

D10a   Girls. *Sunday Times* (1 October 1995). Section 7: 8b.

D10b   Girls. *Granta*, 51 (Autumn 1995): 254–255; fly-title on p. 253. Reprinted in: VV 97–98, etc.; in: *Granta 21*, otherwise *Twenty-One: The Best of Granta Magazine*. Selected by Ian Jack (London, New York Granta Books, 2001) 272–273 (p.271: fly-title).

D11   Latest Reports from the Stock Exchange. *Sunday Times* (2 February 1997), Books: 4.
Reprinted in VV 78–80, dated 1953, with Pinter's note that he had written it in that year, "but lost it. It came to light recently" (VV 78).

D12   Sorry About This. *Areté: The Arts Tri-Quarterly*, 1 (Winter 1999) 18. Reprinted in VV (Grove, 2000).

D13   TESS | A short story by Harold Pinter. *Tatler* (November 2000) 75–76. On p.75, above the text, a large photo of a young woman. Reprinted i

VV (Grove, 2000). Performed as a dramatic sketch, Royal National Theatre, 8 February 2002.

D14 Voices in the Tunnel. *Jewish Quarterly: A Magazine of Contemporary Writing and Culture*, 183 (Autumn 2001) 5.

An imaginative piece based on reminiscences. Reprinted in: *The Golden Chain: Fifty Years of The Jewish Quarterly,* edited by Natasha Lehrer (London, and Portland, Oregon: Vallentine Mitchell, 2003) 37.

E

Prose Non-Fiction: Essays, Articles, and Published Speeches

Essays, articles, and published speeches are bracketed here because an item that was first featured as a speech has often been published in print subsequently as an article or essay. A few items have appeared as separate publications and merit full-scale entries. Where an item has later appeared in a collection, the first such appearance is often noticed, but the item would also be found in successor publications, including American equivalents. In some cases, it has been impractical to pursue the page numbers of items in serials. Where items have been seen, the use of lower case or capitals reproduces what is present on the page. Where they have not been seen, the presentation of titles follows the convention of capitalising initial letters of the more important words.

E1   James Joyce. *Hackney Downs School Magazine,* 160 (Christmas 1946) 32–33.

E2   Speech: "Opposing the Motion 'That a United Europe Would Be the Only Means of Preventing War.'" *idem,* 161 (Spring 1947) 14.

E3   Speech: That the War is Inevitable. *idem,* 162 (Summer 1947) 9.

E4   Speech: Realism and Post-Realism in the French Cinema. *idem,* 163 (Autumn 1947) 13.

E5   Blood Sports. *idem,* 163 (Autumn 1947) 23–24.

E6   Speech: Supporting the Motion that "In View of its Progress in the Last Decade, the Film is More Promising in its Future as an Art than the Theatre." *idem,* 164 (Spring 1948) 12.

E7   [Essay, as an extended letter] A Letter to Peter Wood (30 March 1958).
      "Letter to Peter Wood, director of *The Birthday Party,* written just before rehearsals started for the first production of the play in April 1958" (*VV* 8; text of letter reprinted in full, with the title "On *The Birthday Party* I", 8–11; note by Martin Esslin [1981], 11–12). First published in the *Kenyon Review,* III, No. 3 (Summer 1981): 2–5, with a note by Martin Esslin, editor of the *Kenyon Review.* Also, as "A Letter to Peter Wood (1958)," *Drama,* n.s. 142 (Winter 1981): 4–5. Also in: *Harold Pinter: The Birthday Party, The Caretaker and The Homecoming,* ed. Michael Scott (London: Macmillan, 1986), 79–82.

E8   [Essay, as an extended letter to the editor, see *F1*] *The Play's the Thing* (October 1958) 10–11.
      Reprinted with the title "On *The Birthday Party* II", *VV* 13–15. An extract from this letter, untitled and unsigned, printed on a single leaf, was inserted into the theatre programme for the production of *The Room* and

The Dumb Waiter, at the Royal Court Theatre, premièred 8 March 1960. ["Given a man in a room and he will sooner or later receive a visitor. . . . The more acute the experience the less articulate its expression."]. This extract was reprinted in: Martin Esslin, *Pinter: A Study of His Plays,* 3rd edition (London: Methuen, 1977), 40.

E9   Writing for Myself. *Twentieth Century,* 169 (February 1961) 172–175. This piece was reputedly edited by Richard Findlater on the basis of an interview, with Pinter being dissatisfied by the initial result, and revising it for further publication. Reprinted in revised form in *Plays: Two* (1977), 9–12 (as *"Based on a conversation with Richard Findlater . . ."*).

E10   Speech. "Writing for the Theatre." First published as: "Pinter: Between the Lines." *Sunday Times* (4 March 1962) 25. Delivered at the Seventh National Student Drama Festival, Bristol, 1962. Deals with his concepts of verification and of the uses of language. Reprinted, in a revised and extended form, as: "Writing for the Theatre," in: *The New British Drama,* ed. Henry Popkin (New York: Grove Press, 1964), 574–580; *Evergreen Review,* 33 (August-September 1964): 80–82; *Evergreen Review Reader 1957–1967: A Ten Year Anthology,* ed. Barney Gosset (New York: Grove Press, 1967), [633]–635; *English Dramatic Theories,* Vol. 4, *20th Century,* ed. Paul Goetsch (Tübingen: M. Niemeyer, 1972), 118–124; *Harold Pinter Plays One* (1976), 9–16; VV 16–20. For earlier explorations of the ideas expressed, see *E8, F1, J4.*

E11   Beckett. In: *Beckett at Sixty: A Festschrift,* edited by John Calder (London: Calder and Boyars, 1967), 86. This is in the main a paragraph extracted from a letter to a friend, written in 1954, with the addition of three introductory sentences and a concluding sentence. The paragraph itself is reprinted verbatim in *VV* 45, dated 1954, without the accompanying sentences.

E12   The Birthday Party. In: *Writers' Theatre,* edited by Keith Waterhouse & Willis Hall (London: Heinemann, 1967), 69. This Heinemann Educational Books volume contains extracts from ten plays by contemporary British authors, each preceded by an introductory note by the playwright(s). Pinter selected the middle third of Act II of *The Birthday Party* (from *"Enter MCCANN with bottles."* to the entry of Meg, and her first line: "I brought the drum down. I'm dressed for the party."), which occupies pp. 70–77. The fly-title for Pinter's piece is on p. [67], p. [68] is blank, and his note (a single-paragraph summary of the plot-situation, up to this point) on p. 69, with, below it, "© HAROLD PINTER".

E13   The Knight Has Been Unruly – Memories of Sir Donald Wolfit. *The Listener,* 79 (18 April 1968) 501. This was one of a series of tributes to Wolfit, broadcast on the BBC-1 "Contrasts" programme, by Michael Elliott, Ronald Fraser, Pinter, and Sir Tyrone Guthrie. Pinter's contribution includes comments on Wolfit's acting.

E14   MAC   1968

a. Separate publication, in UK (1968):

[*In open letters:*] MAC | HAROLD PINTER | [*double rule, thick, thin, 6.6 cm.*] | [*Pendragon Press device, in white, reversed out of orange-brown oval, 3.4 × 3.7 cm.*] | EMANUEL WAX | FOR PENDRAGON PRESS | 1968.

21 pp., 1 leaf (unpaginated leaf present in Binding B copies only). 20.9 × 13.5 cm. Bindings: (A) Hardback, quarter-bound with green cloth, rest of boards covered with grey paper; down spine, in gold: "MAC [*Maltese cross*] Pinter Pendragon Press"; endpapers lime green. (B) Hardback, quarter-bound with pale green cloth, rest of boards covered with off-white linen cloth, spine-lettering and endpapers as for A.

Published May 1968 (L accession 22 MAY 68). 2000 copies. On verso of title leaf: "© Harold Pinter 1968 | Library of Congress Catalogue card No. 68-26009 | Designed and printed in Great Britain by | W. S. Cowell Ltd, Buttermarket, Ipswich".

Contents: [1] half-title "*MAC*"; [2] blank; [3] title page; [4] as above; 5–19 text; [20] blank; 21 "BIOGRAPHICAL NOTE" on Anew McMaster; [22] blank; [23] limitation notice: "*This first edition is limited to 2,000 | copies of which 1,000 (numbered 1–1,000) | are intended for sale in the British Isles | and 1,000 (1,001–2,000) in the United | States of America. | This copy is number*"; [24] blank [pp. [23–24] present in Binding B copies only].

Notes: The L copy (Binding A) is signed on p.19 in facsimile "Harold Pinter". A copy owned by William Baker copy (Binding B) is numbered in ink on p. [23] "117", and signed in facsimile on p. 19. The essay has later been reprinted in: *P&P, CP&P* 83–90 (preliminary note, p.82); *VV* 21–27 (preliminary note at head). Dated in these, 1966. Text of a talk given on BBC Radio 3, 17 April 1963, repeated 13 September 1964 and 25 March 1968 (1968 copy of BBC tape, *NSA* M1371R C1), and see *E21*. The book was distributed in the USA by Grove Press.

b. In American periodical (1968):

Mac. *Harper's Bazaar*, 102 (November 1968) 234–235.

c. In anthology (1969):

Mac. *Good Talk 2: An Anthology from BBC Radio*, edited by Derwent May (London: Victor Gollancz Ltd, 1969), 20–27.

d. American reprint (1979):

[*In open letters:*] MAC | HAROLD PINTER | [*double rule, thick, thin, 7.6 cm.*] | [*Pendragon device*] | GROVE PRESS, INC. | NEW YORK

1 leaf, 21 pp., 1 leaf, 1 blank leaf. 20.5 × 12.9 cm. Paperback, stiff paper, pale cream; on outside front: "MAC | Pinter"; outside back and spine blank. Endpapers.

Reprint published in 1979 of 1968 edition. On verso of title leaf: as for 1968, with addition: "Reprinted for Grove Press | by permission of Emanuel Wax | for Pendragon Press, 1968". On p.[i]: "Reprinted for | Grove Press | by | University Microfilms International | Ann Arbor, Michigan, U.S.A. | London, England | [*DLC cataloguing data, LCCN 79-23984*] | ISBN 0-835704858".

Contents: [i] as above; [ii] blank; [1]–[23] as for 1968; [24–26] blank (photo-facsimile of a copy signed by Pinter on p. [19], with the limitation page, p. [23], also present, and the number 1134).

E15   *MEMORIES OF CRICKET | by HAROLD PINTER. Daily Telegraph Magazine* (16 May 1969) 25–26.
Reprinted in: *Cricket '72*, edited by J. A. Bailey and R. J. Roe (London: The Test and County Cricket Board, Lord's Ground, 1972), pp. 26, 28, as "Hutton and the Past". Also, with this latter title, in: *P&P* 78–90, *CP&P* 93–96; *VV* 28–30.

E16   Pinter on Beckett. *New Theatre Magazine*, XI. 3 (May-June 1971) 3.
This issue of the magazine has on the cover "Samuel Beckett Special Issue". Pinter's piece is the text of his short speech of tribute when he opened the Samuel Beckett Exhibition at the University Library, Reading, on 19 May 1971; he also pays tribute to "Dr. [James] Knowlson and his colleagues" who mounted the exhibition. A photographic version of the exhibition would be touring the UK, and this issue of the magazine would evidently be associated with it.

E17   Speech : Hamburg 1970. *Theatre Quarterly*, I: 3 (July-September 1971) 3–4.
Text of speech of acceptance, on 4 June 1970, for the award of the Shakespeare Prize, for his two plays *Landscape* and *Silence*. Reprinted in: *Plays: Four* (1981), pp. [ix]–xiii, as the "Introduction" to this volume; see *I1 (4)* (note in *VV* 203 states this speech was "first published in *Harold Pinter Plays Three*, 1970"; but the latter does not include it, and was first published in 1978). Reprinted, as "On Being Awarded the German Shakespeare Prize in Hamburg," in *VV* 31–34, there dated 1970.

E18   Public and Private: Notes by Harold Pinter. *Manitoba Theatre Centre Newsletter* (1 January 1972) 1–2.
Not seen; status not established.

E19   Pinter on Pinter. *The American Film Theatre / Cinebill*, 1. 2 (October 1973) 5–7.
Remarks made at the time of the Hamburg award ceremony, on the dif-ferences between writing for the stage and for the screen (not included within the speech of acceptance). Within an issue devoted to *The Homecoming*.

E20   [Account of experiences of reading.] In: *Bookmarks,* edited and introduced by Frederic Raphael (London: Jonathan Cape, 1975), 126.
This was a compilation by the Authors' Lending Right Society Ltd,
associated with the Writers' Action Group, British PEN. Pinter's contribution is much shorter than most, simply listing the authors he read during
each decade of his life, to date, ending with "I read a great deal of poetry."

E21   Arthur Wellard (1902–1980): (Somerset, England and Gaieties). In:
Summer Days: Writers on Cricket, edited by Michael Meyer (London:
Methuen London Ltd, 1981), 189–195.
The volume was subsequently issued as an Oxford University Press paperback in 1983. This appreciation had initially formed part of a one-man
show, on BBC radio, "Players," with "Mac," performed in 1981 by
Edward De Souza (NSA B7383/10). Later, Pinter's own reading of the two-
piece programme was broadcast on BBC Radio 3, 17 March 1985.
Reprinted in: *CP&P* 111–118; *VV* 37–42. Dated 1981. Harold Pinter was
initially a player in the Gaieties Cricket Club, a touring team constituted
mainly by show business people, and subsequently became its chairman.

E21A   **ARTHUR WELLARD**   1981

ARTHUR WELLARD | (1902–1980) | (Somerset, England and Gaieties) | Harold
Pinter

11 pp. 21.5 x 13.7 cm. Paperback, off-white: on front cover: "ARTHUR
WELLARD | [swelled rule, 7.5 cm.] | Harold Pinter."

Published 1981. On verso of title leaf: "Harold Pinter © 1981 | Printed by Villiers
Publications Ltd | London NW5".

Contents: [1] half-title "Arthur Wellard"; [2] affixed photograph of team, cap-
tioned: *"Gaieties C. C. is a wandering side which plays club cricket in the | Home
Counties. It was established in 1937. The photograph | was taken in 1975. Arthur
Wellard is seated bottom right.";* [3] title page; [4] as above; 5–11 text; [12] blank.

Note one: The book is printed on laid paper with the watermark of a crown
above "[Cra]nbury".

Note two: It is uncertain whether this publication of it preceded or followed its
publication within the anthology *Summer Days,* issued *circa* 8 August 1981
(*Bookseller,* 8 August 1981, p. 777: cf. E21).

Note three: The copy seen is inscribed in holograph on the title page: "To Tony
| from | Harold"; it was inscribed to Anthony Astbury.

E22   **[CONTRIBUTION TO "JIMMY"]**   1984

"JIMMY" | [*double rule*] | [*publisher's device*] JONATHAN WAX | FOR
PENDRAGON PRESS | 1984

66pp. 21.5 × 14.0 cm. Quarter-bound with blue cloth, boards in oatmeal cloth. Frontispiece by Clare Shenstone.

Published 1984. On verso of title leaf: "*For Thelma Wax,* | *who knew and loved him best.* | © ACTAC (Theatrical & Cinematic) Ltd 1984 | Designed and printed in Great Britain by | W. S. Cowell Ltd, Butter Market, Ipswich".

Anthology of reminiscences of Jimmy Wax, from 47 family members, friends, and clients, edited by Jonathan Wax. Jimmy Wax, who had been Pinter's literary agent, and a good friend, had died in 1981. Literary or theatrical contributors include, in addition to Pinter: Quentin Bell, Michael Codron, David Campton, Christopher Fry, Pam Gems, Philip Mackie, and Heathcote Williams, among others. Pinter's contribution, headed "*Harold Pinter*", on pp.49–50, is reprinted in VV 43–44.

E23   How I Shall Vote. *Observer* (7 June 1987).

E24   The US Elephant must be stopped. *Guardian* (5 December 1987) 10.
       Within feature "Third World Review," as the "THIRD COLUMN." At foot of second column of text: "*Harold Pinter will launch a* | *new Arts for Nicaragua Fund* | *At the Royal Court Theatre* | *tomorrow.*" Reprinted in VV 171–172, with slight variations in punctuation and capitalization, and the date of the US overthrow of the democratically elected Guatemalan government incorrectly given as 1951, rather than 1954.

E25   Language and Lies. *Index on Censorship,* 17: 6 (1988) 2.
       On Nicaragua. Text of an address to the European Conference on City-linking Nicaragua, in Amsterdam, on 28 May 1988. Pinter was at that time chairman of the Arts for Nicaragua Fund, see E29.

E26   Eroding the Language of Freedom. *Sanity,* No. 3 (March 1989):17.
       Sanity is the journal of the Campaign for Nuclear Disarmament. Reprinted in VV 173–174. On the deceptive or meaning-deadening nature of British official rhetoric, especially, but only at its worst extreme, under the Thatcher government. Pinter's article serves as an introduction to a special section on the erosion of civil liberties, with contributions by Adrian Fulford and Ben Webb-Latter profiling Richard Shepherd, a dissident Conservative MP. Marks the relaunch of the National Council for Civil Liberties.

E27   Yanquis Go Home! *The Independent on Sunday* (27 May 1990), Sunday Review section:10–11, 15.

E28   [CONTRIBUTION] "ARTHUR MILLER'S SOCKS"   1990

In: ARTHUR MILLER AND COMPANY | Arthur Miller talks about his work | in the company of | Actors, Designers, Directors, | Reviewers and Writers | *Edited by* CHRISTOPHER BIGSBY | METHUEN DRAMA *in association with* | THE ARTHUR MILLER CENTRE FOR AMERICAN STUDIES

Published 11 October 1990. On verso of title leaf (of copy seen, second printing): "First published 1990 by Methuen Drama | [. . .] | Reprinted 1990 | Copyright © The Arthur Miller Centre for American Studies | [. . .] | ISBN 0 413

64220 8 (Hardback) | 0 413 65050 2 (Paperback) | Printed in Great Britain | by Clays Ltd, St Ives plc | [*conditions of sale statement*]".

Notes: Pinter's contribution, on pp. 4–5, was an account of his visit to Turkey with Arthur Miller in March 1985, on behalf of International PEN, to investigate the plight of imprisoned writers. Reprinted as: "Happy Birthday, Arthur." *Guardian* (17 October 1995), Guardian Features Page: T12. A short account of this visit, dated May 1985, had been included as a "POSTSCRIPT" to the interview with Nicholas Hern, in *One for the Road* (1985), p. 24.

E29   [Article on Nicaragua] *World* (March 1992).
       "Written to accompany a documentary film made by the photographer Susan Meisalas about Nicaragua" and its finally frustrated efforts to resist United States aggression. *World* magazine was a BBC publication. Not seen, but reprinted in part or in full in Billington (334–335).

E30   Blowing up the Media. *Index on Censorship*, 21: 5 (May 1992) 2–3.
       On the difficulty of getting his poem "American Football" published. At the head of the article, reprints the poem. [Described in *TPR 1991–1992* (1993) as an interview with Andrew Graham-Yooll.] Reprinted in *VV* 183–188. See C29d.

E31   Archbishop Romero's Ghost Can Be Avenged. *Observer* (28 March 1993) 24. Reprinted in *VV* 187–189, with the title "The US and El Salvador." A demand that the USA should be brought to justice for its role in El Salvador's civil strife.

E32   A NOTE ON SHAKESPEARE. *Granta,* 59 (Autumn 1993) 252–254.
       Fly-title for article on p.251. Reprinted in *VV* 5–7, dated 1950; but here Pinter says he wrote it in 1951, when touring in Ireland with Anew McMaster.

E33   [Contribution] The New Cold War. *Red Pepper, Green Socialism,* 1 (June 1994) 13.
       Special feature, includes also articles by John Pilger, Carlos Fuentes, Joe Hanlon, William Minter. On p. [3], Pinter is listed among the magazine's "advisers." "The New Cold War" had been the topic of a debate between Noam Chomsky and John Pilger, chaired by Pinter, at the Almeida Theatre, Islington, in May 1994. The host was *Red Pepper.*

E34   **A SPEECH OF THANKS**   1995

a. Separate volume (1995):

HAROLD PINTER *A speech of thanks* | Privately printed for Faber and Faber

9, [1] pp., 1 leaf. [A]⁶. Light card wrapper, with flaps, grey, sewn; on front cover: "HAROLD PINTER *A speech of thanks*", back cover and flaps blank. Endpapers matt black.

Published 1995. Colophon on p. [12]: "The speech was delivered on 15th March

1995. | © Harold Pinter, 1995. | Typeset by Parker Typesetting Service, Leicester | Printed in England by Smith Settle, Ottley, West Yorkshire | One hundred and fifty copies for private circulation | Faber and Faber Limited | 3 Queen Square, London WC1N 3AU".

Contents: [1] title page; [2] "Harold Pinter's speech of thanks on receiving | the David Cohen British Literature Prize for 1995. | The prize is awarded every two years in recognition of a lifetime's achievement by a living British writer."; 3–[10] text; [11] blank; [12] colophon.

b. In periodical (1995):

[Extract from this speech] And thank you, Hackney library. *The Times* (18 March 1995), (Features) 18.

c. In periodical (1995):

Harold Pinter. *Literature Matters* [Newsletter of the British Council literature department], 19 (September 1995) 4–5.

Notes: It was reprinted in full in *TPR 1995 & 1996* (1997): 1–3; and in *VV* 46–49 as "A Speech of Thanks," dated 15 March 1995. Pinter donated £10,000 of the prize money (£30,000) to the Glasgow Citizens' Theatre, to commission new plays. See Billington 369.

E35   A War of Words. *Red Pepper,* 12 (May 1995) 24–25.
         Speech delivered in Sofia, Bulgaria, April 1995, when being awarded an honorary doctorate. Critical of the US assault upon Nicaragua, etc., and the gross misuses of value-words involved. Extract in Billington 371.

E36   Murder is the most brutal form of censorship. *Guardian* (11 November 1995) 1
         Protest about the hanging of the Ogoni writer Ken Saro-Wiwa and eight other Ogoni activists by the Nigerian military junta. See *H29.*

E37   Merry Christmas. *Red Pepper,* 20 (January 1996) 5.
         A Christmas message to readers about the US government's hypocrisy and brutal violence, especially in regard to Central America and the Carribbean.

E38   Caribbean Cold War. *Red Pepper,* 24 (May 1996) 26–27.
         Celebrates the survival of Cuba, comparing its so-called scorn for inter-national law with that of the USA. Reprinted in *VV* 191–193. Cf. *F35.*

E39   Address to Hull University Congregation, 11 July 1996, on the occasion of being awarded an honorary degree.
         Text on website: www.haroldpinter.org/politics/politics_freedom.shtml.

E40   First Person: Picking a Fight with Uncle Sam. *Guardian* (4 December 1996) Section 2, 4.
         About the incompatibility between US public rhetoric and the cruel impacts of the US upon other countries. Filed as: "Opinion: Picking a

Fight with the Bully of the West." *Mail & Guardian* website (16 December 1996, 22 August 1998) (*TPR* [1999]: 187; website no longer current). Reprinted as: "American Foreign Policy: It Never Happened." *Spectre* 1 (1997) 12–13. Also as: "Commentary: Land of the Free? It Never Happened." *Z Magazine* (1 February 1997) 9–10 (also posted online, on *Third World Traveler*, 28 August 1998, as http://www.third-worldtraveller.com/US_ThirdWorld/Never_happened.html, longer version). Also as: "My Best Shot: America the Hun." *Utne Reader*, issue 82 (July/August 1997) 26 (also posted online, *Utne Reader Online: Society*, 22 August 1998, http://www.utne.com, shorter version). Also as: "It Never Happened." *VV* 197–199 (longer version, revised).

E41 Introductory speech, 11 December 1997, reception at Article XIX, London, to launch Julia Guest's Musa Antor Peace Train Photographic Exhibition. Posted on www.haroldpinter.org/politics/Turkey and the Kurds. The Peace Train had set off to go to Turkey to protest against the oppression of Turkish Kurds and others. Frances de Souza and Bianca Jagger also spoke. See *H40*.

E42 That he will be made to face his past is uplifting. *Independent* (10 December 1998) 3.
On decisions relating to the proposed extradition of the Chilean ex-president Augusto Pinochet to Spain, to stand trial for his crimes against humanity. (In the event, a decision by the British Home Secretary Jack Straw would allow Pinochet to escape back to Chile.) See *H47*.

E43 Ian Hamilton. In: *Another Round at the Pillars: Essays, Poems, & Reflections on Ian Hamilton,* general editor David Harsen. Tregarne, Manaccan, Cornwall: Cargo Press, 1999, pp. 41–42.
This volume is described on its half-title as "A Festschrift | for Ian Hamilton's | sixtieth birthday | Limited Edition".

E44 The Kurds have lifted the veil. We have been blind for far too long to the plight of the Kurdish people, says Harold Pinter. It is time we saw their courage and realised that what is at stake is freedom of expression too. *Guardian* (20 February 1999), Saturday Review: 3.
Discusses the reasons for the responses worldwide by Kurdish people to the arrest by the Turkish authorities of the Kurdish guerilla leader Abdullah Ocalan.

E45 A comment on the war by British playwright Harold Pinter. *World Socialist Web Site*, 18 May 1999. www.wsws.org/articles/1999/may1999/readm18.shtml.
An earlier article on this website, by Ann Todd, "Playwright Harold Pinter presents a powerful case in opposition to NATO bombardment of Serbia," dated 7 May 1999, reported on a programme on BBC-TV2 "last Tuesday evening" (i.e., 4 May 1999, see *K41*), in which Pinter and others had denounced US and UK actions in relation to Serbia and Kosovo, and the deliberately misleading representations of them in official media releases.

E46 [Speech] The Nato Action in Serbia. Delivered 25 June 1999, to the Confederation of Analytical Psychologists, in London. Privately printed. Reprinted in the newsletter of The Harold Pinter Society, 1 August 1999. Also in: *The Spokesman*, 65 (1999), issue entitled *Ethical Imperialism: The War after the War*, edited by Ken Coates (Nottingham: The Spokesman for the Bertrand Russell Peace Foundation). Reprinted in: *Masters of the Universe? Nato's Balkan Crusade*, edited by Tariq Ali (London: Verso, 2000), pp.327–336 (volume also includes anti-war writings by Noam Chomsky, Edward Said, *et al.*). Deals with, e.g., use of depleted uranium.

E47 Cruel, inhuman, degrading: leading British playwright Harold Pinter lays bare the excesses of the American penal system. *New Internationalist*, 327 (September 2000) 16.

The text had been broadcast on BBC Radio 4's "Today" programme. It concerns, e.g., the use of restraint chairs, stun guns and stun belts, shackles, and the death penalty.

E48 Aristotle University of Thessaloniki Degree Speech, 18th April 2000. In: *TPR* (2000) [103]–104. Illustration, 105.

Also on website www.haroldpinter.org. Deals with the capacity for "facts" in literary texts to be at once true and not true, and with political concerns, over the United States government's misleading rhetoric relating to its bombing of Serbia and Iraq.

E49 [Speech] Anniversary of Nato Bombing of Serbia. Delivered at the Committee for Peace in the Balkans Conference, The Conway Hall, London, 10 June 2000.

Photocopies distributed by Pinter at: Pinter in London: An International Conference, (*TPR* [2001] 239).

E50 Humanitarian intervention. *Spokesman*, 73 (2001) 47–49; issue entitled *War is peace*, edited by Ken Coates (Nottingham: Spokesman for the Bertrand Russell Peace Foundation, 2001).

Degree speech to the University of Florence, 10 September 2001. Confronts NATO's misuse of language, in its justifications of the bombing of Serbia, with the cruel facts of the innocent civilian casualties caused by the misdirected bombing of the town of Nis on 7 May 1999. "America's brutal and malignant world machine must be recognised for what it is and resisted." Followed by a brief statement to the Italian press made on 13 September 2001, where he denied that he in any way "advocate[d] violence. I was not throwing bombs. I was using words. The atrocities in New York and Washington [on 11 September 2001] are horrific, appalling. No responsible person can regard them in any other light." Other essays in this issue of *The Spokesman* are by Arundhati Roy, Noam Chomsky, Johan Galtung, Achin Vanaik, and Steve Boggan.

E51 Speech at the Edinburgh International Book Festival, 25 August 2002. Extensively reported, with extracts and paraphrases, in: report by Kirsty Scott, "Dark thoughts: Pinter tells of illness and its aftermath," *Guardian*

(26 August 2002): 2; also in: article by Hugh Davies, "Pinter emerges from the 'dark dream' of cancer," *Daily Telegraph* (26 August 2002): 7; also in: "Pinter lambasts Blair," *Times* (26 August 2002): 2; also in: report by Luke Leitch, *Evening Standard* (28 August 2002):17. For a major interview at the Edinburgh International Book Festival, with Ramona Koval of the *Guardian,* published 28 August, see *G117.*

E52   "The War Against Reason". Speech at the House of Commons, October 2002.

Condems Prime Minister Tony Blair's acquiescence in the American drive to control the world's resources. On website www.haroldpinter.org. Printed as: "The War Against Reason." *Red Pepper*, 102 (December 2002) 23.

E53   Speech of introduction, 9 December 2002, to the Kurdish Human Rights Project 10th Anniversary Lecture, given by Noam Chomsky, St. Paul's Cathedral, London.

On website www.haroldpinter.org.

E54   The American administration is a bloodthirsty wild animal. *Daily Telegraph* (11 December 2002) 24.

The main body of an address given on the occasion of receiving an honorary doctorate at the University of Turin, 27 November 2002; full text on website www.haroldpinter.org. Fierce attack on "the nightmare of American hysteria, ignorance, arrogance, stupidity and belligerence," in relation to the prospect of the Bush regime's planned oil war against Iraq. Reprinted in *War.*

E55   Speech at the "Don't Attack Iraq" Lobby, in the Grand Committee Room, Westminster Hall, House of Commons, 21 January 2003.

Text on website www.haroldpinter.org. One of a number of distinguished invited speakers, Pinter was very vehement.

E56   Speech at the Anti-Iraq War Rally, Hyde Park, 15 February 2003.

Text on website www.haroldpinter.org. One of a number of speakers, at the culmination of a march that involved one million people. Pinter declared, "The planned war on Iraq is an act of premeditated mass murder," and recited a new poem, "The Bombs" (see *C44*). Reported in: "Trendies, toffs, students and men with impressive beards unite. Jenny McCartney joins the anti-war demonstration as it snakes through central London." *Daily Telegraph* (filed 16 February 2003; seen on website). Other speakers were: Michael Foot, Bruce Kent, Mick Rix, Charles Kennedy, Tony Benn, Mo Mowlam, Bianca Jagger, Ken Livingstone, and the Reverend Jesse Jackson.

E57   His first act's been running for 50 years now – at 72, he's still going strong. So take a bow, Peter Hall, the great British enabler. *Sunday Times* (22 June 2003), Culture section: 14.

One of a group of tributes to Peter Hall, the others being by Felicity Kendall, Elaine Paige, Thelma Holt, Greg Hicks, Dominic Dromgoole, and Nicholas Hytner, on pp. 14–15.

F

Published Letters to Newspapers, Magazines, etc.

In some cases, the item has been seen in the serial in which it is printed. In others it has not yet been examined, and the reference used may not provide the heading or the page number. Nonetheless, in the interests of comprehensiveness, where an item is known to exist, as much information is provided about it as is currently available.

F1   "A Letter to the Editor" by Harold Pinter. *The Play's the Thing* (October 1958) 10–11.

Related to the "most stimulating" responses of Oxford and Cambridge audiences to *The Birthday Party*, in contrast with the London daily newspaper critics and responding to the editor's queries about Pinter's approaches to writing the play. Reprinted in *VV* 13–15, with the title "On *The Birthday Party* II: Letter to the Editor of *The Play's the Thing*, October 1958"; see above, as *E8*. This drama magazine was published at Cambridge University, 1957–58. Extracts are cited in Billington 94 (as from "the *Cambridge University Magazine*"). The extended letter is of seminal importance; in responding to the editor's request "to discuss the lines I myself am working on," Pinter articulates developing ideas that would be elaborated on in his interview with Gordon Woolford for the BBC, recorded 23 January 1960, on "Writing for the Theatre,"and in his speech at Bristol University in 1962: see *J4*, *E10*.

F2   Pinter's Reply to Open Letter by Leonard Russell. *Sunday Times* (14 August 1960) 21.

Response to Russell's criticism of the laughter aroused by *The Caretaker*: that it is indeed funny, up to, but only up to, a certain point. Leonard Russell was the literary editor of this newspaper; his "open letter" had appeared in late July or early August (Billington 129).

F3   Distressing. *New York Times* (26 April 1970) 180.

Rejects Clive Barnes' assessment that the New York production of *Landscape* and *Silence*, directed by Peter Gill, was greatly inferior to the London production and denies that it betrayed his intentions.

F4   [Letter] *Times* (9 December 1970) 11g.

Also, cf. letter (12 December 1970) 11g.

F5   Mr Losey's screenplays. *Times* (19 October 1972) 17d.

F6   [Letter] *Times* (10 December 1973) 17d.

Comment on the film industry.

F7   Vladimir Bukovsky. *Times* (22 March 1974) 17.
On the imprisonment of Vladimir Bukovsky, in relation to the Soviet practice of incarcerating political prisoners in psychiatric hospitals. This letter was simultaneously sent to the Soviet Ambassador.

F8   [Letter] *Times* (7 June 1975) 13g.

F9   "No Man's Land." *Guardian* (24 February 1977) 10.
Response to letter by John Russell Brown, "Why the NT blackening has to stop" (23 February) 11, relating to a writers' strike. Pinter confirmed he was not a member of the Theatre Writers' Union and added that he did not belong to the Writers' Guild either.

F10   Peace studies. *Times* (24 January 1984) 11e.
Rejects "smear" in a leading article of 19 January, that peace movement people, who include himself, broadly support "communist theory."

F10A Blind Eye on Turkey. *Guardian* (10 January 1986) 6.
Expressing outrage over continuing imprisonment of 18 members of the Turkish Peace Association since 1983. "Why has the *Guardian* been so silent?" Signed by Arnold Wesker and Harold Pinter.

F11   Spiegel and Pinter. *Sight and Sound,* 57: 1 (1987) 73.
Reply to Andrew Sinclair.

F12   "Mountain Language." *Times Literary Supplement* (7–13 October 1988) 1109.
Corrects editorial comments about the nature of the play, which is printed on the following two pages (see A47a): it is not about "the fate of the Kurdish people" and it is not a "parable."

F13   [Letter] *Independent* (30 November 1988) 21.
Justifies assertion he had made to the *Independent* that the UK has become a satellite of the USA, cited in an article by Timothy Garton Ash, "Red war, phony reflections" (25 November) 19.

F13A Freedom of the Vote in Nicaragua. *Times* (18 October 1989) 21g.
Response to leader of 14 October 1989 which predicted the election of February 1990 would be unfair. On the contrary, every effort was being made to ensure its fairness, with official observers from the UN, OAS, and European Community invited. Pinter wrote as Chairman, Nicaragua Solidarity Campaign; and another second letter was presented by Julian Jacobs, its General Secretary.

F14   [Letter] *Time Out* (30 January – 6 February 1991) 146.

F15   Gulf War. *Observer* (3 February 1991) 19.
The USA's disregard for the demands of the International Court of Justice in 1986 that it desist from its illegal operations in Nicaragua, and make reparations, makes a cruel mockery of President Bush's "outrage" over Saddam Hussein's breach of international law.

F16   Bush's Comic Talent. *Independent* (24 May 1991) 22.
President George Bush's deploring the resort to violence, in relation to the assassination of Rajiv Gandi, rings hollow in relation to his own role in

causing the deaths of 150,000 Iraqis.

F17 The Play's the Thing. *Times* (20 January 1992) 13a.
Contradicts Benedict Nightingale's assertion he had written only "three playlets" in the past ten years; he had written five one-act plays, which, "though short, remain plays," and two sketches (perhaps "playlets").

F18 The Living Issue Behind a 500-Year Old Discovery. *Independent*, 1 August 1991: 18.
Response to David Lister's article, "Why Harold Hates Christopher . . . or the Case of the Pinter, the Nina and the Santa Maria," *Independent* (14 July 1992): 8. Celebrations of the five-hundredth anniversary of Christopher Columbus's discovery of the Americas had prompted the emergence of the protest group 500 Years of Resistance, foregrounding the on-going subjugation and dispossession of their indigenous peoples. In July, Pinter had spoken at the launching of this group, at the House of Commons, arguing, along with other writers, that this discovery and its consequences were more to be lamented than celebrated (Billington 237).

F19 U.S. Should Admit Role in El Salvador. *Ottawa Citizen* (29 March 1993) A11.

F20 Reply to Michael Coveney. *Observer* (9 May 1993) 46.
Relates to his friendship with Simon Gray.

F21 "The Trial" upstaged. *Times* (21 June 1993) 15g.
Rejects reports in *The Times* of 18 June (9a) and 19 June (leading article, 13a) that he had been vociferously "irate" about the BBC's inept scheduling of a screening of Orson Welles's film of Kafka's *The Trial* within the same week as the release of his own version. "The truth is that I have said nothing to anybody about the matter."

F22 [Letter] *Times* (19 July 1993) 15e.
Like North Korea, South Korea holds and maltreats political prisoners.

F23 How the Law Lies in Russia. *Guardian* (12 October 1993) 91.

F24 Losey and friends. *Times* (22 January 1994) 15d.
Contradicts Dirk Bogarde's assertion that Joseph Losey had generally alienated his friends. Pinter had enjoyed twenty years of friendship with him, with much affection and admiration, and "we never had a cross word."

F25 [Letter] *New York Review of Books* (9 June 1994) 60.
Response to Jacob Epstein's objections to the film of *Schindler's List*, stresses that his account of "moral and political turpitude" in the twentieth century omitted the wrong-doing of the USA.

F26 US Troops' Ambiguous Role. *Guardian* (27 September 1994), Features: 21.
Response to Chris Dunham's letter of 24 September, relates to their presence in Haiti in relation to the CIA's role in that country's recent history.

F27 [With Antonia Fraser.] Playwrights at the Palace. *Guardian* (13 January 1995), Features: 25.

F28 [Letter] *Times Literary Supplement* (17 February 1995) 15a.

Response to Ken Jowitt's review of Noam Chomsky, *World Orders, Old and New,* in *TLS* (10 February 1995): 3–4.

F29   Socialism Not to Blame . . . or Is It? *Sunday Telegraph* (12 March 1995) 30.

F30   [Letter] *Evening Standard* (30 March 1995) 49.
Repudiates a suggestion in the "Londoner's Diary" in the issue of 27 March of a rift between Salman Rushdie and himself.

F31   A Pinter Drama in Stoke Newington. *Guardian* (9 July 1996) 16.
Concerns a raid by armed British police on a rehearsal by Kurdish actors of *Mountain Language.* Eventually the Metropolitan Police had to pay £55,000 in damages and £100,000 in legal costs (Knowles, in *TPR* [2000]: 190). Reprinted in *VV* 196.

F32   Scenario for the Bugging of a Home. *Times* (8 January 1997) section 1: 17.
About the Police Bill's legalising the bugging of private property: if anyone found police installing bugs in his home, and objected to it, he could be charged with obstructing them. Reprinted in *VV* 200.

F33   Pause for thought. *Sunday Times* (2 February 1997), Section 8: 2a.

F34   [Open letter to Tony Blair, UK Prime Minister.] Writer outraged. *Guardian* (17 February 1998), Features: 17.
Opposes Britain's involvement in the war against Iraq. Reprinted in *VV* 236. In his interview with David Edwards, *G107,* Pinter objected to the trivialising effect of the heading (he's only a writer, and here's what he's outraged about this time).

F35   Breaking the Chains: A State of War with Unlimited Duck in Lime Sauce for the Victor. *Guardian* (15 May 1998), Guardian Home Page: 7.
Cf. "Caribbean Cold War," *E38.*

F36   Derek Newark. *Guardian* (19 August 1998), Guardian Features Page: 16.
Letter responding to the *Guardian*'s obituary, of 14 August 1998. Pinter writes that it had been a "great shock to read of the death of" Newark, whom he had worked with, and regarded as a "great comic actor".

F37   Pinter and Comedy Error. *Sunday Times* (7 February 1999) 18.
Corrects an apocryphal story that the Comedy Theatre would be renamed the "Pinter Theatre"; its origin had simply been a joke by Bill Kenwright, after five successive productions at this theatre had been of Pinter's plays.

F38   Proust found again. *Observer* (14 March 1999) 30.
Responds to a comment on Joseph Losey and the non-filming of Proust. With the screenplay published and still in print, "I remain very proud of what we did."

F39   [One of several letters under the heading "Artists Against the War".] *Guardian* (8 April 1999) 21.
Posted online as "The US is now a highly dangerous force, totally out of control" (last line of letter) by Nikos Sarantakos, on the website

Alternative Information about the NATO WAR in Yugoslavia: Stop the NATO Aggression against Yugoslavia, 2 June 1999, 29 August 2000, http://members.tripod.com/sarant_2/ksindex.html.

F40 Artists against the War. *Guardian* (8 April 1999) 21.
Opposes US action against Serbia, and Blair's support for Clinton.

F41 We Are Bandits Guilty of Murder. *Sunday Telegraph* (2 May 1999) 33.
Refers to forthcoming television programme, on BBC2, "Counterblast," on Tuesday following, 4 May 1999, made by Pinter and the photographer Stuart Urban, protesting about NATO's bombing of Serbia.

F42 A Playwright Rants. *Observer* (*ca.* May 1999) 4.
Disputes an earlier article in the *Observer,* about the ostensible threat to the West represented by the Kurdish organisation PKK, said to be revealed by an unidentified deserter. In the interview with David Edwards, *G107*, Pinter objected to the trivialising effect of the heading given to his letter.

F43 US foreign policy. *Times Literary Supplement* (10 December 1999) 17d.
Contradicts claims the USA "defend[s] democratic institutions" in Latin America, in relation to the overthrow of democratic regimes in Guatemala in 1954 and in Haiti.

F44 My Defence. *Guardian* (31 December 1999) 19.
Reply to an article by Alan Travis. Relates to his conscientious objection to military service in 1949.

F45 On "Heroes and Villains." *Independent* (28 December 2000), Comment: 2.
In the feature article, "Heroes and Villains" (26 December 2000), (Features):1, 7, 33 individuals had nominated their "heroes and villains" for 2000; Pinter, as the eighth of them, had on 13 December nominated as hero Mumia Abu-Jamal, for his dignity, lucidity, defiance, and endurance on Pennsylvania's death row for 18 appalling years; and as villain he ostensibly nominated NATO for its role in the bombing of Serbia and the murder of thousands of innocent people (mainly children) through its blockade of Iraq. However, as he protested in his letter of 28 December, as villain he had specificly nominated Tony Blair, rather than NATO, and his contribution had been editorially censored.

F46 [Letter] *Independent* (*ca.* 2 January 2001).
Complaint about the censorship of his previous contribution (provides full text of it), and also of his letter published on 28 December 2000: its final sentence had been omitted: "How can the Independent justify this act of censorship?" Cf. Stephen Glover, "Is the Independent trying to protect New Labour, or is it just inept?" *Spectator* (24 February 2001), who notes that its letters editor had made no response. Also commented on in *The Observer* (11 February 2001), in relation to a report on the Index on Censorship Awards dinner, where it was noted by "Browser" that, up to that time, Pinter's assault upon the letters editor of *The Independent* had received no attention in the British media.

F47 Library loan. *Times Literary Supplement* (17 February 2001) 17.

Corrects impression created by a statement that the British Library had "acquired" his papers. They had been deposited on loan and "I received no money."

F48   Two tales of human rights. *Guardian* (8 May 2001) 15.

Concerns the USA's use of torture weapons in its prisons and its sales of these weapons worldwide. Such factors are ignored by those who are complaining about the USA's loss of its seat on the UN Human Rights Commission.

F49   [Letter] *Guardian* (2 August 2001) 2.

Contrary to a claim ostensibly made by Henry Porter in the *Guardian* of 1 August, he had never said Slobodan Milosevic, the ex-president of Serbia, was innocent of war crimes, but was "simply challenging the legality of the court that will try him" (i.e., the International Court of Justice in the Hague). [In its "Corrections" column, on 7 August, p.17, the *Guardian* acknowledged that a caption below a photograph of Pinter, in the issue of 1 August, "Milosevic is innocent–Pinter", adjacent to Henry Porter's column (p.7, G2), was erroneous. Pinter had said no such thing, nor was it stated in Porter's column that he had; the editor apologised to both Porter and Pinter.]

F50   Dissenters put the record straight. *Guardian* (28 September 2001) 23.

States that contrary to items that had appeared in the *Guardian*, he had never said "Milosevic is innocent", as indicated on 1 August, nor had he or John Pilger said anything to the effect that "any neighbourhood" struck by a suicide plane on September 11 2001 had somehow "been asking for it," as alleged by Christopher Hitchens in his column on 26 September. Letters also appeared from Hitchens, retracting his comment (he had sought to remove it before his column was printed but had not succeeded), and from Pilger. Editorial apologies also appeared in the "Corrections" column.

F51   In: Comment: Letters to the Editor. They said what? *Observer* (1 September 2002) 26.

On his experience of fighting cancer.

F52   "Dear President Bush". [Within a series of letters, headed: "While we have your attention, Mr. President. . . . (It's not often we get the chance to speak directly to the most powerful man in the world. So as George Bush lands in Britain for his first state visit, we asked 60 Brits and Americans to make the most of it.") *Guardian* (18 November 2003) G2:2–17. Pinter's letter is on p.2. Also in this issue, a six-line poem presumably addressed to the British Prime Minister Tony Blair. Pinter's letter reprinted in the *Observer* (28 December 2003), which also contains, within Bel Littlejohn's column, a poem that appears to be a spoof of Pinter's.

F53   'Waiting for Godot': an unpublished letter. *Areté*, 14 (Spring/Summer 2004): 88–90. Letter addressed to Mick Goldstein.

F54   Bush and Blair 'terrorists', *Spectator* (30 October 2004) 38.

G

Interviews Printed in Newspapers or Magazines

Over the years, Harold Pinter has given a large number of interviews, some of which were published in print or broadcast as such, while others resulted in interview-based articles. Within the second category, sometimes the portion of the article which comprises direct quotation of Pinter's own words is relatively small; only those examples in which it forms a substantial percentage of the article are included here. Moreover, one cannot always tell from the context whether a short quotation comes directly from a recent interview, or is reprinted from some other source. Where no interviewer or author is given, the item is (at least in part) an interview-based article.

For radio and television interviews not published in print, see Sections J and K.

Undoubtably, some printed interviews or interview-based articles exist that have not been identified or located.

G1   Mr. Harold Pinter: Avant-Garde Playwright and Intimate Revue. *Times* (16 November 1959) 4.

G2   With Brian Glanville. "Harold Pinter Interviewed. 'I am a Jew Who Writes.'" *Jewish Chronicle* (11 March 1960) 27.
       Not seen, but information from Keith Feldman. A response to a criticism in this newspaper by Arnold Wesker that *The Birthday Party* should have had an explicitly Jewish setting.

G3   Julian Holland. "The 296 (all-night) Bus to Success." *Evening News* (14 May 1960).

G4   With Philip Purser. "A Pint with Pinter Helps to Dispel the Mystery." *News Chronicle*, (28 July 1960) 6.
       Interview-based article about *Night School* and *The Caretaker*.

G5   With Charles Marowitz. "Theatre Abroad." *Village Voice* (1 September 1960).
       Cited by S. Gale, *Harold Pinter: An Annotated Bibliography* (Boston MA: G K Hall, 1978, p. 149: item 1403). About the meaning of *The Caretaker*.

G6   With Harry Thompson. "Harold Pinter Replies". *New Theatre Magazine*, II: 2 (January 1961) 8–10.
       At foot of p.8: "Harold Pinter was interviewed for New Theatre Magazine by Harry Thompson." The title for the interview was similar to that used for others (e.g., an interview in the previous issue, II: 1 (October 1960): 12–14) was headed "Stephen Austin Replies"); Pinter was replying to the interviewer, not to something that had previously appeared in the magazine.

G7   *Caretaker*'s Caretaker. *Time* (10 November 1961) 76.

G8   People Are Talking About . . . *Vogue,* 139 (15 January 1962) 25.

G9   Pinter Between the Lines. *Sunday Times* (4 March 1962) 25.

G10   With Peter Lewis. "Fascinated by Unsatisfactory People." *Time and Tide* (21 June 1962) 16–17.

G11   Pinterview. *Newsweek* 60 (23 July 1962) 69.

G12   Interview with Harold Pinter. *New York Times* (6 November 1962) 39.

G13   Filming *The Caretaker:* Harold Pinter and Clive Donner interviewed by Kenneth Cavander. *Transatlantic Review,* 13 (Summer 1963) 17–26.
      Reprinted in: *Behind the Scenes,* edited by Joseph F. McCrindle, with an introduction by Jean-Claude van Itallie (London: Pitman Publishing, 1971), 211–222. In: *Focus on Film and Theatre,* edited by James Hurt (Englewood Cliffs, NJ: Prentice-Hall, 1994).

G14   With Jo Durden-Smith, Jonathan Gili, and Misha Donat. "Harold Pinter". *Isis National* (week ending 1 February 1964) 18–20. Film issue.
      Interview relating to his writing the screenplay for *The Servant* and his thoughts about the film. A translation of this into French by Maryse Beaulieu was published as: "Réponses sur The Servant | Harold Pinter", *Positif* (July-August 1985) 47–40. In *Isis,* the interview is followed by the text of a sequence omitted *"from the final version of the film"* (pp.20–21).

G15   With Lee Langley. "From 'Caretaker' to 'Servant.'" *New York Herald Tribune* (1 March 1964), Magazine section: 24.

G16   Trying to Pin Down Pinter: Interview with Marshall Pugh. *Daily Mail* (7 March 1964) 8.

G17   Barry Norman. "Five Desperate Years of Harold Pinter." *Daily Mail* (9 March 1965) 8.
      Interview-based article, in which Pinter disclosed that after the failure of *The Birthday Party* in 1959 an American impresario (Roger L. Stevens) had given him £1000, in a deal which enabled him to carry on as a playwright (see Billington, 126).

G18   Interview with Harold Pinter. *Daily Mirror* (*ca.* 20 March 1965) (clipping seen, but not traced).

G19   With John Russell Taylor. "*Accident.*" *Sight and Sound,* XXXV: 4 (Autumn 1966) 178–179.

G20   With Lawrence M. Bensky. "The Art of the Theatre III: Harold Pinter: An Interview." *The Paris Review,* 10: 39 (Fall 1966) 13–37. [On p.13, photo of Pinter (note on p.10 that it is "by L. M Bensky"); on p. 12, reproduction of typescript page from a draft of *The Homecoming.*]
      Reprinted in: *Theatre at Work,* edited by Charles Marowitz and Simon Trussler (London: Methuen, 1967), pp. 96–109; *The Playwrights Speak,* edited by Walter Wager, with an introduction by Harold Clurman (New York: Delacorte Press, 1967), pp. 171–188; *Writers at Work: The Paris Review Interviews: Third Series,* edited by Charles Plimpton, introduced by Alfred Kazin (New York: Viking, 1967; London: Secker and Warburg,

1968), pp. 347–368 (re-published, Harmondsworth: Penguin, 1977); *Writers at Work: Interviews from The Paris Review,* selected by Kay Dick (Harmondsworth, Mx: Penguin, 1977), pp. 296–314; *Pinter: A Collection of Critical Essays,* edited by Arthur Ganz (Englewood Cliffs, NJ: Prentice-Hall, 1972), pp. 19–33.

G21 With Alain Schifres. "Harold Pinter: Caretaker of Britain's New Theater." *Réalités,* 193 (December 1966): n.p.

G22 Pinter: Violence is Natural: Interview with Harold Pinter. *New York Times* (1 January 1967), Section 2: 1.

G23 Two People in a Room: Playwriting. *The New Yorker,* 43 (25 February 1967) 34–36.
    In "Talk of the Town." Cutting in *PA* Box 67.

G24 Henry Hewes. "Probing Pinter's Play." *Saturday Review,* 50 (8 April 1967) 56, 58, 96–97.
    Article about Pinter and *The Homecoming,* that draws upon an interview, and also cites comments by Paul Rogers, who played Max. Adjacent is a short article by Dr. Abraham N. Franzblau, "A Psychiatrist Looks at 'The Homecoming'" (p.58).

G25 With William Packard. "An Interview with Harold Pinter." *First Stage,* VI: 2 (Summer 1967) 82.

G26 Interview with Harold Pinter. *New York Times* (10 September 1967), Section 2: 3.

G27 Charles Marowitz. "Harold Pinter." *New York Times* (1 October 1967), Section 2: 36–37, 89–90, 92, 94.
    "Biography," includes some direct speech by Pinter, probably from an interview.

G28 With Kathleen Halton. "Funny and Moving and Frightening Pinter." *Vogue* (1 October 1967) 194, 236, 239, 245.

G29 [Interview with Harold Pinter] *New York Times* (27 October 1967), Section 2: 3.

G30 In Search of Harold Pinter: Interview with Kathleen Tynan. Part I. *Evening Standard* (25 April 1968) 7; Part II: We're pretty tight as a family. Nobody just rings at the door and comes in. *Evening Standard* (26 April 1968) 8.

G31 With Patricia Bosworth. "Why He Doesn't Write More." *New York Times* (27 October 1968), Section D: 3.
    Interviewed while directing the New York production of Robert Shaw's *The Man in the Glass Booth*; expressed his dislike of American actors' molestation of the audience and of political double standards.

G32 With Judith Crist. "A Mystery: Pinter on Pinter." *Look* (24 December 1968) 77–78, 80, 83.

G33 Harold Pinter Talks to Michael Dean. *Listener,* 81: 2084 (6 March 1969) 312.
    From "Late Night Line-Up", BBC-2.

G34   In an Empty Bandstand–Harold Pinter in conversation with Joan Bakewell.
       Listener, 82: 2119 (6 November 1969) 630–631.
       Broadcast on BBC-2 TV, in "Late Night Line-Up," 11 September 1969. See
       Radio Times (4 September 1969) 43.

G35   With Richard Roud. "Take Three on The Go-Between." *Guardian* (16
       March 1971), *Arts Guardian*: 8.
       On the film, *The Go-Between*, released in 1971. In the film industry, who
       contributes what to the final product? Interview with Joseph Losey,
       Harold Pinter, and L. P. Hartley.

G36   With Harold Hobson. "I Am Not Concerned with Making General
       Statements." *Christian Science Monitor* (16 March 1971).

G37   With Mel Gussow. "A Conversation [Pause] with Harold Pinter." *New
       York Times* (5 December 1971), Section 6: 42–43, 126–129, 131–136.
       Reprinted in more extended form in Gussow, *Conversations with Pinter*
       (1994): 15–47, including preamble, as "Something to do with the sofa?"
       Gussow notes that it "was reprinted in part in the programme for *Old
       Times* on Broadway and in programmes for various revivals" (p.10).

G38   Peter Nichols. "Mr Pinter accuses Signor Visconti of staging `fiasco': Play
       still belongs to me, Mr Pinter says." *Times* (11 May 1973) 6.
       Protest about the liberties taken in Luchino Visconti's Teatro di Roma
       production of *Old Times*. Pinter flew to Rome to see it, and on 11 May
       held a press conference there (Billington 237–238).

G39   Sydney Edwards. "Beatrix Potter and Mr Pinter." *Evening Standard* (22
       June 1973) 28.
       Within Edwards' "News of the Arts" column. Article about the filming
       of *Butley*, directed by Pinter, partly interview-based, includes one passage
       of direct speech.

G40   Lee Langley. "Genius – A Change in Direction." *Daily Telegraph* (23
       November 1973), Magazine: 30–36.
       Article partly interview-based.

G41   Harold Pinter, Director. *Cinebill* 1: 7 (January 1974) 8.
       Discusses directing of film *Butley*.

G42   Michael Owen. "Pinter's taxi to No Man's Land." *Evening Standard* (11
       July 1975) 20–21.
       Interview-based profile article, relating to directing of Gray's *Otherwise
       Engaged*.

G43   Jack Kroll. "The Puzzle of Pinter." *Newsweek* (29 November 1976)
       75–78, 81.
       Review of *No Man's Land* and biographical overview, evidently with some
       interview-based content (cited as interview-related in Gordon, p. 249).

G44   With Jack Emery. "Just a Simple Little Love Story?" *Radio Times* (16–22
       September 1978) 80–83, 85.
       On *Langrishe, Go Down*, also includes interviews with Judi Dench, David
       Jones.

G45 Sydney Edwards. "To hell and back with Pinter." *Evening Standard* (18 May 1979) 28–29.

G46 With Mel Gussow. "Harold Pinter: 'I Started with Two People in a Pub.'" *New York Times* (30 December 1979), Section 2: 5, 7.
Reprinted in more extended form in Gussow, *Conversations with Harold Pinter* (1994): 49–63, including preamble, as "Two people in a pub . . . talking about the past".

G47 A Rare Interview with Harold Pinter. *San Francisco Chronicle* (2 January 1980) 48.

G48 Mel Gussow. "London to Broadway: How a Culture Shapes a Show." *New York Times* (3 February 1980), Section 2: 1, 35.

G49 John Barber. "Talking with Pinter . . ." *Daily Telegraph* (23 June 1980) 11; "Precise words of Pinter." *Daily Telegraph* (30 June 1980) 11.
Two articles closely based on an interview occasioned by the transfer of Pinter's production of *The Hothouse* from the Hampstead Theatre Club to the Ambassador's Theatre. The second instalment deals with how he writes, his defence of Robert Bolt's *State of Revolution,* his debt to Harold Hobson, his love of reading Proust, and the publication of his new collection of poems, *I Know the Place.*

G50 "Pendennis". "Writing gets less easy for Pinter." *Observer* (13 July 1980) 40.

G51 With Miriam Gross. "Pinter on Pinter." *Observer* (5 October 1980), review section: 25, 27.

G52 With Leslie Garris. "Translating Fowles into Film." *New York Times Magazine* (30 August 1981) 24, 48–54, 69.
Concerns the adaptation of *The French Lieutenant's Woman.*

G53 Michael Owen. "Harold and his lady and a great erotic experience." *Evening Standard* (11 September 1981) 24–25.

G54 Howard Kissell. "Harold Pinter: The Man in the Ironic Mask." *Women's Wear Daily* (23 February 1983) 40.
Cited as interview-related by Gordon (300).

G55 Michael Owen. "Pinter: my split with Hall." *Evening Standard* (7 October 1983) 24–25.

G56 With Bryan Appleyard. "The new light that burns within Harold Pinter." *The Times* (16 March 1984) 13.

G57 With Nick Hern. "A Play and its Politics: A Conversation between Harold Pinter and Nicholas Hern." In *One for the Road* (London: Methuen, 1985), pp.7–23.
Fly-title for interview, p.5, with verso blank. See *A45.b.*

G58 With S[tephen] F[arber]. "Topical Relevance." *New York Times* (10 May 1987), Section 2:25.
Telephone interview, re: *The Dumb Waiter* on ABC-TV.

G59 Sue Summers. "Breaking the Silence." *London Daily News* (19 June 1987) 19.

G60   Togetherness. *New York Times* (22 January 1988), Section C: 6.
Cited as interview-based by Gordon (301).

G60A   With Andrew Graham-Yooll. "Pinter Among the Poets." *South*, 91 (May
1988): 116–117. Relates to Pinter's visit to Nicaragua in February 1988,
for "nine intensive days", which included long conversations with
President Ortega. Protesting against blatant lies about Nicaragua by US
leaders.

G61   Growth of an Angry Playwright. *Observer* (16 October 1988) 13.

G62   With Sue Summers. "A conscientious objector." *Independent* (18 October
1988) 19.
Refers to his going to trial, as an objector, rather than accepting National
Service.

G63   Radical Departures: Harold Talks to Anna Ford. *Listener*, 120, No.3086
(27 October 1988) 5–6.
Edited television interview, broadcast on BBC-TV arts programme
"Omnibus," 21 October 1988. Acknowledges *One for the Road* and
Mountain Language are political in intent and relate to his visit to Turkey
in 1985, and his concern for the plight of the Kurds; they also reflect his con-
cern with Thatcherite authoritarianism in the UK (D. Keith Peacock, *Harold
Pinter and the New British Theatre* [Westport, CT: Greenwood, 1997] 138).

G64   With Mel Gussow. "Pinter's Plays Following Him out of Enigma and into
Politics." *New York Times* (6 December 1988), Section C: 17, 22.
Reprinted in more extended form in Gussow, *Conversations with Pinter*
(1994): 65–79, including preamble, as "Stan, don't let them tell you what
to do."

G65   Michael Ciment. "*Reunion:* Harold Pinter Visually Speaking." *Film
Comment*, XXV, No. 3 (May-June 1989) 20–22.

G66   Lawrence Van Gelder. "Pinteresque Pinter." *New York Times* (28 July
1989), Section B: 4.
Cited as interview-based in Gordon (301).

G67   Michael Owen. "The Hall and Pinter show." *Evening Standard* (4 May
1990) 28.
Deals with Pinter's patching up his split with Peter Hall. Two articles side-
by-side, based on interviews with Pinter and Hall respectively.

G68   Stephen Schiff. "Pinter's Passions." *Vanity Fair* (September 1990) 219–222,
300–303.

G69   Polly Toynbee. "The Master of Strident Silences." *Guardian* (29
September 1990): 23; reprinted in *Guardian Weekly* (14 October 1990) 24.
This is *not* interview-based, because Pinter was angered by the intrusively
personal content of Steven Schiff's interview-article in *Vanity Fair* and
called off a scheduled interview with Toynbee. However, her article contains a good deal of interesting biographical detail.

G70   Polly Toynbee profiles playwright Harold Pinter. *Guardian* (29 October
1990) 23.

G71   [Interview relating to *The Homecoming*.] *Guardian* (12 November 1990) 35.

G72   With Barry Davis. "The *Jewish Quarterly* Interview: The 22 from Hackney to Chelsea: A Conversation with Harold Pinter." *Jewish Quarterly*, 38 (Winter 1991/2) 9–17.

G73   Michael Billington. "Myths in *No Man's Land*." *Guardian* (2 November 1992) 4.
Profile article with some citation.

G74   John Gross. "Genius Revived–Profile: Harold Pinter." *Sunday Telegraph* (8 November 1992) 33.
Cites or paraphrases statements by Pinter within an extensive article.

G75   With Edward T. Jones. "Harold Pinter: A Conversation." *Literature/Film Quarterly*, XXI (1993) 2–9.
Publication of part of an interview in May 1992 about writing the (largely unused) screenplay for Kazuo Ishiguro's *The Remains of the Day*.

G76   With Brian Johnston. "The Oval, 25 August 1990." In: *More Views from the Boundary: Celebrity Interviews from the Commentary Box,* Volume Two, edited by Peter Baxter. London: Methuen, 1993. Re-published London: Mandarin: 1994; Bath: Chivers Large Print, 1994.
One of a series of "conversations" with Johnston for the BBC during 25-minute test-match lunch-breaks. In the Chivers Large Print edition, that with Pinter occupies pp.19–30. See *J45*.

G77   Claire Armistead. "Harold's New Baby." *Guardian* (3 February 1993), Section 2: 2–3.
Based on interview relating to Pinter's new play *Moonlight* being completed and going into rehearsal at the Almeida Theatre. He recalls that he used to send his scripts to Samuel Beckett, who detected a defective speech in *Silence*.

G78   With Steve Grant. "HP SOURCE." *Time Out* (15 September 1993) 16–19.
Also, printed as "Pinter: my plays, my polemics, my pad." *Independent* (20 September 1993), Living: 13.

G79   With Michael Billington, "public discussion" at the Shelbourne Hotel during the Dublin International Writers' Festival, *ca.* September 1993, cited and extracts printed in Billington 92–93, 353–354 (wider publication untraced).

G80   With Mel Gussow. *Conversations with Pinter.* London: Nick Hern Books, 1994.
Gussow (p.156) acknowledges the previous publication of "the first three conversations in part in articles in the New York Times." The fourth piece, dated October 1989, not previously published, is identified as a "discussion at the 92nd Street Y in New York [which] was organised by Karl Kirchway, the head of that group's poetry series", following a one-man presentation of a scene from *The Hothouse* and the whole of *One for the Road:* it is here entitled "[Silence, followed by audience laughter],"

pp.81–93. The final section is the text of four interviews in London in September 1983, and Gussow notes: "Some of the material in those talks appeared in an article in *American Theatre*" ca. 1984. It is here entitled "Even old Sophocles didn't know what was going to happen next".

A translation into Polish of an excerpt from one of the interviews appeared as: "Nawet stary Sofokles nie Wiedzial, co zdarzy sie za chwile." *Dialog: Miesiecznik Poswiecony Dramaturgii Wspolczesnej: Teatralnej, Filmowej, Radiowej, Telewizyj* (Warsaw, Poland), 40: 9 (September 1995) 101–111.

G81   With Fintan O'Toole. "An Unflinching Gaze." *Irish Times* (30 April 1994), Living and Loving Section: 3.

Related to the Pinter Festival at the Gate Theatre in Dublin in May 1994 (Billington 354–356).

G82   With Fintan O'Toole. "Walking into a Dark Room." *Irish Times* (3 May 1994), Arts section: 10 (City edition).

G83   [With B. S. Johnson.] "Evacuees." *TPR* (1994) 8–13.

Text of an interview in 1968, not previously published.

G84   With David Sexton. "The Arts: Life in the old dog yet." *Daily Telegraph* (16 March 1995) 12.

Relates to Pinter's winning the David Cohen British Literature Prize for 1995; see *E34*.

G85   With Kate Saunders. "Pause for Thought." *Sunday Times* (9 July 1995), Section 10: 4–5.

Relates to Pinter's reaching the age of 65.

G86   Mark Lawson. "Interviews without the vampire." *Guardian* (14 July 1995) Section 2: 2.

Compares the declining newspaper literary interview with the rise of interviews in other formats; discusses interviews with Tom Stoppard and Harold Pinter.

G87   Michael Owen. "Funny, but Pinter and Cooney Are Very Similar." *Evening Standard* (6 October 1995) 18.

G88   Harold Pinter and Michael Billington in Conversation at the National Film Theatre, 26 October 1996. In *VV* 50–57.

G89   With Austin E. Quigley. "The Art of Drama. Dean Quigley Interviews Playwright Harold Pinter." *Columbia University Record* (6 December 1996) 27.

Posted on website 13 September 2000: http://www.columbia.edu/cu/record/archives/vol22/vol 22iss11/record2211.27.html.

G90   Michael Billington. *The Life and Work of Harold Pinter* (London: Faber and Faber, 1996).

As well as citing previous interviews, contains some fresh interview material, both paraphrased and in direct speech.

G91   With Mireia Aragay and Ramon Simó. "Writing, Politics, and *Ashes to Ashes*: An Interview with Harold Pinter." *TPR: Annual Essays 1995 and 1996*, 8 (1997) [4]–15.

An edited text of a public interview on 6 December 1996 in the auditorium of the Centre de Cultura Contemporània de Barcelona, during the "Pinter Autumn" festival in Barcelona. An introduction on pp.[4]–5 is followed by the text, pp.5–15. Reprinted in *VV* 58–70.

G92   Harold Pinter: "Interview donnée au Monde du 15 octobre 1997." *Le Monde* (15 October 1997).
Reproduced: http://www.multimania.com/yrol/LITTERA/PINTER/pinter/html, 7 November 2000.

G93   John Francis Lane. "Where, might one ask, have all your nuances gone, Harold?" *Independent* (26 November 1997), Features: 14.
Concerns Pinter's directing of *Ashes to Ashes* in Italian with the Teatro Biondo at Palermo, Sicily; includes some quotation and paraphrases of statements by him.

G94   Colin Brown. "Harold Pinter and Cardinal Hume lead assault on plans for war in the Gulf." *Independent* (13 February 1998) 12–13.
Partly interview-related, partly quoting their addresses to a meeting at the House of Commons opposing plans for another war against Iraq.

G95   With Valerie Grove. "Rebel without a pause." *Times* (14 February 1998) 20a.

G96   With Steven Winn. "Harold Pinter Takes the Stage." *San Francisco Chronicle* (16 June 1998), Daily Datebook: D1.

G97   With John Walsh. "That nice Mr Pinter." *Independent* (8 February 1999), Monday Review section: 1, 8.

G97A   Richard Brooks. "Pinter to attack Nato's 'Bandits'." *Sunday Times* (2 May 1999): 2. Interview-based article previewing "Counterblast" television programme, see *K41*.

G98   Sue Quinn. "Pinter in a rage over play's fate." *Guardian* (13 May 1999) 7. Quotes Pinter over the Gielgud Theatre's decision not to produce his production of Simon Gray's *The Late Middle Classes* in favour of a rock musical.

G99   Jay Rayner. "The Observer Profile: Harold Pinter: Pinter of discontent." *Observer* (16 May 1999) 27.
Some interview-based citation.

G100   Audrey Gillan. "Bombing shames Britain, Pinter tells protesters." *Guardian* (7 June 1999) 4.
Report about Pinter's denunciation of British participation in the bombing of the former Yugoslavia at an anti-war demonstration outside the Imperial War Museum.

G101   With Stephen Moss. "The Guardian Profile: Harold Pinter: Under the Volcano." *Guardian* (4 September 1999), Review Section: 6–7.
Based on an extended interview.

G102   With Mary Riddell. "The NS Interview: Harold Pinter." *New Statesman* (9 November 1999) 18–19.

G103   With Mel Gussow. "The Playwright's Other Pursuit." *New York Times* (30 December 1999), The Arts: E1, 5.

G104 With Elizabeth Sakellaridou. "An Interview with Harold Pinter." *TPR: Collected Essays 1999 and 2000*, 10 (2000) [93]–102.

G105 With Frank Moher. "Pinter on Woolf and Friendship: Frank Moher's Interview with Harold Pinter." *Saturday Night Magazine* (8 July 2000) 28–31.

G106 Patrick Marber. "The man on the stairs." *Sunday Telegraph* (5 November 2000) 6.

G107 With David Edwards. "Unthinkable thoughts (an interview with Harold Pinter)." *Santa Monica Review* (Spring 2000), Magazine of Santa Monica College, California.
Reprinted in: *Squall Magazine* (24 October 2000) (posted on *Squall Magazine Online*, 8 November 2000; http://www.squall.co.uk/squall.cfm?sq=200107030&ct=2.
Concerned with the need to resist the suppression or trivialisation by the mainline media of information and attitudes which conflict with powerful corporate and political interests, taking the cases of the Western assaults upon Serbia and Iraq. Cf. *F42*.

G108 With Anne-Marie Cusac. "Harold Pinter: The Progressive interview." *The Progressive* (March 2001). On website www.progressive.org/intv0301.html.

G109 With Michael Billington. "'The evil that men do': Harold Pinter's political drama tells the world things it would prefer to forget about the prevalence of torture and tyranny. Michael Billington meets him as he prepares to play a sadistic interrogator in One for the Road." *Guardian* (30 June 2001), Review Section: 4.
Relates to the production at the Royal Court Theatre, in a double bill with *Mountain Language*.

G110 With Mel Gussow. *New York Times* (15 July 2001), section 2: 8.
Heading not known; referred to in *G112*. Interview in New York just before the start of the Harold Pinter Festival (16–29 July).

G111 Fiachra Gibbons. "Free Milosevic, says Pinter." *Guardian* (26 July 2001) 1.
Quotes Pinter on his denial of the legality of the trial of the Serb leader Milosevic and his view that the trial is very biased.

G112 With Mel Gussow, and others. "Pinter on Pinter: The Lincoln Center Interview." *TPR 2001–2002* (2002) 14–37.
Symposium, 27 July 2001, near the conclusion of the two-week Harold Pinter Festival (16–29 July) at Lincoln Center, New York. The last of several symposia, this was transferred to the Juilliard School Auditorium because of larger-than-expected audience numbers. Introduced by Nigel Redden, with Gussow in conversation with Harold Pinter, and a number of questions coming from audience members. The published text was transcribed by Susan Hollis Merritt with the assistance of Sean Donnelly.

G113 With Matthew Tempest. "Prosecute Blair and Clinton, urges Pinter." *Guardian* (2 August 2001) 21.

Protest against use of cluster bombs, etc., in bombing of Serbia and killing of civilians in the bombing of the Belgrade television station building. Posted as: "Pinter: I won't be silenced." *Guardian Unlimited* (3 August 2001), possibly in extended form, stressing the invalidity of the trial of Slobodan Milosevic, in the light of the comparable war-guilt of Nato's leaders, for the bombing of Serbia and Kossovo.

G114 Martin Bright. "Released documents show that neo-Nazi violence was ignored amid Cold War hunts for Communists: The day a teenage Pinter defied East End fascists." *Observer* (6 January 2002), News: 3.

Relates to the release of Home Office documents in the Public Record Office, which included a revelation that investigating officers scorned a complaint lodged with the police by Pinter and four teenage friends about being brutally assaulted by a gang of fascists in March 1949, not long after they had been heckling at an open-air meeting of the Union Movement. Reports upon an interview with Pinter about this affair.

G115 Hugh Davies. "Pinter emerges from the 'dark dream' of cancer." *Daily Telegraph* (26 August 2002).

Relates to interview on 25 August.

G116 Kirsty Scott. "Dark thoughts: Pinter tells of illness and its aftermath." *Guardian* (26 August 2002) 2.

Reports Pinter's remarks at the Edinburgh Festival, with some direct quotation.

G117 With Ramona Koval. "On cancer, war and cricket: In his first interview since undergoing surgery for cancer, Harold Pinter talks to Ramona Koval about nearly dying and reveals a new poem." *Guardian* (28 August 2002), Section G2: 2–4.

Edited version of an interview at the Edinburgh International Book Festival, with, at the end of it, the poem "Cancer cells" (dated March 2002) and the new poem "Meeting" (dated August 2002). For reports of Pinter's speech at the Edinburgh Festival, see *E51*. A full transcript of the interview, dated 15 September 2002, is on www.haroldpinter.org. It was broadcast on the Australian Broadcasting Corporation's Radio National programme "Books and Writing" on 15 September 2002.

G118 Curmudgeon of honour. *Daily Telegraph* (*ca.* 29 August 2002; filed on *Telegraph* website for that day).

Relates to award of Companionship of Honour.

G119 With Michael Billington. "'I'm not a theorist - I follow my nose.' Harold Pinter tells Michael Billington about film, politics and editing Shakespeare." *Guardian* (12 October 2002), Review Section: 117.

Edited extract from an on-stage interview (Barbican Screen Talk) at the Barbican Theatre, 9 October 2002, following a special screening of the 1963 film of *The Caretaker*. Related especially to this film, his screenplay for *King Lear*, his work with Joseph Losey, and the "great joy" he has had writing screenplays. Harold Pinter weekend at the Barbican: included also screenings of: *The Servant; Langrishe, Go Down;* and *The Go-Between.*

G120 When Harold met Ronald. Harold Pinter and Ronald Harwood have known each other, as actors and playwrights, for 50 years. Here they discuss celebrity casting, musicals at the National Theatre, and the critics. *Independent* (6 February 2003).

Conversation recorded at Pinter's home. Reprinted as: "Old Times." *RSL* (February 2003) 6–7. (*RSL* is the magazine of the Royal Society of Literature.)

G121 With Fiona Maddocks. "Pinter's War against Bush." *Evening Standard* (5 June 2003) 43.

Publicizing his *War* poems. Having "beaten cancer - now he's battling the nightmare of American belligerence."

G122 Angelique Chrisafis and Imogen Tilden. "Pinter blasts 'Nazi America' and 'deluded idiot' Blair." *Guardian* (11 June 2003) 9.

Report of Pinter's conversation on stage with Michael Billington at the National Theatre, London, on the occasion of his reading from his new poem-collection, *War.*

G123 With Geordie Greig. "My sadness over the son who won't speak to me." *Evening Standard* (7 July 2004) 25–26.

For full version of this, see G124. There was a follow-up to Greig's *Evening Standard* piece by Geoffrey Levy and Gordon Rayner titled "Pinter's Lost Son (A Tragedy in Two Acts)." *Daily Mail* (10 July 2004) 16–17.

G124 With Geordie Greig. "You talkin' to me?" *Tatler,* 299: 8 (August 2004) 108–113.

G125 Kate Kellaway. "Theatre of War: The Iraq war has energised dramatists, with David Hare's new play the latest in a surge of political drama. Pinter, Frayn and others on the front line talk to Kate Kellaway." *Observer* (29 August 2004), Arts Section, p. 5.

H

Miscellaneous: Minor Pieces, Collaborative Writings, Editing, etc.

H1   FOREWORD, LABICHE, *TWO PLAYS*   1962

[*To left, 7 thick vertical rules*] TWO PLAYS | BY EUGENE LABICHE | 90° IN THE SHADE | DUST IN YOUR EYES | ENGLISH VERSION BY | EMANUEL WAX | Forewords by Christopher Fry and | Harold Pinter | [*star*] | [*7 thick horizontal rules, full width of type-page*] | [*star*] | DRAMATISTS | PLAY SERVICE | INC. | [*to right, 7 thick vertical rules*]

Paperback, lettering on front cover identical with that on title page.

Pinter's single-paragraph foreword (unheaded) is on p. 3, signed "HAROLD PINTER"; Fry's is on p. 4. The author of "A NOTE ON THE TRANSLATOR" (pp.5–6), Pinter's literary agent, and friend, Emanuel (Jimmy) Wax, is not identified.

H2   Playwrights in Apartheid Protest. *Times* (26 June 1963) 12.
       One of the signatories to a declaration opposing performances of plays in South African theatres which observed a colour bar.

H2A   CELEBRITIES' CHOICE   1966

Celebrities' Choice | [to left: device of the National Book League, an open book, with emblematic flowers, and beneath it "N B L"] [to right: emblem of National Library Week: a large black dot, and beneath it a black oval with an open book in white in the centre] | 6d | National Book League 7 Albemarle Street London W1.

23 [24] pp. 21.6 x 14 cm. Paperback, stapled.

Published in March 1966. Price 6d. On verso of title leaf: "© NATIONAL BOOK LEAGUE 1966 | Printed in Great Britain | by W. & J. Mackay & Co Ltd, Chatham".

Contents: [1] title page; [2] as above; [3] contents; 4 preface, signed "J.E.M[orpurgo]"; 5-23 text; [24] details of the National Book League.

Notes: Pinter's contribution occupies pp.18–19. He chose specified editions, with in certain cases specified translations, of Samuel Beckett's *Molloy,* John Donne's poems, Fyodor Dostoevsky's *The Brothers Karamazov,* James Joyce's *Ulysses,* and Franz Kafka's *The Castle,* commenting, "My reason for this choice is simply that I like them" (18). B. C. Bloomfield in his *Philip Larkin: A Bibliography, 1933–1994* (London: The British Library; New Castle, DE: Oak Knoll Press, 2002) notes that this booklet accompanied an exhibition of a personal selection of books by twenty-six individuals, in the Stallybrass Galleries of the National Book League premises during the annual National Book Week, 12–19 March 1966 (76).

H3   Edited, with John Fuller, Peter Redgrove. *New Poems 1967*. London: Hutchinson, 1968.
P.E.N. anthology of recent poetry. Fifteen-line "Introduction" [p. 9] signed "H.P. | J.F. | P.R."

H3A   [Contribution to] *Authors Take Sides on Vietnam: Two Questions on the War in Vietnam Answered by the Authors of Several Nations*. Ed. Cecil Woolf and John Bagguley. London: Owen, 1967.
Pinter wrote, simply, "The Americans should not have gone in, but they did. They should now get out, but they won't" (41). This comment was reprinted in *Authors Take Sides on the Falklands: Two Questions on the Falklands Conflict Answered by More Than One Hundred Mainly British Authors*. Ed. Cecil Woolf and Jean Moorcraft Wilson. London: Cecil Woolf, 1982. 141.

H4   Joint introduction to pamphlet, with Arnold Wesker and George Steiner. "Harold Pinter, Arnold Wesker, and George Steiner appeal . . ." *the Jewish Quarterly the only Anglo-Jewish literary magazine in Britain appeals to you* . . . (London: Jewish Literary Trust, 1976), [2].

H5   [Contribution] Gowrie, Xandra and Jacob Epstein. "The 'Lost' Plays of Simon Gray, David Mercer, Peter Nichols, Alun Owen, Harold Pinter . . . and Many Others." *New Review*, 3: 27 (June 1976) 45–49.
The article deals with the tendency of the BBC to wipe television recordings from videotapes so they could be reused, with others being wiped by accident. The attitudes of Actors' Equity (the two year rule) and the Writers' Guild (with a copyright period of 5 or 7 years) did not help. In 1976, belatedly, a BBC Archives Advisory Committee was being instituted; by then a number of plays were irreparably lost, including two out of seven by Pinter and six by Simon Gray definitely gone, with two others doubtful, out of ten.
On p. 46, within a box, there is a statement by Pinter: "Why can't they sell plays at a nominal price to | authors? Since we have no idea | how it's decided at the moment, at least a respon- | sible body could exist. The basic thing is that the BBC | have been acting like dictators and I'm very glad | you're doing this article because it might give them | some idea of their responsibilities. It's pretty | destructive. There's no real plan or system. I don't | think anyone's really thought about it. It isn't a | question of who's well-known and who isn't – it's | a question of whether the damn thing's any good: | The BBC are acting in a very high-handed way in this matter."

H6   Petition *circa* 15 June 1978, calling for the release of the Soviet prisoner of conscience, Eduard Kuznetsov, a Jewish pro-democracy activist and writer who had been sentenced to 15 years' imprisonment mainly for his association with a *samizdat* periodical, the Phoenix Magazine. During his imprisonment, he wrote, and had smuggled out, his *Prison Diaries,* describing his trial and prison conditions.

Pinter was amongst the earliest signatories. The petition was published in several British daily papers (see www.haroldpinter.org/politics/politics freedom.shtml).

H7   FOREWORD, AN UNNATURAL PURSUIT   1985

a. British edition (1985):

AN UNNATURAL PURSUIT | and other pieces | [*rule, 8.8 cm.*] | SIMON GRAY | ff | *faber and faber* | LONDON BOSTON

Journal of the production of Simon James Holliday Gray's play, *The Common Pursuit,* at the Lyric Theatre, Hammersmith, in 1984, directed by Harold Pinter, as well as "other pieces." Pinter's "Foreword" is on p.15. ISBN 0-571-13719-9; ISBN 0-571-13757-1. Book includes photographs of Pinter directing the play.

b. American edition (1985):

AN UNNATURAL | PURSUIT & | OTHER PIECES | SIMON GRAY | St. Martin's Press | New York

First US edition, published 1985, ISBN 0-312-83371-7. Pinter's "Foreward" [*sic*] is on p.15. DLC copyright registration, 8 January 1986 (TX-1-730-199), gives publication-date as 2 September 1985.

H8   100 POEMS BY 100 POETS   1986

a. Hardback edition (1986):

100 Poems | by 100 Poets | AN ANTHOLOGY | *selected by* | HAROLD PINTER, | GEOFFREY GODBERT | *and* | ANTHONY ASTBURY | Methuen . London | Greville Press

1 blank leaf, xiv, 177 pp., 1 blank leaf. 21.6 × 13.4 cm. Hardback, green cloth; lettered down spine, in gold, in three lines: "100 POEMS BY 100 POETS | [*rule*] | selected by | [*rule*] | PINTER · GODBERT · ASTBURY [*across spine, at foot:*] Greville | Press | METHUEN". Endpapers. Dust jacket dark green; on outside front: "[*in yellow, rule, 8.3 cm.*] | [*2 lines in silver:*] 100 | POEMS | [*in white:*] [*rule, 3.3 cm.*] by [*rule, 3.3 cm.*] | [*2 lines in silver:*] 100 | POETS | [*in yellow, rule, 8.3 cm.*] | [*2 lines in yellow:*] AN ANTHOLOGY | selected by | [*in white:*] HAROLD

PINTER | [2 *lines in yellow*:] GEOFFREY GODBERT | & ANTHONY AST-
BURY"; on outside back, at foot, panel in yellow, within it, in black: "ISBN 0-413-
14300-7 | [*bar-code*] | 9 780413 143006"; down spine, in 3 lines: "[*in silver*:] 100
POEMS BY 100 POETS | [*in white*:] [*rule, 1.9 cm.*] selected by [*rule, 1.9 cm.*] | [*in
yellow*:] PINTER · GODBERT · ASTBURY [*across spine, at foot*:] [*3 lines in yel-
low*:] Greville | Press | [*within single-rule frame*:] methuen". On front flap: in white,
but with 4-line initial in yellow, 2 paragraphs about the origins of the selection,
and its nature, at foot: "PRICE NET | £8.95 | IN U.K. ONLY"; on back flap: in
white but with initials "A", "G" and "H" in yellow, 3 paragraphs, about the 3 selec-
tors, Astbury, Godbert, and Pinter, at foot "PRINTED IN GREAT BRITAIN".

Published 30 October 1986 (L accession 3 SEP 86). On verso of title leaf: "First
published in Great Britain in 1986 | by Methuen London Limited, 11 New Fetter
Lane, London EC4P 4EE | and Greville Press, Emscote Lawn, Warwick |
Selection © copyright 1986 | by Harold Pinter, Geoffrey Godbert, Anthony
Astbury. | [*copyrights statement*] | Printed in Great Britain by | Richard Clay (The
Chaucer Press) Ltd, | Bungay, Suffolk | [*cataloging data*] | ISBN 0 413 14300 7".

Contents: [i] half-title; [ii] blank; [iii] title page; [iv] as above; [v] "For George,
Elspeth, Nessie | and in memory of W. S. Graham"; [vi] blank; vii–x
contents; xi–xii acknowledgements; xiii "Introduction"; [xiv] blank;
1–168 texts of poems; 169–172 chronological list of poets; 173–177
index of first lines; [178] blank.

Notes: On p.xiii, "Introduction", signed "Harold Pinter | London, April, 1986",
in which he recounts that the three of them had devised the book during a train
journey to Cornwall and back, on an excursion to Penzance to visit Nessie, the
widow of W. S. Graham; they had decided that each poem should represent its
author's finest work. Methuen gives the publication date as 30 October 1986.

b. Paperback reprint (1987):

Title page as for 1986 hardback, except imprint as: "A Methuen Paperback |
Greville Press".

xiv, 177 pp. 19.3 × 12.4 cm. Paperback, dark green; on front cover: "[*in white,
rule, 7.4 cm.*] | [*2 lines in gold*:] 100 | POEMS | [*in white, rule, 3 cm.*] [*in white*:]
BY [*in white, rule, 3.1 cm.*] | [*2 lines in gold*:] 100 | POETS | [*in light green, rule,
7.4 cm.*] | [*2 lines in pale green*:] AN ANTHOLOGY | selected by | [*in white*:]
HAROLD PINTER | [*2 lines in pale green*:] GEOFFREY GODBERT | &
ANTHONY ASTBURY | [*2 lines in white*:] Greville Press | [*within single-rule
frame*:] methuen"; on back cover: additional information: "Price net £3.95 In
UK only | Methuen paperback | Greville Press Poetry | ISBN 0-413-15840-3 [[*bar-
code*] | 9 780413 158401"; spine as for spine of dust jacket.

Published 1987 (L accession 28 JUL 87). On verso of title leaf: added at head:
"This paperback edition published 1987", ISBN as "0 413 15840 3".

Contents: As for 1986 hardback, except: on [i] information about the editors and their publications; also, no endpapers.

c. Faber paperback edition (1991):

100 POEMS BY 100 POETS | An Anthology selected by | Harold Pinter, Geoffrey Godbert | and Anthony Astbury | ff | *faber and faber* | LONDON · BOSTON | Greville Press

xiv, 177 pp. 19.8 × 12.6 cm. Paperback, standard Faber cover design; on front cover, within white panel, within double-rule frame in black: "100 POEMS | BY | 100 POETS | [*rule, 2.5 cm.*] | *An Anthology* | Edited by | HAROLD PINTER | Geoffrey Godbert | and | Anthony Astbury"; on back cover: publishers, brief account of volume, "UK £7.99 net | Canada $17.99 | ISBN 0-571-16095-6 | [*barcode*] | 9 780571 160952"; on spine, within white panel: "[*2 rules*] | [*down spine:*] 100 POEMS BY 100 POETS | Greville | Press | ff | [*across spine, two rules*]".

Published 3 June 1991 (L accession 19 APR 1991). On verso of title leaf: publication information, "This paperback edition first published in 1991 | [. . .] | Printed in England by Clays Ltd, St Ives plc | [*conditions of sale, CIP record statements*] | ISBN 0-571-16095-6".

Note: Reprinted 1 November 1991, 11 March 1993, 20 June 1994, 18 December 1995, 1 May 1998 (Faber records, 2001).

d. American edition (1987):

[*rule, 7.3 cm.*] | 100 POEMS | [*rule, 3 cm.*] BY [*rule, 3 cm.*] | 100 POETS | [*rule, 7.3 cm.*] | AN ANTHOLOGY | selected by | HAROLD PINTER, | GEOFFREY GODBERT | and | ANTHONY ASTBURY | [*small decorative device*] | GROVE PRESS / NEW YORK

xvi, 176 pp. 20.7 × 13.6 cm. Hardback, quarter-bound in dark grey cloth, boards light green; lettered down spine, in silver, in 2 lines: "100 POEMS BY 100 POETS | [*rule, 0.8 cm.*] selected by PINTER · GODBERT · ASTBURY [*rule, 0.8 cm.*] [*across spine:*] GROVE".

Published 1987. On verso of title leaf: copyright, first publication, and reproduction restriction statements, "Published by Grove Press, Inc. | 920 Broadway | New York, N.Y. 10010 | [*cataloging data*] | Manufactured in the United States of America | First Edition 1987 | 10 9 8 7 6 5 4 3 2 1".

Contents: As for British hardback, except: [xiv] blank; xv "Introduction"; [xvi] blank; and at end, the list of first lines is compressed, to end on p.176.

e. American paperback edition (1992):

Title page as for hardback, except, below decorative device: "[*Evergreen device*] | GROVE WEIDENFELD | NEW YORK" xiv, 176 pp. 20.9 × 13.7 cm. Paperback, light brown; on front cover: lettering mainly in black, but with initial *"P"* of *"Poems"* in red: "AN ANTHOLOGY | *[rectangular yellow panel, with small bands at top right corner in red, within it, in 2 lines:]* 100 Poems | by 100 | *[smaller black panel, within it in white, reversed out of black]* POETS | Selected by | HAROLD PINTER | *[rule, 2.6 cm.]* | GEOFFREY GODBERT | *[small red panel]* | ANTHONY ASTBURY"; on back cover: "*[at top, right:]* $9.95 | *[centred, three paragraphs with critical citations and account of the collection, between second and third, small green panel]* | *[in red, Evergreen device]* | AN EVERGREEN BOOK | Published by Grove Weidenfeld | *[at foot, left:]* Cover design by Carin Goldberg | 7/92 Printed in USA © 1992 Grove Press, Inc. | *[at foot, right:]* *[white panel, within it:]* *[bar-code]* | 9 780802 132796 | ISBN 0-8021-3279-0 | *[to right:]* 90000> | *[bar-code]*"; down spine: "*[in black:]* 100 *[in red:]* POEMS BY *[in black:]* 100 *[in red:]* POETS *[in black:]* PINTER GODBERT ASTBURY".

Published July 1992. On verso of title leaf: copyright and restriction statements, "Published by Grove Weidenfeld | A division of Grove Press, Inc. | *[address, first UK publication data, DLC cataloging data]* | Manufactured in the United States of America | [. . .] | First American Edition 1987 | First Evergreen Edition 1992 | 3 5 7 9 10 8 6 4 2".

Contents: As for Grove hardback.

H9   Charter 88 [1988]
      Document signed by about 6,000 people, including some members of the 20th of June Group (a group of anti-establishment artists so-called because their first assemblage was at Harold Pinter and Lady Antonia Fraser's home in Campden Hill Square, Holland Park, London, on 20 June 1988). It called for, among other things, a Bill of Rights and a written constitution.

H10   Mandrake. "Pinters bow out of the Group." *Sunday Telegraph* (7 May 1989) 13.
      Cites extract from a letter to other members, relating to Pinter and Antonia Fraser's leaving the June 20 Group which had been founded in their house almost a year earlier.

H11   Gotlieb, Vera. "Theatre in Crisis." *Modern Drama,* 33 (1990) 57–58.
      Includes "The Conference Declaration," resolutions of a conference at Goldsmith's College, University of London, 4 December 1988. Signatories included Pinter.

H12   *Salman Rushdie: Is Nothing Sacred?* Sir Herbert Read Memorial Lecture, 6 February 1990. Cambridge: Granta, 1990.
      Because of the *fatwa* against Rushdie, Pinter delivered his lecture for him at the Institute of Contemporary Arts, London on 6 February. Extracts from the speech appeared in the *Guardian* (7 February 1990) 15; also in the *Guardian Weekly* (18 February 1990) 4; and cf. Susan Heller Anderson, "Chronicle . . . Rushdie Speaks (in Pinter's Voice)," *New York*

Times (8 February 1990), Section B: 7; John Walsh, "Wish You Were Here," *Sunday Times* (11 February 1990), Section G: 1.

H13   [Joint letter] Held in Pentonville but not told why. *Independent* (29 January 1991) 16.

On the arbitrary detention of Abbas Cheblak, a Palestinian. Signatories: Martin Amis, Nina Bawden, Angela Carter, Maureen Duffy, David Edgar, Mark Fisher, Antonia Fraser, Victoria Glendinning, David Hare, R. Harwood, Michael Holroyd, Rana Kabbani, Hanif Kureishi, Ian McEwan, Ursula Owen, Harold Pinter, Patrick Seale, and Emma Tennant. At the time of the First Gulf War, the British Government was setting out to round up and deport Iraqi and Palestinian nationals; this letter and other protests halted this programme (Billington 327).

H14   Contribution. "Weighing Up the Rights and Wrongs: Gulf War – The Intellectual View." *Observer* (3 February 1991) 19.

Personal response, along with those of Nadine Gordimer, Gore Vidal, and other well-known people, on the 1991 Gulf War.

H15   [Joint letter] Labour is Failing the Challenge of a Cynical and Unnecessary War. *Guardian* (19 February 1991) 18.

Signatories: Ian Bartholomew and 56 others, including Pinter. Relates to the 1991 Gulf War.

H16   [Joint letter] Easing the Suffering of War. *Guardian* (14 March 1991) 20.

Signatories: Miriam Stoppard and 17 others, including Pinter.

H17   [Joint statement] America's $17bn Debt to Nicaragua. *Independent* (18 June 1991) 16.

Signatories: Helena Kennedy, Harold Pinter, Glenys Kinnock, Tony Benn, Dafydd Elis Thomas, and Christine Oddy (for the Nicaragua Solidarity Campaign), demanding the USA respect the World Court judgement against its "illegal war" and settle Nicaragua's claim for damages.

H18   [Joint letter] *Independent* (29 June 1991) 16.

Signatories: as for *H13*. A further protest about the imprisonment in Pentonville Prison and threatened deportation of Abbas Cheblak, a Palestinian writer and intellectual, as a violation of freedom of speech.

H19   [Joint letter] Mordechai Vanunu: More in Need of Help Than Ever. *Independent on Sunday* (29 September 1991) 21.

Signatories: Peter Benenson, Ken Coates, Bruce Kent, Yael Lotan, Harold Pinter, Jakob von Uexkull, and Andrew Wilski (members of The Mordechai Vanunu Trust). Vanunu had been kidnapped by Israeli agents in 1986 and abducted to Israel, where he was sentenced to 18 years' imprisonment for whistleblowing on Israel's development of nuclear weapons at the Dimona research station.

H20   [Petition] Government Attacks Access to Justice. *Independent* (10 October 1991) 10.

A protest against the British government's proposed changes to immigration legislation that would place further obstacles in the way of those seeking political asylum. An advertisement, promoted by PEN, Amnesty International, the Joint Council for the Welfare of Immigrants, and other organisations. Pinter was one of many signatories.

H21   [Joint letter] Travel Ban on Mikhail Gorbachev Condemned as Abuse of Power. *Guardian* (13 October 1992) 18.
Signatories: Harold Pinter, Antonia Fraser, Vanessa Redgrave, and 14 others.

H22   [Joint letter] Reprisal Murders of Journalists in Turkey. *Independent* (18 January 1993) 16.
Signatories: Edward Albee, Harold Pinter, Antonia Fraser, Arthur Miller, and 6 others. Relates to repression of Kurdish people.

H23   [Joint letter] Turkish Responsibility for Kurdish Fears . . ." *Independent* (28 April 1993) 21.
Signatories: Harold Pinter and 7 others.

H24   **99 POEMS IN TRANSLATION**   1994

a. Paperback (1994):

Faber: Published 13 April 1994, 1300 copies. ISBN 0571-17357.8. Not seen.

b. Paperback edition (1996):

99 POEMS | IN TRANSLATION | An Anthology selected by | HAROLD PINTER | ANTHONY ASTBURY | GEOFFREY GODBERT | ff | *faber and faber* | LONDON · BOSTON | Greville Press

x, 149 pp. 19.7 × 12.4 cm. Paperback, glossy white; on front cover: "ff | POETRY | 99 Poems in Translation | An Anthology | edited by | Harold Pinter | Anthony Astbury | and Anthony Godbert | [*coloured illustration*]"; on back cover: "ff | faber and faber | [*brief account of volume*] | Cover illustration: *The Wine Press* by Henry Matisse | © Succession H. Matisse | DACS 1996 | Price UK £7.99 RRP | Canada $16.99 | $12.95 | ISBN 0-571-17692-5"; on spine: "ff | [*down spine:*] 99 Poems in Translation".

Published 5 February 1996 (O accession 11 JAN 1996). Copies printed 9,882. On verso of title leaf: "Photoset in Sabon by Wilmaset Ltd Wirral | Printed in England by Clays Ltd, St Ives plc".

Contents: [i] half-title; [ii] list of Pinter titles; [iii] title page; [iv] as above; [v] dedication "For the translators"; [vi] blank; vii–x contents; 1–137 text; 138–140 "Chronological List of Poets"; 141–142 "Index of Translators";   143–145   "Index   of   First   Lines";   146–149 "Acknowledgements"; [150] blank.

c. American edition (1994):

99 POEMS | IN TRANSLATION | An Anthology selected by | HAROLD PIN-
TER | ANTHONY ASTBURY | GEOFFREY GODBERT | [*publisher's device*] |
Grove Press | New York

x, 149 pp., 1 blank leaf. 20.8 × 13.3 cm. Hardback, pale green cloth; down spine,
in dark green: "99 POEMS IN TRANSLATION Selected by Pinter · Astbury ·
Godbert [*across spine, publisher's device*]". Dust jacket missing, in copy seen.

Published October 1994. On verso of title leaf: selection copyright statement,
"Copyright of individual poems is as stated in the Acknowledgements", reproduction restriction and first publication statements, "First Grove Press edition,
October 1994 | Printed in the United States of America | FIRST EDITION | [*cat-
aloging data*] | Grove Press | 841 Broadway | New York, NY 10003 | 10 9 8 7 6 5
4 3 2 1".

Contents: [i] half-title; [ii–iii] list of Pinter titles; [iv] blank; [v] title page; [vi]
as above; otherwise as for British edition.

H25 [Joint letter] Radio Daze. *Guardian* (22 March 1994), Guardian Features:
23.
Signatories: Joe Dunlop, Jill Hyem, Guy Jenkin, Harold Pinter, Alan
Plater, David Stafford, Sue Teddern, Peter Tinniswood, and J. C. Wilsher.
Deplores the proposed closure of the BBC Radio "literary unit."

H26 [Joint letter] Vanunu Anniversary. *Independent* (30 September 1994),
Comment: 17.
Signatories: Benedict Birnberg, Peter Benenson, Bruce Kent, Harold
Pinter, Arnold Wesker, Julie Christie, Alexei Sayle, Helena Kennedy, and
Michael Mansfield. See *H19*, *H28*.

H27   **Foreword, ANTHOLOGY OF CONTEMPORARY**   1994
KURDISH POETRY

Anthology | of | Contemporary | Kurdish Poetry | Published by | Kurdistan
Solidarity Committee | and Yashar Ismail | 44 Ainger Road | London NW3 3AT
| tel/fax 071-586 5692 | © December 1994 | ISBN: 0 9524991 X | [*to left: small
black panel, lettering in white reversed out of black:*] LONDON | ARTS BOARD
[*centred:*] We gratefully acknowledge the financial | assistance of the London
Arts Board.

3 leaves, I-VIII [IX-X] 1–48 pp.

Notes: Pinter's Foreword is a single paragraph on p. I, but it is also reprinted on
the back cover. The editors are Estella Schmid, Sheri Laiser, and Kamal
Mirawdeli. The short paperback book contains ten full-page photographs.

H28   [Joint letter] Vanunu and Israel's Secrets. *Sunday Telegraph* (22 January 1995) 26.

Signatories: Julie Christie, Harold Pinter, Alexei Sayle, and Susannah York (Campaign to Free Vanunu and for a Nuclear Free Middle East). In 1995 Pinter proposed a toast at the 40th Birthday Party held for Mordechai Vanunu. See *H19, H26*.

H29   Amnesty International. Page of protest against the execution of Ken Saro-Wira by the Nigerian military junta. *Independent* (18 November 1995) 7. Pinter was one of many signatories. In January 1995, he had gone with a PEN group to the Nigerian Embassy to protest against the imprisonment and prosecution of the Ogoni playwright, Ken Saro-Wiwa. Despite international pressures, in November 1995 the junta went ahead and hanged him, along with eight other Ogoni activists (Billington 373). See *E36*.

H30   [Joint letter] Europe Sells Its Soul for a Euro. *Observer* (17 December 1995), Observer Features: 14.

Signatories include Tariq Ali, Pinter, *et al*. Expresses solidarity with French strikers for "social rights."

H31   [Joint letter] Hollow Reforms in Turkey. *Independent* (2 January 1996), Comment: 10.

Signatories include Tony Benn, MP, Pinter, *et al*.

H32   [Joint letter] The Many Friends of Eyyad Sarraj. *Guardian* (25 May 1996) 26.

Signatories: Kamal Abu Dib Adonis, Hanan Ashrawi, Antonia Fraser, Lord Gilmour, Germaine Greer, Rana Kabbani, Kanaan Makiya, Harold Pinter, Edward Said, and Patick [*sic*] Seale.

H33   [Joint letter] Solidarity with Turkish Writers. *Independent* (31 May 1996), Leader: 17.

Signatories: Julian Barnes and 97 others, including Pinter.

H34   [Joint letter] *Independent on Sunday* (6 August 1996) 14.

Protest against the "proposed execution . . . of Mumia Abu-Jamal in the United States" (Knowles, "From London," *TPR* (1997), p.167). Signatories include Pinter. Cf. *F45*, his contribution to the *Independent* (28 December 2000) 1, 7, nominating this man as a hero for his courage throughout 14 years on death row in Pennsylvania.

H35   [Television joint statement] A Statement from the International Parliament of Writers. "Without Walls" programme, BBC-TV, 14 November 1996.

Speakers included Pinter, among others (*TPR* (1997): 166, 213).

H35A [Endorsement to book of poems] W. S. Graham. *Selected Poems* (London: Faber and Faber, 1996).

Single sentence on back cover: "His song is unique and his work an inspiration."

H36   [Joint letter] UN Closure of Camp Betrays Refugee Rights. *Independent* (22 January 1997), Leader: 13.

Signatories: Lord Avebury (Chairman, Parliamentary Human Rights Group) and 27 others, including Pinter.

H37 [Contribution] "When it comes to the vote . . ." *Red Pepper,* 35 (April 1997) 12, 30.

One of a number of short comments as to what hope is offered by the forthcoming parliamentary election. Pinter finds "the ducking and weaving of Labour in opposition has been despicable"; still, the Tories' return would mean "this country will be doomed."

Also, on p.30, the magazine prints a letter forwarded by Pinter, from W. Probyn, inmate, Littlehey Prey Prison, Huntingdon, referring to a letter by Pinter in the *Times,* December 1996 (i.e., *F32,* 8 January 1997), about excessive powers given to the police and commenting upon their police state methods. A following note by Pinter records that he sent Probyn's letter to the *Guardian,* which refused to print it.

H38 [Joint letter] Editor under arrest: Iran. *Independent* (7 July 1997) 14.

Appeal against the arrest of the Iranian dissident writer, Faraj Sarkuhi, chief editor of the literary review, *Adinah.* Signatories: Sybille Bedford, Lady Rachel Billington, Morris Farhi, Lady Antonia Fraser, Ronald Harwood, Francis King, Harold Pinter, Tom Stoppard, and 42 others of the English Centre of International PEN.

H39 [Joint letter] A Family Blighted by Deportation. *Independent* (10 July 1997), Leader Page: 21.

Signatories: Jeremy Corbin, John Pilger, Paul Foot, Harold Pinter, *et al.* Appeal to the Home Secretary to allow the re-entry into Britain of the family of Abdul and Ade Onibiyo.

H40 [Joint letter] Kurdish Peace Train Plea. *Independent* (29 August 1997), Comment: 13.

Signatories: Estella Schmid and 14 others, including Pinter. Protests against Germany's halting of the Musa Antor Peace Train at the Belgian border, frustrating a Kurdish attempt to influence the Turkish government. See *E41.*

H41 [Petition] Decriminalize Cannabis: Campaign Supporters . . . Add Your Name to the List. *Independent* (5 October 1997), Comment: 1.

Signatories: almost 250 persons, including Pinter.

H42 [Joint letter, published as advertisement] *Jewish Chronicle* (14 November 1997).

Signatories: Pinter and others (British Friends of Peace Now). Opposes Binyamin Netanyahu's conduct of current Middle East peace talks.

H43 Declaration against the Globalisers of Misery. February 1998.

Signatories included Pinter and Ken Loach. No other information currently available.

H43A Owen Barcutt. "Pinter challenges 'ethical' foreign policy: Playwright backs demonstrators found guilty of obstruction during protest over weapons to Turkey." *Guardian* (6 February 1998) 4.

Some direct quotation of his comments both inside and outside the courtroom.

H43B   Sarah Hall. "Funereal air as the left stages Whitehall vigil." *Guardian* (19 February 1998): 12.

Speakers quoted at this demonstration against a threatened war against Iraq included Pinter. It was organised by the Emergency Committee on Iraq, to which he and Lady Antonia Fraser belonged: see public notices in the *Guardian* (11 February 1998): 17; and (17 February 1998): 1.

H44   Comment by Pinter. In: *Suitcase: A Journal of Transcultural Traffic* (UCLA Program in Comparative Literature) [3] ([1] June 1998). Cited by Merritt in *TPR* (2001), p.239.

H45   Petition of Scholars and Writers: Taking a Stand against the Turkish Government's Denial of the Armenian Genocide and Scholarly Corruption in the Academy. 22 August 1998.

Cited Merritt, *TPR, 1997–1998*, p. 187. Signatories included Pinter.

H46   [Joint letter] Open Letter from Harold Pinter and Others. *Observer* (20 September 1998), The Observer News Page : 30.

Condemns the refusal of press credentials for the Labour Party Conference requested by the magazine *Red Pepper*, as a denial of press freedom.

H47   [Joint letter] Two Perspectives on Pinochet. *Daily Telegraph* (6 November 1998) 29.

Signatories: Isobel Allende, Bono (U2 pop group), Costa Gavras, Elizabeth Horman, Ken Loach, Angel Parra, Harold Pinter, Emma Thompson, and Philip Cox. Cited from Merritt (*TPR* [1999]).

In late 1998, General Augusto Pinochet, ex-president of Chile, was detained in England, where he had gone for medical treatment, under house arrest following an application by the Spanish judge, Luiz Garzon, that he be extradited to Spain to stand trial for murder. Following the American-assisted military coup in 1973, in which he had overthrown the democratically elected government of President Salvador Allende, about 3,000 Chileans had been killed, and many thousands had been tortured. Some of these had been Spanish citizens, hence the move to bring him to justice in Spain. In the event, all legal hurdles were passed, except for approval by the Home Secretary, Jack Straw, and Straw allowed him to return to Chile on the questionable ground that he was too ill to stand trial. Nonetheless, some legal moves to bring him to justice continued in Chile. See *E42*.

H48   [Contribution] Sayings of the Week. *Observer* (14 February 1999) 29.

Cited: "I have the feeling that lots of people have wanted to punch me in the face for a very long time."

H49   Foreword. In *Degraded Capability: The Media and the Kosovo Crisis*, edited by Philip Hammond and Edward S. Herman. London: Pluto Press, 1999.

H50   "Foreword by Harold Pinter." In: Kennard, Peter. *Domesday Book: Photopoem. The Critical Image*. Manchester: Manchester UP; New York: St. Martin's, 1999. Cited from Merritt, *TPR* (2001).

H51 [Contribution to:] CARCANET 2000 | *A Commonplace Book* | CAR-CANET

Published in 2000 by Carcanet Press Limited, Manchester. ISBN 1 85754 521 4. Pinter's single-sentence contribution appears on p.53: "A great publishing house!"

H52 [Joint letter] Stop This Holy Slaughter Now. *Observer* (24 December 2000), Observer News Pages.

Signatories: Paul Foot, Harold Pinter, Prof. Edward Said, Prof. Noam Chomsky, Susannah York, Tony Benn, Dr. Ghada Kaimi, Elfi Pallis, and many others.

H53 [Contribution] "My election" series. *Guardian* (14 May 2001) 11.

One of a series of respondents to ten questions. Pinter stated he would, for the first time, be voting for the Socialist Alliance and that he did not consider things had got better under New Labour.

H54 Election 2001. I'm Voting For. *Observer* (3 June 2001) 14.

One of a number of respondents. Pinter: "I support Socialist Alliance. If they had a candidate in Kensington and Chelsea that is how I would vote."

H55 [Joint letter] Stop the war of rich against poor. *Independent* (*ca.* 20 September 2001), Review: 2. [Noted on: www.independent.co.uk].

H56 [Joint letter] Stop the war! *Daily Telegraph* (20 September 2001).

Signatories included Pinter. Response to the destruction of the World Trade Centre towers in New York, appealing for a measured rather than an extreme reaction from the USA and UK.

H57 Joint letter to Signor Silvio Berlusconi, President of Italy, also submitted to the *Independent,* week of 23 February 2002.

Appeal for the extension for a further two years of Dr Mario Fortunato's appointment as director of the Italian Cultural Institute in Belgravia, London. Signatories: Salman Rushdie, Harold Pinter, Hugh Everett, Nick Hornby, Mary Elizabeth Mastrantonio. Not printed in full in the *Independent,* but quoted, in an article by Louise Jury, "Actors and writers rush to defence of Italy's cultural ambassador" (23 February 2002).

H58 [What we think of America] Episodes and Opinions from Twenty-Four Writers.

Granta, 77 (Spring 2002) 66–69.

Includes a blistering attack by Pinter, one of the harshest of the 24 writers' assessments. Pinter recorded a version of his contribution at the ABC London studio, broadcast in Australia on Radio National, "Radio Eye" programme, 30 March 2002.

H59 [Joint appeal] More pressure for Middle East peace. *Guardian* (6 April 2002) 23.

Among other points, includes an appeal "to all people of good conscience" to protest against the Israeli government's onslaught against the Palestinian people. Signatories: Harold Pinter, Benjamin Zephaniah,

Ahdaf Soueif, Andy de la Tour, Susan Wooldridge, and 18 other writers and artists (Artists for Palestine).

H60   Joint letter to the BBC, 13 August 2002, extensively quoted in: Jonathan Petre. "Atheists want voice on Today." *Daily Telegraph* (filed 14 August 2002), seen on website.

Signed by Pinter and over 100 other prominent figures against the ban on secular contributions to Radio 4's "Thought for the Day," in the "Today" programme.

H61   Stars tell Blair: stay out of Iraq. *Guardian Unlimited* (18 September 2002). Celebrities representing the Stop the War Coalition presented a petition opposing aggression against Iraq to 10 Downing Street. Signatories included Pinter.

H62   [Contribution] 100 issues of Red Pepper. *Red Pepper* (October 2002). First of a series of 16 short statements congratulating *Red Pepper* and its editor, Hilary Wainwright, on surviving through to its 100th issue ("In these dark days, Red Pepper is an island of sanity. . ."). Pinter on p. 26.

H63   [Joint letter] Time to free Vanunu. *Guardian* (29 October 2002) 17. Signatories: Bert Birnberg, Bruce Kent, Yael Lotan, Harold Pinter, Andrew Wilski, Susannah York, Campaign to Free Vanunu. See *H19*.

H64   [Joint letter] Hard choices about war. *Guardian* (12 November 2002) 21. Concerns the UN resolution about Iraq. Co-signatories: Alice Mahon, Tony Benn, Jeremy Corbyn, Tam Dalyell, Carol Naughton, Harold Pinter, Mohamed Sawatha, and four others.

H65   **LARKIN, POEMS**   2002

PHILIP LARKIN | [*rule*] | POEMS | SELECTED BY | HAROLD PINTER | GREVILLE PRESS | IN ASSOCIATION WITH THE | DELOS PRESS

23, (1) pp. 21.5 × 13.7 cm. Paperback, pale blue; on front cover: "[*3 lines in dark blue:*] POEMS BY | PHILIP | LARKIN | [*2 lines in black:*] Selected by | Harold Pinter | [*in dark blue, 2 rules, thick and thin, 2.4 cm.*] | [*in black:*] Greville Press Pamphlets"; on back cover: "[*in dark blue:*] ISBN 0 906887 76 3"; down spine, in black: "Poems by Philip Larkin | Greville Press". Endpapers off-white.

Published 2002. On verso of title leaf: publication and copyright statements, for selection and for 13 of Larkin's poems, selected from his *Collected Poems,* at foot: "Printed in Great Britain by Peter Lloyd | at The Holbeche Press, Rugby". On back cover: "ISBN 0 906887 76 5".

Contents: [1] half-title; [2] note, as below; [3] title page; [4] as above; 5–23 text, 13 poems; [24] limitation page.

Notes: On p.[2]: note by Pinter, that he "had wanted to include in this selection four poems from *The Less Deceived*", but had been refused copyright permission. On p.[24]: "Printed in an edition of 300 copies | of which the first fifty are

| numbered and have been signed | by the selector | COPY NUMBER" [William Baker copy numbered "44", signed "Harold Pinter"].

H66 Joint letter. "Send aid to Gaza now." *Guardian* (21 February 2003) 21.
Plea for urgent dispatch of food-aid to ease the humanitarian crises, causing malnutrition in children, etc., in the Gaza strip and the West Bank, initiated by the group "Jews for Justice for Palestinians," signed by 147 "Jews in Britain."

H67 A Manifesto for Peace & Progress. In: *Guardian* (18 March 2003).
An advertisement of the manifesto, inviting people to add their names to the list of signatories, launched by a group of theatre-celebrities headed by Vanessa Redgrave and including Pinter. Opposed to the oncoming invasion of Iraq.

H68   THE DWARFS [*novel adapted as a play*]   2003

The Dwarfs | Kerry Lee Crabbe | adapted from the novel by | Harold Pinter | ff | *faber and faber*

4 leaves, 88 pp. 19.9 × 11.9 cm. Paperback, grey; on front cover: "ff | STAGE-SCRIPTS | The Dwarfs | Kerry Lee Crabbe | adapted from the novel by | Harold Pinter"; on back cover: publisher, 3 paragraphs about the novel and the play, at foot, left: within vertical single-rule frame: "£7.99", vertical: ISBN, bar-code, number; centred: "Discover the brightest and best in fresh theatre | writing with Faber's new *StageScripts*."; on spine: "ff | [*down spine:*] The Dwarfs adapted from Harold Pinter's novel by Kerry Lee Crabbe".

Published April 2003. Price £7.99. On verso of title leaf: "This adaptation first published in 2003 | by Faber and Faber Limited | [*address*] | Typeset by Country Setting, Kingsdown, Kent CT14 8ES | Printed in England by Intype Libra Limited", copyright, Crabbe's right to be identified as author, performing rights, conditions of sale, and CIP record statements, "ISBN 0-571-22104-1", issue numerals.

Contents: [i] half-title, with notes about Pinter and Crabbe; [ii] Faber's Pinter titles; [iii] title page; [iv] as above; [v] first stage performance details (17 April 2003); [vi] blank; [vii] characters, time, and place of action; [viii] blank; 1–88 text.

Notes: The notes on the back cover record that the play was developed at the National Theatre Studio, screened on BBC4 in October 2002, and premièred at the Tricycle Theatre, Kilburn, London, April 2003.

H69   THE CATCH   2003

THE | CATCH | A CORRESPONDENCE | [*rule, 1.3 cm.*] | HAROLD PINTER | [*small ornament, in the shape of an ampersand, 0.5 × 0.4 cm.*] | ALAN WILKINSON | CHARINGWORTH | THE EVERGREEN PRESS | 2003

Unpaginated, [20] pp. 22.7 × 15.6 cms. Hand-sewn. (A) Hardback: special copies: quarter-bound with dark green cloth, extending 2.3 cm across boards, spine unlettered; on boards, marbled paper, with a pattern in red, yellow and different shades of green; on outside front board, glued-on label [5.5 × 7.7 cm.], printed on cream-coloured paper used in the body of the book: "THE | CATCH | | HAROLD PIN-TER | [*small ornament, in the shape of an ampersand, 0.4 × 0.3 cm.*] | ALAN WILKINSON" (lettering of "CATCH" in green and off-white, otherwise black). Endpapers. (B) Paperback: standard copies: wrap-around, dark green paper cover, on front cover, glued-on label, as for hardback. No endpapers.

Published 6 November 2003. 500 copies printed, all copies numbered by hand; 50 copies bound in hardback, and signed on the title page by Harold Pinter and Alan Wilkinson; 450 copies bound in paperback, unsigned. Prices: hardback ("special edition") £60; paperback ("standard edition") £12.50. No ISBN.

Contents: [1–2] blank; [3] half-title: "THE CATCH"; [4] "© Harold Pinter and Alan Wilkinson, 2003"; [5] title page; [6] affixed coloured photograph of "Gaieties C.C. versus Sir Paul Getty's XI, Wormsley 1997." [*8.7 × 10.2 cm.*] ; [7] "Introduction" signed "A.W."; [8] blank; [9]–[16] text; [17] printed letter from Harold Pinter to Alan Wilkinson dated 31 January 2002 with facsimile signature "Harold"; [18] blank; [19] colophon: "Designed, hand-set and printed by | John Grice of the Evergreen Press | in Caslon type on Zerkall paper | in an edition of 500 numbered copies, | the first 50 being specially bound, | and signed by the authors. | [*copy number of 500 added in pencil*] | Boxwood engraving by | Miriam Macgregor"; [20] publishers' imprint: "EVER-GREEN PRESS GL55 6NY".

Note one: Alan Wilkinson, the publisher, comments in an e-mail to William Baker dated 11 March 2004: "I collected my first copies on 6 November 2003 – of the standard edition. John Grice [the printer] is still sewing up by hand copies of the standard edition as the demand requires. The 'specials' came later as they were sent away to be bound.... On 8 January 2004, two years to the day after Harold told me about 'that catch' (see my introduction) I gave a launch party for 'the little green book' at Brooks's my London club, drinks 6.30 to 8.30. At about 8.00 I announced 'Ladies and gentlemen, the London premier of THE CATCH.' The actor Matthew Burton read my questions and Harold his answers. It was superb, especially the timing."

Note two: Alan Wilkinson commented in an e-mail to William Baker dated 26 February 2004: "All the type was hand-set; each sheet, with four pages on each side, was rolled through the little press by hand; and printer John Grice has and is hand-sewing the 450 copies of the standard edition." He noted in a letter to William Baker of 18 February 2004: "The labels for both [special and standard editions] are printed on... cream coloured Zerkall paper used in the body of the book."

Note three: The text concern a fine catch Pinter made while playing for the Gaieties Cricket Club. Wilkinson had heard about it over a drink and on 21 January 2002 wrote to Pinter asking a number of questions about the catch. Pinter replied on 24 and 31 January 2002. The main text consists of Wilkinson's questions and Pinter's answers, followed by the complete text of the letter of 31 January 2002.

Note four: After the text on page [16], there is a black-and-white boxwood engraving of a hand catching a cricket ball. This is directly underneath the words "Great Catch!"

Note five: William Baker owns a "special edition" copy numbered "19/500" and a "standard edition" copy numbered "223/500".

H69A [Endorsement to book of poems] Anne Wilkinson. *Heresies: The Complete Poems of Anne Wilkinson, 1924–1961.* Ed. Dean Irvine (Montréal, Québec: Véhicule Press, 2003). Single sentence on back cover: "Poised, spare, delicate, poignant, Anne Wilkinson's verse reveals a rare poetic sensibility."

H70 [Statement within] "True colours". "In 1937 W. H. Auden and Stephen Spender asked 150 writers for their views on the Spanish Civil War. The result was the book *Authors Take Sides.* Jean Moorcroft Wilson and Cecil Woolf have repeated the exercise, asking writers if they were for or against the Iraq war and whether they thought it would bring lasting peace and stability." *Guardian* (14 February 2004), Review section: 36.

This feature article provides edited extracts from statements by 25 writers, including Pinter. The full texts of 71 writers' statements was published on 7 March 2004 in *Authors Take Sides on Iraq and the Gulf War,* edited Jean Moorcroft Wilson and Cecil Woolf. London: Cecil Woolf, 2004. Pinter's contribution is on pp. 67–68.

I

Editions of Collected or Selected Works

Subsection 1: Plays and Prose

Within this subsection, to avoid over-proliferation of detail, a relatively summary account is provided of contents. Within the volumes of these collected editions, each item is normally preceded by a fly-title and (where appropriate) details for productions or presentations.

I1   PLAYS: ONE [–FOUR]   1976–81

a. Methuen edition, in four volumes (1976–81):

(i:i) Plays: One (1976):
HAROLD PINTER | Plays : One | The Birthday Party | The Room | The Dumb Waiter | A Slight Ache | A Night Out | The Black and White | The Examination | *With an introduction:* 'Writing for the Theatre' | A METHUEN PAPERBACK | Eyre Methuen

256 pp. 17.8 × 11.2 cm. Paperback, glossy black, lettered and ruled in white; on front cover: "Pinter | PLAYS: ONE | [*thin rule, 6.3 cm.*] | THE BIRTHDAY PARTY, | THE ROOM, THE DUMB WAITER, | A SLIGHT ACHE, A NIGHT OUT | [*thin rule, 6.3 cm.*] | [*coloured illustration*] | [*publisher's device*] | METHUEN | PAPERBACKS"; on back cover: "Harold Pinter | 'Our best living playwright' | THE TIMES | [*note on contents of volume*] | [*coloured photo of Pinter, full-length, on the landing of outside stairs*] | [*at foot, left:*] UK 75p | Australia $2.35* | New Zealand $2.65* | Canada $2.95* | *recommended only | [*at foot, right:*] 0 413 34650 1"; down spine: "Pinter PLAYS: ONE 0 413 34650 1 [*across spine, publisher's device*]".

Published 25 March 1976. 75 pp. On verso of title leaf: "Methuen paperback edition | First published in 1976 by Eyre Methuen Ltd", address, first publication and copyright details for items, "This collection © 1976 by H. Pinter Ltd, | Printed in Great Britain by Cox & Wyman Ltd, | London, Reading and Fakenham | ISBN 0 413 34650 1", performing rights and conditions of sale statements.

Contents: [1] half-title, with notes on Pinter and this volume, at foot: "*The front cover shows La Réponse imprévue by René Magritte © by | A.D.A.G.P. Paris, 1976, reproduced by courtesy of the Musées Royaux | des Beaux-Arts de Belgique. The photograph of Harold*

Pinter on the | back cover is by Tony McGrath."; [2] list of titles in the same series; [3] title page; [4] as above; [5] contents; [6] blank; [7] "Harold Pinter : A Chronology" [to 1975]; [8] blank; 9–16 "Introduction | Writing for the theatre | *A speech made by Harold Pinter at the National Student Drama Festival | in Bristol in 1962.*"; [17]–256 texts: The Birthday Party – The Room – The Dumb Waiter – A Slight Ache (stage version) – A Night Out (television version) – The Black and White (short story) – The Examination (short story).

Note one: The text of "Writing for the theatre", as noted on the verso of the title leaf, is the "revised version first published in *The | New British Drama*, Grove Press, New York, 1964". The statement there that *The Black and White* had "first appeared in *Transatlantic Review* in 1966" is incorrect, as it had earlier appeared in *The Spectator* of 1 July 1960 (see D2a).

Note two: This edition was reprinted in 1978 by Eyre Methuen Ltd, in 1981 and 1983 by Methuen London Ltd. Title page for 1981 as for 1976, except imprint as: "The Master Playwrights | METHUEN · LONDON". Binding in 1981 as for 1976, except for minor variations in lettering: e.g., at foot of front cover: "MASTER | PLAYWRIGHTS", and varied colouring of illustration; on back cover, UK price as £1.95.

(i:ii) Plays: One (expanded) (1986):
Inclusion of *The Hothouse*. Title page as for 1981, with the addition of "The Hothouse", following "A Slight Ache". 334 pp. 18 cm. Binding as for 1981 with minor variations, including, e.g., on the front cover, the addition of "THE HOT-HOUSE". ISBN 0 413 34650 1. This edition reprinted in 1987, 1989 (latter by Methuen Drama).

(ii) Plays: Two (1977):
HAROLD PINTER | Plays : Two | The Caretaker | The Dwarfs | The Collection | The Lover | Night School | Trouble in the Works | The Black and White | Request Stop | Last to Go | Special Offer | *With an introduction:* 'Writing for Myself' | EYRE METHUEN | London

248 pp., 4 leaves. 17.7 × 11.2 cm. Paperback, outside glossy black, lettered and ruled in white; on front cover: "Pinter | PLAYS: TWO | [*thin rule, 6.3 cm.*] | THE CARETAKER, | THE COLLECTION, THE LOVER, | NIGHT SCHOOL, THE DWARFS | [*thin rule, 6.3 cm.*] | [*coloured illustration*] | MASTER | PLAYWRIGHTS"; on back cover: as for *Plays: One,* except, at foot: "UK 85p 0 413 37300 2"; down spine: "Pinter PLAYS: TWO 0 413 37300 2 [*across spine:*] [*publisher's device*] | EYRE | METHUEN".

Published 19 May 1977. 85p. On verso of title leaf: "This collection first published in 1977 by Eyre Methuen Ltd," etc., first publication and copyright details

for each item and copyright statement for this collection, printer's imprint as for
Plays: One, "ISBN 0 413 37300 2", performing rights and conditions of sale
statements.

Contents: [1] half-title, 3 paragraphs about Pinter, and this volume, at foot:
"*The front cover shows Réproduction interdite by René Magritte ©
by* | *A.D.A.G.P. Paris, 1977, reproduced by courtesy of the Edward
James* | *Foundation. The photograph on the back cover is by* | *Tony
McGrath.*"; [2] list of volumes in series; [3] title page; [4] as above;
[5] contents; [6] blank; [7] "Harold Pinter: A Chronology" [to 1975];
9–12 "Introduction | Writing for Myself | *Based on a conversation
with Richard Findlater published in* The | Twentieth Century,
February 1961."; [13]–[249] texts: The Caretaker – The Dwarfs (stage
version) – The Collection (stage version) – The Lover (stage version)
– Night School (radio version) – Revue Sketches [five, including:]
Trouble in the Works – The Black and White – Request Stop – Last
to Go – Special Offer; [250] blank; [251] account of series; [252]
account of previous volumes; [253–255] list of Methuen's Modern
Plays; [256] blank.

Notes: Revised edition 1979, reprinted 1981; reprinted 1983, 1984 (by Methuen
London Ltd); reprinted 1988 (by Methuen Drama). On the verso of the title leaf
of the 1991 edition, it is stated that in the 1979 reprint (not seen), the television
version of *Night School* was substituted for the radio version. However, in the
1991 edition volume the text is that of the radio version

(iii) Plays: Three (1978):
HAROLD PINTER | Plays : Three | The Homecoming | Tea Party | The Basement
| Landscape | Silence | Night | That's Your Trouble | That's All | Applicant |
Interview | Dialogue for Three | *With the memoir,* 'Mac', *and the short story,*
'Tea Party' | The Master Playwrights | EYRE METHUEN . LONDON

247 pp., 4 leaves. 17.7 × 11.1 cm. Paperback, glossy black, lettered and ruled in
white; on front cover: "Pinter | PLAYS: THREE | [*thin rule, 5.9 cm.*] | THE
HOMECOMING, TEA PARTY, | THE BASEMENT, LANDSCAPE, | SILENCE
| [*thin rule, 5.9 cm.*] | [*coloured illustration*] | MASTER | PLAYWRIGHTS"; on
back cover: as for *Plays: One,* except at foot: "UK 95p 0 413 38480 2"; down
spine: "Pinter PLAYS: THREE 0 413 38480 2 [*across spine:*] [*publisher's device*]
| EYRE | METHUEN".

Published 4 May 1978. Price 95 p. On verso of title leaf: "This collection first
published in 1978 by Eyre Methuen Ltd," address, first publication and copyright details for each item, and copyright for this collection, printer's imprint as
for *Plays: One,* "ISBN 0 413 38480 2", performing rights and conditions of sale
statements.

Contents: [1] half-title, notes about Pinter and this volume, at foot: "*The front cover shows a detail from* Les amants *by René Magritte, repro-* | *duced by courtesy of Richard S. Zeisler. The photograph of Harold Pinter on* | *the back cover is by Tony McGrath.*"; [2] list of volumes in series; [3] title page; [4] as above; [5] contents; [6] blank; [7] "Harold Pinter : A Chronology" [to 1975]; [8] blank; [9]–247 texts: Mac (preceded by "BIOGRAPHICAL NOTE") – The Homecoming – Tea Party (television version) – The Basement (television version) – Landscape – Silence – Revue Sketches [six, including:] Night – That's Your Trouble – That's All – Applicant – Interview – Dialogue for Three – Tea Party (short story, with introductory note); [248] blank; [249–256] account of series and previous volumes in it, lists of volumes in two series, publisher's note.

Notes: Reprinted in 1986 (by Methuen London Ltd), reprinted 1989 (by Methuen Drama), with price increased to £1.95.

(iv) Plays: Four (1981):
HAROLD PINTER | Plays : Four | Old Times | No Man's Land | Betrayal | Monologue | Family Voices | *With an introduction by the author* | The Master Playwrights | EYRE METHUEN · LONDON

xiii [xiv], 296 pp., 5 leaves. 17.8 × 11.2 cm. Paperback, glossy black, lettered and ruled in white; on front cover: "Pinter | PLAYS: FOUR | [*thin rule, 5.8 cm.*] | OLD TIMES, NO MAN'S LAND | BETRAYAL, MONOLOGUE, | FAMILY VOICES | [*short rule, 5.8 cm.*] | [*coloured illustration*] | MASTER | PLAYWRIGHTS"; on back cover: as for *Plays: One*, except, at foot: "UK £1.95 0 413 48490 4"; down spine: "Pinter PLAYS: FOUR 0 413 48490 4 [*across spine:*] [*publisher's device*] | EYRE | METHUEN".

Published 27 August 1981. Price £1.95. On verso of title leaf: "This collection first published in Great Britain in 1981 | by Eyre Methuen Ltd," etc., details of first publication and copyright for the items contained, "This collection © 1981 by Neabar Investments Ltd | ISBN 0 413 48490 4 | Printed and bound in Great Britain by | Richard Clay (The Chaucer Press) Ltd, | Bungay, Suffolk"; performing rights and conditions of sale statements.

Contents: [i] half-title, with notes about Pinter and this volume, at foot: "*The front cover shows* L'empire des lumières *by René Magritte* | © *A.D.A.G.P. 1981, reproduced by courtesy of the Musées* | *Royaux des Beaux Arts de Belgique, Brussels. The photograph of* | *Harold Pinter on the back cover is by Tony McGrath.*"; [ii] list of Pinter titles; [iii] title page; [iv] as above; [v] contents; [vi] blank; [vii] "Harold Pinter : A Chronology" [extending to 1981]; [viii] blank; [xi]–xiii "Introduction | *A speech made by Harold Pinter in Hamburg, West Germany,* | *on being awarded the 1970 German Shakespeare Prize.*";

[xiv] blank; [1]–296 texts: Old Times – No Man's Land – Betrayal – Monologue – Family Voices; [297–306] list and accounts of volumes in the Master Playwrights series.

Notes: Reprinted in 1984, with title page as for 1981, except imprint "METHUEN – LONDON". Binding varies, with at foot of front cover, and spine, within white box, in black: "methuen"; on back cover, price as £2.50. Contents as for 1981, except chronology extends to 1984, final advertisements differ.

b. Faber edition (1991–93):

(i) Plays: One (1991):
[*All within single-rule border:*] PLAYS: ONE | HAROLD | PINTER | The Birthday Party | The Room | The Dumb Waiter | A Slight Ache | The Hothouse | A Night Out | The Black and White | The Examination | *With an introduction:* | 'Writing for the Theatre' | ff | *faber and faber* | LONDON · BOSTON

xiv, 386 pp. 19.8 × 12.5 cm. Paperback, white, with standard Faber design of black, grey and white triangles, lettering and rules in black; on front cover, within single-rule frame: "ff | [*rule*] | HAROLD | PINTER | [*rule*] | Plays One | [*coloured illustration*]; on back cover, within single-rule frame: "ff | *faber and faber* | [rule] | HAROLD PINTER | Plays One | [*note on contents of volume*] | Cover illustration by Andrzej Klimowski | UK £6.99 | Canada $17.99", ISBN, bar-code, number; on spine, within single-rule frame: "ff | [*rule*] | [*down spine:*] HAROLD PINTER   Plays One".

Published 1991. Price £6.99 (Canada $17.99). On verso of title leaf: "First published in this edition in 1991 | by Faber and Faber Limited | [*address, earlier publication details*] | Printed in England by Clays Ltd, St Ives plc", first publication and copyright details for each item, performing rights, conditions of sale, and CIP record statements, "ISBN 0-571-16074-3".

Contents: As for expanded Methuen (1986), with omission of note on illustration, of the "Chronology", and of final lists of titles in series (instead, final list of "FABER DRAMA" playwrights); on [ii], list of Faber's Pinter titles, instead of titles of series; performance details add those of later productions, for stage or television.

Notes: The four volumes of this edition were initially sold in Canada by Faber and Faber, subsequently co-published in Canada by Penguin Books Canada, Limited (from January 1997, ISBN for *Plays: One*: 0-571-17844-1). Also issued in South Africa, and (later) Australia.

(ii) Plays: Two:
[*All within single-rule border:*] PLAYS: TWO | HAROLD | PINTER | The Caretaker | The Dwarfs | The Collection | The Lover | Night School | Trouble in the Works | The Black and White | Request Stop | Last to Go | Special Offer |

With an introduction: | 'Writing for Myself' | ff | *faber and faber* | LONDON · BOSTON

xi, 238 pp., 1 leaf, 2 blank leaves. Binding style as for *Plays: One*, with, on front and back covers and spine: "Plays Two", and on front cover a different illustration.

Published 1991. Price £5.99, Canada $14.95. On verso of title leaf: as for *Plays: One*, with ISBN 0-571-16075-1.

Contents: As for Methuen, with same variations as for *Plays: One*.

(iii) Plays: Three (1991):
[*All within single-rule border:*] PLAYS: THREE | HAROLD | PINTER | The Homecoming | Tea Party | The Basement | Landscape | Silence | Night | That's Your Trouble | That's All | Applicant | Interview | Dialogue for Three | With the memoir, | *Mac,* and the | short story, *Tea Party* | ff | *faber and faber* | LONDON · BOSTON

1 blank leaf, 3 leaves, 241 pp., 1 leaf, 2 blank leaves. Binding style as for *Plays: One*, with "Plays Three" and different illustration.

Published 1991. Price £5.99, Canada $14.95. On verso of title leaf: as for *Plays: One*, with ISBN 0-571-16076X

Contents: As for Methuen, with same variations as for *Plays: One*; initial blank leaf.

(iv) Plays: Four (1993):
[*All within single-rule border:*] PLAYS : FOUR | HAROLD | PINTER | Old Times | No Man's Land | Betrayal | Monologue | Family Voices | A Kind of Alaska | Victoria Station | One for the Road | Mountain Language | With an introduction | by the author | ff | *faber and faber* | LONDON · BOSTON

xii, 423 pp. 20 cm. Binding style as for *Plays: One,* with "Plays Four" and different illustration.

Published 23 December 1993. Reprinted 30 October 1995, total copies printed 6,636. On verso of title leaf: as for *Plays: One*, with ISBN 0-571-17303-9 (pbk), and note of extended contents.

Contents: As for Methuen, with same variations as for *Plays: One*, but adds: A Kind of Alaska – Victoria Station – Precisely – One for the Road – Mountain Language – The New World Order.

c. Reissued Faber edition (1996):

(i) Plays One:
HAROLD PINTER | Plays One | *The Birthday Party* | *The Room* | *The Dumb Waiter* | *A Slight Ache* | *The Hothouse* | *A Night Out* | *The Black and White* | *The Examination* | ff | *faber and faber*

xiv, 386 pp. 19.7 × 12.6 cm. Paperback, grey, lettering in black but on front cover and spine volume number in white; on front cover: "ff | CONTEMPORARY CLASSICS | Harold Pinter: Plays | 1 | The Birthday Party · The Room | The Dumb Waiter · A Slight Ache · The Hothouse · A Night Out | The Black and White · The Examination | [coloured illustration]"; on back cover: "[to upper left:] [small photo of Pinter] | Photo by Sally Soames | Sunday Times | [centred:] ff | faber and faber | [notes on contents of volume, with citations from newspaper reviews] | Cover illustration by Andrzej Klimowski"; [at foot, left, within white panel:] UK £6.99 RRP | Canada $16.95 | [vertical:] ISBN 0-571-16074-3 | [bar-code] | 9 780571 160747 | [below, vertical:] 90200 | [bar-code]"; on spine: "ff | [down spine] Harold Pinter: Plays | [across spine] 1".

Re-issued 10 September 1996, reprinted 18 November 1997, 24 November 1999, 30 November 2000. Total copies printed, to 2000, 16,837. Price £12.99 (Canada $19.99). On verso of title leaf: as for 1991, except "Re-issued in 1996 as Harold Pinter: Plays One", "Printed in England by Mackays of Chatham PLC, Chatham, Kent | All rights reserved", "This collection © Harold Pinter 1976, 1985, 1991", "ISBN 0-571-17844-8", issue numerals.

Contents: As for first printing, but on p.[i], also note of contents.

(ii) Plays Two:
HAROLD PINTER | Plays Two | The Caretaker, | The Dwarfs, | The Collection, | The Lover, | Night School, | Trouble in the Works, | The Black and White, | Request Stop, | Last to Go and | Special Offer | ff | faber and faber

xi [xii], 238 pp., 1 leaf, 2 blank leaves. 19.8 × 12.5 cm. Paperback, binding style as for Plays One, with different illustration, ISBN, etc.

Reissued 15 January 1996, reprinted 11 March 1997, 1 January 1999, 20 September 2000. Number of copies of the re-issue printed, as of 2001, 10,296. Price UK £12.99 net, Canada $19.99. On verso of title leaf: same kinds of details as for 1991, except: "Reissued in 1996 | Originally published by Eyre Methuen in 1977 | Printed and bound in Great Britain by | Mackays of Chatham PLC, Chatham, Kent", "This collection © Harold Pinter, 1996", "ISBN 0-571-17744-1", issue numerals.

Contents: As for 1991 printing, except on [i] half-title, brief accounts of contents, and of Pinter; and at end, [239] "FABER CONTEMPORARY CLASSICS", list of authors; [239–244] blank.

(iii) Plays Three:
HAROLD PINTER | Plays: Three | The Homecoming | Tea Party | The Basement | Landscape | Silence | Night | That's Your Trouble | That's All | Applicant | Interview | Dialogue for Three | and the short story, | Tea Party | ff | faber and faber | LONDON · BOSTON

3 leaves, 241, [1] pp. 19.8 × 12.6 cm. Paperback, binding style as for *Plays One*, with different illustration, ISBN, etc.

Reissued 10 September 1996 (0-571-17845-6), re-published 2 December 1997 (0-571-19383-8), reprinted 7 February 2000, 19 March 2001 (0-571-16076-X). Copies printed 1996–2001, 8,658. Price £8.99 (Canada $18.99). On the verso of the title leaf: same kinds of details as for *Plays One*, except "Reissued in 1996 as *Harold Pinter: Plays Three* | The first paperback edition of this volume | was published in 1978 | by Eyre Methuen Ltd | Reprinted 1989 (by Methuen London Ltd) | Reprinted 1989 (by Methuen Drama) | Printed in Great Britain by Clays Ltd, St Ives plc", "ISBN 0-571-17845-6".

Contents: As for 1991 volume, except variance as for *Plays Two*, and on p.[242], "FABER DRAMA", list of authors.

(iv) Plays Four:
HAROLD PINTER | Plays Four | *Old Times* | *No Man's Land* | *Betrayal* | *Monologue* | *Family Voices* | *A Kind of Alaska* | *Victoria Station* | *Precisely* | *One for the Road* | *Mountain Language* | *The New World Order* | ff | *faber and faber*

xii, 423 pp. 19.8 × 12.6 cm. Paperback, binding style as for *Plays One*, with different illustration, etc.

Re-issued 10 September 1996, as ISBN 0-571-17850-2, 6,636 copies printed. Neither issue seen.

d. Expanded editions of Plays Three and Plays Four (1997–98):

(i) Plays Three:
Title page includes addition of "*Old Times* | *No Man's Land*".

399 pp. 20 cm. Paperback, style as for 1993 volume.

Published 2 December 1997. Reprinted 7 February 2000, 19 March 2001, total 8,658 copies. Price £12.99, Canada $19.99. ISBN 0-571-19383-8. Not seen.

(ii) Plays Four:
Title page as for 1993, except for deletion of "*Old Times* | *No Man's Land*" and addition (after *The New World Order*) of "*Party Time* | *Moonlight* | *Ashes to Ashes*".

xii [xiii–xiv], 433 pp. 19.7 × 12.6 cm. Paperback, binding style as for 1993, with 2 plays deleted, 3 added.

Published 2 November 1998. Reprinted 9 February 2001, 6,636 copies printed. Price £12.99 RRP, Canada $19.99. On verso of title leaf: as for 1993, except "Reissued as *Harold Pinter: Plays Four* in 1996 | Expanded edition (including *Moonlight* and *Ashes to Ashes*) | first published in 1998 | Photoset by Parker Typesetting Service, Leicester | Printed in England by Mackays of Chatham PLC,

Chatham, Kent", first-publication and copyright details, performing rights and conditions of sale statements, "ISBN 0-571-19384-6", issue numerals.

Contents: Preliminaries as for Methuen, except substituted introduction: "Introduction | *Harold Pinter's speech of thanks on receiving* | *the David Cohen British Literature Prize for 1995*", etc. – Betrayal – Monologue – Family Voices – A Kind of Alaska – Victoria Station – Precisely – One for the Road – Mountain Language – The New World Order – Party Time – Moonlight – Ashes to Ashes.

I2   [AMERICAN EDITION] COMPLETE WORKS   1977–81

a. Black Cat edition (1977–81):

Vol. One:

HAROLD PINTER | *Complete Works: One* | The Birthday Party | The Room | The Dumb Waiter | A Slight Ache | A Night Out | The Black and White | The Examination | *With an introduction:* 'Writing for the Theatre' | GROVE PRESS, INC. | NEW YORK

256 pp. 18.4 × 10.9 cm. Paperback, outside red; on front cover: "[*top left, in yellow:*] Harold | Pinter [*centre:*] [2 *lines in black:*] Complete | Works: One | [*titles of items, as for title page, last as* "Writing for the Theatre", *in white*] | *photo, from American production of* The Birthday Party] [*at top, right, 3 lines in black:*] [*Black Cat device*] | B-402 | $3.95"; on back cover: volume title in white, "by Harold Pinter" in yellow, account of contents and of Pinter in white, "Cover Design: Kenneth R. Deardoff | A Black Cat Book", with Grove Press address and ISBN number, at top right: as for front cover; on spine: "[*in black:*] [*Black Cat device*] | Grove | Press | [*down spine:*] [*in black:*] Complete Works: One [*in yellow:*] Harold Pinter [*across spine, at foot:*] B-402".

Published 1977 [DLC copyright registration, 18 October 1977 (in notice: 1976) (A921783)]. Black Cat series B-402. Price $3.95. On verso of title leaf: copyright and performing rights statements, "First Black Cat Edition 1977 | First Printing 1977 | ISBN: 0-394-17019-9 | Grove Press ISBN: 0-8021-4088-2 | Library of Congress Catalog Card Number: 77-002449 | Manufactured in the United States of America | Distributed by Random House, Inc., New York | GROVE PRESS, INC., 196 West Houston Street, New York, N.Y."

Contents: [1] half-title, account of Pinter and of this volume; [2] list of Grove's Pinter titles; [3] title page [4] as above; [5]–256 as for first Methuen edition (possibly printed from same litho plates).

Vol. Two:

HAROLD PINTER | *Complete Works: Two* | The Caretaker | The Dwarfs | The Collection | The Lover | Night School | Revue Sketches: | Trouble in the Works |

The Black and White | Request Stop | Last to Go | Special Offer | *With an intro-duction:* "Writing for Myself" | Grove Press, Inc. | New York

248 [249–250] pp., 3 leaves. 18.4 × 10.9 cm. Paperback, outside brown; on front cover: "[*at top, left, in yellow*:] Harold | Pinter [*centred*:] [*2 lines in black*:] Complete | Works: Two [*rest in white*:] The | Caretaker | The Collection | The Lover | Night School | Revue Sketches | *Trouble in the Works* | *The Black and White* | *Request Stop* | *Last to Go* | *Special Offer* | Writing for Myself | [*photo, from* The Caretaker, *British cast*] [*at top, right*:] [*Black Cat device*] | B-403 | $3.95"; on back cover: same style and kind of content as Vol. One, with differ-ent Black Cat number, price and ISBN; spine as for Vol. One, with "Two" and "B-403".

Published 1977 [DLC copyright registration 21 November 1977 (DP10827)]. Black Cat series B-403. Price $3.95. On verso of title leaf: first publication and copyright details for this collection and for each item, otherwise as for Vol. One, except "ISBN: 0-394-17020-2 | Grove Press ISBN: 0-8021-4089-0 | Library of Congress Catalog Card Number: 77-77882".

Contents: [1] half-title, account of Pinter and of this volume; [2] list of Grove's other Pinter titles; [3] title page; [4] as above; [5]–[249] as for Methuen *Plays: Two* (possibly printed from same litho plates); [250–255] lists of Grove titles; [256] blank.

Vol. Three:
HAROLD PINTER | *Complete Works: Three* | The Homecoming | Tea Party | The Basement | Landscape | Silence | Revue Sketches: | Night | That's Your Trouble | That's All | Applicant | Interview | Dialogue for Three | *With the mem-oir,* 'Mac', *and the short story,* 'Tea Party' | GROVE PRESS, INC. | NEW YORK

247 pp., 3 leaves, 1 blank leaf. 17.9 × 10.4 cm. Paperback, blue; on front cover: "[*at top, left, 2 lines in yellow*:] Harold | Pinter [*centred*:] [*2 lines in black*:] Complete | Works: Three | [*remainder in white*:] The | Homecoming | Landscape | Silence | The Basement | Revue Sketches | *Night* | *That's All* | *That's Your Trouble* | *Interview* | *Applicant* | *Dialogue for Three* | Tea Party (Play) | Tea Party (Short Story) | Mac | [*photo of* The Homecoming, *with British cast members*] [*at top, right, in black*:] [*Black Cat device*] | B-410 | $3.95"; back cover similar to Vol. One, with different Black Cat number and ISBN; spine as for Vol. One, with "Three" and "B-410".

Published 15 June 1978 [DLC copyright registration 21 June 1978 (PA-25-443)]. Black Cat series, B-410. Price $3.95. On verso of title leaf: first British publica-tion and copyright information for this collection and for each item, otherwise as for Vol. One, except "First Edition 1978 | First Printing 1978 | ISBN: 0-394-17051-2 | Grove Press ISBN: 0-8021-4183-8 | Library of Congress Catalog Card Number: 77-002449 | Library of Congress Cataloging in Publication Data (Revised)", details.

Contents: [1] half-title, account of this volume and of Pinter; [2] list of Grove's
Pinter titles; [3] title page; [4] as above; [5]–247 texts, as for Methuen
Plays: Three (possibly printed from same litho plates); [248] blank;
[249–254] lists of Grove titles; [255–256] blank.

Vol. Four (1981):

HAROLD PINTER | Complete Works: Four | Old Times | No Man's Land |
Betrayal | Monologue | Family Voices | *With an introduction by the author* |
GROVE PRESS | NEW YORK

xiii, 296 pp., 5 leaves. 17.8 × 11.4 cm. Paperback, outside glossy black, lettering
in white; on front cover, lettering and illustration as for Methuen *Plays: Four*;
on back cover, lettering above, and colour photo of Pinter, as for Methuen, but
at top right: "$9.95", at foot left: Black Cat device, "A Black Cat Book | Published
by Grove Press, Inc.", at foot, right, within white panel in black: bar-code,
numerals, ISBN; on spine as for Methuen, except at foot: "[*Black Cat device*] |
Grove | Press".

Published 1981. Price $9.95. On verso of title leaf: copyright and first publica-
tion details for this collection and each item, otherwise as for Vol. One, except
"Published by Grove Press | a division of Wheatland Corporation", address,
"First Black Cat Edition 1981 | ISBN: 0-8021-5050-0 | Library of Congress
Catalog Card Number: 81-47696 | Manufactured in Great Britain", issue
numerals.

Contents: [i] half-title; [ii] list of Grove's Pinter titles; [iii] title page; [iv] as
above; [v]–296 as for Methuen *Plays: Four*; [297–304] lists of Grove
titles; [305] Methuen contact address; [306] blank.

Note: Unlike Vols. One to Three, this volume was manufactured in the
UK, alongside Methuen's *Plays: Four,* with appropriate modifications at either
end.

b. Grove edition, four vols. (1990):

Vol. One:

HAROLD PINTER | COMPLETE WORKS: | ONE | THE BIRTHDAY PARTY
| THE ROOM | THE DUMB WAITER | A SLIGHT ACHE | A NIGHT OUT |
"The Black and White" | "The Examination" | *With an introduction:* "Writing
for the Theatre" | [*publisher's device*] | Grove Press | New York

256 pp. 21.1 × 13.7 cm. Paperback, front and back covers dark violet and white,
spine dark violet; on front cover: "[*in black:*] HAR ["O" *as large dot in orange,
circled by dates* "1954" *and* "1960" *in grey-green*] [*in black:*] LD | PINTER | [*in
white:*] Complete Works | [*to right, at diagonal, in grey-green, as large numeral:*]
1" ; on back cover, lettering in black except for large letter "H" (as initial letter
of "Harold") in grey-green: at top left: "Poetry", at top right: "$14.50", centred:

account of Pinter and of this volume, Grove Press device in orange, at foot, left: "Distributed by Publishers Group West | Cover design by Jo Bonney | 10/90 Printed in USA © 1990 Grove Press, Inc.", at foot, right, within white panel: barcodes, numerals, ISBN; down spine: "[*in black, with individual letters across spine:*] PINTER [*in white:*] Complete Works: [*across spine, in grey-green:*] 1 | [*across spine, in orange, Grove Press device*] | [*down spine, in 2 lines, in black:*] GROVE | PRESS".

Published October 1990. Price $12. On verso of title leaf: copyright, conditions of sale, and performing rights statements, "*Published simultaneously in Canada | Printed in the United States of America*", DLC cataloging data, "ISBN 0-8021-5096–9 (v. 1)", Grove Press address, issue numerals.

Contents: [1] half-title, with "*This book is Volume One of the Collected Works of Harold Pinter*"; [2] Grove's Pinter titles; [3] title page; [4] as above; [5] contents; [6] blank; [7] Pinter chronology [to 1988]; [8] blank; 9–256 introduction and texts line-for-line as for Black Cat edition, Vol. One, but in enlarged font (i.e., does not follow revised Methuen, by including *The Hothouse*).

Notes: This edition was also published in the USA by Grove Weidenfeld, as explicitly an Evergreen edition, and later reprinted by Grove Weidenfeld with more colourful covers. It was co-published in Canada by Publishers' Group West Canada. It came to be marketed in the UK by Avalon Travel Publications.

Vol. Two:
HAROLD PINTER | COMPLETE WORKS: | TWO | THE CARETAKER | THE DWARFS | THE COLLECTION | THE LOVER | NIGHT SCHOOL | REVUE SKETCHES | TROUBLE IN THE WORKS | THE BLACK AND WHITE | REQUEST STOP | LAST TO GO | SPECIAL OFFER | *With an introduction:* "Writing for Myself" | [*publisher's device*] | Grove Press | New York

248, (1) pp., 3 leaves. 19 cm. Binding in similar style to Vol. One, orange and pale green, with black, yellow and brown lettering and numerals, scarlet dot.

Published October 1990. $13. ISBN 0-8021-3237-5. Not inspected.

Vols. Three and Four
Vol. Three: 256 pp. Published October 1990. $13. ISBN 0-8021-5094-7. Contents as for Black Cat edition, Vol. Three. Not seen.

Vol. Four: 296 pp., 4 leaves. Published October 1990. ISBN 0-8021-5050-0. Contents as for Black Cat edition, Vol. Four (1981). Not seen.

Subsection 2: Poetry and Short Prose Works

I3   POEMS   1968

a¹. First edition, first issue:

(i) Paperback copies issue
POEMS | [*rule, 11.6 cm.*] | Harold Pinter | Enitharmon Press | [*rule, 11.6 cm.*] |1968

1 blank leaf, 4 leaves, 24 pp., 1 blank leaf, 1 leaf, 1 blank leaf. 18.7 × 14.6 cm. Slate-grey light card binding, with fold-in flaps; on outside front, lettered and ruled in black: "POEMS | [*rule, 11.6 cm.*] | Harold Pinter"; outside back and spine blank; on front flap: "This first selection of poems by | Harold Pinter has been made from work | published in little magazines during the | nineteen fifties and includes ten poems | previously unpublished in any form together | with an early fragment of dialogue, KULLUS, | which is also unpublished and dates from 1949. | Price 12s. 6d. net".

Published 30 July 1968 (L accession 16 SEP 68). Price 12s. 6d. On verso of title leaf: "*This selection of poems was made by Alan Clodd* | © Harold Pinter 1968 | All Rights Reserved | Printed and made in Great Britain".

Contents: [i–ii] blank; [iii] half-title "POEMS"; [iv] blank; [v] title page; [vi] as above; [vii] "The Enitharmon Press is grateful to Harold Pinter for permission to publish these | poems; with the exception of THE TABLE (1963), all were written between | 1949 and 1958 | First published 1968 by the Enitharmon Press London"; [viii] blank; [ix] "*To Mick Goldstein*"; [x] "Acknowledgements are due to POETRY QUARTERLY, POETRY LONDON, NEW POEMS | 1957, THE TWENTIETH CENTURY, THE WINDOW, THE GLASS and THE OBSERVER where | some of the poems first appeared"; [dates of composition provided below poems are given within round brackets] 1 "NEW YEAR IN THE MIDLANDS" (1950); 2 "THE MIDGET" (1950); 3 "CHANDELIERS AND SHADOWS" (1950); 4 "I SHALL TEAR OFF MY TERRIBLE CAP" (1951); 5 "BOOK OF MIRRORS" (1951); 6 "THE ISLANDS OF ARAN SEEN FROM THE MOHER CLIFFS" (1951); 7 "JIG" (1952); 8 "THE ANAESTHETIST'S PIN" (1952); 9 "YOU IN THE NIGHT" (*c.*1952); 10 "THE SECOND VISIT" (*c.*1952); 11 "STRANGER" (1953); 12 "A WALK BY WAIT-ING" (1953); 13 "POEM" ("I walked one morning with my only wife,") (1953); 14 "THE TASK" (1954); 15 "THE ERROR OF ALARM" (1956); 16 "AFTERNOON" (1957); 17–19 "A VIEW OF THE PARTY" (1958); 20–21 "THE TABLE" (1963); 22–24 "KULLUS" (1949); [25–26] blank; [27] "PRINTED BY DAEDALUS PRESS, | CROWN HOUSE, STOKE FERRY, NORFOLK | DISTRIBUTED

BY ERIC AND JOAN STEVENS, | 2 PROSPECT ROAD, LONDON, N.W.2, ENGLAND"; [28–30] blank.

Note one: A loose errata slip (14.2 × 11.3 cm.) is normally tucked in between pages 13 and 14. It reads: "ERRATUM | On page 13 the third line of the second stanza should read: | Over the boulders and the moonlit hill,". In the poem "I walked one morning with my only wife," as printed, the line reads: "Over the boulderas and the moonlit hill,".

Note two: Manuscripts in *PA* Box 61 provide titles and dates that sometimes differ. "The Second Visit" is dated 1950. "I Shall Tear Off my Terrible Cap" appears as "A Time". The poem "Stranger" ("That you did barter") appears within the second of the three parts of the poem "Episode," which would be printed in full in *Ten Early Poems* (1992), pp. 15–18, and in later collections. As "Stranger" it ends abruptly: "That yours was the practise – | No case." In "Episode," after "That yours was the practice.", this section of the second part of the poem continues for another 9 lines; see *VV* 120.

Note three: 1,700 copies were printed. Of these, 1,050 were bound in grey wrappers, lettered in black, and issued in 1968 at 12s. 6d. 200 copies were "specially bound" (see below). In May 1970, 450 further copies were issued, bound in grey wrappers, with the addition of a blue and white dust jacket, lettered in black, at 12s. 6d. (see below). See *Alan Clodd and the Enitharmon Press: A Checklist of his Publications 1967–1987 and Private Printings 1958–1998*. Compiled by Steven Halliwell with a tribute by Jeremy Reed. London: Stephen Stuart-Smith at the Enitharmon Press, 1998 (ISBN 1-900564-85-8 [copies 1–50], 1-900564-90-4 [copies 51–250]), item 3.

Note four: For earlier printings of some of these poems that have been traced, see Section C. The ten poems said to be "previously unpublished" are evidently: "The Midget," "Book of Mirrors," "The Islands of Aran seen from the Moher Cliffs," "Jig," "The Anaesthetist's Pin," "Stranger," "A Walk by Waiting," "Poem" ("I walked one morning with my only wife"), "The Task," and "A View of the Party." Of the sites of first publication listed in the "Acknowledgements," at least one poem has been traced in each of them, with the exception of *The Observer.*

Note five: "A View of the Party" would be reprinted in *Parties: A Literary Companion,* compiled by Susanna Johnston (London: Macmillan, 1994), pp.253–255. In later re-printings, the poem is divided into two sections, "I", of five stanzas, and "II", of 11 stanzas. In this printing, this section division is absent.

Note six: A proof copy headed "Enitharmon Press Proof" is at TxU-HRC [callmark TEMP P 657p 1968 HRC].

(ii) Specially bound copies issue:

2 blank leaves, 4 leaves, 24 pp., 2 leaves, 2 blank leaves. 18.3 × 14.5 cm. Hardback, quarter-bound with crimson leather, extending to 3.5 cm. of width of each

board, boards bound in black cloth, at junction between leather and cloth a vertical line in gilt; down spine, in gold: "POEMS | HAROLD PINTER". Endpapers.

Contents: As for other issue, but on p. [25]: "200 specially bound copies of this book have been printed, numbered 1 to 200 | All are signed by the author | This is No. . . . . | Published by the Enitharmon Press | 32 Huntingdon Road East Finchley | London N2 England" [a copy owned by William Baker has in black ink the number "63" and the signature "Harold Pinter"]; on p.[27] "PRINTED BY DAEDALUS PRESS, | CROWN HOUSE, STOKE FERRY, NORFOLK".

Note one: The paper for printing the text and the erratum slip is Antique Laid paper, cream-coloured, whereas for the ordinary copies the paper is white. These copies were issued for sale at £7.10s. See *Note three* above.

a². First edition, second issue (1970):

450 copies, of the 1,700 printed in 1968, were not issued at that time; in May 1970, they were issued for sale, at 12s. 6d, with the addition of a blue and white dust-jacket (see *a¹ (i), Note three*). The dust jacket is decorated in blocks of blue and white; on lower front, in black "Harold | Pinter | POEMS"; on back, in black "*Other Books from the | Enitharmon Press*", 5 titles, plus 3 for the Gissing Series; on front flap, as for flap of cover.

b. Second edition, with nine added poems (1971):

(i) Ordinary bindings issue:
POEMS | HAROLD PINTER | LONDON/ENITHARMON PRESS

43 pp., 2 blank leaves. 21.6 × 14 cm. (a) Hardback, bound in pale blue cloth; down spine in gold: "Harold Pinter Poems   Enitharmon". Endpapers. Dust jacket pale blue; on outside front: "Harold Pinter | POEMS", design of three concentric rings, in black and white, with a central black circle, off-centre; on outside back: list of other Enitharmon Press titles; down spine: "Harold Pinter Poems Enitharmon"; on front flap "For this new edition of | Harold Pinter's POEMS (first | published in 1968) nine | poems have been added, six | of which are unpublished | in any form | £1.40". (b) Paperback, design as for dust jacket; text from front flap is on inside front of cover; price as "80p". Omits front endpaper, and one blank leaf at the back.

Published December 1971. Prices: hardback, £1.40; paperback, 80p. On verso of title leaf: "First published in 1968 by the Enitharmon | Press, 22 Huntingdon Road, East Finchley, | London, N.2. | Second edition, with additional poems, | published in 1971. | © Harold Pinter 1971 | All rights reserved. | SBN 901111 21X (wrapped) | SBN 901111 35X (cloth) | Typesetting by Trade Type, Frome. | Printed and made in Great Britain | by Compton Press, Salisbury."

Contents: [1–2] blank; [3] half-title "POEMS"; [4] blank; [5] title page; [6] as above; [7] blank; [8] "*To Mick Goldstein*"; [9] "Acknowledgements are due to *Poetry Quarterly, Poetry London, New Poems 1957, The Twentieth Century, The Window, The Glass, The Observer* and *The Times Literary Supplement,* where some of the poems first appeared. | The selection of poems was made by Alan Clodd"; [10] contents; 11–43 text; [44–48] blank.

Note one: The added poems (with dates of composition provided below the poems given here within round brackets) are "EUROPEAN REVELS" (1950) (p.11, first in sequence), "CHRISTMAS" (1950) (p.14, fourth), "HAMPSTEAD HEATH" (1951) (p.16, sixth), "A GLASS AT MIDNIGHT" (1951) (p. 18, eighth), "THE DRAMA IN APRIL" (1952) (p. 21, eleventh), "CAMERA SNAPS" (1952) (p. 24, fourteenth); "DAYLIGHT" (1956) (p. 32, twenty-second); "ALL OF THAT" (1970) (p. 39, twenty-sixth, following what had previously been the last poem); and "POEM" ("they kissed I turned they stared") (1971) (p. 40, twenty-seventh). Previous publishings are noted in *Section C* for the first, eighth, and ninth of these poems. The prose-poem (or short story) "Kullus" now occupies pp. 41–43.

Note two: 1,450 copies were printed. 510 were hardbound in blue cloth boards, with the light blue dust jacket, as above, issued for sale at £1.40. 800 were bound in light blue wrappers, lettered and decorated as the dust jacket, price 80p. 100 copies were specially bound, as below, price £9.50. See *Alan Clodd and the Enitharmon Press* (as above, *Note three*), item 26. [40 copies unspecified.]

Note three: Bound in before p.9, an errata slip, 8.5 × 10.4 cm.: "ERRATA | On page 22, the title of the poem | should read "JIG" and on page 41 | in the third line from the bottom | for "climed" read "climbed" | *****". On p.22, the heading is "IG"; and on p.41, the line has "climed". Slip not present in TxU-HRC copy.

b(ii). Special copies issue:

21.7 × 13.4 cm. Quarter-bound with black leather, extending 3.1 cm. of width of boards, boards in crimson cloth; at junction between leather and cloth, vertical gilt line; down spine in gilt: "Harold Pinter Poems Enitharmon". Endpapers. Glasserine dust jacket.

Published 1971. Price £9.50 (see above).

Note one: In these copies the errata slip is loose, and measures 7.7 × 10 cm.

Note two: A copy owned by William Baker has on p.[7] in black ink the signature "Harold Pinter", and in green "19/100".

14   POEMS AND PROSE 1949–1977   1978

a. First edition (1978):

Poems and Prose | 1949–1977 | [*curving rules device*] | by HAROLD PINTER |
Eyre Methuen Ltd. London

x, 101, [1] pp. 24.5 × 18.7 cm. Hardbound, brown cloth; spine ruled and lettered
in gold: "[*double rule, thin, thick*] | [*down spine:*] Poems and Prose 1949–1977 |
[*rule*] | [*down spine:*] HAROLD PINTER | [*double rules, thick, thin*] | Eyre |
Methuen". Endpapers pale brown. Dust jacket chocolate brown; on outside
front, lettered in pale brown: "Harold | Pinter | [*photo, within black frame, 7.8
× 6.1 cm.*] | Poems | and Prose | 1949–1977"; outside back, plain; spine lettered
and decorated in pale brown: "[*down spine:*] Harold Pinter Poems and Prose
1949–1977 | [*across spine:*] [*publisher's device*] | EYRE | METHUEN"; on front
flap, in white, three paragraphs about the contents, at foot, right, price [in copy
seen, sticker on top: '£6.95']"; on back flap, small photo of Pinter, biographical
note in white, "Photo: Tony McGrath, courtesy of | The Observer", at foot: "[*in
white:*] PRINTED IN GREAT BRITAIN [*in black:*] ISBN 0 413 38970 7 | [*below
ISBN number, in black, short thick rule*]". [Variant dust jacket: in Baker copy,
variance in colour of lettering: on outside front: "Harold | Pinter" in white; on
spine "Harold Pinter", publisher's device and "EYRE | METHUEN" in white.]

Published 4 May 1978. On verso of title leaf: "This collection first published in
Great Britain in 1978 by Eyre Methuen Ltd., 11 New | Fetter Lane, London EC4
P4EE | Copyright in this collection © 1978 by H. Pinter Ltd | [first publication
and copyright details, including the statement: "'Poem (Always where you are)'
and 'Denmark Hill' first published in this volume"] | ISBN 0 413 38970 7 | Printed
in Great Britain by | W. & J. Mackay Limited, Chatham".

Contents: [i] half-title; [ii] other Methuen titles "*BY THE SAME AUTHOR*";
[iii] title page; [iv] as above; [v] "*To Antonia*"; [vi] blank; vii–viii
contents; [ix] fly-title "Poems | [*curved-lines device*]"; [x] blank; 1–2
"*New Year in the Midlands*"; 3 "*The Midget*"; 4 "*Christmas*"; 5–6
"*Chandeliers and Shadows*"; 7–8 "*Hampstead Heath*"; 9 "*I shall tear
off my Terrible Cap*"; 10 "*A Glass at Midnight*"; 11–12 "*Book of
Mirrors*"; 13 "*The Islands of Aran seen from the Moher Cliffs*"; 14
"*The Drama in April*"; 15 "*Jig*"; 16 "*The Anaesthetist's Pin*"; 17
"*Camera Snaps*"; 18 "*You in the Night*"; 19–20 "*The Second Visit*";
21–22 "*Stranger*"; 23 "*A Walk by Waiting*"; 23–25 "*Poem*" ("I walked
one morning with my only wife"); 26–27 "*The Task*"; 28–29 "*The
Error of Alarm*"; 29 "*Daylight*"; 30–31 "*Afternoon*"; 32–34 "*A View
of the Party*"; 35–36 "*The Table*"; 37 "*Poem*" ("Always where you
are"); 38 "*All of That*"; 39 "*Poem*" ("they kissed I turned they
stared"); 40 "*Later*"; 41 "*Poem*" ("and all the others"); 42 "*Paris*" and
"*I know the place*"; 43 "*Message*"; 44 "*The Doing So*"; 45 "*Denmark*

Hill"; [46] blank; [47] fly-title "Prose | [*curved-lines device*]"; [48] blank; [40] fly-title "*Kullus* | [*device*]"; 51–54 text; [55] fly-title "*The Black and White* | [*device*]"; [56] blank; 57–[58] text; [59] fly-title "*The Examination* | [*device*]"; [60] blank; 61–66 text; [67] fly-title "*Tea Party* | [*device*]"; [68] author's note; 69–73 text; [74] blank; [75] fly-title "*Mac* | [*device*]"; [76] biographical note; 77–84 text; [85] fly-title "*Hutton and the Past* | [*device*]"; [86] blank; 87–90 text; [91] fly-title "*The Coast* | [*device*]"; [92] blank; 93 text; [94] blank; [95] fly-title "*Problem* | [*device*]"; [96] blank; 97 text; [98] blank; [99] "*Lola* | [*device*]"; [100] blank; 101–[102] text.

Notes: Of the poems first published in this collection, "Poem" ("Always where you are") is dated 1964, and "Denmark Hill" is dated September 1977. The poem "Chandeliers and Shadows" has an epigraph restored, not present in *Poems*: "'I'le goe hunt the badger by owle-light: 'tis a deed of darknesse.' | The Duchess of Malfi" (p.5). It has a typo on p.6, "tham" for "them" (line 7 on this page, line 28 in the poem). This is reproduced in CPP (still present in 1991 edition). A proof copy, in orange wrappers, headed "<u>UNCORRECTED PROOF COPY</u>", is at TxU-HRC.

b. American edition (1978):

Poems and Prose | 1949–1977 | [*curving rules device*] | by HAROLD PINTER | GROVE PRESS, INC., NEW YORK

5 leaves, 101, [1] pp. 20.3 × 12.7 cm. (A) Hardback: quarter-bound in black cloth, boards pale yellow, lettered down spine in silver: "Harold Pinter POEMS AND PROSE 1949–1977 Grove Press". No dust jacket seen. (B) Paperback, glossy white; on front cover: "[*in black:*] E-722 [*small publisher's device*] $5.95 | [*remainder in mid-brown:*] HAROLD | PINTER | [*thick rule, 12.2 cm.*] | [*space*] | [*thick rule, 12.2 cm.*] | POEMS | PROSE ['AND' within the 'O' of 'PROSE'] | 1949–1977"; on back cover: "[*in black:*] E-722 [*small publisher's device*] $5.95 | [*in mid-brown, thick rule, 11.6 cm.*] | [*all in black, in 2 columns:*] [*at head of left column, photo of Pinter, captioned at upper left side, lettered down,* "Photo: Tony McGrath"] | [*account of the content of the book and of Pinter, with, at foot of second column:*] Cover Design: Kenneth R. Deardoff | An Evergreen Book | Published by Grove Press, Inc. | 196 West Houston Street | New York, N.Y. 10014 | ISBN: 0-394-17070-9"; on spine: "[*3 lines in black:*] [*small publisher's device*] | Grove | Press | [*down spine, in mid-brown:*] POEMS AND PROSE 1949–1977 HAROLD PINTER [*across spine, at foot, in black:*] E-722".

Published 1978. Price $5.95. On verso of title leaf: copyright statements, details of previous publication of poems and prose pieces, reproduction restriction statement, "First Edition 1978 | First Printing 1978 | ISBN: 0-394-50290-6 | Grove Press ISBN: 0-8021-0164-X | Library of Congress Catalog Card Number: 78-56046 | First Evergreen Edition 1978 | First Printing 1978 | ISBN: 0-394-17070-9

| Grove Press ISBN: 0-8021-4219-2 | [*same LC number, cataloguing data*] | Manufactured in the United States of America | Distributed by Random House, Inc., New York | GROVE PRESS, INC., 196 West Houston Street, New York, N.Y. 10014".

Contents: As for British edition.

I5   **I KNOW THE PLACE**   1979

I Know The Place | Poems by | HAROLD PINTER | [*publisher's device*] | The Greville Press, Warwick

Unpaginated, [28] pp. Printed as [1]⁸ 2⁸, with the recto of the eighth free leaf signed "2"; the first leaf of the first octavo gathering and the last leaf of the second are used as paste-down endpapers. Hardback with black textured material pasted over boards; down spine, in gilt: "I KNOW THE PLACE [*space*] HAROLD PINTER".

Published 1979 (L accession 10 Oct 79).

Contents: [1] half-title "*I Know The Place*"; [2] blank; [3] title page; [4] "Drawings by Michael Kenny"; [5] "This is a limited edition of | 500 copies of which this is copy | number | [*at foot of page:*] © Booker Books Limited"; [6] attached drawing; [7]–[27] text, on rectos only, with all versos blank [although three have illustrations attached]: [7] "*Stranger*", dated 1953; [9] "*Poem*" ("I walked one morning with my only wife,"), dated 1953; [10] attached drawing; [11] "*The Error of Alarm*", dated 1956; [13] "*Daylight*", dated 1956; [15] "*Poem*" ("Always where you are"), dated 1964; [16] attached drawing; [17] "*All of That*", dated 1970; [19] "*Poem*" ("they kissed I turned they stared"), dated 1971; [21] "*Later*", dated 1974; [22] attached drawing; [23] "*Paris*", dated 1975; [25] "*I Know the Place*", dated 1975; [27] "*Denmark Hill*", dated September, 1977; [28] "Printed in Great Britain by Tomes of Leamington" .

Note one: On pp. [6], [10], [16], [22], small leaves bearing reproductions of Michael Kenny's pastel-coloured drawings are pasted at one edge to the inner edge, near the gutter, to face the poems to which they relate.

Note two: On p.[5], the L copy is numbered "67" and signed, below, "Harold Pinter"; a copy owned by William Baker is numbered "155" and signed. The poem "I Know the Place" was at some time printed separately on a card, 14 × 9 cm. (at foot, "© Greville Press").

16   COLLECTED POEMS AND PROSE   1986

Collected | Poems and Prose | [curled-rules device, 2.4 cm.] | HAROLD PINTER | Methuen . London

x, 116 pp., 1 leaf. 19.0 × 12.2 cm. Paperback, across outside, in full colour, picture of cricketers playing in a rural setting; on front cover: "COLLECTED | POEMS AND PROSE | [rule, with diamond in centre, 10.9 cm.] | Harold Pinter | [at foot, within small black panel, with white inner frame, in white:] methuen"; on back cover, at foot, centre, within white panel: "ISBN 0-413-60670-8 | [barcode] | 9 780413 606709", at foot, right: "PRICE NET | £3.95 | IN UK ONLY | A METHUEN PAPERBACK | POETRY | LITERATURE | COVER: DAVID INSHAW | THE CRICKET GAME"; down spine: "[in black:] HAROLD PINTER [in white:] COLLECTED POEMS AND PROSE [within black panel, in white:] methuen".

Published 10 April 1986. Price £3.95. On verso of title leaf: "This collection first published in Great Britain in 1986 | by Methuen London Ltd., | [. . .] | ISBN 0-413-60670-8 | Printed in Great Britain | by Hazell Watson & Viney Limited | Member of the BPCC Group | Aylesbury, Bucks".

Contents: [i]–45 as for 14; 46 "The Ventriloquists"; 47 "Poem" ("The lights glow"); 48 "Ghost"; 49 "Before They Fall"; 50 "Partners"; [51] fly-title "Prose"; [52] blank; [53] fly-title "Kullus"; [54] blank; 55–56 text; [59] fly-title "The Black and White"; [60] blank; 61–62 text; [63] fly-title "The Examination"; [64] blank; 65–70 text; [71] fly-title "Tea Party"; [72] blank; 73–77 text; [78] blank; [79] fly-title "Mac"; [80] biographical note; 81–88 text; [89] fly-title "Hutton and the Past"; [90] blank; 91–94 text; [95] fly-title "The Coast"; [96] blank; 97 text; [98] blank; [99] fly-title "Problem"; [100] blank; 101 text; [102] blank; [103] fly-title "Lola"; [104] blank; 105–106 text; [108] fly-title "Arthur Wellard"; [109] blank; 110–116 text; [117] sources for poems, "'Partners' first published in this volume. | Copyright © 1986 by Harold Pinter"; [118] sources for prose (added: "Arthur Wellard").

17   COLLECTED POEMS AND PROSE   1991

a. First edition (1991):

HAROLD PINTER | Collected Poems | and Prose | ff | faber and faber | LONDON · BOSTON

viii, 118 pp., 1 leaf. 19.3 × 12.4 cm. Paperback, patterning made by recurrences of "ff" in darker grey, on light grey background; on front cover: rectangular white panel, with, within double border in black: "HAROLD | PINTER | [rule, 2.8 cm.] | Collected Poems | and Prose | [portrait of Pinter]"; on back cover,

within white panel, within double border: "ff | faber and faber | HAROLD
PINTER | Collected Poems and Prose | [*account of this volume, 12 lines*] | Cover
illustration by Sue Linney | UK £5.99 net Canada $14.99 | ISBN 0-571-16090-5 |
[*bar-code*] | 9 780571 160907"; on spine, within white panel: "[*two rules, thin
and thick*] | [*down spine:*] HAROLD PINTER Collected Poems and Prose
[*across spine:*] ff | [*two rules, thick and thin*]".

First published 1991. Price £5.99 net ($14.99 in Canada). On verso of title leaf:
"To Antonia | First published in 1991 | by Faber and Faber Limited | [. . .] | This
edition is an expanded version of Collected Poems and Prose | first published in
1986 by Methuen London Ltd | being an expanded version of Poems and Prose
1949–1977 | first published in 1978 by Eyre Methuen | Printed in Great Britain
by Clays Ltd, St Ives plc | [. . .] | Copyright in the collection © 1978, 1986, 1991
by H. Pinter Ltd | Copyright in individual poems and prose pieces is itemized on
the last two | pages of this book. | [*authorship identification, conditions of sale
statements, etc.*] | ISBN 0-571-16090-5".

Contents: [i] half-title, with brief note about Pinter; [ii] other Faber titles "*by
the same author*"; [iii] title page; [iv] as above; [v]–vi contents; [vii]
fly-title "Poems"; [viii] blank; 1–45 as for *I4, I6*; 46 "*Joseph Brearley
1909–1977* | *(Teacher of English)*"; 47 "*The Ventriloquists*"; 48
"*Poem*" ("The lights glow"); 49 "*Ghost*"; 50 "*Before They Fall*"; 51
"*Poem*" ("I saw Len Hutton in his prime") and "*Restaurant*"; 52 "*It
Is Here* | (for A)*"; [53]–118 prose as for *I6*, with page numbers greater
by two; [119–120] details of previous publishings.

Notes: One poem, "Partners", has been dropped and four added, with the
"Joseph Brearley" poem added on p. 46 and the others at the end of the poetry
section. This volume was reprinted 9 September 1997.

b. American edition (1996):

HAROLD PINTER | Collected Poems | and Prose | GROVE PRESS | New York

xii, 129 pp., 1 blank leaf. 20.2 × 12.9 cm. Paperback; front cover patterned in
black and mauve, with large letters, in mauve or black: "HAR | OLD | PIN |
TER", superimposed on second quarter: "[*3 lines in yellow:*] HAROLD
PINTER | COLLECTED | POEMS | [*in black:*] & | [*in yellow:*] PROSE"; back
cover white: at top left: "Poetry"; at top right: "$11"; centred: 4 paragraphs
about the poems, and Pinter; at foot, left: "Grove Press books | are distributed
by | Publishers Group West | Printed in the U.S.A. 0196"; at foot, right: "[*bar-
code*] | 9 780802 134349 | ISBN 0-8021-3434-3 | [*to right, second bar-code, above
it:*] 51100X"; spine upper portion black and lower portion white, lettered down:
"[*in mauve:*] HAROLD PINTER [*in white:*] COLLECTED POEMS & PROSE
[*across spine, in black, publisher's device*] [*down spine, in mauve:*] GROVE
PRESS".

Published 1996. Price $11. On verso of title leaf: copyright details, note of status as expanded version, as above, reproduction restriction statement, note of first publication in UK in 1991, "FIRST GROVE PRESS EDITION, JANUARY 1996 | Printed in the United States of America | [*cataloguing data*] | Grove Press | 841 Broadway | New York, NY 10003 | 10 9 8 7 6 5 4 3 2 1".

Contents: [i] half-title; [ii] blank; [iii] title page; [iv] as above; [v] "*To Antonia*"; [vi] blank; vii–ix contents; [x] blank; [xi] fly-title "Poems"; [xii] blank; 1–52 texts of poems, as for Faber edition; 53–54 "*Poem*" ("This man has a nose and two eyes"); 55 "*American Football*"; 56 "*God*"; [57] "*Poem*" ("Don't look"); [58] blank; [59]–124 prose as for *16* [51]–116 (i.e., with pagination increased by 8); [125–126] poems, first publication and copyright details; [127] prose, first publication and copyright details; [128] blank; [129] brief note about Pinter; [130–132] blank.

18   TEN EARLY POEMS   1992

Harold Pinter | [*swelled rule, 8.8 cm.*] | TEN EARLY POEMS | GREVILLE PRESS PAMPHLETS

19 pp., 1 leaf, 1 blank leaf. 21.5 × 13.9 cm. Yellowish-cream paper wrapper, with folded-in flaps, loose over plain white card binding; on outside front wrapper: "Harold Pinter | [*two rules, thin, thick, in red, 10.5 cm.*] | TEN EARLY POEMS | Greville Press Pamphlets"; on outside back of wrapper: "Newly-discovered | early poems | by Harold Pinter | £5.50 net | ISBN 0 906887 50 X | [*vertical, at right, adjacent to spine:*] Ten Early Poems by Harold Pinter | Greville Press".

Published 1992 (L accession 12 OCT 92). On verso of title leaf: "First published in this edition 1992 | by the Greville Press, Emscote Lawn, Warwick | © Harold Pinter, 1992 | Printed in Great Britain by Peter Lloyd | at The Gamecock Press, Rugby".

Contents: [1] half-title "TEN EARLY POEMS"; [2] blank; [3] title page; [4] colophon; [5] "I rediscovered these poems by chance. | They represent my earliest work. | HAROLD PINTER"; [6] blank; [all poem titles in capitals] 7 "NIGHT'S EASE", dated 1949; 8 "SLEEP OF A BISHOP", dated 1949; 9 "AT THE PALACE OF THE EMPEROR AT DAWN", dated 1949; 10 "POEM" ("Sights are sounds but not the cretin picture:"), dated 1949; 11 "ONCE, IN A VENTRILOQUIST EVENING", dated 1949; 12 "LINES TO AN ACTRESS", dated 1951; 13 "THE WORM THAT ATE A BUILDING DOWN", dated 1951; 14 "OTHERS OF YOU", dated 1951; 15–18 "EPISODE", dated 1951; 19 "THE IRISH SHAPE", dated 1951; [20] blank; [21] "Printed in an edition of 500 copies | of which the first fifty are | numbered and have been signed | by the author | [space for signature] | COPY NUMBER"; [22–24] blank.

Note one: The poem "Episode" is in three parts, I, II, and III. The second, II, includes 2 stanzas, and then "HE: | That you did barter"; that is, it includes 28 lines of verse which in *Poems* (1968) were published as a separate poem, "STRANGER", dated 1953. However, there the last lines are:

That yours was the practice –

No case.

Here the passage is more extended, with nine lines of text in place of "No case."

Note two: A copy owned by William Baker has inscribed on the title page, below the title, in holograph: "To William | Baker | All the best | Harold Pinter". On p.[21] it has the signature in holograph "Harold Pinter", and the number "49" written and crossed out, with "50" substituted.

I9   **VARIOUS VOICES**   1998

a. British edition (1998):

HAROLD PINTER | Various Voices | PROSE, POETRY, POLITICS | 1948–1998 | ff | *faber and faber*

3 leaves, 205 pp., 6 blank leaves. 23.4 × 15.2 cm. Hardback, dark green cloth; down spine in white: "HAROLD PINTER Various Voices [*space*] [*across spine, at foot:*] ff". Endpapers, pale cream (as for text-sheets). Dust-jacket: outside front multi-coloured, outside back and flaps green; on outside front, reproduced painting of Pinter, facing half-right, with as lower background a pile of books and papers, upper background orange-red, at upper right, lettered in white: "Harold Pinter | Various Voices | Prose, Poetry, Politics 1948–1998", at lower right, in white: "ff"; on outside back, in black, three paragraphs about this volume, as "Pinter's own selection of his prose, poetry and political writings", at foot, left: "ff", at foot, right, within white panel: "ISBN 0-571-19576-8 | [*barcode*] | 9 780571 195763"; on front flap, title and text of poem "Death", at foot, right: "UK £16.99 RRP | Canada $34.99"; on back flap: lists of Pinter's plays and screenplays, "Jacket Painting of Harold Pinter | by Justin Mortimer courtesy of the | National Portrait Gallery, London".

Published 15 February 1998. Price £16.99. On verso of title leaf: "This collection first published in 1998 | by Faber and Faber Limited | [*address*] | Photoset by Wilmaset Ltd, Birkenhead, Wirral | Printed in England by Clays Ltd, St Ives plc | All rights reserved | This collection © Harold Pinter, 1998 | [*author-identification and CIP record statements*] | ISBN 0-571-19576-8".

Contents: [i] half-title; [ii] list of titles "by the same author"; [iii] title page; [iv] as above; [v] contents; [vi] blank; [1] fly-title "[1]"; [2] blank; [3] contents, for prose, non-fiction, not political; [4] blank; 5–7 "A Note on Shakespeare"; 8–12 "On *The Birthday Party* I", followed by a note by Martin Esslin (1981); 13–15 "On *The Birthday Party* II"; 16–20 "Writing for the Theatre"; 21–27 "Mac"; 28–30 "Hutton and the Past"; 31–34 "On Being Awarded the German Shakespeare Prize | in Hamburg"; 35–36 "On the Screenplay of *A la recherche du temps perdu*"; 37–42 "Arthur Wellard"; 43–44 "Jimmy"; 45 "Samuel Beckett" (two notes); 46–49 "A Speech of Thanks", for the David Cohen British Literature Prize; 50–57 "Harold Pinter and Michael Billington in Conversation | at the National Film Theatre, 26 October 1996"; 58–70 "Writing, Politics and *Ashes to Ashes*", interview with Mireia Aragay and Ramon Simó, 6 December 1996; [71] fly-title "[II]"; [72] blank; [73] contents, prose fiction; [74] blank; 75–77 "Kullus"; 78–80 "Latest Reports from the Stock Exchange"; 81–82 "The Black and White"; 83–87 "The Examination"; 88–91 "Tea Party"; 92 "The Coast"; 93 "Problem"; 94–95 "Lola"; 96 "Short Story"; 97–98 "Girls"; [99] fly-title "[III]"; [100] blank; [101] contents, poetry; [102] blank; 103–104 "School Life", 1948; 105 "At the Palace of the Emperor at Dawn"; 106 "Once, in a Ventriloquist Evening"; 107 "New Year in the Midlands"; 108 "The Midget"; 109 "Christmas"; 110–111 "Chandeliers and Shadows"; 112 "Hampstead Heath"; 113 "I Shall Tear off my Terrible Cap"; 114 "A Glass at Midnight"; 115 "Book of Mirrors"; 116 "The Islands of Aran Seen from the Moher Cliffs"; 117 "Others of You"; 118–121 "Episode"; 122 "The Irish Shape"; 123 "The Drama in April"; 124 "Jig"; 125 "The Anaesthetist's Pin"; 126 "Camera Snaps"; 127 "You in the Night"; 128 "The Second Visit"; 129 "A Walk by Waiting"; 130 "Poem" ("I walked one morning with my only wife"); 131 "The Task"; 132 "The Error of Alarm"; 133 "Daylight"; 134 "Afternoon"; 135–137 "A View of the Party"; 138–139 "The Table"; 140 "Poem" ("Always where you are"); 141 "All of That"; 142 "Poem" ("they kissed I turned they stared"); 143 "Later"; 144 "Poem" ("and all the others"); 145 "Paris"; 146 "I know the place"; 147 "Message"; 148 The Doing So"; 149 "Denmark Hill"; 150 "Joseph Brearley 1909–1977 | (Teacher of English)"; 151 "The Ventriloquists"; 152 "Poem" ("The lights glow"); 153 "Ghost"; 154 "Before They Fall"; 155 "Poem" ("I saw Len Hutton in his prime"); 156 "It Is Here | (for A)"; 157 "American Football | A Reflection upon the Gulf War", 1991; 158 "God", 1993; 159 "Poem" ("Don't look"), 1995; 160 "Cricket at Night", 1995; 161 "The Other Guy", 1995; 162 "Order", 1996; 163–164 "The Old Days", 1996; 165 "Death | (Births and Deaths Registration Act 1953)", 1997; [166] blank; [167] fly-title "[IV]"; [168] blank; [169] contents, political prose pieces; [170] blank; 171–172 "The US Elephant Must Be Stopped | *Guardian*, 5 December 1987"; 173–174 "Eroding the Language of Freedom"; 175–182 "Oh, Superman | Broadcast for *Opinion*, Channel 4, 31 May 1990"; 183–186 "Blowing up the Media" (begins with title and text of "American Football"); 187–189 "The US and El Salvador"; 190 "Pinter: Too Rude for Convicts | by Alan Travis, Home Affairs Editor, *Guardian,* | 9 June 1995"; 191–193 "Caribbean Cold War"; 194–195 "*Mountain Language* in Haringey | by Duncan Campbell, *Guardian*, 21 June 1996"; 196 "A Pinter Drama in Stoke Newington | Letter to the *Guardian*, 9 July 1996"; 197–199 "It Never Happened"; 200 "Scenario for the Bugging of a Home | Letter to the Editor of *The Times*, 8 January 1997"; 201–202 "An Open Letter to the Prime Minister | *Guardian*, 17 February 1998"; 203–205 "Acknowledgements", for previous publication and copyright, for "PROSE", "PROSE FICTION", "POETRY", and "POLITICS"; [206–218] blank.

Note: DLC copyright registration 11 July 2001 (TX-5-419-463).

b. American edition [1999]:

HAROLD PINTER | Various Voices | PROSE, POETRY, POLITICS | [*publisher's device*] | GROVE PRESS | New York

3 leaves, 205 pp. 21 × 13.7 cm. Hardback, green cloth; down spine, in gold: "VARIOUS VOICES   HAROLD PINTER [*across spine:*] GROVE | PRESS". Dust jacket: outside mainly red, with flaps white; on outside front: "[*in yellow*] VARIOUS VOICES | [2 *lines in grey*] HAROLD | PINTER | [in yellow] PROSE, POETRY, POLITICS | [*portrait of Pinter, looking half-right, against a background of piles of books and papers*]"; on outside back: "[*in yellow*] [*quotation about Pinter, by Martin Gottfried*] | [*in grey*] Praise for VARIOUS VOICES | [*in yellow*] [3 *passages of quotations from newspaper critiques*]", portrait of Pinter, in partial mirror image of that on outside front, at foot, right, within white panel, in black: "[*bar-code*] | 9 780802 116437 | 0-8021-1643-4", at right, second bar-code, above it "52300"; down spine" "VARIOUS VOICES Harold Pinter [*publisher's device*] GROVE PRESS"; on front flap, in black: "$23 | [*account of Pinter and the content of this volume*]"; on back flap, lists of Pinter's plays and screenplays, in two columns, at foot: "Jacket design by Charles Rue Woods | Jacket painting by Justin Mortimer/ courtesy of | the National Portrait Gallery (London) | Grove Press books | are distributed by | Publishers Group West | Printed in the U.S.A. 0299".

Published 1999, probably in January (see *Notes*). Price $23. On verso of title leaf: "Copyright © 1998 by Harold Pinter | [*copyright and reproduction restriction statements*] | First published in 1998 by Faber and Faber Limited | Printed in the United States of America | FIRST AMERICAN EDITION | [*cataloguing data, including ISBN 0-8021-1643-4*] | Grove Press | 841 Broadway | New York, NY 10003 | 99 00 01 02 10 9 8 7 6 5 4 3 2 1".

Contents: As for British edition.

Notes: An uncorrected proof copy (owned by William Baker) has a paper cover, with the outside front as for the dust jacket, the outside back and spine white. On the outside back, a quoted passage about Pinter by Martin Gottfried, and four paragraphs about Pinter, and this volume. Below, within a single-rule box: "UNCORRECTED ADVANCE PROOF FROM GROVE/ATLANTIC, INC.", with the probable publication date given as January 1999. The verso of the title-leaf lacks the cataloguing data.

I10   POEMS . . . CHOSEN BY ANTONIA FRASER   2002

POEMS BY | *Harold Pinter* | CHOSEN BY | ANTONIA FRASER | [*decorative device*] | GREVILLE PRESS PAMPHLETS | IN ASSOCIATION WITH | DELOS PRESS

1 leaf, 19, (1) pp. 21.5 × 14 cm. Paperback, plain white card, with wrapper, pale yellow on outside; on outside front of wrapper, in brown: "Poems by | HAROLD | PINTER | Chosen by | Antonia Fraser | [*swelled ornamental rule, 4.9 cm.*] | Greville Press Pamphlets"; on outside back: "ISBN 0 906887 78 X"; down spine: "Poems by Harold Pinter | Greville Press"; flaps white, plain.

Published 2002. On verso of title leaf: "First published in this edition 2002", publisher's name and address, copyright and previous publication details, "Printed in Great Britain by Peter Lloyd | at The Holbeche Press, Rugby".

Contents: [1] half-title; [2] "For Edna O'Brien | our friend"; [inserted leaf, off-white, recto blank, on verso:] photo, captioned: "*Harold Pinter and Antonia Fraser after their wedding,* | *27 November 1980*"; [3] title page; [4] as above; [5] "Foreword", signed "ANTONIA FRASER | 21 *April* 2002"; [6] blank; 7 "Paris"; 8 "Later"; 9 "I know the place"; 10 "Message"; 11 "Denmark Hill"; 12 "Joseph Brearley 1907–1977"; 13 "Poem" ("The lights glow"); 14 "Ghost"; 15 "Before They Fall"; 16 "Cricket at Night"; 17 "Death"; 18 "Cancer Cells"; 19 "It is Here"; [20] limitation statement.

Notes: On p.[20]: "Printed in an edition of 300 copies | of which the first fifty are | numbered and have been signed | by the selector | [*asterisk*] | COPY NUMBER" [William Baker copy numbered "48", signed in holograph by Harold Pinter, Antonia Fraser]. As noticed on p. [4], all the poems except "Cancer Cells" have been reprinted from *VV.*

I11   THE DISAPPEARED AND OTHER POEMS   2002

Harold Pinter | [*rule, 12.6 cm.*] | The Disappeared | and other poems | [*rule, 12.6 cm.*] | IMAGES BY TONY BEVAN | [*small ornament, 1.7 × 5.3 cm.*] | ENITHARMON EDITIONS | 2002

2 blank leaves, 51 pp., 1 leaf, 2 blank leaves. 31.2 × 22.2 cm. Hardback: regular copies: brown textured cloth; on front board, glued-on plate (Bevan image); outside back plain; on spine, white label, lettered down spine "Pinter   The Disappeared   Enitharmon". *De luxe* binding not described.

Published 1 October 2002. 240 copies printed (see *Notes*). On verso of title leaf: "Published by Stephen Stuart-Smith | Enitharmon Editions, 36 St George's Avenue, London N7 0HD | Text © Harold Pinter and Neabar Investments Limited 2002 | Images © Tony Bevan 2002 | I S B N 1 900564 98 (*De luxe*) 1 900564 04 1 (regular) | [*sources for selection, author's identification right, and further copyright and performance right statements*] | Printed and made in Great Britain".

Contents: [a-d] blank; [1] plate; [2] blank; [3] half-title; [4] plate; [5] title page; [6] as above; [7] plate; [8] blank; 9 contents; [10] blank; 11 "The Disappeared"; 12 "Death"; 13 "Order"; 14 "Poem: 'Don't look'"; [15] plate; 16 "Cricket at Night"; 17 "God"; 18 "It is Here"; [19] plate; 20 "Ghost"; 21 "Poem: 'The lights glow'"; 22 "Joseph Brearley 1909–1977"; [23] plate; 24 "Message"; 25 "Paris"; 26 "I Know the Place"; [27] plate; 28 "Later"; 29 "All of That"; 30 "Poem: 'Always where you are'"; [31] plate; 32–33 "The Table"; 34 "Daylight"; 35 "The Error of Alarm"; 36 "The Second Visit"; [37] plate; 38 "The Drama in April"; 39 "The Irish Shape"; 40 "The Islands of Aran Seen from the Moher Cliffs"; 41 "Book of Mirrors"; 42 "A Glass at Midnight"; [43] plate; 44 "Hampstead Heath"; 45 "Chandeliers and Shadows"; [47] plate; 48–49 "New Year in the Midlands"; 50 "The Midget"; [51] plate; [52] blank; [53] publisher's note; [54–58] blank. [The plates, reproductions of Bevan images, 14.5 × 12.7 cm., are affixed at the inner edges to otherwise blank pages.]

Note one: The Enitharmon Press's note on p. [53], largely repeating its pre-publication announcement (which had forecast publication on 1 October 2002), states:

The text of The Disappeared and other poems has been designed | and printed by Sebastian Carter of the Rampant Lions Press, | Cambridge. It is set in 14 pt Hunt Roman and the paper is | 160 gsm Arches Vélin. The books have been bound and | slipcased by The Fine Bindery in Northamptonshire.

The plates in the text, reproducing paintings by Tony Bevan | made between 1986 and 2002, have been printed by | Expression Printers Ltd.

The *De luxe* edition consists of seventy-five copies and | twenty *hors commerce* copies, signed by Harold Pinter and | Tony Bevan and numbered 1–75 and i–xx. With each copy | is a signed and numbered original etching by Tony Bevan, | printed at Hope Sufferance Press on 350 gsm Zerkall natural | white. There are also ten artist's proofs, numbered AP i–x.)

The regular edition consists of one hundred signed copies | and twenty-five *hors commerce* copies, numbered 76–175 and | xxi–xlv. A further twenty sets of sheets, numbered 176–195, | have been reserved for binders.

This is number.

The pre-publication announcement specifies that the text is hand-set, and gives the prices: *De luxe* copies: "Pre-publication £400 Post-publication £475 | Fully insured postage : UK £15, Europe £18, rest of world £25"; regular copies: "£100 | Fully insured postage : UK £12, Europe £15, rest of world £18"; sets of sheets for binders: "£100."

Note two: The sources statement on the verso of the title leaf reads: "This selection has been made by Harold Pinter and | Stephen Stuart-Smith from the contents of Poems | (Enitharmon Press, 1968; second edition 1972) and from | poems first published in the following books and journals: | *Bananas*, the *Guardian*, *New Poems 1957*, *The New Review*, *Poetry* | *London*, *Poetry Northwest*, *Soho Square II*, the *Sunday Times*, | *Ten Early Poems* (Greville Press Pamphlets, 1992), and the | *Times Literary Supplement*."

Note three: A *De luxe* copy owned by William Baker is numbered (on p.[53]) "40", and signed by Harold Pinter and Tony Bevan.

I12   WAR   2003

HAROLD PINTER | [*thick rule, 10 cm.*] | WAR | ff | *faber and faber*

Unpaginated, [24] pp. 21.5 × 13.1 cm. Paperback, crimson card, plain, with slate-grey wrapper; on outside front of wrapper: "HAROLD PINTER | [*thick rule, 9.9 cm.*] | WAR | ff"; on outside back, within single-rule frame: "www.faber.co.uk | [*rule*] | ISBN 0-571-22131-9 | [*two bar-codes with numerals*]"; on front flap: notes on Pinter's "response to world events", and on the contents of this pamphlet, at foot, right: "UK £5.00 RRP"; on back flap: note on Pinter.

Published 26 June 2003. Price £5. On verso of title leaf: "First published in 2003", publisher's name and address, "Typeset by Faber and Faber | Printed in England by Character Print and Design Ltd", copyright, author-identification, performing rights, conditions of sale, and CIP record statements, "ISBN 0-571-22131-9", issue numerals.

Contents: [1] half-title; [2] blank; [3] title page; [4] as above; [5] "Acknowledgements"; [6] blank; [7] contents; [8] blank; [9]

"Meeting", dated August 2002; [10] "After Lunch", dated September 2002"; [11] "God Bless America", dated January 2003; [12] "The Bombs", dated February 2003; [13] "Democracy", dated March 2003; [14] "Weather Forecast", dated March 2003; [15–17] "Turin Speech | On the occasion of the award of an Honorary Degree | 27 *November 2002*"; [18] blank; [19] "American Football | A reflection upon the Gulf War", dated August 1991; [20] blank; [21] "Death", undated; [22] blank; [23] Faber's Pinter titles; [24] blank.

Note: "Weather Forecast," "Democracy," "The Bombs," "God Bless America" reprinted in *Red Pepper*, 116 (February 2004): 17.

J
Sound Items

This section covers radio talks by Harold Pinter, radio interviews, and various other programmes or events in which he participated and for which he may have generated some text, either for a radio broadcast or for a stand-alone sound recording. It covers those items for which there is no corresponding print-publication item. Where there is one, the item is normally covered in the relevant section, with a note about radio broadcasting and/or, as appropriate, in *Appendix One* (the recording of *Various Voices* is, however, included here as a major sound-recording item of special interest). This section excludes items for which he was clearly simply an actor, narrator, or director, although where doubt exists an item is included rather than excluded. In some cases, the information that can be provided at this time is incomplete, with certain details such as precise dates of broadcast missing, but in the interests of comprehensiveness, these items are listed with whatever data are presently available. Where known, references are included to material in the British Broadcasting Corporation's Written Archives Centre (*WAC*), in the *Radio Times* (*RT*), and in the National Sound Archives in the British Library (NSA). The on-line National Sound Archives catalogue (accessible via www.cadensa.bl.uk) includes some further items that may be worthy of inclusion, but does not provide sufficient detail, nor, in many cases, dating (many of the items are, in any case, recordings of Pinter plays or poems or Pinter's reading the works of other authors and hence are not eligible for inclusion here).

J1 "Focus on Football Pools," BBC, Light Programme, live broadcast, 19 September 1950.
Speaker. Documentation at *WAC*.

J2 "Focus on Libraries," BBC, Light Programme, live broadcast, 31 October 1950. Speaker.

J3 Author of new play "The Birthday Party" interviewed. Within "In Town Tonight" programme, BBC Home Service, broadcast 17 May 1958. Typescript in *WAC*, LE 162.

J4 Interview with Gordon Woolford, "Writing for the Theatre." Within "Caribbean Literary Magazine" series. BBC Overseas Service, recorded 23 January 1960, broadcast date unknown.
Documentation in *WAC*.

J5 Interview, within "Critic at Large" series, BBC, General Overseas Service, recorded 1 February 1960, broadcast date unknown.
Documentation in *WAC*.

J6   Interview with John Sherwood. "Profile: A Playwight." Within the "Rising Generation" series. BBC European Service, recorded 29 January, broadcast 3 March 1960, repeated 20 March 1960.
      "Duplicated manuscript exists" (S. Gale, *Harold Pinter: An Annotated Bibliography*, p.11: item 85), evidently at WAC. Associated with the broadcast on the BBC Third Programme of *A Night Out* on 1 March 1960. See *RT*, 146: 1894 (26 February 1960): 3. Quoted by Martin Esslin, in *The Peopled Wound: The Plays of Harold Pinter* (London: Methuen,1970), pp.35–36, 38–39.

J7   Interview with O. Webster, on his work as a playwright. Within "Today"programme, "Voices in the Air", BBC Home Service, recorded 23 May, broadcast 26 or 30 May 1960, also broadcast 2 June 1960.
      Typescript in WAC; and see BBC printed *R. P. Permanent Library Catalogue, Supplement* 1, p.534 – LP26098. Interview related principally to *The Caretaker*.

J8   Interview: "Author and Playwright", in the "In Town Tonight" programme, BBC Home Service, recorded 9 June, broadcast 11 June 1960.
      Documentation at WAC.

J9   Interview with Hallam Tennyson, "Dateline London," BBC General Overseas Service, recorded 19 July, broadcast 7 August 1960.
      "Duplicated manuscript exists" (S. Gale, *Harold Pinter: An Annotated Bibliography*, p.11: item 86), evidently at WAC.

J10   Interview with Kenneth Tynan. In "People Today" programme, BBC Home Service, recorded 19 August, broadcast 28 October 1960.
      RT, 149:1928 (20 October 1960): 60 (short description of interview on p.54). Produced by Anthony Smith. "Duplicated manuscript exists" (S. Gale, *Harold Pinter: An Annotated Bibliography*, p.11: item 87): typescript at WAC, T617.

J11   "London Echo: An Interview with John Wain." BBC General Overseas Service, recorded 14 October 1960, broadcast date unknown.
      Documentation at WAC.

J12   Interview, on *The Caretaker*. Within "London Mirror" series. BBC Light Programme, recorded 6 January, broadcast 14 January 1961.
      Documentation at WAC.

J13   Interview. Within "The World of Books" programme. BBC Radio 4, recorded 17 February, broadcast 18 February 1961 (10.10 pm).
      On taking over a role in *The Caretaker*. Documentation in WAC. *RT*, 150: 1945 (February 1961): 12.

J14   Interview with Carl Wildman. "Writing and Producing Plays for Radio and Theatre: Carl Wildman interviews Donald McWhinnie and Harold Pinter." Within the "Talking of Theatre" series. BBC Network Three, recorded 27 February, broadcast 7 March 1961.
      See *RT*, 150: 1947 (2 March 1961) 36. Typescript at WAC, T533/534.

J15   Performer in: Eugene Ionesco, *Victims of Duty*, BBC Third Programme, recorded 25 July, broadcast 21 August 1961, producer Martin Esslin. 8.50–10 pm.

J16   Personal anthology, Pinter's introducing and reading his own choice of poetry, BBC Third Programme, broadcast 30 October 1961, 9.45–10.15 pm. Repeated 7 October 1962, 10.25–11 pm.

J17   Talk, about air. Within "Midweek" programme, BBC Home Programme, 22 August 1962. 1.40–2 pm.

J18   Theatre: A Discussion. London: Argo, 1962. LP recording, one sound disc, 33 1/3 rpm, 12 inch, PLP 2138.
       Features interviews by Walter Harris, with Noel Coward, Albert Finney, Sir Peter Hall, Sean Kenny, Siobhán McKenna, Harold Pinter, Sybil Thorndike, Kenneth Tynan, Peter Ustinov. Produced by Richard Francis. NSA 1LP0054507 ARGO.

J19   Extract from speech, within "Drama Conference," event within Edinburgh Drama Festival, BBC Third Programme, broadcast 3 September 1963, 10.45–11.05 pm.; also a talk: "On Films," Home Programme, 15 September 1963, 2.30–3 pm.

J20   Interview with Philip Oakes. Within programme "On Films." BBC Home Service, recorded 27 September, broadcast 6 October 1963.
       Relates to forthcoming films, *The Caretaker* and *The Servant*; interviews also with Clive Donner, Joseph Losey. *RT* (6 October 1963) 20. Typescript at WAC, T385.

J21   "Harold Pinter talks to Paul Mayersberg and Laurence Kitchin about his recent work for the cinema and the theatre." Introduced by Paul Hona. BBC Third Programme. "New Comment" programme. Broadcast 8 October 1963. Repeated Third Programme, 22 December 1963.
       RT, 161: 2082 (3 October 1963) 37. Typescript at WAC, T359.

J22   Interview with Paul Mayersberg. "The author in search of collaborators." BBC radio, Third Programme, 26 February 1964.
       One of sixteen participants. On the director's role in contemporary cinema. Typescript at WAC (T333). NSA NP598W, NP599W.

J23   Interview with Nan Winton. Within "In Town Today" programme, introduced by Nan Winton and Michael Smee. BBC Radio 4, broadcast 14 March 1964.
       RT, 162: 2105 (14 March 1964) 12. Typescript in WAC.

J24   Desert Island Discs. Castaway. Introducing his own selection of music. BBC Home, broadcast 14 June 1965, 1.10–1.45 pm.

J25   Interview with Mercy Appet. On subject of apartheid in South Africa, within programme "Focus on Africa," BBC Overseas Service, recorded 7 May 1965, broadcast 11 May 1965.

J26   [Short talk, within a series.] "What Makes a Dramatist." BBC, broadcast 20 June 1966.

J27   Interview: "A World of Sound," BBC Home, broadcast 14 November

1966, 10.30–11pm. Previously broadcast in the World Service, 14 March 1966.

J28 Interview. Within the "Lively Arts" programme, introduced by Derek Hart. BBC Home Service, broadcast 27 November 1966.
On writing the screenplay for *The Quiller Memorandum,* currently showing at the Odeon, Leicester Square. Typescript at WAC (T297). NSA LP 30483.

J29 Interviewed by John Bowen, BBC Radio 3, broadcast 26 July 1967.
On Pinter's directing of Robert Shaw's *The Man in the Glass Booth.*

J30 Interviewed by Patricia Brent. "H. Pinter becomes a Manager." Within "Today" programme, BBC Radio 4, broadcast 11 September 1969.

J31 "Personal Anthology" of poems, selected and read by Vivien Merchant and Harold Pinter, in programme "'With Great Pleasure': The Pinters", BBC Radio 4, recorded 25 February 1970, broadcast 24 May 1970.
See *RT,* 187, no. 8248 (21 May 1970) 27. NSA P574W.

J32 Interview with Jacky Gillott. Within "Options" programme, BBC Radio 4, recorded 16 September 1970, broadcast 20 September 1970.
Studio interview, relating to *The Tea Party* and *The Basement.* T137/138. Documentation at WAC.

J33 Interview with Alan Haydock. Within "Options" programme, BBC Radio 4, broadcast 15 November 1970.
Recorded at the Mermaid Theatre; relates to production of Joyce's *Exiles,* directed by Pinter. The broadcast included one extract from the play in performance. Documentation at WAC.

J34 Interview with Jacky Gillott. Within "Options" programme, introduced by Philip Oakes. BBC Radio 4, broadcast 6 June 1971.
Also featured as: "Pinter on Pinter," within series "The Interval." BBC Radio 4, 13 June 1971: extended version of the interview first broadcast on 6 June. See *Radio Times* (3 June 1971) 25; also, issue of 10 June, p.25. Relates to the opening of *Old Times* at the Aldwych Theatre. NSA M477R.

J35 Interview on his hostile criticism of Luchino Visconti's production of *Old Times* for the Teatro di Roma in Italy, on "Kaleidoscope" programme, BBC Radio 4, broadcast 10 May 1973.

J36 Pinter on Pinter with excerpts from his plays. Centre for Cassette Studies, 1974. One cassette tape (40 minutes).
Features an interview with Pinter, and scenes from five of his earlier plays.

J37 "Pinter on Cricket," BBC radio, *ca.* July 1977.
No further information currently available.

J38 Boom, also Collage of lines and words. Recorded 3 December 1983.
Pinter as writer and speaker. Recorded at the Young Vic. NSA C92/5, items 36 and 34.

J39 The Night of the Day of the Imprisoned Writer. Reading of Poetry and Prose Directed by Harold Pinter in Aid of the PEN Writers in Prison Fund. LP disc, 1982.

Recorded live at the Duke of York's Theatre, 4 October 1981. NSA 1LP0190378; RCA RED SEAL BL 25406; also on tape, C125/36.

J40 One of six speakers, PEN Writers' Day, 23 March 1985.
Discussion of the morning's lectures and presentation of PEN awards. Held in the Purcell Room, Royal Festival Hall, London. Session chaired by Francis Henry King. NSA C125/39.

J41 Pinter in conversation with Benedict Nightingale, 25 September 1985, ICA.
NSA C95/124. For 1983 interview, see *K24*.

J42 Interview: on the occasion of Pinter being awarded an honorary fellowship of Queen Mary College, University of London, early May 1987. National Film Theatre audiotape interview; copy of tape in British Film Institute Library.

J43 One of five speakers, PEN Writers' Day, 9 April 1988.
Discussion of the morning's lectures, and presentation of PEN awards. In the Lady Mitchell Hall, Cambridge. Session chaired by Antonia Fraser. NSA C125/93.

J44 One of six speakers, PEN Writers' Day, 4 March 1989.
Discussion of the morning's lectures, and presentation of PEN awards. In the Purcell Room. Session chaired by Antonia Fraser. NSA 125/119.

J45 Interview with Brian Johnston, in "A View from the Boundary" series, BBC Radio 3, within Test Match Special programme (medium wave only), 25 August 1990.
One of a series of "conversations" during test match lunch-breaks. See *RT* (20–25 August 1990) 52. Published in 1993 in *More Views from the Boundary*; see *G76*.

J46 Interview with Paul Allen. Broadcast on "Kaleidoscope" programme, BBC Radio 3, 7 October 1990.
Re-broadcast as part of the 4-hour Sunday evening programme "Harold Pinter at 60–A Birthday Party," Radio 3, 10 October 1990, which included, among other items, Pinter reading the close of Samuel Beckett's *The Unnameable* (Billington 323). NSA B7382. Cf. also "Late Show" celebration of Pinter's 60th birthday, NSA V705/02.

J47 Remembering and forgetting [1995].
Talk about dramatisation of Proust's *Remembrance of Things Past*. NSA H6343/8. [No other details currently available.] Cf. *W34(7)*.

J48 Interview with Michael Billington, at the Cheltenham Festival of Literature, broadcast on "Night Waves," BBC Third Programme, 17 October 1996.

J49 *Various Voices: Prose, Poetry, Politics 1948–1998*. Read by the author. London: Penguin, 1998. In series: "Faber Penguin audio books"; ISBN 0140868461. Two sound cassettes, ca. 120 minutes.
NSA ICA0028849. Also in *NSA*: excerpts read by Pinter, platform performance, Lyttleton Theatre, 1998: 1CDR0000254, C274/126.

J50   Acceptance speech, as one of the two recipients of the Golden Pen award for Distinguished Services to Literature, PEN International Writers' Day, 1 May 2001, function at the Café Royal, Piccadilly.

Pinter devoted part of his speech to attacking the failings of the Labour Government's "ethical" foreign policy. *NSA* 125/348. The other recipient was D. J. Enright.

J51   Comment, on BBC Radio 4, 1 August 2002.

Relates to his motives for adding his signature to a petition calling for the release of the Serbian leader, Slobodan Milosevic, from the International Court of Justice at the Hague. Reported in an article by Hugh Davies, "Blair loved bombing Serbia, says Pinter," *Daily Telegraph* (2 August 2002; seen on *Telegraph* website), which also refers to a recent statement by Pinter published in the *New York Times* [not located].

K

Audio-Visual Materials

This section covers television and film items for which there is no print-publication equivalent, so that they are not given notice in other sections or in *Appendix One* (e.g., it does not include transmissions or recorded forms of Pinter's screenplays or television plays). It does not normally include Pinter's participation as an actor, narrator, or director unless he is also the author of some feature of the text. In many cases, copies of films or video cassettes are available at the British Film Institute, London *(BFI)*. As with *Section J*, some items are included with available information, although all relevant details are not known.

K1   Interviewed about *The Caretaker,* on "Monitor." BBC-TV, transmitted 5 June 1960, 10–10.55 pm.

K2   Participant within "Wednesday Magazine" programme. BBC-TV, transmitted 18 January 1961, 2.45–3.30 pm.

K3   Participant in discussion on playwrights. Within "Tonight" programme, BBC-TV, 13 February 1961, 6.50–7.29 pm.

K4   Interviewed about *The Birthday Party.* Within "View" programme, BBC-TV, 3 January 1962.

K5   Participant within "Wednesday Magazine" programme, BBC-TV, 29 June 1962.

K6   Participant within "Tonight" programmme, BBC-TV, 19 September 1963, 6.50–7.29 pm.

K7   Interviewed about *The Servant,* within "Monitor" programme, BBC-TV, 10 November 1963, 9.50–10.35 pm.

K8   Interviewee, with John Kershaw. Independent Television, 1964 (S. Gale, *Harold Pinter: An Annotated Bibliography*, p.12: item 90; no further details available).

K9   Participant in "Late Night Line Up" programme, BBC-TV, 12 and 15 May 1963.

K10   [Interview] Profile; No. 1 Harold Pinter. Directed by Jim Goddard. ABC Television. First broadcast 3 November 1965. Recording in BFI.

K11   Participant in "Line-Up Review" programme, BBC2, 15 July 1966, from 10.20 pm.

K12   Interview (Pinter and Robert Shaw) with Michael Billington, BBC-TV, July 1967.
      Live interview, on the night following the opening night of Shaw's *The Man in the Glass Booth,* directed by Pinter (Billington 194). Exact date not known.

K13   [Interview] The Pinter Puzzle. WNDT-TV, Channel 13, New York, 1967 (S. Gale, *Harold Pinter: An Annotated Bibliography*, p.32: item 306; no further details available).

K14   Participant in discussion, within "Contrasts" programme, BBC1, 20 March 1968, 11.15–11.45 pm.

K15   In "The Actor." A CBS Television special, 1968 (S. Gale, *Harold Pinter: An Annotated Bibliography*, p.12: item 91; no further details available).

K16   Participant within "Late Night Line Up" programme, BBC2, 3 February 1969, 11.00 pm.

K17   Participant in discussion on the film of *The Homecoming*. Within "Release" programme, BBC2, 1 March 1969, 10.20–11 pm.

K18   Participant within "Line Up" programme, BBC2, 11 September 1969, 10.55 pm.

K19   *Pinter People*, directed by Gerald Potterton, Gerald Potterton Productions, produced in November 1969, for NBC's "Experiment in Television." See *Appendix One*, W11 (6). Includes interview and animated cartoon renditions of early sketches.

K20   Director: film: Simon Gray, *Butley*, completed 28 May 1973, released in USA, January 1974, in American Film Theater series, for American Express Films (brief note about it by Pinter in *American Film Theatre / Cinebill* (January 1974). Broadcast on BBC TV, October 1974 (exact date and channel not known). Film in BFI. Also available on video: DVD video: New York: Kino on Video, 2003 (one videodisc; includes associated items); also in: American Film Collection 1 (6 videodiscs; New York: Kino on Video, 2003).

K21   Interviewee, "South Bank Show," directed by Andrew Snell, first broadcast 22 April 1978, London Weekend Television. Video in BFI.

K22   Interviewee, with Melvyn Bragg. On "The South Bank Show." London Weekend Television (ITV), 7 November 1981.

K23   Participant in: *Poets against the Bomb*, directed by Francis Fuchs, GB 1981; CND Poetfilm.
Copy in BFI/BFL.

K24   Harold Pinter with Benedict Nightingale. In series "Writers in Conversation," No. 27. 1983. VHS, one video cassette (55 minutes). London: ICA Video; Northbrook, IL: The Roland Collection of Films on Art.
Relates especially to *One for the Road*.

K25   Interviewee in: "Admit Me, Chorus, to this History," in series "All the World's a Stage," directed by Henry Hastings. BBC2, first transmitted 22 April 1984, 8.40–9.35 pm.
Recording in BFI.

K26   Interview with John Tusa. In "Saturday Review" programme, BBC2, 28 September 1985, 7.10–8 pm.

K27   Participant: "Nicaragua: Poets as Politicians," series "The South Bank

Show," directed by Tony Knox, first transmitted 27 March 1988, London Weekend Television.

K28   Participant in: "Omnibus" programme, directed by Daisy Goodwin, 1988, BBC1, broadcast 21 October 1988, 10.20–11.20 pm.

K29   Participant in: "Two Dogs and Freedom: A Concert for the Children of South Africa," series "Signals," BBC-TV, directed by David Heather, first transmitted 4 January 1989; John Blair Film Company.

K30   Oh, Superman. Television talk, for "Opinions" series, Channel 4, first broadcast 14 September 1989, repeated 31 May 1990. Clark Productions. Text printed in 1998 in *VV* 175–182.

K31   Presenter of play: "Wake for Sam" [i.e., Samuel Beckett], BBC2, broadcast 8 February 1990, 10.15–10.30 pm.

K32   Participant in: "Graham Greene 1904–1991", BBC-TV, broadcast 7 April 1991.

K33   Interviewee, in "A Very British Picture." BBC2, first broadcast 19 September 1993, 8.05–9.05 pm. Series: "Hollywood, UK: British Cinema in the Sixties". In BFI.

K34   Interviewee in: "Gielgud: Scenes from Nine Decades." In: BBC1 programme "Omnibus." First broadcast 12 April 1994, 10.00–11.00 pm. Revised version first broadcast 23 May 2000.
      First broadcast two days after Sir John Gielgud's death. Notably, he had acted Spooner in *No Man's Land*.

K35   Without Walls: Celebration of Sir Donald Wolfit. Channel 4, 3 May 1994, 9–9.30 pm.
      Introduced by Ned Sherrin; other speakers included: Paul Bailey, Donald Sinden, Ronald Harwood. *NSA* V2963 CH4.

K36   Participant in: episode in "London Stage." London Weekend Television. First broadcast 8 October 1995.

K37   Acceptance speech on being awarded a special prize for his contribution to the theatre. Laurence Olivier Awards programme for 1995. Broadcast BBC-TV, 18 February 1996. [Knowles, in *TPR* (1997), p.167.]

K38   Interviewee, with Sir Jeremy Isaacs. On "Face to Face." BBC2 Television, 21 January 1997.

K39   Participant in: "Michael Redgrave: His Father," directed by Roger Michell. In "Omnibus" session, BBC1, first broadcast 13 July 1997.
      Evidently this was a complementary section of the programme "Michael Redgrave – My Father," in which the main speaker was Corin Redgrave, the actor's son.

K40   Participant in: episode, "The South Bank Show," directed by David Thomas. London Weekend Television. First broadcast 29 November 1998.

K41   Participant in "Counterblast" programme, BBC2, 4 May 1999, 7.30 pm. Speaking out against NATO's war in the Balkans, with photos by Stuart Urban.

K42   Interviewee, with Nigel Williams, BBC2, "Arena" programme, on occasion of Pinter's 70th birthday celebrations, 1 October 2000, organised by the English Centre for International Pen, Soho Theatre, London.

K43   Interviewee, within two-part "Arena" programme on Pinter's life and career, composed and compiled by Nigel Williams, BBC2 and 4, 27 October 2002.

Part of two-week season "Pinter at the BBC," from 26 October 2002, across BBC Two, BBC Four, BBC Radio and BBC1. On BBC Four: season of Pinter's plays, films, and talks, including a newly filmed production of *The Dwarfs* by BBC Fictionlab.

K44   Interviewee, with Mark Lavsa, BBC2, "Newsnight Review" programme, 13 June 2003; pre-recorded at Pinter's home; on his poems about war. [It was followed by a discussion of these poems by Bill Buford, Germaine Greer, and Mark Kermode.]

APPENDIX ONE
Individual Literary Works

This appendix presents the annals of Harold Pinter's more substantial or significant literary works, in the genres of drama (including screenplays) and prose fiction (including only those short stories with a relatively complex "history"). It does not cover unpublished items, in the main sequence, although a few of these are noticed at the end. Worthy of special mention among these, however (and not listed there), is the early autobiographical piece "Queen of All the Fairies," reminiscences of his youth in Hackney, of which a carbon copy, 8 typed pages (rectos only), is in the Pinter Archive, Box 60, along with several drafts or fragments of unpublished short stories and sketches.

Unlike that of Malcolm Page's admirable *File on Pinter* (London: Methuen Drama, 1993), the concern of this appendix is with the genesis and textual forms taken by Harold Pinter's works, and it does not provide the more extended kinds of documentation that he offers for early dramatic productions, for the stage, radio or television, or for films. Nor is it concerned with critical reception.

The items are ordered in terms of the estimated order of their composition, that is, of the completion of their composition, taking into account information from the "Chronology" published in the 1976–81 Methuen edition of Pinter's collected plays, from Billington's biography, and from the www.haroldpinter.org website (information condensed in the *Chronology* section in the present work). It differs somewhat both from the order of publication, and from the order of first performance, presentation or release.

For each item, details are provided in an estimated temporal sequence; but translations into other languages, where they occur, are provided as the last part of each entry, in a separate temporal sequence. This listing of translations offers information readily available; it does not claim to be comprehensive (acknowledgement for much of this information is made to Steven H. Gale's *Harold Pinter: An Annotated Bibliography*).

Notes on manuscripts and other composition-related documents in the Pinter Archive in the British Library are more extensively itemized than those in the finding-list compiled by Dr Sally Brown, yet, for the screenplays, substantially less detailed than those provided by Steven H. Gale and Christopher C. Hudgins in: "The Harold Pinter Archives II: A Description of the Filmscript Materials in the Archive in the British Library," *TPR: Annual Essays 1995–1996* (1997): 101–142. An article in the preceding volume by Susan Hollis Merritt, "The Harold Pinter Archive in the British Library," reproduces the finding-list, and provides in a discursive form information about the contents of a number of the boxes (*TPR : Annual Essays 1994* [1995]: 14–53). The legal pads referred to, frequently used by Pinter for handwritten drafts, are long foolscap pads of yellow paper, with much of the writing in black ink or ballpoint.

For the screenplays, and subsequent films, in addition to materials in the Pinter Archive and the British Film Institute, another significant cache is detailed by Steven H. Gale in: "Harold Pinter Materials in the Margaret Herrick Library at The Academy of Motion Picture Arts and Sciences Center for Motion Picture Study," *TPR (2001–2002)*: 213–219. The Center is in Beverly Hills, Los Angeles, California. The Library has, for the Pinter films, stills, scripts, files of newspaper clippings, published books, a typescript copy of the Proust screenplay dated October 1972, and, most important, two files relating to the filming of *The Birthday Party*. Only the last of these is listed below; for the others, reference can be made to Gale's article, and to the documentation in his edited volume *The Films of Harold Pinter* (Albany, NY: State University of New York Press, 2001) and his *Sharp Cut*.

With performance, presentation, or publication, the concern here is normally only with the first occurrence. For stage-productions, this means that the British première is normally the only one to be noticed, although in some cases the first New York production has been noticed. Likewise for publication, only the first British edition in which a work appeared has always been noticed. No attempt has been made to document the subsequent reproduction of films in video cassettes or, more recently, in DVD videodiscs. Nonetheless, a search of appropriate databases, such as *WorldCat*, will readily discover that most of the films for which Pinter supplied screenplays have been reproduced in one or both of these forms.

W1: *Kullus* [short story] *(1949):*

1.   Manuscripts, etc., in *PA* Box 60, comprise: two drafts, one in ink, one in typescript, within orange folder, written 1949. The character Kullus reappears in the story *The Examination* (written in 1955; see *D1*), and is named in the poem "The Task"(written in 1954).

2.   Published in: *Poems* (1968); *P&P; VV.*

W2: *The Dwarfs* [novel] *(1952–56):*

1.   Composed 1952–1956. Although the novel remained unpublished until *ca.* 10 October 1990, and had been significantly revised in 1989, Pinter's "AUTHOR'S NOTE" states,
This [further] work consisted mainly of cuts. I cut five chapters which seemed to me redundant and reorganized or condensed a number of other passages. Despite this reshaping, the text is fundamentally that written over the period 1952–1956.... In 1960 I extracted some elements from the book and wrote a short play under the same title. The play is quite abstract, mainly, I believe, because I omitted the essential character of Virginia from it.

In an important (as yet unpublished) radio interview with Paul Allen, recorded on 28 September 1990 (broadcast within a "Kaleidoscope" programme, 7 October 1990: NSA: B7335/09; also B7382/01), he went further, acknowledging that in retrospect he thought the excision of Virginia had been "a mistake," in that she was "the linchpin" to much of what happened. Despite having been marginalized and systematically humiliated, she can finally say, to Mark, of Pete, that she is free of him, and "He hasn't harmed me. I've survived" (p.162). In a work primarily about male bonding, she emerges, then, as the first of Pinter's unexpectedly strong and self-aware female characters.

Martin Esslin, in *The Peopled Wound* (1970), first pointed to the seminal importance of this novel: it "represents a veritable storehouse of raw material from which much of Pinter's later work is drawn" (cited by Gillen, *TPR* II.1 [p.1], from *Pinter the Playwright*, p.172).

2.   Manuscripts, etc., in *PA* Box 40:
   (a) Holograph draft, in hardback exercise book.
   (b) Holograph draft, in loose gatherings detached from exercise books.
   (c) Typescript draft, 120 pp.

3.   Manuscripts, etc., in *PA* Box 11 [previously in Box 14]:
   (a) Typescript draft, 265 pp.; on last page dated "1952–1956 | Revised 1989".
   (b) Copy of published novel (1990), with dust jacket intact; on title page, holograph list of extracts read by Pinter, in a public reading of extracts selected by him, at the National Theatre; an identical holograph list of extracts is present on a card, inserted before the title page, held in place with a glide-clip.
   (c) Photocopy of typescript with corrections.
   (d) Photocopy of typescript of earlier version, 125 pp.

4.   Manuscripts, etc., in *PA* Box12:
   (a) Holograph draft in bound notebook, early hand, with additional dialogue, ca. 200 pp.
   (b) Holograph draft in bound notebook, ca. 200 pp.
   (c) Typescript, carbon copy, 145 pp.

5.   Manuscripts, etc., in *PA* Box 13:
   (a) Typescript, with numerous holograph deletions and revisions.
   (b) Typescript, second version, November 1989, with deletions and revisions.
   (c) Uncorrected advanced proofs, Faber 1990.

6.   A chapter from the manuscript was published in *TPR*, II: 1 (1988): 5–7; identified here as Chapter 10, but the text is of Chapter 9 in the novel as published in 1990.

7.   Published by Faber, 1990: see *D8*.

8.   Pinter read selected extracts at the National Theatre. Recording of this event: NSA: B7382/07.

9.   Adaptation as a play, by Kerry Lee Crabbe, screened BBC-TV4, October 2002, premièred as stage-play, 17 April 2003, Tricycle Theatre, Kilburn, London; see *H68*.

10.   Translation into Greek: *Hoi nanoi: mythistorema*. Metaphrase, Paulos Matesis. Athena: Eudoseis Kastaniote, 1991.

11.   Translation into German by Johanna Walser and Martin Walser: *Die Zwerge: Roman*. Reinbek bei Hamburg: Rowohlt, 1994.

12.   Translation into French: *Les nains*. Roman: traduit de l'anglais par Alain Delahaye. Paris: Gallimard, 2000. Series: Du monde entier.

W3: *The Black and White* [short story] *(1954–55):*

1.   Composition dated in *Plays: One* chronology, etc., 1954–55, first published 1 July 1960 (see *D2a*). Later in *Plays: One* (1976); *P&P* (1978), etc.

2.   In 1959, provided basis for stage sketch; see *W11*.

W4: *The Examination* [short story; adapted as a sketch] *(1955):*

1.   Composition dated in *VV*, etc., 1955. Manuscript, undated, in *PA* Box 60: holograph draft, mainly in blue ballpoint, with alterations in black ink, but with passage on pp.6–7 in pencil; ten pages of text, on six leaves torn from an exercise book, with other notes and doodling on the versos of the first and last leaves. The story concerns the narrator's failed interrogation of the character Kullus, who had earlier appeared in the short story "Kullus," written in 1949, although the latter remained unpublished until 1968 (see *D4*).

2.   First published in *Prospect* (1959): see *D1a*.

3.   Read by Harold Pinter on radio, BBC Third Programme, recorded 25 June 1962, broadcast 7 September 1962; producer Michael Bakewell; MT 31434.

4.   Mounted as a dramatic sketch, 12 March 1978, by the Ambiance Lunch-Hour Theatre Club, at The Almost Free Theatre, London; published in: *Ten of the Best: British Short Plays*, edited by Ed Berman. London: Inter-Action Imprint, 1979. See *A38*.

W5: *The Room (1957):*

1.   Stage play, written in 1957, first performed 15 and 16 May 1957, directed and produced by Henry Woolf, in the Drama Department of Bristol

University, in a double-bill with *The Rehearsal* by J. G. Severns. Only relevant extant manuscript: typescript at BBC WAC, submitted 31 May 1957, re-submitted 18 May 1958 (evidently for possible use in adapted form as a radio play).

2. Performed during first week of January 1958, directed by Duncan Ross, at the National Student Drama Festival in Bristol.

3. First professional production: premièred 21 January 1960, Hampstead Theatre Club, directed by Harold Pinter; in a double-bill with *The Dumb Waiter*; transferred to the Royal Court Theatre, opened 8 March 1960, re-directed by Anthony Page, with 3 cast changes (Vivien Merchant retained the role of Rose; Henry Woolf, who had played Mr Kidd at Bristol, retained this role at Hampstead).

4. Published in: *The Birthday Party and Other Plays* (Methuen, 1960); *The Room* (French, 1960); *The Birthday Party and The Room* (Grove, 1961); *The Room and The Dumb Waiter* (Methuen, 1966); *Plays: One* (Methuen, 1976); *Celebration and The Room* (2000).

5. Television productions: (UK) Granada, broadcast 5 October 1961, directed by Alvin Rakoff; (USA) ABC, broadcast 26 December 1987, directed by Robert Altman.

6. First New York production, opened 14 October 1961.

7. Translated into Italian by Elio Nissim, as *La Stanza*, in: *Il Gardiano e altri drammi*. Milan: Bompiani, 1962. Also includes *Il Calapranzi* ("The Dumb Waiter").

8. Translated into Dutch, in: *De Kamer, De Dienstlift, De Huisbewaarder, Die Collectie, De Minnaar*. Amsterdam: Uitgeverij De Bij, 1966.

9. Translated into German by Willy H. Thiem, in: *Die Geburtstagsfeier, Der stumme Diener, Das Zimmer, Die Zwerge: Vier Dramen*. Hamburg: Rowohlt, 1969.

10. Translated into Japanese, by Tetsuo Kishi, in: *Pintá Gikyoku Zenshu* ["Collected Plays of Pinter"]. Tokyo: Takeuchi Shotem, 1970.

11. Translated into Spanish, as *La Habitación*, in: *La habitación, Un ligero malestar, Une noche de juerga, Los enanos, Solicitante, Paisaje, Silencio, Noche*. Madrid: Editorial Cuadernos para el Diálogo, 1976.

W6: *The Birthday Party (1957):*

1. Manuscripts or early typescripts for the stage play are evidently not extant.

2. Stage play, opened at the Arts Theatre, Cambridge, 28 April 1958; 19 May, transferred to London, closing after one week. [Script submitted to BBC, by ACTAC, 20 November 1957, as "The Party."]

3. American copyright registration, as an unpublished script: Library of Congress, 10 August 1959 (DU49518).

4. Published: as *The Birthday Party* (Encore, 1959); in *The Birthday Party and Other Plays* (Methuen, 1960), etc.; large print edition published *ca.* 1972 by the Canadian Institute for the Blind, in 25 copies.

5. Television production, by Associated Rediffusion Television, first presented 22 March 1960, directed by Joan Kemp-Welch.

6. Stage play revived by the Royal Shakespeare Company at the Aldwych Theatre, 18 June 1964, directed by Harold Pinter; sound recording of this production, recorded 25 November 1964: *NSA*: T49W-T50W T1–2.

7. Manuscripts, etc., for the screenplay, in *PA* Box 5:
    (a) Duplicated typescript, as prepared for film, stapled, within black card covers; on title page: "THE BIRTHDAY PARTY | a screenplay | by | HAROLD PINTER | This script is the property of ACTAC Ltd [etc.]"; numerous changes, cuts, and marking of places for inserts, in holograph, in pencil or red pencil; include moving the "party action" in Act II from the kitchen to the parlour.
    (b) Another copy of same, black card covers, with slot cut in front cover to reveal title below; on the title page, at top right, in black biro: "<u>Pinter</u>"; no markings till p.129, thereafter a number of them, mainly for cuts.
    (c) Another copy, similarly bound; on the title page, top right: "H. P."; many cuts throughout, in pencil, and additional markings to expedite use as a filming script.

8. Two files in the Margaret Herrick Library (see headnote, above), within the William Friedkin Collection:
    (a) A copy of the Samuel French (British) acting edition, with Friedkin's holograph alterations, and notes of camera shots and stage directions, for the film.
    (b) A notebook, with orange covers, with Friedkin's notes, mostly in pencil, for shooting the film.

9. Film released in USA, 9 December 1969; in UK, February 1970. Directed by William Friedkin. Copyright for screenplay: Continental Distributors, 1968.

10. Adaptation as radio play, BBC, planned from May 1969 onward (in association with a BBC "Harold Pinter Festival" in February 1970). Broadcast Radio 4, 2 February 1970, directed by Charles Lefeaux. A 7-minute extract from this was to be broadcast within the Radio 4 Schools programme "Speak," 14 January 1974 (provisional date).

11. New television production, BBC2, directed by Kenneth Ives, first broadcast 21 June 1987, within "Theatre Night" programme; repeated on BBC2, 14 May 1989; see *Radio Times* (13–19 May 1989): 25.

12. Translation into Polish by Adam Tarn, as *Urodziny Stanleys,* in: *Dialog,* No. 10 (1960).

13. Translation into Turkish by Memet Fuat: *Dodumgünü Partisi.* De Yayinwevi, 1965.

14. Translation into Czech by Milan Lukěs, as *Norozeniny,* in: *Anglicke Absurdni Divaldo.* Prague: Orbis, 1966. Together with *Navrat Domu* (*The Homecoming*).

15. Translation into Portuguese by Artur Ramos and Jaime Salazar Sempaio: *Feliz Aniversario.* Lisbon: Preto, 1967.

16. Translation into French: *L'Anniversaire; pièce en trois actes de Harold Pinter; traduite de l'anglais par Eric Kahane.* [Paris]: Editions Gallimard, 1968. Series: Théâtre du monde entier. DLC copyright registration: 15 June 1968 (DFO-1621).

17. Translation into German by Willy H. Thiem, as *Die Geburtstagsfeier:* see *W5 (9).*

18. Translation into Japanese by Koji Numasawa, as *Basudei Pati:* see *W5 (10).*

W7: *The Dumb Waiter (1957):*

1. Stage play, written in the summer of 1957 (Billington 75), premièred 28 February 1959, Frankfurt am Main, Germany.

2. Stage play, first British production, presented 21 January 1960, Hampstead Theatre Club, transferred to the Royal Court Theatre, 8 March 1960, in a double-bill with *The Room:* see *W5 (3).* First American production: Guthrie Theatre, Milwaukee, 22 July 1962; New York production: Cherry Lane Theatre, 26 November 1962, in a double-bill with *The Collection.*

3. Published: in *The Birthday Party and Other Plays* (Methuen, 1960); as *The Dumb Waiter* (French, 1960).

4. Television play, broadcast BBC2-TV, 23 July 1985; see *Radio Times,* 247: 3218 (22–26 July 1985): 49.

5. Translated into Italian by Elio Nissim, as *Il Calapranzi,* in: *Sipario,* 16 (July 1961): 48–54. Reprinted in collection, 1962: see *W5 (7).*

6. Translated into Serbo-Croatian, as *Bez Pogovora,* in: *Avangardna Drama.* Belgrade, 1964.

7. Translated into Spanish by Manuel Barbera, as *El Monteplatas,* in: *El Cuidor, El Amante, El Monteplatas.* Buenos Aires: Nueva Vision, 1965.

8. Translated into Swedish by Lars Göran Carlsson, as *Mathissen,* in: *I En Akt,* edited by Ingvar Holm. Stockholm: Aldus, 1966.

9. Translated into Dutch, as *Die Dientslift:* see *W5 (8).*

10. Translated into German by Willy H. Thiem, as *Der stumme Diener:* see *W5 (9).*

11. Translated into Japanese by Tetsuo Arakawa, as *Damu Weita:* see *W5 (10).* Also, by Kobo Abe, as *Damu [Wiet]a,* in *Umi* (February 1975).

12. Translated into Portuguese by Luis de Stau Moneiro, as *O Monte Cargas,* in: *Tempo de Teatro,* No. 3 (n.d.).

W8: *"Something in Common" (1958):*

Unproduced radio play: a typescript submitted 14 April 1958, in BBC WAC as "Untitled Play", is probably of this work. Billington's statement that it was submitted in July 1958 is evidently erroneous; there was much dispute within the BBC as to whether the play should be produced, with Donald McWhinnie, Barbara Bray and Michael Bakewell championing it; but in the event it was not, partly because of a disagreement over the fee to be paid (eventually written off, 29 June 1960). Instead, in July, Pinter was commissioned to write another play, which became *A Slight Ache* (see below), and evidently drew upon this play (Billington 95–96). Documentation in Pinter Scriptwriter File I (1957–62), BBC WAC.

W9: *A Slight Ache (1958):*

Largely composed in "the summer of 1958" (Billington 95–96)

1. Radio play: commissioned by the BBC Third Programme, July 1958; broadcast 29 July 1959; directed by Donald McWhinnie, *NSA* T11062/01 TR1 (advertised cast lists "Baron, David" [Pinter's stage-name] as Barnabas, a wholly silent character).

2. Publication in *Tomorrow,* No. 4 (1960). Ian Hamilton, in an interview in 2001, spoke of starting the magazine *Tomorrow* while a student at Keble College, Oxford. During his National Service in the Royal Air Force at München-Gladbach in Germany, in the Information Service, he had been impressed by, and had favourably reviewed for forces radio, a production of *The Room* presented within a local drama festival. Accordingly, several years later, he wrote to Pinter asking for a contribution to the magazine, and was sent *A Slight Ache* as a radio play script. He recalled:

    "It doubled the size of the issue. In order to promote the magazine I decided that the play could work very well as a stage play too. So I mounted this production.

"*Where, at Keble?*

"No, no. At the Mechanics Institute. And Harold came and saw it and that's how we became friends. Indeed the play went on to become a stage play put on in the West End. But originally it was a radio play.

"*Pinter didn't take any part in the production?*

"Not at all; he just grandly came to inspect it. But he was pleased and all that."

("'You Muddy Fools': In the months before his death Ian Hamilton talked about himself to Dan Jacobson," *London Review of Books*, 24: 2 (24 January 2002): 3–14; quotation from p.7 [second part of interview, in issue 24: 4 (21 February 2002), has no mention of Pinter]).

Forced to cease publication of *Tomorrow* after issue no. 4 because he "just didn't have the money" to pay the printer (p.7), Hamilton subsequently launched the *Review*, which ran from 1962 to 1972, with support from others but with himself as editor, and then, in 1974, the *New Review*. Meanwhile, from 1965–66, he had begun employment with the *Times Literary Supplement*, becoming its poetry editor, and would also become, for a time, poetry editor for the *Observer* (pp.7–8). He would then be one of the founding supporters of the *London Review of Books* in 1979, continuing on as a member of its editorial board and a contributor. He died of cancer on 27 December 2001. Pinter's contributions to several of these serials would have been expedited through his growing friendship with Hamilton.

3. Stage play, directed by Donald McWhinnie, premièred at the Arts Theatre, 18 January 1961, as part of a triple-bill called *Three*; transferred to the Criterion Theatre. Revival by the RSC at the Aldwych Theatre, 17 October 1973, directed by Peter James, in double-bill with *Landscape*; recorded 11 January 1974: *NSA*. First New York production: Writers' Stage Theatre, 9 December 1964.

4. Pinter's stage-version of the play: first published in *A Slight Ache and Other Plays* (Methuen, 1961): television version published in revised edition, 1968.

5. Television production, BBC2, 6 February 1967, directed by Christopher Morahan, as the first of three Pinter plays presented in this month (with *A Night Out* and *The Basement*); see *Radio Times*, 174: 2256 (2 February 1967): 21, with a write-up by Michael Bakewell on p.19.

6. Radio play, new recording, 15 May 1970 (TLN 19/DEO91), for BBC Radio 4, "Wednesday Afternoon Theatre," broadcast 20 May 1970 (repeat, Radio 4, 24 November 1972).

7. American radio play: Radio Theatre of Chicago production, directed by Yuri Rasovsky. [Chicago:] All Media Drama Workshop, 1976. One sound

cassette, 48: 50 minutes. Analog, stereo. Also, DLC holds two copies of a single sound tape reel (59 minutes).

8.   Sound recording: Sydney: Australian Broadcasting Commission, 1976. In "World Theatre Season" series. 1 sound cassette, 55 minutes.

9.   Translated into Italian by Laura del Bono and Elio Nissim, as *Un leggero malessere*, in: *Teatro Uno,* edited by L. Codignola. Turin: Einaudi, 1962. Also in this volume: *Una serata fouori (A Night Out).*

10.   Translated into German by Willy H. Thiem, as *Ein leichter Schmerz,* in: *Der Hausmeister, Eine Nacht ausser Haus, Abendkurs, Ein leichter Schmerz.* Hamburg: Rowohlt, 1969.

11.   Translated into German by Renate Esslin and Martin Esslin, same title, in: *Dramen.* Hamburg: Rowohlt, 1970.

12.   Translated into Japanese by Yushi Odashima, as *Kasuka na Itami:* see W5 *(10).*

13.   Translated into Spanish as *Un ligero malestar:* see W5 *(11).*

W10: *The Hothouse (1958):*

1.   Written Winter 1958, but put aside; the play as produced in 1980 would have only "a few changes during rehearsal, mainly cuts" (author's note in 1980 theatre programme).

2.   Manuscripts, typescripts, in *PA* Box 25:
    (a) Typescript, in old manila folder, loose leaves, with corrections in type and in red ballpoint and black ballpoint; on title page (with underlining in red:) "<u>THE HOTHOUSE</u> | a play in two acts | by | <u>Harold Pinter</u>"; noted on title page in ink: "<u>Final Draft</u> | Discarded Play".
    (b) Photocopy of this typescript, with some cuts and alterations in black biro, and an added leaf after the title page, with a description of the set, on two levels, with four rooms; some stage directions deleted or changed; in black spring-binder.
    (c) Typescript, clean carbon copy; loose leaves, within a clear plastic envelope. Incorporates changes made in (b).
    (d) "CAMERA SCRIPT" for the BBC2-TV television production in 1981, directed by Pinter, produced by Louis Marks; 147 pages, leaves held together at top left corner with split-pin clip. Pages 1–67 on yellow paper, 68–137 on green, 138–147 on blue. Typescript, with some small changes in black biro or ink. On first page on top right in holograph "H. P." Rehearsing and recording 20–23 February 1981.
    (e) Also in this box: letters, or copies of letters: Diana Franklin (ACTAC), 2 December 1980, to Mr Rossi Snipper, Magic Theatre; Francis Gillen to Pinter, 23 February 1981; Pinter to Gillen, 4 March 1981.

2. Stage play, Hampstead Theatre Club production, directed by Harold Pinter, opened 24 April 1980; production transferred to the Ambassadors Theatre, 25 June 1980.

3. Television production, 1981, first presented on BBC2, 27 March 1982. *NSA*: T4888 BW.

4. First published: *The Hothouse* (Methuen, 1980).

5. The Random House Archives have a copy of a 1980 edition, marked up with cuts and revisions, with three typescript pages of "NEW COPY" (to be inserted on pp.59, 68, 72, 75, 78, 89, 145, evidently in place of cut passages), with revisions carried out *ca.* 11 March 1982.

W11: *Revue Sketches (1959):*

Sketches for stage revues: *Trouble in the Works, The Black and White, Request Stop, Last to Go, Special Offer*

1. Manuscripts, etc., in *PA* Box 60:
    (a) Typescripts, within pink folder labelled "REVUE | SKETCHES": (i) "INTERVIEW"; (ii) "The Black and White": early draft, intermediate in shift from prose monologue to dramatic dialogue, with no speech prefixes; (iii) "GUEST FOR BREAKFAST", a sketch in which the unexpectedly early return of the husband interrupts his wife's entertaining a commercial traveller for breakfast [no performance traced]; (iv) Untitled version of "That's All".
    (b) Other dramatic fragments in folders in this box possibly provided ideas for other sketches or plays that were completed and performed.

2. First stage performances:
    (a) *One to Another,* revue including *The Black and White* and *Trouble in the Works,* opened at the Lyric, Hammersmith, 15 July 1959. (John Russell Taylor, in *The Angry Theatre,* p.333, notes that "the sketches came about more or less by accident; Disley Jones, who had worked on *The Birthday Party,* found himself involved in planning a new revue, *One to Another,* and asked Pinter if he would care to contribute. Pinter thought about it and then turned one of his early monologues into a dialogue, 'The Black and White,' which he followed with 'Trouble in the Works' for the same show." He then went on to write the three for *Pieces of Eight,* and subsequently *Applicant,* adapted from a scene in *The Hothouse.*)
    (b) *Pieces of Eight,* revue including *The Last to Go, Request Stop,* and *Special Offer,* and also an unpublished sketch "Getting Acquainted," opened at the Apollo Theatre, London, 23 September 1959. Sketches by Peter Cook, with additional material by Harold Pinter, Sandy Wilson, John Law, and Lance Mulcahy. Directed by Paddy Stone;

devised by Michael Codron and Paddy Stone; presented by Michael Codron.

3. *Pieces of Eight,* as LP 33 1/3 rpm. recording, with the original cast, produced for records by Hugh Mendl. Decca Stereo SKL 4084; of the Pinter sketches, this includes only *The Last to Go,* performed by Kenneth Williams and Peter Reeves. Record also as Decca DFE 8548, Decca LK. 4337.

4. Pre-publication American copyright registration as "A Collection of Sketches by Harold Pinter", unpublished script: Library of Congress, 31 December 1959 (DU50243). Re-registered 24 August 1987 (RE-347-298).

5. "Trouble in the Works" and "Last to Go" were televised in 1959 (date not known) for the BBC's "Monitor" fortnightly Arts programme.

6. Radio productions, BBC: Sketches: series of 3 programmes: broadcast 28 April, 12 May, and 26 May 1964. Series 1 and 3 recorded 22 and 23 April 1963. Typescripts at WAC.

7. Television film, *Pinter People*, produced and directed by Gerald Potterton, Gerald Potterton Productions, Inc., in November 1969 for NBC's "Experiment in Television." The film included an interview with Pinter and animated-cartoon renditions of five early sketches, *Trouble in the Works, Request Stop, Applicant, The Black and White*, and *Last to Go*, interspersed with live action shots of London and Londoners. The voices were provided by Harold Pinter, Donald Pleasence, Vivien Merchant, Richard Briers, Kathleen Harrison, and Dandy Nichols. Colour, 16 mm. soundfilm. Running time 58 minutes. Copy of video in BFI. Associated booklet, compiled by Ruth M. Goldstein, *A Discussion Guide for The Film Pinter People* (New York: Education Department, Grove Press [1970]), 23, [1] pp. Broadcast by BBC2, 20 February 1970; see *Radio Times*, 186: 2414 (12 February 1970) 45.

8. Publishings include: "Request Stop" reprinted in *The Playmakers: One,* compiled by Roger Mansfield (Huddersfield, UK: Schofield & Sims, 1976) pp.95–97, with "The Applicant" in *The Playmakers: Two*: see *W12 (3)*.

9. *The Black and White:* radio broadcast, BBC, within programme "Show of the Week," directed by Beryl Reed, 11 September 1965.

10. *Trouble in the Works:* radio broadcast, BBC, within programme "Lines from my Grandfather's Forehead," Radio 4, 15 February 1971. Also, repeated within the programme "Funny Writing 4", World Service, 12/15 March 1973.

11. *[The] Last to Go:*
    (a) Radio play: BBC: Recorded for BBC World Service, on TBU 502679, directed by John Parry, cast: F. Payne, Henry Woolf. Broadcast on

World Service, World of English, no.29, on 12, 13 and 14 March 1967. Also used within BBC Sunday Magazine, "This English," no. 393, in English on Radio, 20 August 1967, with four further transmissions.

(b) Broadcast on Radio 4, 6 February 1974, from "Pieces of Eight" on LP disc, Decca LK. 4337; also on Radio 4, 6 November 1974, within programme "Celebration: Kenneth Williams": see (3).

(c) Radio play BBC: recorded 12 December 1975; broadcast 25 September 1976. *NSA* 7382/04.

(d) Extract published in: Peter Smart and John Taylor, *Seventh Form English* (Auckland, New Zealand: Longman Paul, 1980).

12. Four sketches translated into Italian by Elio Nissim: in: *Sipario,* 27 (April 1972): 86–88.

W12: *Radio Sketches (1959 [-63?]):*

That's Your Trouble, That's All, Applicant, Interview, Dialogue for Three

1. Manuscripts, etc: see above, *W11* (1).

2. As radio works, presented on the BBC Third Programme in February-March 1964: see *W11* (6).

3. *The Applicant*: Recording, *NSA* 035R3 BD1. Reprinted in: *The Playmakers: Two,* compiled by Roger Mansfield (Huddersfield: Schofield & Sims, 1976), pp. 111–115 (see above for "Request Stop" in *The Playmakers: One*). Translation into Spanish, as *Solicitante:* see *W5 (11)*.

4. *That's All*: BBC: recorded 12 May 1967, for Dick Emery Show, broadcast Radio 2, 22 May 1967.

W13: *A Night Out (1959):*

1. (a) Radio play, BBC Third Programme, recorded 25 February 1960, broadcast 1 March 1960: see *Radio Times,* 146: 1894 (26 February 1960), with comment, p. 3. Produced and directed by Donald McWhinnie, with Pinter (as "David Baron") playing Seeley and Vivien Merchant The Girl. Repeated on 24 March 1960, Third Programme: see *RT,* 146: 1897 (18 March 1960), p.43: below the cast-list and a brief account of the play is the note:
"The author, whose works for the theatre have aroused considerable controversy, says of his radio writing:
I am no more consciously setting out to do extra-special things on radio than I am on the stage. I write instinctively for whatever medium I am working in, and much of what I am apparently trying to convey I only learn about afterwards from the critics. I have found no limitations in writing for radio."

Repeated 25 February 1970, as part of Radio 4 "Afternoon Theatre Harold Pinter Festival": see *RT,* 186: 2415 (19 February 1970):39. Repeated June 1974 (day unknown), BBC World Service drama, in version edited to 45 minutes.

(b) Script, submitted as one of the BBC's Italia Prize entries (1961), by Douglas Cleverdon; see *A9*. Two copies in InU-L, copy seen owned by William Baker.

(c) Sound recording, "A Night Out, a new play for radio": BBC Transcription Service, 1963; LP recording, 2 sound discs (100 minutes), analog 33 1/3 rpm. 12 inch. Standard No. 104179-104182. Also on one of discs: "Bold Nelson's praise: a garland of stories and songs from the time of Trafalgar," compiled by A. L. Lloyd.

2.   Televised, A.B.C. Armchair Theatre, ABC-TV, 24 April 1960. Directed by Philip Saville, with Pinter as Seeley, Vivien Merchant as The Girl.

3.   Stage play, Comedy Theatre, 2 October 1961, within a triple-bill called *Counterpoint*; transferred from the Gate Theatre, Dublin; directed by Leila Blake.

4.   Published in: *A Slight Ache and Other Plays* (Methuen, 1961) (television version).

5.   Television play broadcast, BBC-2 TV, 13 February 1967, as one of three Pinter plays broadcast in this month, with *A Slight Ache* (6 February) and *The Basement* (20 February); see *RT,* 174: 2257 (9 February 1967): 25, with a write-up by Michael Bakewell on p.19.

6.   New radio production, BBC World Service, recorded 18/19 May 1974.

7.   American radio production, by Yuri Yasovsky for Chicago radio theatre. Chicago: All-Media Dramatic Workshop, 1976. National Radio Theatre of Chicago Collection.

8.   Translated into Danish by Klaus Rifbjerg: *En Tur i Byen.* Fredensborg: Arena, 1962.

9.   Translated into Italian by Laura del Bono and Elio Nissim, as *Una serata fouori:* see *W9 (9).*

10.   Translated into German by Willy H. Thiem, as *Einer Nacht ausser Haus:* see *W9 (10).*

11.   Translated into German by Renate Esslin and Martin Esslin, same title: see *W9 (11).*

12.   Translated into Japanese by Yushi Odashima, as *Yoasobi:* see *W5 (10).*

13.   Translated into Spanish as *Una noche de juerga:* see *W5 (11).*

W14: *The Caretaker (1959):*

1. Manuscripts, etc., in InU-L, "Pinter mss." (not seen; citing information and quoted material from the on-line catalogue):
    (a) First draft, typescript, 50 pp., 25 cm.: "Carries holograph additions and revisions. Differs considerably from final draft."
    (b) Second draft, typescript, 74 pp., 25 cm.: "Carries holograph revisions and holograph and typewritten additions. Differs slightly from final draft."
    (c) Final draft, typescript, 88 pp., 25 cm.: "A few holograph additions. Differs slightly from printed play under the same title", i.e., the Encore edition (1960).

2. Manuscripts, etc., in *PA* Box 6:
    (a) Typescript, final draft, for first version of stage-play, 88 pp., within red cover; on title page: "[underlining in red] THE CARETAKER | a play in three acts | by | Harold Pinter"; on this page, in holograph, in ink: "Final Draft"; a few changes and cuts, in red ballpoint [text includes, at the end of Act II, within Aston's monologue, further text as to how the ECT machine was switched on; and at the start of Act III, Davies' complaint that he needs a decent bread-knife includes a demand for "a good solid loaf of bread, that I can cut with a knife," rather than the sliced loaf Aston had bought him, which "fell to pieces in my hand"];
    (b) Duplicated typescript of screenplay version, 84 pp., bound with split-pin clips, in red folder; on title page: "THE CARETAKER | DRAFT SCREENPLAY FROM THE PLAY | by | HAROLD PINTER | October 15th, 1962"; begins with brief episode in the street with Aston and Davies talking briefly, and then a flashback to a sequence in the café, which is cut, with an alternative version on tipped-in leaves, in which they talk about what had happened, as in the stage version;
    (c) Loose notes, holograph, in ink or pencil; concern possible series of shots, outdoors and indoors;
    (d) Single leaf, with Act III dialogue by Mick and Aston [also, in folder, stray leaf from early typescript draft of *No Man's Land*];
    (e) Breakdown of scenes for screenplay, mimeographed, 13 pp., in orange cover: "THE CARETAKER | DOMESTIC VERSION | EXPORT SCRIPT | 14th June, 1963 | Printed in England", some holograph alterations.

3. Stage play, directed by Donald McWhinnie, opened 17 April 1960, at the Arts Theatre, London; 30 May 1960, transferred to the Duchess Theatre, London.

4. Promptbook, for the first American production, at the Lyceum Theatre, New York, opened 4 October 1961 (as London production): stage manager's script: typescript with corrections in manuscript; in *PA* Box 67.

Also, another stage-manager's script, with corrections and notes in an unidentified hand, is in the Billy Rose Theatre Collection, New York Public Library.

5. Radio play; BBC, first broadcast 20 March 1962; proposal initiated 9 May 1961, contract for radio adaptation by Pinter signed 19 December 1961. Typescript at WAC. Repeat, Radio 4, 29 September 1969.

6. (a) Film, released 21 December 1963, in the UK. Screenplay by Harold Pinter; director Clive Donner; producer Michael Birkett. Produced through a special one-off company, Caretaker Films Ltd, with funding raised by private subscription. Distributed by British Lion Films Ltd. Copy of film or video in NSA. Viewing copy and copy of script at BFI.

(b) Released in the USA, 20 January 1964; distributed by Lion International Ltd; Janus Films, with the alternative title *The Guest* (because a film produced by Hall Bartlett called *The Caretakers* had been released in the USA in the fall of 1963). Copies in DLC: 11 reels, 35 mm.; 3 reels, 16 mm. A copy of a poster for this film is owned by William Baker.

7. Original soundtrack recording for this film released as 2 LP's: Parts 1 and 2: LP 0180771; Parts 3 and 4: LP 0180772. Oriole MG 20093-4, Oriole Records Ltd. Copy in NSA. Sleeve has information about the production and direction of the film. Additional narration spoken by Harold Pinter.

8. First published as *The Caretaker*: Encore, 1960; Methuen, 1960.

9. An extract (Mick's speech, from early in Act III: "Yes, you're quite right. . . . It wouldn't be a flat it'd be a palace") was included in a BBC Educational Publication, accompanying a Radio 4 series of school broadcasts, "Inquiry", for Autumn 1972 and also in the requisite radio programme.

10. Television productions: ITV, 1966; BBC1, broadcast 7 June 1981.

11. Translation into Danish by H. C. Branner: *Vicevaerten*. Fredensborg: Arena, 1961.

12. Translation into Spanish by T. R. Trives, as *El Portero,* in: *Primero Acto,* January 1962. And see also W7 *(6).*

13. Translation into Italian by Elio Nissim, as *Il Gardiano:* see W5 *(7).*

14. Translation into Hungarian by Tibor Bartos, as *A Gondnok,* in: *Mai Angol Drámák.* Budapest: Europa, 1965.

15. Translation into German: *Der Hausmeister, Deutsch von Willy H. Thiem.* In: *Theater heute,* 1 (1961): i-xvi; also in: *Spectaculum,* 8 (1965): 231–282; also, see W9 *(10).* Also, translated by Renate and Martin Esslin: see W9 *(11).*

16. Translation into Czech by Milan Lukeš: *Správce*. Prague: Orbis, 1966.

17. Translation into Dutch, as *De Huisbewaarder:* see *W5 (8)*.

18. Translation into Spanish by Josefina Vidal and F. M. Lorda Alaiz, as *El Conserje*, in: *Teatro Inglés*. Madrid: Aquilar, 1966. Also, by Manuel Barbera as *El Cuidor:* see *W7 (7)*.

19. Translation into French by Eric Kahane, as *Le Gardien*, in: *La Collection, suivi de L'Amant et de Le Gardien de Harold Pinter; traduit de l'anglais par Eric Kahane*. Paris: Editions Gallimard, 1967 (DLC registration 30 May 1967 [DFO 1559]). Also in: *L'Avant-scène du théâtre*, No. 441 (15 January 1970): 1–30.

20. Translation into Japanese by Tetsuo Kishi, as *Kanrinin*, in: *Shingeki*, October 1968; also, in revised form, see *W5 (10)*; also in: *Gendai Sekai Engeki*, Vol. 7. Tokyo: Hakusuisha, 1970.

21. For a study of the early texts, see Gerald M. Berkowitz, "Pinter's Revisions of *The Caretaker*," *Journal of Modern Literature*, 5, no. 1 (February 1976): 109–116.

W15: *Night School (1960):*

First written as a play for television; adapted as a radio play

1. Manuscript in *PA* Box 37:
   Typescript, with some alterations in pencil, "1st Draft"; two extra leaves at end with holograph passages of dialogue. At first entitled "My Nephew". Names and ages of characters: "Annie 60. Millie 60. Desmond 45. Rene 25".

2. Television play, Associated Rediffusion Television, broadcast 21 July 1960, directed by Joan Kemp-Welch.

3. Radio play, BBC: commissioned *ca.* 15 February 1966; delivered 10 August 1966; broadcast, Radio 3, 25 September 1966, directed by Guy Vaesen. Repeated Radio 4, 19 May 1969, *ca.* November 1972, 9 March 1973 [provisional, Radio 4: "Selected for Friday"]; also repeated *ca.* September 1973, Radio 4, "Selected for Friday" programme. Typescript, documentation, at BBC WAC. Entered for the Italia Prize in 1967.

4. First published in *Tea Party and Other Plays* (1967). According to Billington, Pinter had excluded the play from earlier volumes "on the grounds that it was too mechanically 'Pinteresque'" (135).

5. Translation into German by Willy H. Thiem, as *Abendkurs:* see *W9 (10)*; also by Renate and Martin Esslin, same title: see *W9 (11)*.

6. Translation into Japanese by Koji Numasawa, as *Naito Sukuru:* see *W5 (10)*.

W16: *The Dwarfs* [as a play] *(1960):*

First written as a radio play in 1960, derived from the novel (see W2)

1. Manuscripts, etc., in *PA* Box 14:
    (a) Holograph and typescript partial drafts, 7 pages: 5 holograph, 2 type-script, with holograph alterations.
    (b) Typescript draft, with alterations in type or ink, on text pages (rec-tos), or (in ink only) on facing versos; two leaves inserted after p.[1]: first has a typed list of 16 "scenes," noting the characters in each (scenes 9, 11, and 16 include "Dwarfs"); second lists in ink 20 scenes, with page numbers in the draft; title as heading on first page; within a fawn manila folder inscribed "Second Draft".
    (c) Typescript draft, with a few alterations in ink or pencil; on title page: "[underlining in red] THE DWARFS | a play for radio | by | [under-lining in red] Harold Pinter"; within same folder, but typescript inscribed on first page "3rd Draft".
    (d) Printed script of stage play version, with text on rectos (with some marking or alterations in holograph) and some re-writings in holo-graph on facing versos; 2 leaves, 25 pp., 1 leaf; on title page: "THE DWARFS | by | Harold Pinter | [at foot, right:] Michael Codron Ltd | 117/119, Regent St., | London, W.1."; after title page, blank leaf, pale blue; after p.25, pale blue leaf, with, on recto, at foot, right: "Scripts printed by: | FRANELL ENTERPRISES | 51, Maida Vale | London, W. 9. | Tel : LORds 0461"; bound in red folder with split-pin clips.
    (e) Typescript, two copies: "[underlining in black:] THE DWARFS | [two lines, underlining in red:] amendments to Methuen 1966 paperback edition of | A SLIGHT ACHE & OTHER PLAYS".

2. Radio play, BBC Third Programme, broadcast 2 December 1960; repeated 20 December; documentation at WAC; initiated 24 April 1960; produced by Barbara Bray. *RT* (2 December 1960) 61 (note by Michael Bakewell refers to Tynan interview, broadcast 28 October, see *J10*; and see extract cited in *RT*, p.52). Martin S. Regal, *Harold Pinter: A Question of Timing* (Basingstoke, Hampshire: Macmillan; New York: St Martin's Press, 1995) notes that both the original sound recording and the typescript have disappeared from the BBC shelves (144, n.11).

3. Radio play first published in: *A Slight Ache and Other Plays* (London: Methuen, 1961).

4. Stage play, New Arts Theatre, London, 18 September 1963, directed by Harold Pinter, assisted by Guy Vaesen; in a double-bill with *The Lover*.

5. First stage-play version, with revisions deriving from this production, published in *A Slight Ache and Other Plays* (Methuen, 1966). Second

stage-play version, with further revisions, published in Methuen's edition of this volume in 1968.

6. Television production in the USA: Channel 13, Public Broadcasting, Boston, 28 January 1968.

7. Translated into German by Willy H. Thiem, as *Die Zwerge*: see W5 *(9)*.

8. Translated into Spanish as *Los Enanos;* see W5 *(11)*.

W17: *The Collection (1961):*

1. Manuscripts, etc., in *PA* Box 7:
    (a) Typescript draft of television screenplay, photocopy, untitled, but labelled in pencil on first page: "THE COLLECTION | 1ST DRAFT | (TV)"; organised in shots; numerous crossings-out and speeches or parts of them re-written; Bill and Harry already have their names, but James originally named Jack, and Stella first named Myra, by Act II named Susan; scenes in dress-shop and in taxi; on last pages: list of hotel shots, schema of play (partly typed, partly handwritten).
    (b) Typescript of early draft, loose leaves in brown folder, now re-titled "A GLASS EYE".
    (c) Typescript, of television version; on title page: "[underlining in red:] A GLASS EYE | A Play for Television | by | [underlining in red:] Harold Pinter | [lists of characters and sets:] | This play should be produced with no musical background whatsoever."
    (d) Typescript, marked in ink and pencil with cuts; on title page: "A GLASS EYE [crossed through in ink, and "THE COLLECTION" written in ink above] | a play for television | by | Harold Pinter | [at foot, right, note that the script is the property of ACTAC (Theatrical & Cinematic) Ltd.]".
    (e) Another copy of this typescript, carbon copy, within black covers, text unmarked; on cover, original title crossed out, and "THE COLLECTION | First version" added in ink.
    (f) Typescript, bound with metal clips, within yellow folder: later version of television play.
    (g) Several typescripts involving progressive revising of television play to stage play;
    (h) Typescript, stage version; on title page: "[underlining in red:] THE COLLECTION | a play in one act | by | [underlining in red:] Harold Pinter"; added on title page, in ink, at top right: "TO COPY | Final Draft".
    (i) Printed script, stage version, bound in yellow folder, with three split-pin clips; noted as "Typed and reproduced by | L. G. Quinney Ltd. | 72, Wardour Street, London. W.1", and that the script is the property of ACTAC (Theatrical & Cinematic) Ltd.

2.   Television play, Associated Rediffusion Television, London, first presented 11 May 1961, directed by Joan Kemp-Welch. New production, Granada Television, 5 December 1976; video cassette of this released: Simon & Schuster Video.

3.   Stage play, first presented 18 June 1962 by the Royal Shakespeare Company at the Aldwych Theatre, co-directed by Harold Pinter and Peter Hall; in double-bill with Strindberg's *Playing with Fire*. First New York production, Cherry Lane Theatre, 26 November 1962, directed by Alan Schneider; in double-bill with *The Dumb Waiter*.

4.   Radio play: BBC Third Programme, recorded 8 November 1962, broadcast 9 November 1962, directed by Cedric Messina. Has scenes in boutique, taxi (Jimmy spying on house), etc., not in stage play. *NSA* P79R C1. Documentation in WAC, scriptwriter's file. [Earlier recording, 11 March 1962.]

5.   Published in: *The Collection and The Lover* (Methuen, 1963) (stage version).

6.   Translation into German: *Die Kollektion*. Deutsch von Willy H. Thiem. *Theater heute*, 12 (1962): i-viii. Also published in: *Die Heimkehr, Der Liebhaber, Die Kollektion, Teegesellschaft, Tiefparterre*. Hamburg: Rowohlt, 1967.

7.   Translation into Italian by Elio Nissim and Lauro del Bono, in: *Sipario*, 18 (April 1963): 56–63.

8.   Translation into French: *La Collection*, adaptation de Eric Kahane. *L'Avant-scène du théâtre*, 357 (1966): 7–19 [*Mise en scène revue de la semaine* (Paris: Bruneau, 1966)]. Reprinted, see *W14 (19)*.

9.   Translation into Dutch, as *Die Collectie*: see *W5 (8)*.

10.   Translation into Japanese by Toshio Tamura, as *Korekushon*, in: *Gendai Engeki*, No. 1, January 1967.

11.   Translation into Spanish by Luis Escobar, as *La Colleccion*, in: *Primero Acto*, No. 83, 1967. With *El Amante*.

W18: *The Lover (1962):*

1.   Manuscripts, etc., in *PA* Box 33:
   (a) Partial draft, for television, typescript 16 pp., holograph in ink 2 pp. (second act unfinished); on first page, in type "The Lover", in ink "1st Draft"; shows Richard after his first exit from the house "in Armstrong Siddeley. Driving gloves | on. Away."
   (b) Typescript, top copy, 34 pp. (extra leaf, headed "38", carbon copy of typescript, alternative version of text on page 33); title page, in typescript: "THE LOVER" [underlining in red], in ink: "2ⁿᵈ Draft".

(c) Typescript, carbon copy, stapled, 37 pp. (extra page "38" really belongs to this copy, and p. 39 is missing); on title page, in typescript: "<u>THE LOVER</u> | a play for television | by | <u>Harold Pinter</u>"; in ink: "<u>Final Draft</u>".

(d) Printed copy, with numerous alterations and added stage directions in pencil; three leaves [third is blank], 40 pp., one leaf; on title page: in typescript: "<u>THE LOVER</u> | a play for television | by | <u>Harold Pinter</u> | [at foot, right] Michael Codron Ltd | 117/119, Regent St., | <u>London, W1</u>"; in ink, at top, right: "Pinter | Who?"; bound in blue folder with two split pins, on front cover: "THE LOVER | by | Harold Pinter"; following the title page leaf and leaf with character list [etc.], there is a blank leaf, thin paper, pale blue; after p.40, there is a similar leaf, pale blue, with, at foot, right: "Scripts printed by: FRANELL ENTERPRIZES | 51, Maida Vale | London, W.9 | Tel: LORds 0461"; alterations in pencil include crossing through of final stage direction, relating to bongo drum.

2. Television production, Associated Rediffusion Television, first presented 28 March 1963. Directed by Joan Kemp-Welch (Richard: Alan Badel; Sarah: Vivien Merchant; John: Michael Forest). NSA V997/01 0:11'10".

3. Stage play, first presented 18 September 1963, Arts Theatre, directed by Harold Pinter; in a double-bill with *The Dwarfs*. First New York production: Cherry Lane Theatre, 5 January 1964, in double-bill, directed by Alan Schneider.

4. Published in: *The Collection and The Lover* (Methuen, 1963), television version; the second edition of this volume (1964) prints the stage version.

5. Translation into French by Eric Kahane: *L'Amant*, in: *L'Avant-scène du théâtre*, No. 357 (1966): 21–32. Reprinted: see *W14 (19)*.

6. Translation into Italian by Elio Nissim, in: *Sipario*, 19 (April 1964): 45–51.

7. Translation into German by Willy H. Thiem: *Die Liebhaber*, in: *Theater heute*, No. 6 (1965): 60–64. Reprinted: see *W17 (6)*.

8. Translated into Spanish by Manuel Barbera, as *El Amante*: see *W7 (7)*. Also, by Luis Escobar, same title: see *W17 (10)*.

9. Translated into Dutch, as *De Minaar*: see *W5 (8)*.

10. Translated into Polish by B. Taborski, as *Kochanek*, in: *Dialog*, No. 8 (1966).

W19: *The Servant [screenplay] [1962]:*

Adaptation from a novel by Robin Maugham (London: Falcon, 1948)

1. Manuscripts, etc., in *PA* Box 52:
   (a) Holograph notes on first 8 scenes, two loose pp., pad paper.
   (b) Holograph notes, scenes 6–32, 5 loose pp.

(c) Typescript, outline of 45 scenes, 6 loose pp.

(d) Typescript, 131 scenes, 34 loose pp.

(e) Typescript, with alterations, 82 pp., headed "THE SERVANT | HAROLD PINTER | Adapted from the novel by Robin Maugham".

(f) Typescript, carbon copy, 18 pp., headed "THE SERVANT | Page Corrections".

2.   (a) Film released by Elstree Distributors Ltd, 14 November 1963; directed by Joseph Losey. Screenplay copyright: Springbok Productions, 1971. Anglo-EMI Film Distributors Ltd. "Acclaimed for Best Screen Writing by the Los Angeles Film Critics and won both the New York Film Critics Award and the British Screenwriters Guild Award" (Keith D. Peacock, *Harold Pinter and the New British Theatre* [Westport, CT: Greenwood, 1997] p. 185). Copies of film and press-book at BFI. Copy of release script of screenplay at InU-L. Cf. S. Gale, *Sharp Cut*, p. 208, n. 22.

(b) Dialogue and continuity release script at Cambridge University Library, West Room, classmark: 1989:12:4. Dated in catalogue: 1963. On title page: "THE SERVANT | A SPRINGBOK PRODUCTION | Dialogue Continuity | REEL FOOTAGES" [footages follow for Reels 1–6, (A) and (B) for each – i.e., 12 reels] bound in pink light card covers, blank with two clips.
Duplicated (presumably mimeographed) typescript, text and pagination on rectos only; pages paginated separately for each reel (9, 7, 7, 10, 8, 7, 6, 5, 6, 10, 5, 8 pp.) Unmarked script.

3.   Published in: *Five Screenplays* (Methuen, 1971).

4.   Radio play, BBC; text adapted from screenplay by Guy Vaesen; received 19 May 1969; broadcast 26 October 1970, Radio 4 (repeat 28 July 1972). Typescript in WAC. Tape: TLN22/DF686, dated 8 June 1970. See *RT* (22 October 1970): 31 (and see short feature article, p.4). Devised for "Harold Pinter Festival," October 1970.

5.   Radio play (shortened version), 1972; BBC; text adapted from screenplay by Guy Vaesen (Drama Department [Radio]), who was producer. Pre-recorded 2 June 1972 (TLN22/DF686); re-edited with announcements (DD45H), 28 July 1972; broadcast Friday 28 July 1972, BBC Radio 4.

6.   Film shown on television, BBC2-TV, 3 June 1989, within series "Pinter on Screen"; see *Radio Times* (3–9 June 1989): 23.

W20: *Mac* [prose reminiscence] *(1963):*

1.   Manuscript (copy of typescript) in *PA* Box 28.

2.   Written for radio, 1963, as a tribute to the Irish actor-manager Anew MacMaster; BBC, recorded with Pinter as speaker, broadcast 17 April

1963, repeated 13 September 1964; re-recorded, Third Programme, 25 June 1968: copy of tape, *NSA* M1371R C1.

3. Read in 1981 on BBC as one of a two-piece programme "Players," using the 1968 tape, and with Edward de Souza reading the other piece, "Arthur Wellard": as Pinter's recollections of two great "players" from the worlds of cricket and theatre. *NSA* B7382/10. Re-recorded, for Radio 3, 17 March 1985, broadcast 25 June 1968, with Pinter as the reader of both pieces (*NSA* TLN 21/DC618).

4. Published in 1968, as *Mac*, see *E14*.

W21: *The Pumpkin Eater* [screenplay] *(1963):*

Adaptation of novel by Penelope Mortimer

1. No manuscript material in *PA*.

2. Film released 15 July 1964, first presented by Romulus Films, directed by Jack Clayton. US copyright: Columbia Pictures Industries, Inc., 1971. Film received a British Film Academy Award (Peacock, 185); featured at Cannes Film Festival. Viewing copy of film and press-book at BFI.

3. Published in: *Five Screenplays* (Methuen, 1971).

W22: *Tea Party* [as short story] *(1963):*

1. Manuscripts, etc., in *PA* Box 53:
   (a) Holograph draft, partial, on leaves from a small exercise book.
   (b) Notes, two legal-pad leaves and one typed leaf.
   (c) Three drafts of short story.
   (d) BBC recording script (short story), duplicated typescript, cover leaf plus six leaves, with text on rectos only; headed on cover leaf: "TEA PARTY" | by | Harold Pinter | Transmission: For future use in the Third Programme | Rehearsal (Thursday) 23rd April 1964 6.00–7.00 | RECORDING Thursday 23rd April 1964 7.00–7.30 pm | STUDIO: LANGHAM (Phillips) | R.P. REF.: TLO 37259 | READER: HAROLD PINTER | Produced by Michael Bakewell". A few directions added in holograph, in ink, by Pinter for himself as reader.

2. Short story commissioned by *Playboy*, in 1963, but not published till issue of January 1965. See *D3a*.

3. Short story on radio: Harold Pinter as reader, BBC Third Programme, recorded 23 April 1964, broadcast 2 June 1964, 29 August 1964. KF T29980. *NSA* T11052/01 TR1; item 29980; original tape no. 37259, copied for NSA 1993. Also broadcast in monthly "Theatre Magazine" programme, 1 February 1971.

4.   Short story published in anthology: *The Edge of the Chair,* edited by Joan Kahn (New York: Harper & Row, 1967; London: Arlington Books, 1968). Also in: *Poems and Prose 1949–1977 (14a).*

W23: *Tea Party* [as television play] *(1964):*

1.   Manuscripts in *PA* Box 25:
       (a) Two drafts of television play: one headed in holograph, "1st Draft", one leaf, 25 pp., densely typed; the other headed "Tea Party | 2cnd Draft", one leaf, 41 pp.
       (b) Typescript, carbon copy, television play, two leaves, 63 pp., two leaves of "Additions to text"; headed on first page: "TEA PARTY | a play for television | by | Harold Pinter".

2.   Television play, commissioned in 1964 by the BBC, for the European Broadcasting Union; in series "The Largest Theatre in the World," broadcast 25 March 1965.

3.   Article, *Radio Times,* 166: 2158 (18 March 1965): 47: that "within the space of a single week *Tea Party* will be seen and heard – but in different languages, different productions – in France, Belgium, Luxembourg, Switzerland, Germany, Austria, Spain, Holland, Denmark, Sweden, and Norway as well as in Britain." Quotes Pinter's statement that "the fact that it had to be translated into all these languages" had affected his approach "not at all." His previous plays had been translated; and "The experience that it describes is not confined to these islands." He had, however, taken out a reference to cricket, because people in other countries "might find it too baffling." Programme entry, p.51.

4.   As a stage play: adapted by Richard Lee Marks and Henry Jaffe, for a production at the Eastside Playhouse, 334 East 74 Street, New York, opening October 10, 1968. Bound typescript, [iv], 77 leaves (text on rectos only); copy at TxU-HRC.

5.   Pinter's stage adaptation: Duchess Theatre, 17 September 1970, directed by James Hammerstein; in a double-bill with *The Basement.*

6.   Published in: *Tea Party and Other Plays* (Methuen, 1967).

7.   Translation into German by Willy H. Thiem, as *Teegesellschaft:* see *W17 (6).*

W24: *The Homecoming (1964):*

1.   Manuscripts, etc., in *PA* Box 24:
       (a) Typescript, carbon copy, 49 pp., in red springback folder; some crossings out and substitutions, in black biro.
       (b) Typescript, clean copy; bound in red card covers with black tape

around spine, and protecting edges; rehearsal script for stage. On front cover, printed: within single-rule box: "The | Homecoming"; below box: "By HAROLD PINTER". Text corresponds to first Methuen edition (1965).

(c) Printed screenplay; in pale blue paper wrappers; 104 pp. On front page: "THE ELY LANDAU ORGANISATION LIMITED | THE HOMECOMING | by | Harold Pinter | 2nd October, 1972". Divided into 287 shots, text as for second revised Methuen, numerous small holograph alterations. No printer identified.

2. Facsimiles of manuscript notes and of a page of the typescript were published in *The London Magazine*, n.s. 100 (July-August 1969). The text of an "early draft" of the play in holograph was reproduced in facsimile in *TPR: Annual Essays 1994*, 7 (1994): 1–7. An "early typed draft" with holograph notes was reproduced in *TPR: Annual Essays 1995–1996*, 8 (1997): 16–27. Another, described as the "first draft," in typescript with holograph alterations, was reproduced in *TPR: Annual Essays 1997–1998*, 9 (1999): 1–30, together with an essay by Francis Gillen: "Pinter at Work: An Introduction to the First Draft of *The Homecoming* and Its Relationship to the Completed Drama" (pp. 31–47).

3. Stage play opened in London 3 June 1965, by the Royal Shakespeare Company, at the Aldwych Theatre, preceded by a provincial tour. Premièred 25 March 1965, New Theatre Cardiff [*RSC* Promptbook]. Revived 2 May 1978, Garrick Theatre, directed by Peter Hall.

4. Published by Methuen 10 June 1965; revised edition 1966; further revised 1967.

5. Film released 1973, in the USA, by American Express Films, Inc., & the Ely Landau Organization, Inc. in association with Cinevision, Ltd. 114 min. sd. color, 35 mm. © AFT Distributing Corporation. LC copyright registration 29 October 1973 (LP42934). Released in the UK in 1976.

6. Motion picture sound track made available: (a) 1973; two LP sound discs, analog, 33 1/3 rpm, 12 inch (95 min.); New York: Caedmon Records, TRS 362; LCCN 73-750955; (b) two sound cassettes, Caedmon, same LCCN.

7. The film broadcast on BBC TV2, 27 November 1994. *NSA* V3255/3. Videotape, 1 VHS cassette, PAL col. mono.

8. Translation into German by Willy H. Thiem, as *Die Heimkehr*, in: *Theater heute*, No. 11 (1965): 67–76. Reprinted, see *W17 (6)*.

9. Translation into Polish by Adam Tarn, as *Powrot do Dumo*, in: *Dialog*, No. 12 (1965).

10. Translation into French by Eric Kahane, as *Le retour*, in: *L'Avant-scène*

du théâtre, no.378 (1967): [7]-29. Re-published as: *Le retour; traduit de l'anglais par Eric Kahane.* Paris: Editions Gallimard, 1969 (DLC registration 30 May 1969 [DFO 1704]).

11.   Translation into Japanese by Makoto Sugiyama, as *Kikyo*, in: *Konnichi no Eibei Engeki*, Vol. 4. Tokyo: Hakusuisha, 1968.

12.   Translated into Czech, see *W6(14)*.

W25: *The Quiller Memorandum* [screenplay] *(1965):*

Adaptation from a novel by Adam Hall, *The Berlin Memorandum* (London: Collins; New York: Simon and Schuster, 1965). American edition, *The Quiller Memorandum*: see S. Gale, *Sharp Cut*, pp. 431–432.

1.   Material in *PA* Box 48:
     (a) Typescript, headed "Berlin Memorandum," 51 pp. (rectos), plus 3 sides in black pen, and additions in pencil.
     (b) Typescript, 156 pp.
     (c) Printed script of screenplay, 92 pp., with numerous changes in pencil, red ballpoint and black ballpoint; on title page: "THE QUILLER MEMORANDUM | SCREENPLAY BY | HAROLD PINTER | AN IVAN FOXWELL PRODUCTION | to be directed by | MICHAEL ANDERSON | [to right] Pinewood Studios. | Bucks | April 1966".

2.   Film first presented by The Rank Organization, 10 November 1966; directed by Michael Anderson. Screenplay copyright: Ivan Foxwell Productions, Ltd. Copies of film and press-book at BFI. Two variant copies of script at InU-L (156 leaves and 198 leaves).

3.   Published in: *Five Screenplays* (Methuen, 1971).

4.   Film shown on television, BBC2-TV, 20 May 1989; see *Radio Times* (20–26 May 1989): 25, on the same evening as a showing of *The Go-Between*.

W26: *Accident* [screenplay] *(1965–66):*

Adaptation from a novel by Nicholas Mosley, *The Accident* (London: Hodder and Stoughton, 1965; reprinted Elmwood Park, IL: Dalkey Archive Press, 1985).

1.   Manuscripts, etc., in *PA* Box 1:
     (a) Holograph drafts, about 200 pp. in red, black, or blue ballpoint, in three exercise books, first labelled "Accident 7/6", second without cover, third includes some scenes omitted from the film.
     (b) Drafts and working notes, holograph, some loose leaves; also, 6 leaves of typescript, with alternative sequences; one leaf is a photocopy of a page, the original of which had been given to a Mr. Colin Huggett,

of Cookham, Maidenhead, Berks., "As he had requested a page of manuscript | to add to his collection."

(c) Typescript, partial draft, pp. 2–41 (p.1 missing), with duplicates of pp.34–37.

(d) Typescript, duplicated, 4 leaves, labelled "Joseph Losey | 1st August, 1966 | Time lapses and transitions for Sunday at Stephen's sequence"; starts "<u>page 33, scene 143</u>", goes to "scene 338 (New Shot)".

(e) Typescript, full clean draft; 2 leaves, [1]-77 pp.; loose foolscap pages; on title page: "[*red underlining*;] <u>ACCIDENT</u> | A screenplay | [*black underlining*;] <u>Harold Pinter</u>".

2.   Film first presented 9 February 1967 by London Independent Producers (Distribution) Ltd.; directed by Joseph Losey. Copyright for screenplay: London Independent Producers (Distribution) Ltd. "Received the Cannes Film Festival Special Jury Prize" (Peacock, *Harold Pinter and the New British Theatre*, p. 185). Copies of film and press-book at BFI.

3.   Published in: *Five Screenplays* (1971).

4.   Dialogue and continuity release scripts at Cambridge University Library, West Room, shelfmark: 1999:12:58. Dated in catalogue: 1965. No title page. Bound in yellow light card covers, with three clips. On front cover, in red: "'ACCIDENT'| DIALOGUE AND CONTINUITY | RELEASE SCRIPT". Duplicated typescript, text and pagination on rectos only; paginated separately for pages for each of 12 reels; before each reel's pages, a pink leaf with reel number, footage, not included in pagination. Pagination for 12 reels: 11, 13, 11, 11, 11, 8, 9, 5, 10, 14, 8, 9, pp. One handwritten correction noticed: on R7 | 9: "Cow" changed to "car" in black biro.

W27: *The Basement [1962–66]:*

1.   Manuscripts, etc., in *PA* Box 2:

(a) Three quarto leaves, typescript with notes in black ink, headed "THE COMPARTMENT". Verso of third leaf blank. This is prose narrative, with a narrator, "I", an unnamed girl, and a third character, not at first present, named as Kullus (i.e., this is a version of the short story "Kullus").

(b) Three leaves, typescript, carbon copy, part of a letter, for which the first page is missing, about difficulties in writing the screenplay script; includes tentative outline of scenes, characters, plot; ends on p.3: "Exhausted. | Yours,".

(c) Two small leaves, holograph in pencil on first three, fourth blank: series of scenes.

(d) Four loose leaves, foolscap, holograph, written on both sides in blue biro: alternative or additional passages, headed "*The Compartment*".

    (e) Four leaves, typescript with holograph addenda or alternative passages.

    (f) Typescript draft, 19 pp. of screenplay, first three leaves missing.

    (g) Typescript, for screenplay, loose quarto leaves held together with glide clip, headed: "<u>THE COMPARTMENT</u> | Harold Pinter". 23 pp. See S. Gale, *Sharp Cut*, pp. 148–152.

2.   First text, as *The Compartment:* Shooting script for film production (never filmed): New York: Grove (Evergreen) Press, 1962. Bound with screenplay by Eugene Ionesco, *The Hard-Boiled Egg*.
Copies at: BFI (Paper store 791.451.6 HAR), DLC, WAC (submitted 15 May 1964).

3.   Second text, as television play, *The Basement,* broadcast, BBC-2 TV, 20 February 1967, in series "THEATRE 625"; see *Radio Times*, 174: 2258 (16 February 1967): 21 (third of Pinter plays to be presented in this month, with *A Slight Ache* on 6 February and *A Night Out* on 13 February); replay BBC2, 9 July 1967; produced by Michael Bakewell.

4.   Published in: *Tea Party and Other Plays* (Methuen, 1967).

5.   Stage adaptation, Duchess Theatre, premièred in London, 17 September 1970, directed by James Hammerstein; in a double-bill with *Tea Party*. First New York production, this double-bill, Eastside Playhouse, 15 October 1968 (Malcolm Page, *File on Pinter* [1993], p. 75).

6.   A screenplay based on *The Basement*, with the title *Fast Friends*, was written by Richard Lee Marks, with Henry Jaffe, at the Eastside Playhouse; the script in the British Library is in the revised form of 25 October 1970 (accessioned 15 JUL 94), 2 leaves, 94 pp., 1 leaf; on recto of last leaf: "Printed by | SCRIPTS LIMITED | [. . .] | 8 GERrard STREET | LONDON W1 | GERRARD 2087 /8".

7.   Translation into German by Willy H. Thiem, as *Tiefparterre:* see W17 (6).

W28: *Landscape (1967):*

1.   Manuscripts, etc., in *PA* Box 28:
    (a) Holograph notes, in ink, four foolscap leaves; notes relating to bottles and barrels of beer in a pub; in folder inscribed "<u>Landscape</u> | Draft".
    (b) Holograph partial draft, in ballpoint, on three quarto legal pad leaves; Beth's early speeches; in same folder.
    (c) Typescript, first full draft, with alterations and additions in ink or ballpoint; pages numbered [1]-17; it ends with B's recollection of A's banging the gong after Sykes's death: "[typescript] There's not a soul in the house. Not a soul. Except me. I'm not in the army. [added in ink or ballpoint] There's nothing cooked anyway. No steak. No pie.

No joint. No spuds. Bugger all." He took off A's chain, with keys, etc. Much of A's final speech, following, recollecting being on the beach, is re-written in holograph.

(d) Typescript draft, carbon copy; two leaves, 28 pp.; in fawn manila folder.

(e) Typescript draft, with many deletions; in pink folder, inscribed: "LANDSCAPE | FIRST DRAFT | (PHOTOCOPY)"; speech prefixes in ballpoint only, characters still as "A" (woman) and "B" (man).

(f) Typescript draft, carbon copy; in fawn manila folder, inscribed "2nd | Draft"; characters now Beth and Duff; Duff's phrase changed to "Fuck all.".

(g) Typescript draft, another carbon copy of same, but with many holograph alterations, and "pause" added between paragraphs of Beth's speeches; in fawn manila folder, inscribed "2cnd Draft".

(h) Printed stage script, three leaves, [1]-28 pp., one leaf; on title page: "LANDSCAPE | by | Harold Pinter"; bound in black folder, with two split pin clips, and slot in front cover to reveal title; after p.28, a pale blue leaf, with, on the recto: "Printed by | SCRIPTS LIMITED | [printer's device: figure of Mercury, encircled with words] | 8 GERRARD STREET | LONDON W.1. | GERrard 2087/8".

(i) Duplicated typescript, for radio production; two leaves, 29 pp.; noted on the title page: recording 15 April 1968: rehearsals at Stratford 12–15 April, recording 15 April; transmission 25 April 1968, BBC Third Programme, with a repeat on 12 May 1968 [Peggy Ashcroft as Beth, Eric Parker as Duff]. Repeated Radio 3, 12 December 1972. [The manuscript here called "(d)" is reproduced in photofacsimile in *TPR 2001–2002*, pp.38–54, followed by an article by Francis Gillen, '"The Shape of Things": *Landscape* in Draft, Text, and Performance,' pp.[55]-64.]

2. The stage-play was written in 1967–68, for the Royal Shakespeare Company. However, it was deemed unacceptable for public performance by the Lord Chamberlain's Office because of the presence of the phrases "gloomy bugger" and "Fuck all"; Pinter was prepared to replace the second but not the first, considering "bugger" as commonly used "very *mild*," and that "there is no possible or proper alternative to the word bugger, as it is used in the play" (letter to Sir George Farmer, Chairman of the RSC, 27 February 1968; cited in Peacock, pp.98, 100). His refusal meant the play was banned from stage-performance.

3. Presented on radio, BBC Third Programme, in full, 25 April 1968, directed by Guy Vaesen; repeated on Radio 3, 12 December 1972. Copy of typescript at WAC.

4. Published by Pendragon Press, July 1968.

5.   Stage-play, in full, opened as part of a double-bill with *Silence,* 2 July 1969, RSC at the Aldwych, following the abolition of the 1843 Theatre Act, which had given the Lord Chamberlain's Office its power of censorship. Directed by Peter Hall. First New York production, 2 April 1970, Forum Theater, Lincoln Center, with *Silence.*

6.   Published by Methuen, July 1969, in the volume *Landscape and Silence* (with the sketch *Night*).

7.   The theatre program for the first German production of the play (Hamburg, January 1970), mistakenly included the text of a letter from Pinter to its director, Hans Schweikart, in which he said he had come to feel that "the man on the beach," in a situation in the past to which Beth often refers, "is Duff. I think there are elements of Mr. Sykes in her memory of this Duff, which she might be attributing to Duff, but the man remains Duff. I think that Duff detests and is jealous of Mr. Sykes, although I do not believe that Mr. Sykes and Beth were ever lovers." (Cited in Martin Esslin, *The Peopled Wound: The Work of Harold Pinter* [New York: Doubleday, 1970], p.187n.).

8.   Sound recording: Sydney: Australian Broadcasting Commission, 1976. 1 sound cassette, 50 minutes.

9.   First television production, BBC2, 4 February 1983.

10.   Stage-production at Gate Theatre, Dublin, opened 19 May 1994, directed by Harold Pinter (Beth: Penelope Wilton; Duff: Ian Holm). Sound recording of this production, *NSA* V3589/1 0:5'32".

11.   Television production, derived from this stage-production, broadcast BBC2-TV, 21 October 1995.

12.   Translation into German by Renate Esslin and Martin Esslin, as *Landschaft:* see *W9 (11).*

13.   Translation into Spanish, as *Paisaje:* see *W5 (11).*

W29: *Silence (1968):*

1.   Manuscripts, etc., in *PA* Box 28:
      (a) Holograph draft, on quarto or foolscap legal pad leaves; within fawn manila folder; within pink folder inscribed "SILENCE".
      (b) Early draft, partly typescript, partly holograph; within same pink folder.
      (c) Typescript draft, carbon copy, two leaves, 29 pp., with one page of holograph on legal pad leaf; within same pink folder.
      (d) Typescript, carbon copy, with changes and deletions in ballpoint, 27 pp.; headed "SHADOWS"; within blue folder; characters as "GIRL", "MAN 1", and "MAN 2",

(e) Typescript draft, carbon copy, or photocopy; two leaves, 36 pp.; within the pink folder; characters as finally named.

2. Printed rehearsal script, bound photocopy, text on rectos only, [ii], 29 pp., "Printed by | Scripts Limited | 8 Gerrard Street | London W.1"; copy at TxU-HRC.

3. Stage play, premièred 2 July 1969, in double-bill with *Landscape*, RSC at the Aldwych Theatre. New York, 2 April 1970, with *Landscape*, as above.

4. Published in: *Landscape and Silence* (Methuen, 1969).

5. Radio broadcast, BBC Radio 3, 2 August 1970; recording of *Silence* from Harold Pinter Festival, produced by Guy Vaesen. *NSA* NP 1586W. And see *Radio Times* (30 July 1970): 25. Repeated, Radio 3, 19 August 1970; *NSA* T11053/01 (dubbing for *NSA* of loaned BBC tape T33890, 17 September 1993).

6. Sound recording with music by Michael Mantler:
   (a) Published text with music; 59 pp. © Watt Works, Inc. DLC copyright registration, 22 December 1976 (EU42090).
   (b) Recording (1977): Silence: music, an adaptation of the play by Harold Pinter. By Michael Mantler, with Carla Bley (as Ellen, also, piano, organ), Robert Wyatt (as Bates, also, percussion), Kevin Coyne (as Rumsey), Chris Spedding (guitar), and Ron McClure (musician). Watt/ECM Watt/5 LP. Original German pressing (1977): 2313 105. Phonodisc (2s. 12 inch 33 1/3 rpm. rep. stereo.) Gatefold cover. © Watt Works, Inc. DLC copyright registration 15 February 1977 (N41200).

7. Spanish translation, provisionally scheduled for the BBC Latin American (Spanish) Service, 30 January 1972.

8. Translation into Spanish, as *Silencio*: see W5 *(11)*.

9. Translation into German, as *Schweigen*: see W9 *(11)*.

W30: *Night (1969):*

1. Manuscripts, etc., in *PA* Box 28:
   (a) A copy of a typescript headed "Shadows" and "Girl and Man," 27 pp., may relate to the genesis of *Night*.
   (b) Typescript, with re-writings in ballpoint; five quarto pages.
   (c) Typescript draft, carbon copy; two leaves, [1]-12 pp.; headed "<u>NIGHT</u> | Harold Pinter".
   (d) Printed copy; two leaves, [1]-13 pp.; on title page: "NIGHT | Harold Pinter"; in black folder, fastened with two split-pin clips; printer not identified, but similar style as for Scripts Limited.

2. Stage-play, first presented by Alexander H. Cohen Ltd., within an enter-

tainment entitled *Mixed Doubles,* at the Comedy Theatre, 9 April 1969. Performers: Vivien Merchant, Nigel Stock.

3. Published in: *Landscape and Silence* (Methuen, 1969); *Mixed Doubles* (Methuen, 1970).

4. Radio play, broadcast BBC Radio 3, 15 September 1970 (recorded 18 June 1970; TLN 24/DD972): *NSA* NP 1590 C3. Same performers.

5. Translation into Spanish, as *Noche:* see *W5 (11).*

W31: *The Go-Between* [screenplay] *[first draft 1964, second revised script 1969]:*

Adaptation of a novel by L. P. Hartley, *The Go-Between* (London: Hamish Hamilton, 1953)

1. Manuscripts, etc., in *PA* Box 21:
    (a) Folder containing holograph notes on passages and scenes from the novel.
    (b) Holograph notes on scenes and images.
    (c) Draft outline, holograph, 104 pp.
    (d) Short typescript draft, with holograph text on legal pad leaf.
    (e) Holograph notes, 3 pp., legal pad leaves.
    (f) Holograph script outline and notes, on legal pad.
    (g) Typescript draft, with some scenes and lines deleted in ink.
    (h) Two copies of typescript draft, one with alterations.
    (i) Near-final typescript draft of revised script.
    (j) Printed screenplay, bound, two leaves, 118 pp.; on title page: "THE GO-BETWEEN | A screenplay | by | Harold Pinter | based on the novel by L. P. Hartley | [at foot, right:] for Joseph Losey | January 27th 1969". See S. Gale, *Sharp Cut,* pp. 195–199.

2. Screenplay completed 1969, film released in July 1977 as a World Film Services Production presented by EMI/MGM; directed by Joseph Losey. E.M.I. Film Productions, Ltd. 116 minutes, colour. DLC copyright registration 25 May 1971 (LF 88). Released in the USA by Columbia Pictures. It was awarded the Grand Prix (Palme D'Or) at Cannes, May 1971, awards in 1971 from the Society of Film and Television Arts (including Best Film, and Best Screenplay), and a British Film Academy Award. Copies of film and script at BFI. Copy of script at InU-L.

3. Published in: *Five Screenplays* (Methuen, 1971).

4. Film shown on television, BBC2-TV, 20 May 1989; see *Radio Times* (20–26 May 1989): 25 (with *The Quiller Memorandum* following on the same evening).

W32: *Old Times (1970):*

1. Manuscripts, etc., for stage play, in *PA* Box 41:
   (a) Typescript draft with some changes in ink, also some leaves of holograph draft; characters as "A", "B", "C"; lyrics of songs used.
   (b) Typescript draft with some changes in ink.
   (c) Typescript (possibly gestetnered), in black light-card covers, bound with two split pins, with a rectangular slot on the front cover to reveal the title, on the title page.
   (d) Another copy owned by William Baker. On first leaf inscribed in blue biro: "To Frances [Roe: costume designer] | with best wishes | Harold Pinter" and with a purple felt tip pen "Thank you | for 'All that you did!' | Vivien Merchant" with name underlined.

2. Manuscripts, etc., for screenplay, in *PA* Box 42:
   (a) Holograph drafts and notes, on legal pad, for alternative sequences.
   (b) Three typescripts (carbon copies) of screenplay, headed: "OLD TIMES | A screenplay | by | Harold Pinter"; latest copy has at foot, right: "All enquiries should please be sent to | ACTAC (Theatrical and Cinematic) Ltd | 16 Cadogan Lane | London SW1". 139 pp.; divided into shots, with first six dramatising episodes in the past.

3. First stage production, Royal Shakespeare Company at the Aldwych Theatre, 1 June 1971, directed by Peter Hall.

4. Radio presentations: recorded within "Classic 2" series, *ca.* August 1974; another production, broadcast BBC Radio 4, 16 March 1998: *NSA* H9772/1.

5. Television productions: BBC2, broadcast 22 October 1975, directed by Christopher Morahan; BBC2, broadcast 26 October 1991.

6. Sound recording: Sydney: Australian Broadcasting Commission, 1976. In "World Theatre Season" series. 1 sound cassette.

7. Published by Methuen, 17 June 1971.

8. Translation into French: *C'etoit hier; traduit de l'anglais par Eric Kahane.* Paris: Editions Gallimard, 1971 (DLC copyright registration 30 October 1971 [DFO 1860]).

9. Translation into Polish by B. Taborski, as *Dawne Czasy,* in: *Dialog,* No. 2 (1972).

10. Translation into Italian by Romeo de Baggis, in: *Sipario,* 27 (April 1972): 76–85.

11. Translation into Japanese by Tetsuo Kishi, as *Mukashi no Hibi,* in: *Chikuma Sekai Bungaku Taikei,* Vol. 85. Tokyo: Chikuma Shobo, 1974.

W33: *Langrishe, Go Down* [first written as screenplay] *(1970):*

Adaptation of the novel by Aidan Higgins

1.　Manuscripts, etc., in *PA* Box 29:
 (a) Holograph and typescript partial drafts, etc.; within green folder inscribed "Langrishe notes".
 (b) Holograph notes, on scene sequence, etc.; in yellow folder.
 (c) Letter, James Callan Jones to Pinter, 19 October 1976, about television production.
 (d) Camera script for television production, duplicated; two leaves, 155 pp.; first leaf blue, remainder white; on title page leaf: "BBC – 2 | COLOUR ALL FILM [to right] Project No : | 2158 / 2714 | [centred] '"LANGRISHE, GO DOWN" | by | Harold Pinter | Based on the novel by Aidan Higgins | [list of production team] | TO BE FILMED ON LOCATION WEEKS 23 – 27 1978 | in Waterford and Dublin'. [Another copy of this camera script is at InU-L, Pinter mss., Box 46, folder 6.]

2.　On 18 June 1976, Guy Vaesen, at the BBC, tried to initiate the adaptation of the screenplay as a radio drama for the thirtieth anniversary of Radio 3. The rights were held by a Mr. Max Rosenberg of Amicus Productions in the USA.

3.　The film was never made. Instead, the work was produced for BBC television in 1978, directed by David Jones. Broadcast, BBC2, 20 September 1978, as "Play of the Week"; see *Radio Times,* 220: 2862 (16–22 September 1978): 57: write-up, with Pinter, Judi Dench and the director David Jones interviewed by Jack Emery: "Just a simple little love-story?", pp. 80–83, 85 (p.81: photo of Pinter; part of p.82: production still with Judi Dench as Imogen, Jeremy Irons as Otto Beck).

4.　Published in: *The French Lieutenant's Woman and Other Screenplays* (Methuen, 1982).

W34: *The Proust Screenplay: À la Recherche du Temps Perdu [screenplay, not filmed, 1972]:*

Adaptation from the novel by Marcel Proust, in collaboration with Joseph Losey and Barbara Bray.

1.　Manuscripts, etc., in *PA* Box 47:
 (a) Typescript draft, old photocopy, with some interpolated typescript leaves, and some holograph changes in black ballpoint; 221 pp., plus extra pages.
 (b) Typescript, first draft, 11 May 1972, 19 pp., some changes; in envelope marked "10 copies Black Friday".

2. At TxU-HRC, in Pinter Collection, Box 2:
   a) Typescript in French translation by Barbara Bray, at TxU-HRC, Pinter Collection Box 2. Bound copy, 29.3 × 20.8 cm., [ii], 242 pp., typed and paginated on rectos only. On final leaf, p.242, two handwritten directions in French. According to a note by Walter Reuben, Inc, rare book dealer, "This project . . . was intended to be shot in French."
   b) Also in this box, bound typescript of version in English, 33.2 × 20.5 cm., [ii], 221 pp. Dated on final leaf "October 25.72". Pencilled note on first leaf: "Earlier version | Oct 1972 | 24 pages cut". On p.84, small handwritten change to dialogue notes the presence of the film script "dated Oct. 25, 1972 in the Gregory Peck Collection, Margaret Herrick Library, Academy of Motion Pictures Arts and Sciences, Beverly Hills, Calif" (S. Gale, *Sharp Cut*, p. 440, n. 6).

3. Also at TxU-HRC, uncorrected proof copy, 24.7 × 18.8 cm., in off-red paper wrappers.

4. Published as *The Proust Screenplay* (New York: Grove Press, 1977), and (London: Eyre Methuen, 1978).

5. Adaptation for radio by Michael Bakewell, directed by Ned Chaillet, music by Stephen Warbeck, recorded 1995, NSA H6344/1 0:2'35". Noted by Billington as "very successful" (267). Broadcast BBC Radio 3, 31 December 1995.

6. Radio play adaptation (different?) by Pinter, Michael Bakewell, broadcast BBC Radio 3, 11 May 1997. Pinter as narrator. NSA H8807/1. 0:01'36".

7. Radio broadcast talk by Pinter, about the dramatisation of Proust, "Remembering and Forgetting," 1995, NSA H6343/8 2:39':30". Cf. J47.

8. Stage-play adaptation, as *Remembrance of Things Past*, by Di Trevis and Harold Pinter, premièred 23 November 2000, Cottesloe Theatre at the Royal National Theatre, directed by Di Trevis; published by Faber, London, 2000.

W35: *Monologue [1972–73]*:

1. Manuscripts, etc., in *PA* Box 60:
   (a) Holograph partial draft, mainly on small-sized pad leaves, includes some dialogue; in folder labelled "Monologue", that also contains various dramatic fragments.
   (b) Typescript, five copies, two of them headed "REHEARSAL SCRIPT"; in brown manila folder, labelled "MONOLOGUE" (Camera rehearsals 29 December 1972; also in this box, list, in pencil and ink, of 30 names of individuals to whom copies should be sent, including Mick Goldstein, Henry Woolf, etc.).

2.   Television presentation, BBC-2 TV, 13 April 1973; performed by Henry Woolf as "Man", directed by Christopher Morahan; see *Radio Times* (5 April 1973): 55.

3.   Stage-performance by Woolf "a few months later... at the Orange Tree [which] played much better" (Woolf, cited in Billington 237).

4.   Published: *Monologue* (Covent Garden Press, 1973).

5.   Radio presentation, BBC, 1975; performed by Pinter as "Man", produced by Guy Vaesen. NSA M563R TR162 [also listed as M5631R TRK.2].

6.   Sound recording: Sydney: Australian Broadcasting Commission, 1978. 1 sound cassette, 15 minutes.

W36: *No Man's Land (1974):*

1.   Manuscripts, etc., in *PA* Box 38:
     (a) Typescript draft, carbon copy, in black spring-binder [the general's withdrawal is corrected to "von Kleist's"].
     (b) Typescript, possibly gestetnered, bound in blue covers with two split pins.

2.   Manuscripts, etc., in *PA* Box 39 [*No Man's Land* II]:
     (a) Holograph notes and passages of dialogue, on slips and legal pad leaves, with some leaves of typescript interspersed.
     (b) Typescript, "1st Draft", first two pages are old photocopies, characters as A, B, C, D.
     (c) Typescript, "2cnd Draft".
     (d) Typescript, "2cnd Draft", copy.

3.   Copy of Actac typescript, 5 + 53 pp., at TxU-HRC (Pinter Collection, Box 2).

4.   First stage presentation, National Theatre at the Old Vic, 23 April 1975; transferred to Wyndham's Theatre, from 15 July 1975.

5.   Radio presentation, BBC, *ca.* 12 February 1976 (repeated January 1980). Extract from this used in "Sir John Gielgud in his Greatest Roles," compiled by Hallam Tennyson and introduced by Ralph Richardson, Radio 4, 15 April 1979.

6.   Television production, Granada Television Ltd, by Sir Peter Hall, broadcast 3 October 1978.

7.   Sound recording: sound track of this production: *Harold Pinter's No Man's Land*. New York: Caedmon, 1982, two LP sound discs (80 minutes): TRS 369; LCCN 82-740056. Also as *Sir John Gielgud and Sir Ralph Richardson in Harold Pinter's "No Man's Land"*, two sound cassettes, CP 369, same LCCN.

8.   Published 3 April 1975 (Eyre Methuen).

W37: *The Last Tycoon (1975):*

1.   Manuscripts, etc., in *PA* Box 30:
        (a) Typescript draft, 120 pp. plus title leaf, in tan folder, headed "THE
        LAST TYCOON", on title leaf "First Draft Screenplay", dated
        "March 5" [1974].
        (b) Typescript and holograph items, in tan folder headed "NOTES".
        (c) Card, and typescript draft, "2nd version L. T. with notes for 3rd
        revision", dated May 31, 1974, 117 pp. plus title leaf.

2.   Manuscripts, etc., in *PA* Box 31:
        (a) Typescript, with alterations in ink, 91 pp., in grey-green folder,
        headed "THE LAST TYCOON | HP FIRST DRAFT".
        (b) Typescript, 120 pp., some alterations, in tan folder headed "Last
        Tycoon | 1st Draft | Mar 5".
        (c) Typescript, 117 pp., some alterations, in grey-green folder headed
        "Last Tycoon | May 31".
        (d) Typescript, #19, 117 pp., in blue binder headed "THE LAST
        TYCOON", dated July 1, 1974.

3.   Manuscripts, etc., in *PA* Box 32:
        (a) Typescript notes, in green folder headed "TYCOON – THE LAST
        TYCOON | Notes, | 1st January, | 1974 | H. Pinter", 12 pp. and 5 pp.
        For a discussion of this and other drafts, see S. Gale, *Sharp Cut,* p.
        441–442, n. 7.
        (b) Typescript, with some holograph changes, 124 pp., dated 1 November
        1974, in oxblood folder headed "The Last Tycoon".
        (c) Typescript and holograph notes, in oxblood folder headed "The Last
        Tycoon | November 1974 | Notes".

4.   Copy of bound typescript, with holograph annotations in an unidentified
        hand, dated 11 August 1975, and note "rev. 10.16.75" [in effect, 16–23
        October 1975]; 1 leaf, 117 pp.; 33 × 22.1 cm.; now at TxU-HRC, Pinter
        Collection, Box 1 [Reg. no. 13540].

5.   Copy of unmarked film script, at InU-L.

6.   Film released 1977. Directed by Elia Kazan.

7.   Published in: *The French Lieutenant's Woman and Other Screenplays*
        (Methuen, 1982).

8.   Film shown on television, BBC2-TV, 10 June 1989; see *Radio Times*
        (10–16 June 1989): 27.

W38: *The Coast* [short story] *(1975):*

1.　　In *PA* Box 60, single leaf: translation, "La Côte," by Eric Kahane.

2.　　Published in *P&P* (1978); see *14.*

W39: *Problem* [short story] *(1976):*

1.　　Manuscripts, etc., in *PA* Box 60:
　　　(a) Typescript, within same blue folder as for *Lola*.
　　　(b) Also within this folder, copy of proof, probably from the *Transatlantic Review*.

2.　　Published in *P&P* (1978); see *14.*

W40: *Lola* [short story] *(1977):*

1.　　Manuscripts, etc., in *PA* Box 60:
　　　(a) Typescript drafts, within blue folder.
　　　(b) Also in this folder, copy of proof, for publication in *The New Review*.

2.　　Published in *P&P* (1978); see *14.*

W41: *Betrayal (1978):*

1.　　Manuscripts, etc., in *PA* Box 3 ["Betrayal I"]:
　　　(a) Holograph notes and passages of dialogue, in blue biro, on loose legal pad leaves; names of characters vary, from A, B, and C, to Susan, Jack, and Chris, to Judith, Patrick, and Stephen, to Emma, Robert, and Jerry; one section has E and J (for Emma and Jerry); one leaf, typescript, with alterations in ink, has details of characters; in blue folder inscribed "Torcello | Notes".
　　　(b) Single leaf, typescript, lists of characters [Emma, Stephen, Patrick] and of 9 sequences [1977 back to 1968]; in same folder.
　　　(c) Typescript of dialogue-passages and notes, with holograph changes [characters: Lucy, Jerry, Nick], six leaves, with first leaf numbered "2"; also, some loose leaves, of dialogue-passages, with characters as Lucy, Jerry, Robert; in same folder.
　　　(d) Typescript draft, with some leaves photocopies, in blue folder inscribed "Torcello | 1ˢᵗ Draft | copy".
　　　(e) Typescript draft, with, on title page: "A White Wedding | by | Harold Pinter | Second Draft"; in dark pink folder inscribed "Torcello / 1ˢᵗ Draft" [i.e., the contents differ from the inscription; the characters are Emma, Jerry, Robert].
　　　(f) Typescript, partial draft, loose quarto leaves, odd pages, numbered; on title page: "Wedding Ring | by | Harold Pinter | Second Draft"; in "Torcello | Notes" folder.

(g) Typescript, draft entitled "Betrayal"; some leaves only [pp.1, 99, 103G, 104, 105, 109–111], A4 size, held together with glide-clip, in brown folder.

(h) Holograph list of 9 sequences [1974–1968], dated "24.1.78", headed "Betrayal"; in "Torcello | Notes" folder.

(i) Typescript, photocopy, 4 pp., "TEATR POWSZECHNY, WARSAW | – Programme Notebook | Translation of entries"; in "Torcello | Notes" folder.

(j) Note on timing, on single leaf, dated "24.1.78", all in Pinter holograph.

2. Manuscripts, etc., in *PA* Box 4 ["Betrayal II"]:

(a) Typescript, two carbon copies, leaves headed "<u>BETRAYAL: NOTES</u>"; one copy has notes in black ink; another dated "19 January 1981".

(b) Typescript, parts of draft, four A4 leaves, blue paper, held together with a glide-clip; small slip at the front, with [typed]: "I enclose a set of the new pages for Mr | Pinter's script to be inserted. | Thanks. | <u>With the Compliments of</u> | HORIZON PICTURES (GB) LIMITED".

(c) Holograph draft, in ink, on legal pad leaves, headed "<u>Betrayal</u>"; some pages numbered.

(d) Typescript draft, on A4 leaves held together with a glide-clip; headed: "<u>BETRAYAL</u>".

(e) Typescript notes, carbon copy.

(f) Typescript draft, carbon copy, 125 pp.; on title page: "BETRAYAL" | a screenplay | by | Harold Pinter | First Draft [crossed through in ballpoint, "Final Draft" written above; below, in pencil "with additions of", crossed through in ballpoint] | [at right] 21 March 1981 [crossed through in ballpoint; "20 December 1981" written below in ballpoint, and crossed through; "2 March 1982" written above, in ballpoint"]; the text is preceded with a page giving characters, ages of their children, in the years covered by the nine scenes.

(g) Typescript, some extra pages, with substituted material.

3. Stage-play first presented 15 November 1978, National Theatre (Lyttleton Theatre), directed by Peter Hall.

4. Film released in 1983, directed by David Jones; videotape, 1 VHS cassette. PAL col. mono. *NSA* V2240/02. Pinter received Oscar nomination for best screenplay, 1983. Copy of press-book at BFI.

5. Film shown on television, BBC TV2, 13 May 1989; see *Radio Times* (13–19 May 1989): 21.

6. Radio presentation, BBC Radio 3, 9 October 1990, directed by Ned Chaillet, Pinter in role of Robert. Recorded at start of October 1990. *NSA* B7392/01 0:09':55.

7.   Sound-recording of stage-performance: Royal National Theatre: Lyttleton Theatre, 23 November 1998. *NSA* H11098.

8.   Published by Eyre Methuen, 16 November 1978 (stage version).

Note: For discussion of the various drafts and "one sheet of carbon paper with the title 'Robert'" at the *PA*, see S. Gale, *Sharp Cut*, pp. 445–446.

W42: *The French Lieutenant's Woman* [screenplay] *(1970–1980):*

Adaptation of novel by John Fowles

1.   Manuscripts, etc., in *PA* Box 16:
      (a) Typescript draft, with some pencil alterations, 59 pp., dated December 27 [1978], in green folder, headed "Remaining Sheets | First Draft | Top Copy".
      (b) Similar draft, carbon copy, with some alterations in ink, 58 pp., in green folder, headed similar but "Carbon".
      (c) Typescript, carbon copy, 180 pp., in brown folder, headed "FLW No. 3, April 26" [1979], some handwritten alterations.
      (d) Typescript draft, carbon, 136 pp., in pink folder headed "French Lieutenant's Woman | FIRST DRAFT".
      (e) Typescript, final draft, in blue folder headed "Film"; on title leaf: date June 28, 1979, "Parlon Productions, | 11 Charlton Gardens, | England's Lane, | London N.W.3. 4YB".

2.   Manuscripts, etc., in *PA* Box 17:
      (a) Holograph drafts and notes, 11 pp., in green folder labelled "F.L.W. Notes".
      (b) Holograph drafts and notes, in green folder labelled "CORREC-TIONS. FLW".
      (c) Holograph and typescript drafts and notes (some within separate folders) within large green folder, headed "PRESENT | Carbon copy".

3.   Manuscripts, etc., in *PA* Box 18:
      (a) Typescript draft, 28 pp., and various loose pages.
      (b) Typed and holograph, 7 pp., clipped, script alterations.
      (c) Typed and holograph, 6 pp., script with alterations.
      (d) Typed text, three photocopies, 13 pp., headed "HORS D'OEUVRE" (John Fowles, July 1980), discusses adaptations.
      (e) Holograph, 5 pp., and typescript, 10 pp., in green folder, headed "Old Half Pages".
      (f) Typescript of near-final shooting script, with holograph alterations, headed "FRENCH LIEUTENANT'S WOMAN – SAVINGS".

4.   Manuscripts, etc., in *PA* Box 19:
      (a) Typescript draft, photocopy, 162 pp., in brown folder labelled "F.L.W.".

(b) Typescript draft, with some holograph changes, in tan folder headed "The draft I typed from | FLW | 219 pp. | & my corrections | No. 4 | & correctioned pages | June '79", title page dated June 17, 1979.

(c) Typescript draft, 51 pp., in tan folder headed "FLW | RETYPES FROM FINAL VERSION".

(d) Typescript and holograph, six items, in green folder headed "Sequences".

(e) 8 pp., loose, script alterations and notes.

(f) "New Continuity", 4 pp., stapled.

5. Manuscripts, etc., in *PA* Box 20:

(a) "The French Lieutenant's Woman An Appreciation of the Film" by Donald Spots, typescript, 16 pp.

(b) Two letters and release form for video cassette, 1982–83.

(c) Clipped: "Correspondence", between 29 October 1980 and 24 November 1981.

(d) Typescript draft, with some changes in ink, in green folder, headed "FLW | No.4 | June 1979 | This is the uncorrected version – | without emendations | ie: for pages", 159 pp. with cover.

(e) Typescript draft, with some holograph alterations, in green folder, headed "FLW | No. 4 | June 27, 1979", 201 pp.

6. Later typescript draft, text unmarked, dated "November 3, 1979 Revisions April 22 1980"; at foot of title page: "Parlon Productions | 2 Lower James Street, | Golden Square, | London, W1R 3PN"; 1 leaf, 163 leaves; photocopy at TxU-HRC, Pinter Collection Folder 1.

7. Film released 1981. Directed by Karel Reisz. Copy of script at BFI.

8. Published as: *The Screenplay of The French Lieutenant's Woman* (Jonathan Cape, in association with Eyre Methuen, 1981); also in: *The French Lieutenant's Woman and Other Screenplays* (Methuen, 1982).

9. Film shown on television, BBC2-TV, 27 May 1989; see *Radio Times* (27 May-2 June 1989): 39.

W43: *Family Voices (1980):*

1. Manuscripts, etc., in *PA* Box 15:

(a) Typescript draft, two copies, both with holograph changes, not all identical in both copies.

(b) Typescript draft, three copies, clean copies; 23 pp.; two copies loose, in manila folders, one copy bound in grey-black binder with metal spring-clip.

(c) Typescript of radio play, gestetnered; on title page: "BRITAIN'S NATIONAL THEATRE | in | FAMILY VOICES | [underlined in red pencil or crayon;] A new play by Harold Pinter | Rehearsal: Thursday 8th January 1981 | Reh /Record: Friday 9th January 1981 | Transmission: Radio 3 Thursday 22nd January 1981 | Cast [listed] | Directed by Peter Hall | Radio production by John Tydeman | <u>THIS BROADCAST MATERIAL IS THE COPYRIGHT OF THE AUTHOR.</u> | <u>THIS TRANSCRIPT MAY NOT BE COPIED OR SOLD.</u>"; this copy has holograph markings in ink, as directions for the actors and director; on the title page, at top right, in holograph: "HP".

(d) Typescript, stapled carbon copy, on title page: "<u>Family Voices</u> | a play | by | <u>Harold Pinter</u>"; on recto of preceding leaf: "Property of | ACTAC (Theatrical & Cinematic) Ltd | 16 Cadogan Lane | London SW1X 9EA | 01-235 2797".

(e) In folder, letters between Pinter and John Tydeman: Pinter to Tydeman (carbon copy), 14 January 1981 (regrets *Radio Times* identified characters as Father, Mother, Son, rather than as "Voice 1", "Voice 2", and "Voice 3"); Pinter to Tydeman (carbon copy), 15 January; Tydeman to Pinter, 6 February.

2.   Radio play, broadcast BBC2, 22 January 1981; NSA NP4631 BW BD1. National Theatre cast, directed by Peter Hall (Voice 2: Peggy Ashcroft). Recorded 9 January 1981.

3.   Stage play ("platform performance"), National Theatre, opened 13 February 1981. Subsequently presented 14 October 1982 within a triple-bill, *Other Places,* with *A Kind of Alaska* and *Victoria Station,* Cottesloe Theatre, National Theatre, directed by Peter Hall.

4.   Published in: *Family Voices* (Next Editions, 1981); *Other Places* (Methuen, 1982).

W44: *Victoria Station (1982):*

1.   Manuscripts in *PA* Box 60:
(a) Holograph in ballpoint, early partial draft, three leaves; in this draft, the driver, "G3", knows he's in Pont Street, and is being asked to pick up passengers from Platform 15, off the 4.54 from Hove, "Lady and gentleman. Name of Jones."; within folder "FRAGMENTS | – BITS AND PIECES".

2.   Manuscripts, etc., in *PA* Box 58:
(a) Holograph draft, legal pad; characters as "A" [Controller], "B" [Driver].
(b) Typescript draft, with many changes in ink; 19 pp.; at end, in ink: "Light out in office | Silence | Light out in car"; characters as "MAN" and "DRIVER".
(c) Typescript, carbon copies, with changes in pencil; 2 leaves, 20 pp.; labelled on first page in ink "1ˢᵗ Draft".

(d) Typescript, same, with changes in ink; e.g., on second leaf, "Man in office" – "Man" crossed through, "Controller" substituted; but this change not made in speech prefixes.

(e) Typescript, later draft; 2 leaves, 21 pp.; "CONTROLLER" substituted in speech prefixes.

3. Stage play, first presented 14 October 1982, as part of a triple-bill, *Other Places*, with *Family Voices* and *A Kind of Alaska*, Cottesloe Theatre, National Theatre, directed by Peter Hall. Presented 13 March 1984, Lyric Theatre Studio, Hammersmith, in a double-bill with *One for the Road*, both directed by Harold Pinter. Presented 7 March 1985, in a triple-bill, with *A Kind of Alaska* and *One for the Road*, Duchess Theatre, directed by Kenneth Ives.

4. Published in: *Other Places* (Methuen, 1982).

5. First New York production, 3 April 1984, Manhattan Theatre Club, within *Other Places*, with *One for the Road* and *Victoria Station*, directed by Alan Schneider.

6. Radio play, BBC Radio 4, 16 March 1998: *NSA* H9772/2.

W45: *A Kind of Alaska (1982):*

1. Manuscripts, etc., in *PA* Box 27:
    (a) Holograph drafts, legal pad. Speech prefixes A, B, change partway through to Pauline, Deborah; separate group of pages numbered "19/" etc., W, M (Woman, Man), then P, D.
    (b) Typescript draft, with some changes in biro; two leaves, 38 pp.
    (c) Typescript draft, carbon copy; two leaves, 43 pp.
    (d) Typescript, as for (c), with extra leaf headed "Note to A KIND OF ALASKA".
    (e) Typescript partial draft, with many changes in holograph, in ink; within green folder; with note "This play was stimulated by the memory of O. Sacks 'Awakenings'".
    (f) Television script, 1984, duplicated typescript, on yellow paper; two leaves, 45 pp.; headed on first leaf: "CAMERA SCRIPT PROD. NO 4277 | VTR. NO. 4277/84 | "A KIND OF ALASKA" | BY | HAROLD PINTER | [at foot:] Copyright Central Independent Television plc, 1984 | PRODUCER LYNN HORSFOLD | DIRECTOR KENNETH IVES | CAST | DEBORAH – – – – DOROTHY TUTIN | HORNBY – – – – PAUL SCOFIELD | PAULINE – – – – SUSAN ENGEL | [short rule] | Schedule – entire filming on WED / THUR. 18/19th, JULY".

2. Stage play, first presented 14 October 1982, as part of a triple-bill, *Other*

Places, with *Family Voices* and *Victoria Station,* at the Cottesloe Theatre, National Theatre, directed by Peter Hall. Subsequently presented 7 March 1985, within *Other Places,* with *Victoria Station* and *One for the Road,* Duchess Theatre, directed by Kenneth Ives.

3.   Published in: *Other Places* (Methuen, 1982).

4.   First New York production, as for *Victoria Station.*

5.   Television production, Central Television, broadcast 16 December 1984, directed by Kenneth Ives.

6.   Sound recording: Sydney: Australian Broadcasting Commission Radio, 1992. In "International Playhouse" series, production directed by Walter Acoste. One sound cassette, 40 minutes.

W46: *Victory* [unproduced but published screenplay] *(1982):*

Adaptation from Joseph Conrad's novel, *Victory,* in collaboration with Richard Lester. See S. Gale, *Sharp Cut,* pp. 273–288.

1.   Manuscripts, etc., in *PA* Box 59:
     a) Holograph notes and text on legal pad, with some typescript pages.
     b) Chapter-breakdowns of Conrad's novel, 2 copies in typescript.
     c) Photocopies of photos of South American townscapes.
     d) Typescript headed "First Draft 11 June 1982", 129 pp., with some holograph changes in ink.
     e) Carbon copy of typescript, 2 leaves, 146 pp.; on recto of cover leaf: "VICTORY | a screenplay | by | Harold Pinter | based on the novel by | Joseph Conrad | 24 November 1982".
     f) Copies of several letters to Richard Lester: see S. Gale, *Sharp Cut,* pp. 393–395.

2.   Screenplay "rejected by Universal" (Billington 290).

3.   Published in: *The Comfort of Strangers and Other Screenplays* (1990), see B7.

W47: *Precisely (1983):*

1.   Manuscripts, etc., in *PA* Box 60:
     (a) Various drafts, in ink or typescript, in yellow folder; also in this folder, letters to and from Susannah York, dated 11 and 17 March 1983, concerning the Peace Movement's efforts, and schedule "Life: A Theatrical Show for Nuclear Disarmament," 2 pp., for "Options" programme, includes details of *Precisely.*
     (b) Typescript, single leaf, two copies, within folder labelled "Precisely",

that also contains other items.

2.   Performed as a sketch within the anti-nuclear-weaponry show, *The Big One,* in the Apollo Victoria Theatre, 19 December 1983.

3.   Published in: *The Big One* (Methuen, 1984); see *A44.*

W48: *One for the Road (1983–84):*

1.   Manuscripts, etc., in *PA* Box 43:
      (a) Holograph script, legal pad, characters as A [the interrogater, Nicholas], B [the prisoner, Victor], C [wife, Gila], D [boy, Nicky].
      (b) Typescript, clean, top copy, 26 pp. (rectos only), dated January 1984; within folder with spring-clip. Names of characters as Roberts [Nicholas], Marsh [Victor], Kathy [Gila], Boy [Nicky].
      (c) Typescript, top copy, with holograph changes in pencil, 24 rectos.

2.   Stage play, first presented 13 March 1984, Lyric Theatre Studio, Hammersmith, in a double-bill with *Victoria Station,* both directed by Harold Pinter. Subsequently presented as part of the triple-bill *Other Places,* with *Victoria Station* and *A Kind of Alaska,* opened 7 March 1985, at the Duchess Theatre, directed by Kenneth Ives.

3.   Published as *One for the Road* (Methuen, 1984).

4.   Television production, broadcast BBC2-TV, 25 July 1985; see *Radio Times,* 247: 3218 (20–26 July 1985): 63. Write-up by Michael Billington, "Pauses for Pinter," on p.9.

W49: *Turtle Diary* [screenplay] *(1984–85):*

Adaptation from the novel by Russell Hoban

1.   Manuscripts, etc., in *PA* Box 57:
      (a) Typed dialogue changes, 4 pp., in brown folder.
      (b) Correspondence with Russell Hoban, 12 April 1984.
      (c) Typed outline of action for scenes, 10 pp., stapled.
      (d) Holograph notes, etc., three copies of (c), within pink folder.
      (e) Holograph notes, passages of dialogue, and drafts for various scenes, on legal pad leaves, variously dated.
      (f) Typescript, noted as "FIRST DRAFT January 84", 141 pp., some alterations in pencil.

2.   Film went into production, for UBA (United British Artists), and was released, 1985. Directed by John Irvin. See S. Gale, *Sharp Cut,* p. 289.

3.   Published in: *The Comfort of Strangers and Other Screenplays* (Faber, 1990).

W50: *Reunion* [screenplay] *(1987–88):*

Adapted from novel by Fred Uhlman, *No Coward Soul*

1. Manuscripts, etc., in *PA* Box 49:
    (a) "Konrad's Letter", 74 pp., typed, explaining his actions.
    (b) Holograph notes, with outlines of early scenes, 12 pp., on legal pad and notebook paper, dated June 14.
    (c) Random holograph notes, 6 pp., dated June 4.
    (d) Two loose leaves, pink paper, holograph dialogue for one scene.
    (e) Two leaves, clipped, headed "Structure".
    (f) Typescript notes on German history since 1932.
    (g) Holograph notes of alterations, 10 pp., legal pad leaves.
    (h) Holograph notes for several scenes, 3 pp., dated Nov. 22.
    (i) Typescript notes, 8 pp., correspond to (b).
    (j) Typed outline of scenes, 11 pp., dated 21 September 1987.
    (k) Holograph passage on dialogue on three cards.
    (l) Typescript, 86 pp., in plastic envelope, corrected Sept. 1, 1987.
    (m) Further groups of leaves, typescript or holograph, with notes or passages of dialogue, dated through to July 11.

2. Manuscripts, etc., in *PA* Box 50:
    (a) Typescript of novel by Fred Uhlman, "NO COWARD SOUL | The Diary of Konradin von Hohenfels | London | 1961".
    (b) Typescript draft, inscribed "First Draft | September 2, 1987"; 2 leaves, 103 pp.
    (c) Memo, typed, about names, and sundry letters, notes, and short drafts of scenes.
    (d) Holograph notes and alternative passages, on legal pad leaves.
    (e) Memorandum, typed, about German names that should not be used, and suggested alternatives.
    (f) Letter to Pinter from "Jerry", February 7, 1988, relating to the use of a coin as a vehicle of a symbolic "reunion".
    (g) Typescript draft, 99 pp. (with interpolated leaf after title page: "2–1"); title page typed "Second Draft Screenplay | by | Harold Pinter | October 13, 1987"; pp. 2–97 headed "Additional Ending", dated 13 Oct. 1987 (latter occupies 3 typed sides).
    (h) Typescript draft, with some holograph markings in biro; 4–1 to 4–106 pp, with various additional pages, including unpaginated leaf at end, headed "Alternative Ending | (Both endings to be shot)"; on title page: "REUNION | a screenplay | by | Harold Pinter | adapted from the novel by | Fred Uhlman | February 22, 1988"; bound in spiral binder, with clear plastic front cover, light white card back cover.

3. Film directed by Jerry Schatzberg; released in 1990.

4.   Published in: *The Comfort of Strangers and Other Plays* (Faber, 1990); ©
      1989 Les Films Ariane.

W51: *The Heat of the Day* [screenplay for television] *(1988):*

1.   Manuscripts, etc., in *PA* Box 23:
      a) Typescript, 1 leaf, 149 pp., within spiral-bound covers (clear plastic
          front, white card back), with, on recto of first leaf: "THE HEAT OF
          THE DAY | by | Harold Pinter | adapted from the novel by | Elizabeth
          Bowen | 26 April 1988"; some holograph changes.
      b) Typescript, 1 leaf, 152 pp., within plastic folder; title leaf as above,
          but dated "1 July 1988".
      c) Granada Television camera script, duplicated typescript, on blue
          paper, held together with a split pin; 16 leaves, 188 pp.; rehearsals
          scheduled "4–14 Oct 88", filming "17 Oct – 6 Dec 88"; unmarked copy,
          except for "FINAL" on title leaf; directed by Christopher Morahan.

2.   First broadcast, Granada Television, 30 December 1989: PBS Masterpiece
      Theatre, 30 September 1990. See S. Gale, *Sharp Cut*, p. 373.

3.   Published 1989, by Faber and Faber: see *B6*.

W52: *Mountain Language (1988):*

1.   Manuscripts, etc., in *PA* Box 36:
      (a) Holograph draft, legal pad.
      (b) Typescript draft, unpaginated, with many changes in ink, or in
           pencil.
      (c) Typescript draft, with changes in ink, 16 pp.
      (d) Typescript, four copies; two leaves, 17 pp.; bound in spring-binders
           with clear plastic covers; several copies have changes in ink or pencil;
           one copy has in ink on title page "HP, Reading – 22 June".
      (e) Television production camera script, duplicated typescript on yellow
           paper; on first page: "[to left:] BBC-2 SPECIAL | CAMERA SCRIPT
           | [to centre:] [double-underlined:] MOUNTAIN LANGUAGE |
           WRITTEN AND DIRECTED | by | [double-underlined:] HAROLD
           PINTER | PRODUCER LOUIS MARKS | MONDAY NOVEMBER
           4TH, 1988 | rehearse/record" [the ordering of pages indicates the
           scenes were not shot in the final order].
      (f) Faber page proofs, two sets, one with changes, dated 14 June 1988.

2.   Stage play, first presented 20 October 1988, National Theatre (Lyttleton
      Theatre), directed by Harold Pinter.

3.   Published in *Times Literary Supplement* (7–13 October 1988); as
      Mountain Language (Faber and Faber, 10 October 1988).

4.   Stage play, recorded, 2 November 1988, enactment by Pinter, with A. Fraser, R. Harwood, International PEN English Centre Studio; performance followed by questions from the floor. *NSA* C125/105 BD 1.

5.   Television production, broadcast BBC-TV2, 11 December 1988, directed by Harold Pinter. *NSA* 2381/03: V258/03 1:55'35".

W53: *The Handmaid's Tale* [screenplay] *(1987–89):*

Adapted from a novel by Margaret Atwood

1.   Manuscripts in *PA* Box 62:
      (a) Script, 12 December 1986.
      (b) Script, 2 February 1989.
      (c) Script, undated.

2.   Manuscripts, etc., in *PA* Box 63:
      (a) Extensive file of press-cuttings.
      (b) Five rough scene outline fragments, dated July 3, September 7, September 29, January 14, February 7.

3.   Manuscripts, etc., in *PA* Box 64:
      (a) Early scene outline.
      (b) "Skeleton," October 1.
      (c) Outline, October 8, 1986, similar to (b).
      (d) Typescript draft labelled "Early", incomplete.
      (e) Draft, 17 October 1986.
      (f) Typescript, "Second Draft, Nov. 17, 1986".

4.   Pinter began work on this project in 1986; but when Karel Reisz was replaced by Volker Schlöndorff as director, Pinter gave the latter freedom to make whatever changes he wished, and so many were made that Pinter has not published the screenplay, not considering it authentically his own work (Billington 304). See also S. Gale, *Sharp Cut*, pp. 316–321.

5.   Film released in the USA by Cinecom Entertainment Group, in association with Cinetudes Film Production and Odyssey/Cinecom International. Directed by Volker Schlöndorff, produced by Daniel Wilson.

6.   Film released on video, 1990: New York: HBO Video. ISBN 1559831963. One video cassette, VHS (109 minutes).

W54: *The Comfort of Strangers* [screenplay] *(1989):*

Adapted from the novel by Ian McEwan

1.   Manuscripts, etc., in *PA* Box 8:
      (a) Holograph notes and fragments of dialogue, on note cards and yellow legal pad, in red folder, labelled "Dec. 21" [1988].

(b) Five series of notes and partial drafts on legal pads, dated Jan. 3, Jan. 17, undated, Feb. 19, Feb. 25.

(c) Typescript draft, near completion, with some cuts, undated. See S. Gale, *Sharp Cut*, p. 452.

(d) Bound script, dated 14 March 1989.

(e) Holograph drafts, apparently of revisions for final version, on legal pad, dated April 9.

2. Manuscripts, etc., in *PA* Box 9 ["The Comfort of Strangers II"]:

(a) Holograph draft, photocopy, headed "Jan 3" [1989]; unpaginated, shots numbered 1–98.

(b) Typescript draft, labelled 7 February 1989, with additional holograph text on legal pad leaves.

(c) Typescript draft, dated February 9.

(d) Typescript draft, undated, 103 pp.

(e) Typescript draft, undated, 136 pp.

(f) Typescript of a new, unused scene.

3. Manuscripts, etc., in *PA* Box 10 ["The Comfort of Strangers III"]:

(a) Bound typescript dated 24 April 1989.

(b) Typescript draft, final version, dated July 17, 1989.

(c) File of letters between Pinter and the director, Paul Schrader, including several emended typescript pages, also holograph proof-correcting notes on two legal pad leaves.

4. Film released 1990, directed by Paul Schrader: Skouras Pictures.

5. Published in: *The Comfort of Strangers and Other Screenplays* (Faber, 1990).

W55: *The Remains of the Day* [screenplay, mainly not used, not published] *(1990):*

1. Screenplay being worked on in 1990, as an adaptation of Kazuo Ishiguro's novel; Pinter had bought an option, which he sold on to Mike Nichols; however, Columbia acquired the rights, and its producers Ismail Merchant and James Ivory engaged Ruth Jawer Jhabvala to write the script, in which however "seven or eight scenes" from Pinter's script were retained, although he declined to have his name among the credits (Billington 324). See also S. Gale, *Sharp Cut*, pp. 367–368.

2. Manuscripts, etc., in *PA* Box 51:

(a) Holograph draft, 4 legal pads, 3 loose leaves.

(b) Typescript draft; one leaf, 38 pp.

(c) Typescript draft; one leaf, 88 pp., with extra leaves at front, numbered 1A–1D; in blue folder, inscribed "First Draft Screenplay", dated 25.1.1990.

(d) Typescript, same, with numerous holograph changes in red or blue ballpoint, and pencil.

(e) Typescript draft, in binder, with holograph alterations, and additions on yellow legal pad leaves; 137 pp.; title page: "Draft Screen play | 18 October 1990".

(f) Typescript draft; dated 29 October 1990; in spiral binder.

(g) Typescript draft, 165 pp. + 3 pp., in binder; "Revised 24 January 1991".

W56: *The New World Order [sketch] (1991):*

1.   Manuscripts, etc., in *PA* Box 36:
      (a) Draft in typescript and holograph [latter on legal pad leaves].
      (b) Photocopy of same.
      (c) Typescript draft, with changes in ink and pencil.
      (d) Typescript, two copies; 1 leaf, 8 pp.; on title page: "THE NEW WORLD ORDER | A sketch | by | Harold Pinter".

2.   First public presentation, April 1991, at the Pinter symposium at Ohio State University, Columbus, Ohio.

3.   Stage play, presented 20 July 1991, Royal Court Theatre Upstairs, directed by Harold Pinter.

4.   Published in: *Granta,* 37 (Autumn 1991):251–254. Cf *A48b.*

W57: *The Trial (1989–92):*

Adapted from novel by Franz Kafka

1.   Manuscripts, etc., in *PA* Box 54:
      (a) Holograph script, dated July 26, on three legal pads.
      (b) Partial draft.
      (c) Full typed filmscript, with some corrections in pen.

2.   Manuscripts, etc., in *PA* Box 55:
      (a) Screenplay dated 21 August.
      (b) Three copies of screenplay dated 29 August, one of them including cards with notes for corrections.
      (c) Galley proofs for single-volume edition, with handwritten note by Pinter.

3.   Manuscript in *PA* Box 56:
      (a) Complete script, in plastic binding, within folded manila envelope. See S. Gale, *Sharp Cut,* pp. 452–453.

4.   Commissioned 1989, for the director Istvan Szabo; but in 1992 the rights came to BBC Films, with Louis Marks as producer, and David Jones as

eventual director; both participated intimately with Pinter in the decisions that shaped the film. Marks had been debating them with Pinter since 1984.

5. The film was made by BBC Films and Europanda Entertainment B.V. in 1992. Copy of script at BFI.

6. For the development of this film-project, see Louis Marks, "Producing *The Trial:* A Personal Memoir," in *The Films of Harold Pinter,* edited by Steven H. Gale (Albany, NY: State University of New York Press, 2001), pp. 109–121, and see Gale, *Sharp Cut,* pp. 337–349.

W58: *Party Time (1992):*

1. Manuscripts, etc., of stageplay and television screenplay, in *PA* Box 44:
    (a) Holograph drafts, legal pad.
    (b) Typescript draft, with changes in ink, noted on first leaf as "1st Draft" (characters still as "A", "B", etc).
    (c) Typescript, 20 pp., noted on first leaf as "2nd Draft", with changes in ink (characters named);
    (d) Typescript draft, 1 leaf, 39 pp., with holograph changes.
    (e) Typescript draft, 2 leaves, 40 pp., on front "Theatre", underlined twice, with slip "PARTY TIME X12".
    (f) Typescript, several duplicated copies, bound with spiral binder and clear plastic covers, two leaves, 44 pp.; on title page leaf: "PARTY TIME | a play | by | HAROLD PINTER | [at foot, left:] Harold Pinter | c/o Judy Daish Associates | 83 Eastbourne Mews | London W2".
    (g) Duplicated television screenplay script: "PICTURE BASE INTER-NATIONAL | CAMERA SCRIPT "PARTY TIME" | BY | HAROLD PINTER | 13–22 Aug 1992 | Record – 23–25 Aug 92 | TRANSMIS-SION: T. B. A." Mainly on blue paper, with three leaves detailing recording order in pink. One leaf, a-b, three leaves, 8–49 pp., re-numbered in black biro 1–49 (with numbers in circles). Here, pages 36–41 are displaced to the end.
    (h) Typescript, several duplicated copies, bound with spiral binder and clear plastic covers, four leaves, 47 pp.; on title page leaf: "PARTY TIME | a screenplay | by | HAROLD PINTER | [at foot, left:] Harold Pinter | c/o Judy Daish Associates | 83 Eastbourne Mews | London W2 | [at foot, right:] | Picture Base International | 13/14 Golden Square | London W1". These copies have: on the second leaf, recto: "*Party Time* first performed by Almeida Theatre Company on 31 October 1991 at the Almeida Theatre, London"; on the third leaf, recto: "*Party Time* was adapted by the author for television in 1992 and was trans-mitted on November 17th of that year. This is the version published here. The television production was produced by Michael Custance, designed by Grant Hicks and directed by Harold Pinter."

2.   First rehearsed reading, April 1991, at the Pinter symposium at Ohio State University, Columbus, Ohio.

3.   Stage play, first presented 31 October 1991, Almeida Theatre, in a double bill with *Mountain Language,* both directed by Harold Pinter.

4.   Stage play published 4 November 1991; television version published 10 April 1994.

5.   Television film broadcast BBC Channel 4, 17 November 1992, directed by Harold Pinter; see *Radio Times* (14–20 November 1992): 83.

W59: *Moonlight (1992–93):*

1.   Manuscripts, etc., in *PA* Box 34 ("Moonlight I"):
    (a) Holograph partial drafts, on cards or on paper slips (varying from 12.2 × 7.3 cm. to 12.8 × 7.6 cm.), and also on legal pad.
    (b) Holograph, legal pad, headed "kellaway dialogue"; characters as A, B.
    (c) Typescript, top copy, some changes in ink, other changes on interleaved slips in ink; page 1 numbered "24", and sequence follows to page "42".
    (d) Typescript, photocopy, with many changes in black ink; added in ink on first page: "[within single-rule box:] FIRST | DRAFT"; 48 pp. (pages 1–3 are numbered in type "24", "25", "26"; these numbers are crossed through in ink, and "<u>1</u>", "<u>2</u>", "<u>3</u>" added in ink; thereafter numbered correctly, through to p.48).
    (e) Typescript, with some changes in ink; two leaves, 72 pp.; on recto of first leaf: "<u>MOONLIGHT</u> | a play | by | <u>Harold Pinter</u>"; on this page, in ink: "2cond Draft".
    (f) Four new pages, in holograph, numbered "New 66", "New 67", "New 68", and "New 69".

2.   Manuscripts, etc., in *PA* Box 35 ("Moonlight II"):
    (a) Typescript, labelled in ink on first (title) page: "<u>2cond draft</u>", two leaves, 72pp.
    (b) Photocopy of this typescript.
    (c) Typescript, with a few changes in ink; three leaves, 90 pp.; headed on first (title) page: "MOONLIGHT | by | Harold Pinter"; labelled on this page, in ink: "<u>Penultimate version</u>"; starts and ends with monologues by Bridget.
    (d) Photocopy of (c), with changes in ink, especially deletions.
    (e) Typescript, copy in ring-binder with clear plastic covers, with slip at front "reconverted [*sic*] | May 1993", and loose leaf, headed 'CHANGES TO "MOONLIGHT"'.
    (f) Typescript, bound; three leaves, 94 pp.; labelled in ink "Version 1".

3.   Stage play premièred 7 September 1993, Almeida Theatre.

4.   Published 6 September 1993 (Faber).

W60: *Ashes to Ashes (1995–96):*

1.   Manuscript in *PA* Box 60, within orange folder, on legal pad leaves, in ballpoint, draft of dialogue between "M" (male) and "G" (female), appears to be for an early form of this play.

2.   Manuscripts, etc., in *PA* Box 67:
     (a) Holograph partial draft, on legal pad.
     (b) Rough draft, part-typescript, part-holograph.
     (c) First and second full drafts, typescript with changes in ink.
     (d) Third draft, typescript, changes in ink.
     (e) Typescript, in spiral binder: on title page: "<u>ASHES TO ASHES</u> | a play | by | HAROLD PINTER", 3 leaves, 51 pp. On p.51, dated "February 1996". On title page, pencil note: "Make 15 copies".

3.   Stage play, first presented 12 September 1996, Royal Court Theatre company at the Ambassadors Theatre Upstairs, directed by Harold Pinter.

4.   Published *ca.* September 1996 (Faber).

5.   Stage play presented in Italy, 1997, as *Ceneri alle Ceneri*, translated by Alessandra Serra, directed by Harold Pinter.

6.   Stage play presented in France, 1998, translated by Eric Kahane, directed by Harold Pinter.

7.   Video recording: New York Roundabout Theatre Production, 1999: NYPL # NCOV 2.

W61: *The Dreaming Child* [screenplay, published but not yet filmed] *(1997):*

1.   Commissioned in 1997 by Julia Ormond, as part of her 20th Century Fox development deal; based on a short story by Karen Blixen ("Isak Dinesen"). Film not yet made.

2.   Manuscripts in *PA* Boxes 70–73 (not seen).

3.   Published in: *Collected Screenplays Three* (2001).

4.   Discussed in: Francis X. Gillen, "Isak Dinesen with a Contemporary Social Conscience: Harold Pinter's Film Adaptation of 'The Dreaming Child'," *The Films of Harold Pinter*, ed. Steven H. Gale (2001), pp.147–158.

W62: *Celebration (1999):*

1.   Manuscripts, etc., in *PA* Box 74:
     (a) Holograph drafts on legal pad, and photocopies of such drafts.

(b) Printed draft, 3 leaves, 50 pp., plus holograph additions; headed on title leaf: "ANNIVERSARY | by | Harold Pinter". Identified in ink on this page as: "First | Draft | Aug 25 | 99".

(c) Later printed draft, 3 leaves, 51 pp.; headed on title leaf: "CELEBRATION | by | Harold Pinter | August 1999".

2. Stage play premièred 16 March 2000, Almeida Theatre, in double-bill with *The Room*.

3. Published, 20 March 2000, in: *Celebration & The Room* (Faber, 2000).

W63: *Press Conference* [sketch] *(2001–02):*

1. The sketch was first performed in the Lyttleton Theatre, National Theatre, as part of two brackets of Pinter sketches, as 6 pm performances, preceding the 8 pm programme: on 8 February 2002, *Sketches I:* "That's Your Trouble", "The Black and White", "Tess", "Trouble in the Works", "Press Conference"; on 11 February 2002, *Sketches II:* "Last to Go", "Special Offer", "That's All", "Night", "Press Conference." In "Press Conference," Pinter played the role of the Minister, with the other cast members as the press corps. The other new sketch, "Tess," a monologue, has been published as a short story: see *D13*.

2. Published: *Press Conference* (Faber, 2002).

UNPUBLISHED ITEMS

W64: *Unperformed or Uncompleted Sketches, or Short Stories:*

Manuscripts in *PA* Box 60:

"Death A Play in One Act by Sean Pinter"; draft in typescript (carbon) and ink, with miscellaneous notes; "Interview", 3 pp. (apparently not the sketch published as "Interview"); "Guest for Breakfast", 3 pp.; "two housewives in a park shelter", 3 pp. "The Gathering," 5 pp.; "Woman sitting at table," 7 pp.; "T E T", dated 19.3.60, 13 pp., typed plus 2 sides in ink; drafts in holograph, "The Circus" and "uxorious caravan", on 2 leaves, recto and verso.

W65: *Lolita [screenplay] [1994]:*

Adaptation of the novel by Vladimir Nabokov

1. Manuscripts in *PA* Boxes 65, 66: not seen.

2. Pinter began work in 1994 on the screenplay for a new film for the director Adrian Lynne; however, in January 1995 he learnt his script would not be used. Another was commissioned from David Mamet; however, the script eventually used was by Stephen Schiff (Billington 358–361).

3. See Christopher C. Hudgins, "Harold Pinter's *Lolita:* 'My Sin, My Soul'."
    In: *The Films of Harold Pinter*, ed. Steven H. Gale, pp.123–146.

4. Extracts from script in: "Scenes from 'Lolita'." *Areté*, 5 (Spring/Summer
    2001): 5–16.

W66: *God's District [sketch] [1997]:*

Monologue, written for the intimate revue *Then Again* . . ., Lyric Theatre,
Hammersmith, March 1997.

Unpublished, as yet, in June 2003. Information as of June 2003, from
www.haroldpinter.org/prose/fiction/hml.

W67: *The Tragedy of King Lear (2000):*

Adaptation for film of William Shakespeare's play. Planned to be directed by Tim
Roth, with Dixie Linder as producer (information as of June 2003, from
www.haroldpinter.org/film): "eighty-eight page script (sixty scenes plus thirteen
numbered subscenes)". S. Gale, *Sharp Cut*, p. 372 and pp. 370–372.

APPENDIX TWO
Textual Revisions and Promptbooks

A. REVISIONS

This section deals briefly with variances in print-published texts of Harold Pinter's plays (variant texts in manuscript or typescript are noticed in *Appendix One*). It takes cognizance only of changes in dialogue, not in stage-directions or in set-descriptions, which are often more extensive and "theatrical" in acting editions. It is concerned only with extensive variances, not with small numbers of minor verbal changes.

Harold Pinter's re-workings of his plays have taken two guises: revisions of texts of stage-plays, involving some cuts and re-writing; and adaptations of texts of works written for one medium for performance in some other medium, producing different versions of the works. Noting of publication primarily deals with the British standard reading editions; these are generally followed by derivative editions, and by American (Grove) editions and printings.

1. *The Birthday Party*
Two stage-play texts: the first published in 1959–64 (*A1.a–b, A4, A11.a–b*); and the second from 1965 onward (*A1.c, A11.c*), initially in the "Second edition, revised" of *The Birthday Party* (Methuen, 1965). Most changes are cuts, sometimes with minor re-writing to cover them. Variances to the ending, including altering Stanley's clothing. Discussion in: Charles A. Carpenter, "'What Have I Seen, the Scum or the Essence': Symbolic Fallout in Pinter's *The Birthday Party*," *Modern Drama*, 17: 4 (December 1974): 389–402.

2. *The Caretaker*
Two stage-play texts: the first published in 1960–61 (*A2.a–b, A10.a*); the second from 1962 onward (*A2.c, A10.b*), initially in the "Second edition, revised" of *The Caretaker* (Methuen, 1962). Revisions mainly cuts, but with some re-working. Also, a number of small changes between *A2.a* and *A2.b*.

3. *A Slight Ache*
Radio play version [1960] (*A5.a–b*); stage-play version, from 1961 (*A12.a–b*). The Samuel French edition (*A5.b*) has substantially more directions than *A5.a*. Very extensive re-writing for the stage version.

4. *The Dwarfs*
Radio-play version, 1961 (*A12.a; A13.a*, 1st to 7th printings); first text of stage-

play version (*A12.b; A13.b*, 8th to 13th printings); revised text of stage-play version (*A12.c; A13.b*, 14th printing onward). Versions discussed in: Mary Jane Miller, "Pinter as a Radio Dramatist," *Modern Drama*, 17 (1974): 403–412; Steven H. Gale, *Butter's Going Up: A Critical Analysis of Harold Pinter's Work* (Durham, NC: Duke UP, 1977), pp. 263–265; Scott Giantvalley, "Toying with *The Dwarfs*: The Textual Problems with Pinter's 'Corrections'," in: *Harold Pinter: Critical Approaches*, ed. Steven H. Gale (Rutherford, Madison and Teaneck: Fairleigh Dickinson University Press; London and Toronto: Associated University Presses, 1986), pp. 72–81.

5. The Lover

Television-play version 1963 (*A14.a*); stage-play version 1964 onward (*A14.b*). Extensive re-working for the stage.

6. The Homecoming

Two main stage-play texts: the first published in 1965 (*A20.a*); the revised text in 1966 (*A20.b; A20.f*). Mainly cuts, but also some re-writing. Further revisions, mainly cuts, in 1967 (*A20.c¹*). Some unauthorised changes were introduced to the British acting edition (*A20.j*), by Samuel French's editor, of a bowdlerising nature, affecting some dialogue and stage directions in Act II. Pinter objected to these very strongly, and all but one were eventually reversed in later printings (see *A20.j, Note one*).

7. No Man's Land

Stage-play text, one minor change and two cuts, between the first edition, 1975 (*A36.a*) and the revised edition, also 1975 (*A36.b*), on pp. 20, 20–21, 33.

8. Betrayal

Stage-play text: first edition, 1978 (*A37.a*); revised edition, 1980 (*A37.b*). Four minor changes noted, on pp. 34, 86, 108 and 136.

B. PROMPTBOOKS

1. Royal Shakespeare Company promptbooks for Pinter's plays at the Shakespeare Centre, Stratford-upon-Avon (there is also a promptbook for the production of James Joyce's play *Exiles*, directed by Pinter).

(1) The Collection [1962]

Pale blue card binding, black around spine. Text in typescript on rectos, stage-directions, etc., on facing versos, typed or in pencil; also, interleaved small leaves bear more notations. On title page:

THE COLLECTION | A play in one act | By | Harold Pinter | Royal Shakespeare Company | at the Aldwych Theatre | Directed by Peter Hall & Harold Pinter | 1962

(2) The Birthday Party [1964]

Black ring-binder book, lined paper, with pages from two copies of an issue of the play's first edition (1960–1963), with the first stage version, pasted on versos, with stage-directions and other notations in Pinter's holograph in pencil on rectos. Very interesting cuts and re-writings, usually corresponding to changes found in the revised edition. On verso of title leaf: leaf pasted on, with cast details. On title leaf:
BIRTHDAY PARTY | Prompt Book Aldwych Theatre 1964 | First Performance: June 18 | Directed by Harold Pinter. For the Lord Chamberlain's response to the text dated 18 May 1960, see D. Shellard, S. Nicholson, M. Handley, *The Lord Chamberlain Regrets...A History of British Theatre Censorship* (2004), pp. 160–161.

(3) The Homecoming [1965]

Clipped leaves, within brown manila folder, with printed pages in large type pasted on rectos, and notations in pencil or biro on both versos and rectos. Some cuts and changes correspond to those in the second, revised edition; others do not. On title page: lists of characters, acts, times of scenes, at foot:
R. S. Co. Prompt Book | 1965 Provincial Tour & Aldwych (1st Perf.: March 25, | New Theatre, Cardiff | 1966/67 U. S. Tour | Directed by Peter Hall

(4) The Dumb Waiter [1967]

Hardback exercise book, with lined paper, with pages pasted on rectos from Samuel French (London) edition, stage-directions, etc., on versos. One cut, on p. 22. On title page, in ink:
The Dumb Waiter | RSC Theatre ground | 1st perf: May 19, 1967 | Director: David Jones

(5) Landscape & Silence [1969]

Hardback ring-binder book, greyish texturing on boards, green around spine. Texts in typescript [printed?], large font, with lines well-spaced, on leaves pasted on to rectos; stage-directions and other notations on rectos and on facing versos. Some cuts and re-writings. On first title page: "SILENCE | by | Harold Pinter". On second title page: "LANDSCAPE | by | Harold Pinter".

(6) Old Times [1971]

Black ring-binder book, blank paper, text in large font, with lines well-spaced, on printed leaves pasted on to rectos, notations in pencil on facing versos. Some interesting changes to dialogue and to printed stage-directions, especially towards the end. On title page:
OLD TIMES 1971 | Directed by Peter Hall | 1st perf. April 26 at Oxford Playhouse | 1st perf. At Aldwych June 1

(7) A Slight Ache [1973]

Black ring-binder book, unlined paper, with pages of printed edition pasted on rectos, with stage-directions, etc., in pencil on versos. Some cuts and re-writings. On title page:
R. S. C. | Tour & Aldwych, 1973 | A SLIGHT ACHE | by Harold Pinter | Presented with "Landscape" | Prompt Book | Directed by Peter Jones | Tour: April 21 – June 22 | Aldwych: Oct. 17, etc.

(8) Landscape [1973]

Purple-covered ring-binder, with pages from the second Methuen edition of *Landscape and Silence* pasted on to rectos, notations on versos and rectos. Some changes to dialogue. On title page:
R. S. C. | Tour & Aldwych | LANDSCAPE | by Harold Pinter | Prompt Book | Presented with "A Slight Ache" | Revival of Peter Hall production at the | Aldwych | Tour: April 21 – June 22 | Aldwych: Oct. 17, etc

(9) The Caretaker [1995]

Text of play: photocopy of second stage-play text, from Methuen *Plays: Two*, paginated [39]-110. Quite a few cuts and changes to dialogue and stage directions. On title page:
CARETAKER – | TOP, 1995 | Directed by Danny Carrick

II. Royal National Theatre promptbooks at the RNT Archive, Salisbury House, 1–3 Brixton Road, Kennington Park, London.
   This Archive has files including promptbooks and other documents for plays by Pinter (some directed by him, some by other persons), and also for plays by other dramatists directed by Pinter. The latter category includes: *Next of Kin,* by John Hopkins, Old Vic (1974); *Blithe Spirit,* by Noel Coward, Lyttleton (1974); *Close of Play,* by Simon Gray, Lyttleton (1979); and *The Trojan War Will Not Take Place,* by Jean Giraudoux, English version by Christopher Fry (1983). The former category includes:

(1) No Man's Land [1975–76]

Prompt "Bible" Scripts, ref. no. 891. Directed by Peter Hall; opened Old Vic, 23 April 1975; transferred to Wyndham's, 15 July; transferred to Lyttleton, 12 April 1976 [use of other theatres needed because of delay in completion of South Bank building]. File includes annotated text, envelope containing production documents, etc., and three folders.

(2) Betrayal [1978]

Ref. no. 143. Directed by Peter Hall; opened Lyttleton, 15 November 1978. File includes annotated text and a number of production documents. In text, before each scene, elaborate stage plan and placements; precise descriptions of physical movements of actors.

(3) The Caretaker [1980]

Ref. no. 178. Directed by Kenneth Ives; opened Lyttleton, 11 November 1980. File includes annotated text, and a number of production doocuments.

(4) Other Places: Family Voices, Victoria Station, A Kind of Alaska [1982]

Ref. no. 210. Directed by Peter Hall, opened Cottesloe, 14 October 1982. File includes annotated texts, and envelope containing various production documents.

(5) Mountain Language [1988]

Ref. no. 301. Directed by Harold Pinter; opened Lyttleton, 20 October 1988. File includes annotated text and seven folders of production documents.

(6) The Birthday Party [1994]

Ref. no. 376. Directed by Sam Mendes; opened 17 March 1994. File includes annotated text and eight folders of production documents. Programme includes full text of poem "A View of the Party."

(7) The Homecoming [1997]

Ref. no. 408. Directed by Roger Michell; opened Lyttleton, 23 January 1997. File includes annotated text and ten folders of production documents.

(8) Betrayal [1998]

Ref. no. 427. Directed by Trevor Nunn; opened Lyttleton, 24 November 1998. File includes annotated text and eight folders of production documents.

Note: Promptbooks and other documents not yet available in Archive for: *Remembrance of Things Past* (directed by Di Trevis; opened 23 November 2000), adapted by Pinter and Di Trevis; or for *No Man's Land* (directed by Harold Pinter; opened 6 December 2001).

III. Promptbook in the National Theatre Museum, London
The Birthday Party, Prospect Theatre production, date not given. Uses leaves from French's edition.

IV. Promptbook in the Pinter Archive, Box 67.
The Caretaker, produced at the Lyceum Theatre, New York, opened 4 October 1961. Stage manager's script, with corrections in ms. Another copy of this is in the Billy Rose Theater Collection, New York Public Library Reserve Collection.

INDEX I:
Works by Harold Pinter

This index lists references to all of Harold Pinter's writings, published and unpublished, and also to audio-visual materials, films made from his screenplays, and sound materials. They are arranged under the categories employed in Sections A to K, but with these categories rearranged in terms of the alphabetical order of their headings. Interviews and interview-based articles, and some kinds of items in the "Miscellaneous" section, were only partially authored by him. References to works in dramatic form directed by Pinter, including his own, are found in *Index II*, as are translated from his works, and the titles of regular radio or television programmes in which he appeared in certain episodes. Some titles listed also appear in *Index II*, when used for other purposes. Reference for items are given in the form of assigned item-numbers within the various sections and not of page-numbers.

FICTION

INTERVIEWS, AND INTERVIEW–BASED ARTICLES, PRINTED IN NEWSPAPERS OR MAGAZINES

MISCELLANEOUS: MINOR PIECES, COLLABORATIVE WRITINGS, EDITING, ETC.

PLAYS AND SKETCHES FOR THE STAGE, RADIO AND TELEVISION

UNPUBLISHED OR INCOMPLETE ITEMS, & ALTERNATIVE TITLES

INDEX II
General Index

This index covers all aspects of Harold Pinter's bibliographical history apart from his own published and unpublished works. It includes, for instance, work he had directed and individually itemizes radio and television programmes he has participated in. References to items are given in terms of assigned item numbers within the various sections instead of page numbers. Abbreviations listed in the "List of Abbreviations" are employed here following the items referred to, for instance, "British Broadcasting Corporation Written Archives Centre (WAC)".